THE LAW OF ARBITRATION
IN SCOTLAND

THE LAW
OF ARBITRATION
IN SCOTLAND

ROBERT L. C. HUNTER WS, FCIArb
Lecturer in Private Law, University of Aberdeen

T & T CLARK
EDINBURGH

Copyright © Robert L. C. Hunter, 1987

Typeset by C. R. Barber & Partners, Fort William
Printed and bound by Billing & Sons, Worcester

for

T. & T. CLARK LTD
59 George Street, Edinburgh EH2 2LQ

First printed 1987

British Library Cataloguing in Publication Data

Hunter, Robert L.C.
The law of arbitration in Scotland.
1. Arbitration and award—Scotland.
I. Title
344.1107′9   KDC904
ISBN 0–567–09480–4

In Memoriam D.M.H.
(1928–1986)

'Twa traivellers, as they were walking,
'Bout the Chameleon fell a-talking, ...
Says ane, 'Tis a strange Beast indeed,
Four-footed, wi a Fish's heid;
A little Bowk, wi a lang Tail,
And moves far slawer than a Snail;
Of Colour like a Blawart blue; —
Reply'd his Nibour, That's no true;
For weel I wat his Colour's Green,
If ane may true his ain twa Een;
For I in Sun-shine saw him fair,
When he was dining on the Air. —
Excuse me, says the ither Blade,
I saw him better in the Shade,
And he is blue. — He's Green I'm sure. —
Ye leed. — And ye're the Son of a Whore. —
Frae words there had been Cuff and Kick,
Had not a Third come in the Nick,
Wha tenting them in this rough Mood
Cry'd Gentlemen, whit! are ye wood?
Whit's ye'r Quarrel, an't may be speer't?
Truth, says the tane, Sir, ye shall hear't;
The Chameleon, I say, he's Blue;
He threaps he's Green. — Now, whit say you?
Ne'er fash yersels about the Matter,
Says the sagacious Arbitrator,
He's Black. — Sae nane o ye are richt,
I view'd him weel wi Candle-licht;
And have it in ma Pocket here,
Row'd in ma Napkin hale and feer.
Fy! said ae Cangler, Whit d'ye mean?
I'll lay ma Lugs on't, that he's Green.
Said th'ither, were I gawn tae Death,
I'd swear he's Blue wi ma last Breath.
He's black, the judge maintain'd ay stout;
And tae convince them whop'd him out:
But tae Surprise of ane and a',
The Animal wis White as Snaw,
And thus reprov'd them, — Shallow Boys,
Away, Away, make nae mair noise;
Ye're a' three wrang, and a' three richt,
But learn tae awn yer Nibours Sicht
As good as yours. — Yer Judgment speak,
But never be sae daftly weak
T'imagine ithers will by Force
Submit their Sentiments tae yours;
As things in various Lichts ye see,
They'll ilka ane resemble me.'

Allan Ramsay (1684–1758)

CONTENTS

PART B
ORDINARY ARBITRATION CONTRACTS

Contents

Contents

PART C
ARBITRATION PROCEEDINGS AND THE DECREE ARBITRAL

Contents

Contents

PART D
QUASI-ARBITRAL AND EQUITABLE PROCEDURES

Contents

APPENDICES

FOREWORD

I have, with complete honesty, but often with intent upon tactical advantage for my clients, advised arbiters that I can find no Scottish authority on particular issues. That has permitted me, thereafter, to present arguments based on such a selection of English authority as might be helpful to my clients, or such 'common sense' arguments as I thought to be advantageous!

I fear that, with the publication of this book, my advantage will be lost, for my opponent will have at his disposal not only a careful examination of authority, but also the succinct expression of Mr Hunter's own views. In addition, the book presents a history of arbitration as well as dealing with the arbitration process in many different fields.

Although one often hears criticism of arbitration procedures as being very expensive and time-consuming, in my view the advantage of having a skilled arbiter far outweighs the disadvantage of having to pay for his services. For example, in the assessment of loss arising from disruption caused during building and engineering works, the assistance of an arbiter skilled in the art of assessment of quantum is not only helpful, it is essential.

Mr Hunter has set out to fill the gap on our shelves for a modern Scottish book on arbitration, and has equipped arbiters, arbiters' clerks and parties to arbitrations with a book of persuasive authority which is both comprehensive and, as far as I can judge, accurate.

Alex M. Hamilton

PREFACE

The last substantial work on the law of arbitration in Scotland — Irons and Melville's *Treatise* — was published in 1903. Since then only two short books have appeared — that by Sheriff Guild, published in 1936, and the recent '*Synopsis*' by Mr Weir. J. M. Bell's *Treatise*, the second edition of which was published in 1877, remains of almost institutional authority, but is even more seriously outdated than *Irons and Melville*. The arbitration law of Scotland has not developed as much during this century as has that of England, but textbooks have not kept up with the changes that there have been, and it has been recognised for some time that a new work is needed.

My main intention in writing this book has been to provide a detailed account of modern Scots arbitration law and practice comprehensible to an arbiter without a professional qualification in law but possessing at least the legal education normally required by such professional bodies as the Chartered Institute of Arbitrators (Arbiters), and also by foreign lawyers and traders. I hope that those who use this work will consider that these intentions have been adequately fulfilled. A potential readership beyond the Scottish legal profession has required that a fuller explanation be given of some matters than would otherwise have been necessary, as well as the provision in the text of a translation of most of the Latin phrases which have been used.

Because I believe that the modern Scots law of arbitration cannot be properly understood, and its future development properly directed, without some reference to its historical and jurisprudential foundations, I have inserted at the beginning of the work an outline of these matters based, so far as the historical section in Chapter Two is concerned, on new studies.

Scots arbitration law serves a relatively small community living on the periphery of commercial and political affairs. It is therefore inherently less dynamic than that of more populous and powerful countries, and it does not have the impetus to reform which a separate legislature can often bring to small jurisdictions. English arbitration law, by contrast, serves one of the greatest centres of commercial arbitration in the world, and English concerns naturally dominate the legislature of the United Kingdom. Scots arbitration law therefore runs the risk either of stagnation or subservience to its greater neighbour. It might be argued that latterly it has been the rather parochial scope of arbitration practice in Scotland that has helped to protect this branch of law from the anglicisation that has occurred in many othe legal fields. Be that as it may — the fact that English arbitration law is largely based on a modern statutory 'code', whereas Scots law is based more on juristic articulation of principle and judicial decision, has also played a part — the continued preservation of the distinct character of Scots arbitration law requires the writer of a textbook of this subject to pay special attention to principles derived from native sources and, where these fail, to seek guidance from the wide range of authorities accessible by means of historical and comparative study rather than from precedents derived from a single foreign source, however prestigious and convenient.

So far as my personal limitations have allowed I have sought to follow this prescription. I have tried to read all the Scottish arbitration cases in all the formal law reports, looking at them afresh rather than through the minds of previous writers, and have also sought to glean as much information as possible from other printed and documentary sources. For obvious reasons not every case noted has been cited in this book. Some decisions seemed to me merely to reiterate what was already accepted; others dealt with points of no contemporary and slight historical importance. The labour of reading, noting and indexing every known decision of the Scottish courts on a point of arbitration law has nevertheless not been fruitless, for it has sometimes yielded *dicta* which, even if *obiter*, have pointed the way to solutions of problems which had apparently not occurred to previous Scottish textbook writers and which, if the textbooks on the arbitration laws of other countries are any guide, are of some contemporary importance.

Because of the relatively small number of cases on arbitration law that nowadays reach the Scottish courts, native authority is lacking on quite a number of important questions which have in recent years been the subject of litigation or legislation elsewhere. I have tried to suggest how these questions might best be decided consistently with the traditions of Scots law and contemporary convenience, and have sought guidance from the widest range of sources which were available to me either in English, French or Latin, the only languages of which I have any knowledge. Because of the great differences in this field between English and Scots law I have deliberately treated the decisions of English courts — even of the House of Lords in English appeals — as of no greater formal authority than decisions of superior courts of other Western European countries. Indeed, given that Scots law shares with the laws of those countries a common basis in the writings of the great civil and canon law jurists of the mediaeval and renaissance periods, and given that the economy of Scotland is becoming more and more closely integrated with the continent of Europe, I have taken the liberty, where English and continental approaches differed, to give greater weight to the latter unless practical considerations or post-renaissance developments on the continent made this policy inappropriate.

This preface would be incomplete without a mention of at least some of those who have contributed to any merit this book may have. I am particularly grateful to the Committee of the Scottish Branch of the Chartered Institute of Arbitrators (Arbiters). Their forbearance has been remarkable, for I have taken far longer to finish the work than they had every right to expect. I hope that the completed text will prove useful to their members. I suspect that I also owe a debt to certain colleagues in the Scottish legal world who had thought of writing a textbook on this subject, but forebore to tread on what on they regarded as my patch, turning their minds to other topics. It may be that the academic and professional world is the poorer because of their courtesy, if it has thus been deprived, for the time being at least, of a better book than this one, but for my part I thank them.

I owe a special debt to Professor Frank Lyall, head of the Department of Public Law at the University of Aberdeen, who read drafts of each chapter and made many invaluable suggestions. Among others who read other sections or provided advice or information or both and whose assistance I have greatly appreciated are Professor A. E. Anton, Mr William Fraser, solicitor, Aberdeen, Mr A. M. Hamilton CBE, solicitor, Glasgow,

Mr Robert Howie, Advocate (whose unpublished research paper on the decree arbitral I found most stimulating and informative), Dr Bill McBryde, Dr Leslie MacFarlane, Mr A. D. Mackay, solicitor, Edinburgh, Mr D. F. McQuaker, solicitor, Glasgow, Mr G. F. Robertson FRICS, Edinburgh, Dr Alan and Dr Alida Wilson and Dr Jenny Wormald. A few of those who encouraged and assisted me are now 'hid in death's dateless night': among them are my sister Miss D. M. Hunter, formerly of Register House, Edinburgh, the late Dr Judith Hook, who read a draft of the historical chapter, and two Fellows of the Institute, Mr W. Gilmour, and Mr Garth Green. Though they are beyond personal thanks, they are not beyond public recognition. The errors in and inadequacies of this work — and some will inevitably be noted if book reviewers run true to form — are of course my responsibility. To Mrs Smith and Mrs Wood, who each typed some early drafts, and to the unknown workers — especially those in Greenock — who designed and made the IBM wordprocessor and its associated software and Epson printer without which the final draft might never have been produced, my thanks are also due.

I have tried to state the law as at 1 May 1987.

R. L. C. H.
Faculty of Law,
University of Aberdeen.

TABLE OF CASES

B. *Decisions of the Commission of the European Communities*

C. *Cases from other jurisdictions*

Tables of Cases

STATUTORY PROVISIONS

A. *Applicable within Scotland*

[1] This Act when in force was ignored by Scottish Courts and may not have applied to Scotland.

Tables of Statutory Materials

TABLE OF ABBREVIATIONS

Citation of Cases

To those who are not Scots lawyers, the system of citation of cases may be unfamiliar. A useful guide may be found in Gloag W. M. and Henderson R. C., *Introduction to the Law of Scotland*, (8th edn. by Wilkinson A. B. and Wilson W. A.) Edinburgh 1980, x–xii. Sources in italics in the Table of Cases in the present work will be found among the items listed below.

Other abbreviations

Aaron, *Disp. Proc.*	Aaron B., *Dispute Settlement Procedures in Five Western Countries*, Berkeley, California, 1969.
Abdn. Recs.	Dickinson W. Croft (ed), *Early Records of the Burgh of Aberdeen 1317, 1398–1407*, (Scottish History Society) (3rd series) Edinburgh, 1957.
ACAS Role	*The ACAS Role in Conciliation, Arbitration and Mediation*, ACAS, London.
Acta Sessionis (Stair)	Shearer I. H. (ed), *Selected Cases from Acta Dominorum Concilii et Sessionis 1532–33*, (Stair Society), Edinburgh 1951.
ADA	Thomson T. (ed), *The Acts of the Lords Auditors of Causes and Complaints*, Edinburgh, 1839.
ADC	Thomson T. and others (eds), *The Acts of the Lords of Council in Civil Causes*, Edinburgh, 1839 & 1918.
APS	Thomson T. and Innes C. (eds), *The Acts of the Parliaments of Scotland*, Edinburgh, 1814–75.

Balfour, *Practicks.* Balfour, Sir James, *Practicks,* McNeill P. G. B. (ed), (Stair Society), Edinburgh, 1962.

Bankton, *Inst.* McDouall A. (Lord Bankton), *An Institute of the Laws of Scotland in Civil Rights,* Edinburgh, 1751–3.

Bell, *Comm.* Bell G. J., *Commentaries on the Law of Scotland and the Principles of Mercantile Jurisprudence,* 1800, 7th edn. Edinburgh, 1870.

Bell, *Prin.* Bell G. J., *Principles of the Law of Scotland,* 1829, 9th edn., Edinburgh, 1877.

Bell J. M., *Arb.* Bell J. M., *The Law of Arbitration in Scotland,* (2nd edn.) Edinburgh, 1877.

Carn. Ct. Bk. Dickinson W. Croft, *Court Book of the Barony of Carnwath 1523–42,* (Scottish History Society) (3rd Series), Edinburgh, 1937.

Carruthers, *Stiles.* Carruthers, *A compend or abreviat of the most important Ordinary Securities of, and concerning Rights . . . Collected from the Stiles of several Writers to Signet,* Edinburgh, 1702.

Concannon, 'ACAS Arb.' Concannon H., 'The growth of arbitration work in ACAS', in (1978) 9(1) *Industrial Relations Journal* 12.

Concannon, 'Dismissal Arb.' Concannon H., 'Handling dismissal disputes by arbitration', in (1980) 11(2) *Industrial Relations Journal* 13.

Cooper, *Sel. Pap.* Cooper, Lord, *Selected Papers,* Edinburgh, 1957.

Cooper, *Sel. Scot. Cas.* Cooper, Lord, *Select Scottish Cases of the Thirteenth Century,* Edinburgh, 1944.

D. Mommsen T. and Krueger P. (eds) and Watson A. (Tr.), *The Digest of Justinian,* Philadelphia, 1985.

Dallas, *Stiles.* Dallas G., *System of Stiles,* Edinburgh, 1697.

Dobie, *Sh. Ct. Pr.* Dobie W. J., *The Law and Practice of*

	the Sheriff Courts in Scotland, Glasgow, 1952.
Domke, *Comm. Arb.*	Domke M., *The Law and Practice of Commercial Arbitration*, Illinois, 1968, with cumulative supplement 1983.
Dunf. Recs.	Beveridge E. (ed.), *The Burgh Records of Dunfermline*, Edinburgh, 1977.
Erskine, *Inst.*	Erskine J., *An Institute of the Law of Scotland* (orig. edn. 1773) (9th edn.) Edinburgh, 1871.
Fowler, *Forms.*	Fowler L., 'Forms of Arbitration', in Kuttner S. (ed), *Proceedings of the International Congress of Mediaeval Canon Law 1972*, Vatican City, 1976.
Gill, *Agr. Hold.*	Gill B., *The Law of Agricultural Holdings in Scotland*, Edinburgh, 1982.
Gladstone, *Vol. Arb.*	Gladstone A., *Voluntary Arbitration of Interest Disputes*, International Labour Office, Geneva, 1984.
Gloag, *Contract.*	Gloag W. M., *The Law of Contract*, 2nd edn., Edinburgh, 1929.
Guild, *Arb.*	Guild D. A., *The Law of Arbitration in Scotland*, Edinburgh, 1936.
Halliday, *Conveyancing.*	Halliday J. M. *Conveyancing Law and Practice in Scotland*, Edinburgh, 1985.
Hawker & Ors., *ICE Arb.*	Hawker G., Uff J. and Timms C., *The Institution of Civil Engineers' Arbitration Practice*, London, 1986.
Holmbäck, *Arb. Swe.*	Holmbäck U., *Arbitration in Sweden*, Stockholm, 1977.
Holmbäck, *Arb. Swe. 1984.*	Holmbäck U., *Arbitration in Sweden (2nd edn.)*, Stockholm, 1984.
Hostiensis, Comm.	Hostiensis, *In Primum Decretalium Librum Commentaria*, Venice 1581, republished Turin, 1965.
Irons, *Arb.*	Irons J. C. and Melville R. D., *Treatise on the Law of Arbitration in Scotland*, Edinburgh, 1903.
Julien, *Ev. Hist.*	Julien A. R., 'Evolutio historica

	compromissi in arbitros in iure canonico', 1937 *Apollinaris* 187–201.
Lee, *Int. Comm. Arb.*	Lee E., *Encyclopaedia of International Commercial Arbitration*, London, 1986.
McBryde, *Contract.*	McBryde, W. W., *The Law of Contract in Scotland*, Edinburgh, 1987.
Mackenzie, *Inst.*	Mackenzie, Sir G., *The Institutions of the Law of Scotland*, Edinburgh, 1684.
MacLaren, *Ct. of Sess. Pr.*	MacLaren J. A., *Court of Session Practice*, Edinburgh, 1916.
Maxwell, *Ct. of Sess. Pr.*	Maxwell D., *The Practice of the Court of Session*, Edinburgh, 1980.
Miller, *Arb.*	Miller P. L., *The Law of Arbitration in Scotland*, Glasgow, 1917.
Mustill, *Comm. Arb.*	Mustill M. J., and Boyd S. C., *The Law and Practice of Commercial Arbitration in England*, London, 1982.
Parker, *Arb.*	Parker J., *Notes on the Law of Arbitration*, (2nd edn) Edinburgh, 1845.
Pitcairn, *Trials.*	Pitcairn R., *Criminal Trials in Scotland from 1488 to 1624*, Edinburgh, 1833.
Regiam Maj.	Cooper, Lord (ed), *Regiam Majestatem*, (Stair Society), Edinburgh, 1947.
Robert, *Arb.*	Robert J., *Arbitrage Civil et Commercial*, 4th edn., Paris, 1967.
Robert & Carbonneau, *Arb.*	Robert J. & Carbonneau T. E., *The French Law of Arbitration*, New York, 1983.
Robinson and others, *Eur. Leg. Hist.*	Robinson O. F., Fergus T. D. and Gordon W. M., *An Introduction to European Legal History*, Abingdon, 1985.
Russell, *Arb.* 1982.	Walton A. and Victoria M. (eds), *Russell on the Law of Arbitration*, (20th edn), London, 1982.
Sanders, *Aut. cl. comp.*	Sanders P., 'L'autonomie de la clause compromissoire', in Winqwist C-H

	in (1985) 23(3) *British Journal of Industrial Relations*, 415.
Wormald, 'Blood Feud'.	Wormald J. M., 'Blood Feud, Kindred and Government in Early Modern Scotland', 87 *Past and Present* (1980) 54 ff.
Wormald, *Community*.	Wormald J., *Court, Kirk and Community*, London, 1981.
Wormald, *Manrent*.	Wormald J., *Lords and Men in Scotland: Bonds of manrent 1442–1603*, Edinburgh, 1985, 47.
Zack, *Griev. Arb.*	Zack A. M. & Others, *Grievance Arbitration: a practical guide*, International Labour Office, Geneva, 1977.

PART A
FOUNDATIONS

CHAPTER ONE

THE NATURE OF ARBITRATION

Introduction

1.1. To define arbitration under Scots law in a satisfactory manner is not easy for a number of reasons. No statutory definition exists, and no judicial or juristic formulation has won general acceptance. To make matters worse, the word 'arbitration' has long been used to refer to various types of extracurial proceeding which differ from one another in important respects. There have of course been numerous attempts at formulating a definition.[1] One of the most successful is that of Professor D. M. Walker who states[2] that arbitration is

'the adjudication of a dispute or controversy on fact or law or both, outside the ordinary civil courts, by one or more persons to whom the parties who are at issue refer the matter for decision.'

No attempt to encapsulate the essence of a complex institution in one pithy sentence can be entirely adequate, but this definition is helpful in that it picks out three important features of arbitration — *first*, that it is mainly a procedure for handling disputes; *second* that its normal outcome is a decision; and *third* that while it is a form of adjudication it is not part of the ordinary court system. Professor Walker's formulation may be interpreted as containing also a suggestion that arbitration is normally voluntary.

1.2. Arbitration being a form of adjudication, this chapter — the first of two dealing with the foundations of the institution — is concerned with exploring the implications of this assumption,

---

[1] Bankton, *Inst.* I.23.2; Irons, *Arb.* 1. Some writers define a submission but not arbitration — e.g. Bell J. M. *Arb.* para. 2; Erskine, *Inst.* IV.3.27; Parker, *Arb.* 4; Weir, *Arb.* 21. Guild, *Arb.* and Miller, *Arb.* do not attempt definitions of arbitration or submission, but Guild discusses the nature of arbitration at some length in his first chapter.

[2] *Prin.* I.60.

describing the various forms of procedure which in Scots law are regarded as arbitration, and with clarifying the distinctions between arbitration and other procedures. Since it is a cardinal assumption upon which this work is based that the institution cannot be properly understood, and the purpose and meaning of many of its particular rules comprehended, without an appreciation of its jurisprudential nature and history, chapter two is devoted mainly to an account of the history of arbitration in Scotland and ends with a brief discussion of the advantages and disadvantages of arbitration as compared with litigation in the ordinary courts. Most of the remainder of the work — parts B and C — seeks to expound in detail the modern Scots law relating to the ordinary form of arbitration. Quasi-arbitral procedures, including special statutory regimes which are too various to deal with in detail here and of which accounts are in some cases available elsewhere in specialist works,[3] are discussed in Part D. It is difficult, of course, to grapple with the jurisprudential nature of arbitration entirely in the abstract, and therefore a brief preliminary description of the procedures which in Scots law are regarded as arbitration is appropriate, and this follows immediately below.

Forms of arbitration

1.3. The most important modern form of arbitration procedure in Scots law, which in this work will generally be referred to as '*ordinary arbitration*', has four main features. *First*, there must be a *dispute*[4] between two or more parties. *Second*, resort to arbitration is *voluntary* being based upon a contract[5] or set of contracts, these being first between the parties in dispute, and then between those parties jointly and the third party, the '*arbiter*', who has agreed to decide the matter. The terms of these contracts are contained mainly in a document called a '*submission*' or '*minute of reference*' or in an '*arbitration clause*' attached to another contract. The parties cannot, of course, submit to arbitration any matter upon which they have no power to transact, and which is solely within the power of a public court to decide. *Third*, the arbiter to whom the matter at issue is referred is regarded as exercising an inferior

---

[3] See e.g. Gill, *Agr. Hold.* chaps. 34, 35.
[4] *Albyn Housing Society Ltd* v. *Taylor Woodrow Homes Ltd* 1985 S.L.T. 309.
[5] Bell J. M., *Arb.* para. 2.

jurisdiction, and as such is subject to the supervision of the ordinary courts.[6] He or she is required by the courts to conform to the principles of natural justice, though otherwise a wide discretion in matters of procedure is permitted.[7] *Fourth*, the arbiter is required to *decide* the whole matters submitted to him or her by means of a *'decree arbitral'* or *'award'*, and in so doing must not merely adhere to some rule, principle, criterion or standard; he or she must not contravene the law.[8] Though the power of the arbiters over the submitters is based on contract, there is thus a jurisdictional as well as a contractual element in arbitration.[9] The function of arbiters is in some respects similar to that of judges deciding cases in the ordinary courts. Like judges they may, when faced with an issue on which existing positive law provides no clear solution, seek assistance from an equitable principle, 'but only a principle which is consistent with the existing system'.[10] Arbiters and judges are equally at liberty in deciding questions of fact to have regard to criteria or standards derived from scientific or professional knowledge as well as common sense, though disputes referred to arbitration probably turn on questions of fact more frequently than disputes litigated in the ordinary courts, since arbitration is often resorted to on the ground that an arbiter with particular technical knowledge can be selected to decide the issue.

1.4. This modern form of arbitration has, as will be shown in more detail in chapter 2, developed out of two forms of arbitration that existed in mediaeval Scots law. The first, which for convenience may be called *'legalistic arbitration'*, was a formal type of procedure, very similar to that of an ordinary court, conducted by an arbi*ter* who handed down a decision strictly in accordance with law.[11] The second, which for convenience may be called *'equitable arbitration'*, was an informal type of procedure conducted by an arbi*trator* who dealt in an equitable fashion with disputes and questions involving not only legal claims but also extralegal grievances and appraisals and the filling of gaps left in

[6] *Forbes* v. *Underwood* (1886) 13 R. 465 per L. P. Inglis at 467, approved in *Brown* v. *Hamilton District Council* 1983 S.L.T. 397 at 414–5.
[7] *Christison's Tr.* v. *Callendar-Brodie* (1906) 8 F. 928 at 931.
[8] *Mitchell-Gill* v. *Buchan* 1921 S.C. 390 at 395.
[9] On these elements in arbitration, see Robert, *Arb.*, 257.
[10] MacCormick D. N., 'Formal Justice and the Form of Legal Arguments', in Lloyd, Lord (ed), *Introduction to Jurisprudence* (5th edn), London 1985, 1193.
[11] See para. 2.12 below.

agreements. The equitable judgement of an arbitrator was sought in complex disputes between kindreds where, as in some modern industrial disputes, a global decision was required with which the parties could feel satisfied as being generally fair, even if not justified on strict legal grounds. It was at one time very common for a person to be appointed to act both as arbiter and arbitrator, a practice which helped to blur the distinction between the two offices. By the late seventeenth century the terms arbiter and arbitrator had become hopelessly confused, with the result that the arbiter gained much of the freedom and many of the functions of the arbitrator. Subsequently the term 'arbitrator' fell almost entirely into disuse, while the obligation to judge the substantive issues strictly according to law was reimposed on the arbiter. Equitable arbitration and the office of arbitrator (as formerly understood) have in this century never been mentioned in a legal context in Scotland, but they have never been abolished and arguably there remains a need for them as situations exist with which ordinary arbitration, in spite of its considerable flexibility, cannot effectively deal, such as industrial disputes between employers and trade unions.

1.5.   Some procedures are so similar to ordinary arbitration that they are normally discussed in a work of this kind. Only a few of the quasi-arbitral procedures in existence will however be considered. The closest to ordinary arbitration is the procedure known as *'judicial reference'*. This is resorted to where parties engaged in litigation agree that the matter in issue or some aspect of it would be more conveniently determined by some person other than a lawyer holding public judicial office, or by some procedure which, though still of an adjudicatory nature, is more informal or more flexible than that of the ordinary courts. To such an agreement, expressed in the form of a joint minute lodged in process, the court is usually willing to interpone its authority. The third party, known as a *'judicial referee'*, holds a position analogous to that of an arbiter, but acts under the authority of the court. He or she is usually nominated by the parties and the rules governing the conduct of the reference are in most respects indistinguishable from those applicable to ordinary arbitration, but the decision is issued not in the form of an award but of a report to the court.

1.6.   Other quasi-arbitral procedures consist of *special régimes* created by legislation for dealing with particular types of dispute.

4

It is very difficult to generalise about them because of their variety. Most, but not all, are compulsory, in the sense that if a matter is within the scope of the régime concerned the parties are not permitted to have recourse to any other forum — even the ordinary courts — to obtain a decision on the substantive matter in issue, though they are in some régimes allowed to select the arbiter or arbitrator. (Due largely to the influence of English legal terminology the terms 'arbiter' and 'arbitrator' are used somewhat indiscriminately in this context.) In many régimes the procedure is quite closely regulated though the award is usually enforced in the same manner as an ordinary decree arbitral. These statutory quasi-arbitral régimes might be described as combining features of both ordinary arbitration and administrative tribunals.

Arbitration as a form of adjudication

1.7.   The judicial character of arbitration in Scots law has often been emphasised. Arbitration proceedings, says the ancient Scots law book *Regiam Majestatem* 'are framed on the model of the judicial process'.[12] The nineteenth century jurist J. M. Bell asserted that 'it is avowedly in the character of a private judge that the arbiter is resorted to by both parties'.[13] The dicta of judges in the ordinary courts are to the same effect. 'Arbiters', stated Lord Chancellor Eldon in a Scottish appeal to the House of Lords,[14] 'ought to go into the room as judges'; and more recently Lord President Clyde remarked that in Scots law an arbiter is 'the final *judge* both of fact and law'.[15] There can be no serious question, therefore, that arbitration under Scots law is a form of adjudication. The notion of adjudication is however itself complex and requires some elucidation.[16] Since judicial dicta on this matter are not very helpful it is necessary to go beyond them and engage in jurisprudential analysis.

1.8.   Adjudication has four distinctive characteristics which are best exemplified in the defended action brought in ordinary courts

[12] Bk. II, Ch. 1, sec. 1, (Stair Society edn. p. 105).
[13] *Arb.* para. 13.
[14] *Maule* v. *Maule* (1816) 4 Dow App. 363 at 380.
[15] *Mitchell-Gill* v. *Buchan* 1921 S.C. 390 at 395.
[16] For a full discussion see Beyleveld D. and Brownsword R., *Law as a Moral Judgment*, London, 1986, chap. 9.

of law. Disputes or doubts which have arisen between people who are actually or potentially at odds are placed before a third person. That person then hands down a decision which he or she has reached by the application of rules or principles — including conventions of language and largely unwritten rules which underlie perceptions of 'fact' — to the facts found. The findings of fact are based on evidence presented in a procedure which has given to each party an equal opportunity of influencing the outcome, assuming approximately equal capacity to present a case either personally or through a representative. That decision is binding upon the litigants. This type of case has *two factual features* — a question at issue between two or more parties, and the determination of that question by a decision which is binding upon them — and *two moral requirements* — the impartiality of the third party and the fairness of the procedure. These are linked by the parties' need to trust the system. In the context of a dispute, no free and selfrespecting person will appeal to, or agree to be bound by a decision of, someone who is suspected of bias or arbitrariness or who habitually conducts proceedings in an unfair manner. At least, no such person will so act unless he or she believes that any bias is in his or her favour, or that the adjudicator is firmly under his or her control, and it is almost inconceivable that all parties to a dispute will entertain such beliefs simultaneously. If corruption in ordinary judges and unfairness in court procedure is other than exceptional it betokens weakness or tyranny in political government; and though submission to an arbiter who has an interest in the outcome may exceptionally be acceptable within a relationship of great personal trust and friendship,[17] it normally suggests unscrupulous use of superior physical, economic, or social power. It is a serious blemish on Scots arbitration law that a party or the agent of a party may competently be appointed arbiter.[18]

1.9. Adjudication, then, is a procedure for fairly determining questions at issue between two or more parties. Such questions do not necessarily involve disagreement. The parties may simply both be in *doubt* on some matter which affects their relations and which

---

[17] As when, in *Njal's Saga*, Gunnar appointed Njal to determine a question between them: Magnusson M. and Palsson H. (Tr.), *Njal's Saga*, Penguin edn., Harmondsworth, 1970, 100.
[18] *Buchan* v. *Melville* (1902) 4 F. 620.

requires resolution even though it has not yet been made the subject of any disputed claim or controverted proposition. Usually, however, the parties are in conflict; a *dispute* or controversy — the terms are interchangeable — has arisen between them. A dispute may for present purposes be defined as a situation in which a claim is made or a proposition asserted by one party and knowingly rejected or denied by the other.[19] Since it is normally a dispute which requires adjudication, it will be convenient henceforth to use the term 'dispute' to mean also a case in which the parties are merely in doubt.

1.10. The importance of the existence of a question at issue should be clearly recognised as essential to adjudication. People sometimes oppose each other and resort to verbal abuse, wilful obstruction (such as a refusal to pay an undisputed debt) and even violence, without there being any disputed claim or proposition which could be the subject of an adjudicator's decision. It has been consistently held by the Scottish courts that arbitration requires a dispute.[20] It seems at first sight as if the need for the existence of a dispute is peculiar to arbitration, rather than a feature of all forms of adjudication, since the ordinary courts regularly deal with undefended cases, where there is normally[21] no question for the court to decide. In such cases, however, the court acts not as adjudicator but merely as part of the system of law-enforcement.

1.11. In non-legal terms, a *'decision'* may be said to be a rational act of choice by which the state of ambiguity inherent in a question is terminated.[22] Rationality has in this context two fundamental requirements — first, that the question must be stated with

---

[19] This is consistent with Scots judicial decisions, on which see paras. 6.2–6.5 below.

[20] *Parochial Board of Greenock* v. *Coghill* (1878) 5 R. 732; *Mackay and Son* v. *Police Commissioners of Leven* (1893) 20 R. 1093; *Caledon Shipbuilding and Enginering Co Ltd* v. *Kennedy* (1906) 14 S.L.T. 133; *Brown* v. *Simpson* (1910) 1 S.L.T. 183; *Woods* v. *Co-operative Insurance Society* 1924 S.C. 692, 1924 S.L.T. 529; *Brodie* v. *Ker* 1952 S.C. 216; *Redpath Dorman Long Ltd* v. *Tarmac Construction Ltd* 1982 S.L.T. 442; *Albyn Housing Society Ltd* v. *Taylor Woodrow Homes Ltd* 1985 S.L.T. 309.

[21] In some types of case, such as those relating to status, there is a question.

[22] 'An essential prerequisite of an occurrence of decision is the existence of a motivating state of ambiguity. . . . Thus in problem $Q = a/b$, the ambiguity can be stated in the form, 'which act shall we take?' White D. J., *Decision Theory*, London, 1969, 1.

reasonable precision, and second, that the ultimate act of choice must be linked to that question by a set of identifiable cognitive operations[23] involving the application of some rule, principle, criterion or standard. In adjudication, where there is a question at issue between two or more persons, these operations are usually, but need not be, fully articulated. For example, when a person experienced in a certain trade determines, in a dispute between two merchants, that goods which he has inspected are not of merchantable quality he does not usually, and may not have the verbal skill to, say why he or she has come to this conclusion. There must nevertheless be 'faith that what is intuited is something that would appear rational if it could be brought to adequate expression'.[24] The rules, principles or standards upon which a conclusion is based need not be part of a pre-existent set to which alone the adjudicator may have recourse,[25] but at least they must be consistent with, and recognised by appropriately experienced persons or by the community generally as appropriately included among, such a set.[26] Neither law nor equity is a closed system; both develop with the society they regulate, and some of the developments may be controversial. The process by which an adjudicator selects from among the available rules, principles and standards and interprets the rules that are applicable may be affected by current social pressures or impulses deep within his or her own mind,[27] but provided that the norms upon which the choice is based are legitimate, and provided the reasoning erected thereon is logical or at least generally accepted as such, the outcome can properly be regarded as a decision.

1.12. Judicial dicta on the meaning of 'decision' outside the context of a particular statutory provision are rare, but such statements as there are seem at least not inconsistent with the views

---

[23] *Ibid.*

[24] Fuller L., 'The Forms and Limits of Adjudication' in Hart and Sachs (eds), *The Legal Process*, 10th edn, London 1958, 421.

[25] Sartorius R., 'Social Policy and Judicial Legislation', in (1971) 8 *American Philosophical Quarterly*, 151.

[26] MacCormick D. N., 'Formal Justice and the Form of Legal Arguments', in Lloyd, Lord (ed), *Introduction to Jurisprudence*, (5th edn), London 1985, 1193.

[27] 'It is difficult to escape the conclusion that the choices which the [legal] system leaves the judge free to make are influenced by the judge's personality, his accumulated social and philosophical makeup, and his sense of the public mood.' Lord McCluskey, Reith Lecture 1, in *The Listener*, 6th Nov. 1986.

here expressed on this matter. For example, a New Zealand judge has remarked[28] that

> 'the word "decision" implies the exercise of a judicial determination as the final and definite result of examining a question.'

Not all decisions made by a person who is an adjudicator involve disputed questions; the question may be raised in the mind of the adjudicator alone. A decision may be an interlocutory order,[29] which need not necessarily have been expressly asked for or objected to by a party.

1.13.   When someone decides a disputed question it is obviously necessary for the decision to be promulgated to the parties. Though the forms in which a decision may be expressed are innumerable, in principle the utterance always amounts to saying 'I decide that ...' a claim is upheld or rejected, a suggested proposition approved or disapproved. This gives the decision of an adjudicator a special character: it *makes* the situation to be what the decider says it is, at least within the social or legal setting of the decision. The facts are just as they have been 'found' to be; the obligations of the parties, previously doubtful, are now established. The situation can be effectively changed only if and when the decision is revoked or quashed; hence, because of the operation of judicial precedent, it is said in connection with the decision of points of law by appellate courts that 'when a judge makes a mistake it becomes the law of the land'.

1.14.   The requirement of *impartiality* — sometimes expressed through the old maxim '*nemo judex in re sua*' ('no-one may be judge in his own cause') — is particularly important, for an impartial adjudicator will probably conduct proceedings fairly. An impartial person is one who is not so swayed by the interests of a social or political group of which he or she is a member, or by personal interest, as to substitute in his or her own mind a different basic question from the question actually presented by the parties for decision. For example, where the parties seek a determination of the question, 'Does A owe £100 to B?', an impartial person will not mentally substitute for this some such question as 'How can I

---

[28] *Winter and Calder* v. *Winter* [1933] N.Z.L.R. 289 per Reed J. at 295.
[29] *Medallion Holidays Ltd* v. *Birch* [1985] I.R.L.R. 406.

ensure that A does not have to pay?' To do so would lead a biased adjudicator first to formulate the preferred outcome and then either to ignore the requirement of logical reasoning altogether or to construct (or unquestioningly adopt from the argument of the preferred party) a plausible set of propositions which appear to support that outcome. It is to prevent the most blatant forms of bias that it has long been established in Scots law that personal financial[30] or close family[31] interest will normally disqualify a judge from sitting.

1.15. Absolute impartiality is probably impossible for human beings. As Lord Justice Scrutton once observed,[32]

'It is very difficult sometimes to be sure that you have put yourself into a thoroughly impartial position between two disputants, one of your own class and one not of your own class.'

Though his Lordship had in mind the problems arising in disputes between employers and workers, similar difficulties arise in disputes between persons of different race, sex, religion or national origin. The problems are compounded by the fact that often the law does not yield any clear result, so that the adjudicator may, without losing sight of the question posed by the parties, legitimately take account of what he or she considers to be sound public policy, such as the need to encourage employers to maintain high standards of safety in their operations. Adjudication achieves best results where the positions of the parties are easily interchangeable and their views of public policy and general morality broadly similar, as is generally the case in disputes between mercantile buyers and sellers of goods. Elsewhere, all that can be expected is that persons acting in a judicial capacity make themselves as aware as Lord Justice Scrutton clearly was of the dangers that exist.

1.16. A *fair procedure*, broadly speaking, is one in which the parties are treated equally, each being given an equal opportunity to influence the outcome. Unless the issue is of such a nature that an investigation by the adjudicator is all that is required to produce a well-informed decision,[33] or the value of the disputed matter is so

[30] *Smith* v. *Liverpool, London and Globe Insurance Co.* (1887) 14 R. 938.
[31] *APS* 1594 c. 216; *APS* 1681 c. 13.
[32] 1 *Cambridge Law Journal* (1921–3), 8.
[33] *MacGregor* v. *Stevenson* (1847) 9 D. 1056.

small that it would be inappropriate to go to the expense of a hearing, each party must be given an equal opportunity to present evidence and argument.[34] Though fairness does not always require that parties be allowed to have professional or lay representatives to present their cases,[35] representation must not be arbitrarily denied[36]; steps must be taken, so far as reasonably practicable, to ensure that each party is made aware in sufficient time of the case to be met, and of such matters as the place and time of hearings and dates for lodging documents and other productions.[37] The spirit of the old maxim '*audiatur et altera pars*' ('let the other side be heard also') must be heeded, and justice must not only be done, it must be seen to be done.[38]

1.17.   Two main *types of procedure* may be identified. They are —

(a) '*adversarial*' (or 'contentious') procedure, in which it is the responsibility of the parties to present evidence and argument to the adjudicator; and
(b) '*investigatory*' (or 'inquisitorial') procedure, in which it is the responsibility of the adjudicator to seek out the facts and discover what rules or standards should apply and how they should be interpreted.

The character of most systems is formed by one of these models, though without excluding features from the other. In general, the procedure of the ordinary courts in Scotland follows the adversarial pattern, but this does not mean that investigation is inconsistent with a judicial role. Statutory tribunals such as, for example, the social security appeal tribunals, often have to investigate the case before them.[39] Ordinary arbitration in modern Scotland usually follows the broad pattern of the ordinary courts,[40] but an arbiter is 'the complete master of procedure'[41] subject to the general duty to act fairly. Thus in a complex case the adversarial model is usually adopted, and the arbiter hears evidence and argument presented by the parties; whereas in a dispute over an

---

[34] *Sharpe* v. *Bickersdyke* (1815) 3 Dow App. 102.
[35] *Glagow Corporation* v. *Paterson and Sons Ltd.* (1901) 3 F. (H.L.) 34.
[36] *Walker* v. *AUEW* 1969 S.L.T. 150.
[37] *Walker* (*supra*).
[38] *Barrs* v. *British Wool Marketing Board* 1957 S.C. 72.
[39] R(SB) 38/85 para. 20.
[40] As did legalistic arbitration in the mediaeval period: see para. 2.12 below.
[41] Guild, *Arb.* 56.

uncomplicated matter such as the quality of goods, the arbiter simply investigates the matter personally.

Arbitration and related concepts

1.18. **Amicable composition**. As explained above, in mediaeval law there existed two forms of arbitration, legalistic and equitable, conducted respectively by an arbiter and an arbitrator. The office of arbitrator was often not clearly distinguished from that of *amicable compositor*. Strictly speaking, the latter was not in any sense a judge but rather a *mediator* whose function was not to decide the dispute but to use his or her good offices to induce the parties to arrive at an agreement, an '*amicabilis compositio*'.[42] Where a mediator or arbitrator is a person of high social standing[43] his or her mere proposals may possess almost compulsory authority in relation to the parties. Given that court decrees were often difficult to enforce in mediaeval society,[44] the practical difference between an agreement reached on the basis of a proposal by an amicable compositor/mediator and a decision by an arbitrator/judge was blurred, and the offices themselves became confused.[45] The process of confusion was no doubt assisted by the practice of appointing a person to act as arbiter, arbitrator and amicable compositor in the same dispute. In modern times mediators certainly exist, but are never referred to as amicable compositors, and the term has fallen out of use. Amicable composition is not, in Scotland at least, a form of arbitration.

1.19. **Consultancy and agency**. It sometimes happens that parties who have a difference of opinion or mutual doubt on some matter that affects their relations, request a third party to investigate and report to them upon it, but without binding themselves to accept his or her conclusions. Such a practice, which may for convenience be called *consultancy*, differs from adjudication because the third party — the consultant — does *not* *decide* the matter, and from mediation in that there is *no* obligation

---

[42] See para. 2.15 below.
[43] As in the dispute between Gilbert Earl of Cassilis and James Gordon of Lochinvar, which was devolved upon the Regent of Scotland, Mary of Guise, in 1555: *Wigt. Chrs.* 75.
[44] Wormald, 'Blood Feud', *passim*; Wormald, *Manrent* 128.
[45] E.g. *Sprout v. Crannoch*, 1398, *Abdn.Recs.* 21.

on the consultant to *promote agreement* between his or her clients. Where parties do agree to be bound, but the third party is not required either expressly or impliedly to apply rules or standards of any kind, the proceedings cannot be regarded as adjudication (because of the absence of standards), or mediation or consultancy (because the parties are bound by the decision). Arguably this kind of transaction, which sometimes occurs when gaps have to be filled in long-term business contracts, results in a contract whose terms are established by the third party as the *agent* of both the principals, not their arbiter. The outcome, whatever its apparent form, is not an award or decree arbitral.

1.20. **Reference**. It has been suggested that a distinction should be drawn between ordinary arbitration and a reference. The latter is said[46] to involve

'the determination of some incidental point material to a question between the parties about which they may be otherwise more or less agreed; as where two persons, in order to remove any doubt or difficulty existing in their minds, or that may appear to stand in the way of some treaty or transaction in which they are mutually concerned, agree'

to place it before a professional person. The former is said by contrast to involve 'a decision either in law or fact as to the rights of parties'. It has also been suggested[47] that

'there is in our law a clear distinction between two classes of submissions; between a reference of the price or value of the subject of the contract and a reference of a dispute.'

This purported distinction arises out of the debasement of the traditional distinction between arbiters and arbitrators. Though the distinction was originally drawn in order to avoid the consequences of certain rules of law, the underlying reasons for it no longer exist, as will be shown below.[48] There are of course occasions on which a third party is asked simply to apply his or her professional knowledge and experience to determine authoritatively a question of fact, and in which he or she needs merely to make observations or conduct tests without seeking

---

[46] Irons, *Arb.* 1.
[47] *Calder* v. *Mackay* (1860) 22 D. 741 per LJC Inglis at 743.
[48] Para. 1.22.

information from any other person. It often happens however — and whether it will cannot usually be foreseen — that more is required, in particular that information has to be obtained by the expert from others. Also, an expert may be faced with unexpected questions of general law or of the proper interpretation of a contract between the parties. If there were truly a distinction in law between arbitration and reference, the question of jurisdiction which would then arise would relate not simply to the terms of the contract between the parties, but to the legal category into which that contract fell. It is submitted that to regard arbitration and reference as distinct types of contract is to make some problems of jurisdiction more complicated than they need to be. The use of the term 'reference' in an arbitration contract should be regarded simply as an indication — not conclusive proof — that the parties did not intend to confer on their arbiter a power to decide questions of law or to hear evidence or argument.

1.21. **Valuation.** A distinction is also sometimes drawn between ordinary arbitration and valuation.[49] The reasons are similar to those which lie behind the supposed distinction between arbitration and reference. Judges have sometimes sought to maintain the distinction in order to emphasise that persons appointed to determine a matter simply by the exercise of professional skill were free from any obligation to take evidence and hear parties.[50] It is, however, quite unnecessary to do so, because judges have also emphasised the procedural freedom of ordinary arbiters.[51] Also, greater confusion is created by the exaltation of the concept of valuation into a separate legal category than is created by the supposed distinction between arbitration and reference. A valuer is after all simply a professional person whose expertise lies in estimating the market value of things; he or she is just one of a great number of kinds of technical expert who can be called upon to determine a question by making observations and applying scientific knowledge or standards derived from professional experience, though no doubt reference to valuers is extremely common. If a special category were required — and it is submitted that it is not — the category of reference would be more appropriate. The decision of the House of Lords in the Scottish

[49] Guild, *Arb.* 3.
[50] E.g. *Nivison* v. *Howat* (1883) 11 R. 182; *Gibson* v. *Fotheringham* 1914 S.C. 987; *Cameron* v. *Nicol* 1930 S.C. 1.
[51] *Christison's Tr.* v. *Callendar-Brodie* (1906) 8 F. 928 per Lord Dunedin at 931.

case of *Stewart* v. *Williamson*[52] provides some support for the view that no distinction exists between ordinary arbitration and valuation, though it could be argued that the decision should not be regarded as applicable beyond the context of section 11 of the Agricultural Holdings (Scotland) Act 1908.

1.22. **Reference, valuation, and legal policy.** There are a number of reasons why distinctions were drawn in the past between ordinary arbitration on the one hand and reference and valuation on the other. Some have been briefly touched on in the preceding paragraphs. In some cases, especially in connection with construction contracts, judges clearly sought to prevent persons whose expertise lay in fields other than law from deciding questions of law,[53] though in view of the fact that, then as now, arbiters normally employ a solicitor as clerk in all but the simplest cases such a policy was and is unnecessary to protect the parties. In other cases the motive was to avoid the application of the rule which was in force until removed by the Arbitration (Scotland) Act 1894 whereby an arbitration agreement which did not name the arbiter was invalid.[54] The rise of a class of technical experts who undertook to determine some types of dispute for a fee was a reason for restricting so far as possible the scope of the rule which formerly existed that arbitration was a gratuitous contract,[55] and one way of doing this was to seek to create a separate category of proceeding to which the rule did not apply. The restrictions on the payment of arbiters no longer apply.[56] Where the reason which gave rise to a common law rule no longer exists, the rule itself may disappear — in the words of the old maxim, '*cessante ratione legis, cessat lex ipsa*', a principle which appears to be acknowledged in Scots law.[57] In so far, therefore, as a rule of law once existed distinguishing ordinary arbitration from reference or valuation on any of the abovementioned grounds it may be said to have disappeared with the causes which gave rise to it. Attempts were also made to limit the effect of the 1695 legislation which restricted the grounds on which arbitral awards were challengeable.[58]

---

[52] 1910 S.C. (H.L.) 47.
[53] E.g. in *Calder* v. *Mackay* (1860) 22 D. 741.
[54] E.g. in *Smith* v. *Wharton-Duff* (1843) 5 D. 749 per Lord Mackenzie at 751–2.
[55] E.g. in *Jolly* v. *Young* (1834) 13 S. 188.
[56] *Macintyre Brothers* v. *Smith* 1913 S.C. 129 per Lord Kinnear at 132.
[57] *Beith's Trs.* v. *Beith* 1950 S.C. 66; Smith T. B., *Sh. Comm.* 40.
[58] E.g. in *Robertson* v. *Clephan* (1756) 5 Bro. Supp. 852.

Though the 1695 legislation is still in force, those attempts were rejected,[59] and do not provide a ground for the retention of a distinction between ordinary arbitration on the one hand and either reference or valuation on the other.

1.23. Only two issues of policy which could reasonably have a bearing on the distinction remain, and only one of these is of any importance or difficulty — the question of the immunity of arbiters from liability for negligence. The other is created by section 9 of the Sale of Goods Act 1979, which provides that where a valuer appointed under a contract of sale to fix the price of the goods fails to do so the sale agreement is avoided. In Scotland such a valuer would normally come within the definition of an arbiter, and it does not seem that in that context any difficulties could arise from this provision.

1.24. The immunity of arbiters, by contrast, is a difficult and controversial matter. It is not regulated by statute and has never been directly raised in the Scottish courts, though it has been the subject of some judicial dicta.[60] The question is therefore still open so far as this legal system is concerned, though it is probable that arbiters are under Scots law immune from suit in relation to their awards, but not otherwise. As is indicated in chapter 8 below, where the matter is discussed more fully, some reasons of public policy can be adduced for granting this limited immunity to those who, without holding any public judicial office, decide disputed or doubtful questions which are at issue between two or more persons. Since those reasons relate to the existence of a dispute, the problem of distinguishing for this purpose between arbitration and valuation, as is done in England,[61] or arbitration and reference, does not arise.

1.25. **Certification**. The distinction between arbitration and certification is of real practical importance as well as some difficulty. Experts are often asked to certify that some work has been satisfactorily executed, or that a contractor is entitled to a certain payment, or that some object is of a certain quality or

---

[59] *Morrison* v. *Aberdeen Market Co.* (1847) 9 D. 910.
[60] *McMillan* v. *Free Church of Scotland* (1862) 24 D. 1282 per Lord Curriehill at 1295.
[61] *Arenson* v. *Casson Beckman Rutley & Co.* [1975] 3 All E.R. 901.

standard, or that the accounts of a certain business are in order. The contracts out of which certification procedures arise differ widely in their terms. Some state clearly that the expert's certificate binds both the parties to the contract; others may appear at first sight to bind both parties, but another clause providing explicitly for arbitration may deprive the certificate of binding effect;[62] others may bind only one party, or even neither. It is a necessary, but not a sufficient, condition of the arbitral quality of a certificate that both parties are bound by its terms.

1.26.   Scottish authorities on the subject of certification are inconclusive. In two cases the judges refer (*obiter*) to the grounds of challenge of the validity of certificates in terms which suggest that they do not regard certification as arbitration. In *MacDonald* v. *Malcolm*[63] Lord Curriehill thought the grounds were 'fraud or malversation', and Lord Deas thought that 'gross dereliction of duty', 'abuse of powers' and 'errors or omissions distinctly specified' were 'grounds of objection' which 'ought to be enquired into'; and in *Robertson* v. *Jarvie*[64] Lord President Dunedin remarked that parties could not complain 'unless they urge something exceedingly specific against the architect's measurement, or accuse him of fraud or of committing some specific blunder which could be expressed in so many words'. Such grounds are substantially wider than those upon which an arbiter's award may be reduced in terms of the legislation of 1695 as interpreted by modern case law.[65] *Muir* v. *Turnbull and Findlay*[66] contains an *obiter dictum* to the effect that certification is not arbitration, though opinion is reserved, while *Chapman and Son* v. *Edinburgh Prison Board*[67] suggests that the opposite view is correct. The remaining Scots case dealing with certification[68] is consistent with either opinion.

---

[62] See *Port Glasgow Magistrates* v. *Scottish Construction Ltd.* 1960 S.L.T. 319 at 320; *Inverdale Construction Ltd (In Liquidation)* v. *Meikleriggs Housing Society Ltd.* 1978 S.L.T. 81.

[63] (1855) 17 D. 1033.

[64] (1907/8) 15 S.L.T. 703.

[65] Especially *Adams* v. *Great North of Scotland Railway Co.* (1890) 18 R. (H.L.) 1 per Lord Watson at 7–9; *Holmes Oil Co.* v. *Pumpherston Oil Co.* (1891) 18 R. (H.L.) 52 per Lord Watson at 55.

[66] (1906) 22 Sh. Ct. Rep. 324.

[67] (1844) 6 D. 1288.

[68] *Craib and Tannahill* v. *Stewart* (1905) 21 Sh. Ct. Rep. 295.

1.27. In these circumstances it is necessary to consider English authorities. Their effect[69] is summarised by Russell.[70] It appears that in England the tests for determining whether a certificate is an arbitral award include

'(a) whether the certificate is intended to embody a decision that is final and binding on the parties. If it is, then it is in effect an award.

(b) whether (in the case that the determination is left to an agent of one of the parties) the agent is or is not intended to function independently of the principal. If he is not, it cannot be arbitration.

(c) whether the 'certifier' has merely to decide whether the requirements of a contract have been met, or whether he is entitled to impose a standard of his own'.

There can be no doubt that the certificate must, to bear any likeness whatever to an arbitral award, be binding on both parties. Clearly also, in giving a certificate, the expert must act independently, though this was clearly not intended[71] to mean that the parties may not appoint the professional adviser of one of them as arbiter. (In Scots law it is competent to appoint a servant or professional adviser of a party as arbiter, provided the relationship is known to the other at the time of the appointment and not objected to.)[72] The third test is more puzzling. The central question in many arbitrations is whether the requirements of the contract have been met, and in such circumstances it would be improper for an arbiter to take the view that the specifications laid down in the contract were too low or too high, whatever his professional opinion might be. It is therefore difficult to see why a certificate should not count as an arbitral award merely on the ground that the certifier could not impose his own standard.

1.28. In view of the unsatisfactory state of the authorities, the matter has to be considered on the basis of principle, so far as Scotland is concerned. Taking as an example the situation in which

---

[69] In particular the effect of *Minster Trust* v. *Traps Tractors* [1954] I W.L.R. 963.

[70] *Arb.* 1982, 57.

[71] By Lord Devlin in *Minster Trust Ltd.* (*supra*).

[72] *Crawford Brothers* v. *Commissioners of Northern Lighthouses* 1925 S.C. (H.L.) 22 per Lord Buckmaster at 30; *Buchan* v. *Melville* (1902) 4 F. 620; Bankton, *Inst.* I.23.14.

a contractor claims an interim or final payment under a construction contract, there is initially *no dispute* between the contractor and the employer, for at that stage neither the employer nor any agent of his has rejected the claim. There is not even any question in the minds of the parties, for the contractor must be presumed to believe that the claim is sound, and the employer (or his or her agent) has only just received it for consideration. Disputes or questions may arise between the presentation of the claim and the issue or refusal of a certificate, but it would be odd to suggest that a dispute or question submitted to arbitration arose *only during* the arbitration proceedings. Further, many claims do not give rise to any dispute at all. If the supervising expert is conscientious, there will naturally be questions in her or his own mind, but in arbitration it is the *parties* who must be in doubt or conflict. In such cases there is, in effect, nothing to adjudicate, and since arbitration is a form of adjudication, the process of certification cannot then be arbitration. In addition, it is common practice in connection with large construction projects for a great deal of the routine work of checking the contractor's claim to be done not by the supervising expert personally but by a member of his or her staff. Now, though in Scots law an arbiter may like any other judge take advice on a complex question of fact or law,[73] the arbiter's authority may not be delegated.[74] It therefore appears that unless those practices are wrong and should be abandoned (which would be highly inconvenient) certificates issued in such circumstances are not arbitral awards. In some cases there may also be some doubt whether the certifier has a contract with both the parties. There may be a contract with one party (the employer in a construction contract) in terms of which he agrees to issue a certificate in specified circumstances; that party may have agreed with the other signatory of the contract that the certificates of that expert shall in certain circumstances be conclusive evidence of a certain fact, such as the sufficiency of works, so that no dispute can arise except as to the validity of the certificate itself;[75] but it does

---

[73] *Caldedonian Railway Co.* v. *Lockhart* (1860) 3 Macq. App. 808 per Campbell L.C. at 812.

[74] *Stark* v. *Thumb*, (1630) Mor. 6834, referring to 'the civil law and reason', perhaps consciously departing from the slightly different canon law, under which delegation was permissible if the submitters had expressly so provided: Hostiensis, *Comm.* X. 1.43.13, Fol. 209–210.

[75] Pike, A., *I.Mech.E./I.E.E. Conditions of Contract*, London 1984, 75 and 85, discussing clause 31(ix) of those conditions.

not therefore follow that the expert has a contractual relationship with both contracting parties, and arbitration implies the existence of such a contract.

1.29. It is suggested therefore that while it is not impossible for a certificate to be an arbitral award, the absence of a dispute or question between the parties at the outset of the certification procedure, or the acceptance of the certifier's power to delegate aspects of the investigation to subordinates, or the absence of a contractual relationship between the certifier and one of the parties bound by its terms, or the fact that the certificate is not binding on one or both of the parties, will prevent many certificates from having an arbitral character.

1.30. **Domestic tribunals**. Many voluntary associations provide in their constitutions for the establishment of private tribunals to determine disputes between members arising out of club activities or to impose penalties on members who have broken club rules. Such tribunals provide a form of adjudication, but though their jurisdiction is voluntary, being based on the members' agreement to adhere to the constitution of the association, they do not necessarily act as arbiters. A distinction may be drawn between proceedings which are disciplinary and may lead to the imposition of a penalty, and those which deal with other types of dispute arising between members. The former have been held not to be arbitration[76] whereas the latter may be.[77]

1.31. **Statutory régimes**. Ordinary arbitration has developed, so far as some types of dispute are concerned, into a statutory régime. Some of these régimes, such as that dealing with disputes between landlords and tenants of agricultural holdings, have retained the title of arbitration while also coming within the ambit of the Scottish Committee of the Council on Tribunals.[78] The probable reason why they continue to be regarded as arbitration is that the parties retain some freedom, for example in the selection of the person who is to determine their dispute. Other régimes, such as that dealing with questions of compensation for lands taken for

[76] *McMillan* v. *Free Church* (1859) 22 D. 290 at 324.
[77] *Salvesen* v. *Young* 1965 S.L.T. (Sh. Ct.) 81.
[78] Tribunals and Inquiries Act 1971, Schedule 1 Part II.

public purposes, have become fully fledged statutory tribunals.[79] For the former, the title 'arbitration' remains not inappropriate even where the jurisdiction of the statutory 'arbiters' is compulsory, because on matters for which statute makes no provision the rules of ordinary arbitration apply.[80]

Conclusion

1.32. Though methods of dealing with disputes are difficult to categorise as they tend in practice to shade into one another, it is possible to establish a reasonably clear distinction between ordinary arbitration and other types of procedure. Professor Walker's definition quoted at the beginnig of this chapter[81] apparently sought to comprehend quasi-arbitral procedures as well as ordinary arbitration, arguably an impossible task, but it requires very little amendment to make it serve for the latter alone. In the light of the foregoing discussion ordinary arbitration may be defined as

'the adjudication of a dispute or question of law of fact or value by one or more persons not acting as ordinary public judges, to whom the parties who are at issue or in doubt agree to refer the matter for decision, it being within their power of transaction.'

---

[79] E.g. the Lands Tribunal for Scotland established under the Land Compensation Act 1963.
[80] *Mitchell-Gill* v. *Buchan* 1921 S.C. 390 per L. P. Clyde at 395.
[81] Above, para. 1.1.

CHAPTER TWO

THE HISTORY OF ARBITRATION IN SCOTLAND

Introduction

2.1. The history of arbitration and related procedure in Scotland may for convenience be divided into three sections relating to the following periods:-

(i) from prehistoric times to the eleventh century AD;
(ii) from the twelfth century to the middle of the seventeenth; and
(iii) from the middle of the seventeenth century to the present day.[1]

2.2. Of the first period little can be said because comparatively little is known.[2] Probably there were persons or assemblies exercising judicial functions with a sufficient degree of formality to be regarded as courts.[3] If so, it would make sense to regard as arbiters or arbitrators those to whom disputes were otherwise referred by agreement, but little evidence remains of their activities. The Celtic peoples in Scotland certainly accorded respect to the 'britheamh', a person learned in the customary law who seems to have acted in both a consultative and an adjudicatory capacity,[4] and the Nordic had their 'birleymen' for the settlement of disputes between neighbours.[5] Both of these survived into recorded history. It is probable that the informal systems of settling disputes within kin groups or 'names' by the head of the name, and between members of different names by their respective heads or some independent person of high standing, existed in the

---

[1] 1987.
[2] Robinson O. F. and others *Eur. Leg. Hist.*, 258.
[3] *Ibid.*, 258–9.
[4] Cameron J., *Celtic Law*, Glasgow, 1937, 12–7, 162, 193–5; Duncan A. A. M., *Scotland; The Making of the Kingdom*, Edinburgh, 1975, 106.
[5] *Carn.Ct.Bk.* Appendix A, cxiii–cxvi.

first period as they undoubtedly did in the second, though they do not reveal themselves in documents until the fifteenth century, when lordship, hitherto largely territorial, was reinforced by written personal bonds[6] which often contained what amounted (from the point of view of the formal legal system) to equitable arbitration agreements.

2.3. The second period is of enormous importance in Scottish legal history. It saw both the reception of the civil and canon law systems, and the establishment of a formal court structure. Until recently, historians, especially legal historians, concentrated upon these developments and paid relatively little attention to informal systems of dispute settlement. In the last few years, however, the balance has begun to be redressed.[7] While it has long been known that legalistic arbitration was firmly established in Scotland by the beginning of the thirteenth century, the considerable part played in Scottish society by more informal systems of dispute settlement, and the strikingly co-operative relations that existed between the ordinary courts and both legalistic and equitable arbitration are now becoming more apparent.

2.4. During the third period the law of arbitration in Scotland has been shaped primarily by the courts. Parliament and the jurists — notably J. M. Bell — have also had a role to play, but it has been a subordinate one. If quasi-arbitral statutory regimes are left out of account, the legislature has intervened in Scots arbitration law only three times in the last three hundred years, through the Articles of Regulation 1695 section 25, the Arbitration (Scotland) Act 1894 (which consisted of only seven short sections, three of which were formal), and the Administration of Justice (Scotland) Act 1972 section 3. There has been no codifying statute on the model of the English Arbitration Acts. Scots arbitration law as it now exists might be described as the creation mainly of mediaeval juristic architects and nineteenth century judicial and Parliamentary building contractors, with some rather hasty, do-it-yourself additions by seventeenth and twentieth century

---

[6] Wormald, *Manrent*, 47.
[7] See e.g. Brown J. M., 'The exercise of power' in Brown J. M. (ed), *Scottish Society in the Fifteenth Century*, London, 1977; Lenman B. and Parker G., 'Crime and Control in Scotland 1500–1800', in 1980 *History Today*, 13,15; Rae T. I., *The Administration of the Scottish Border 1513–1603*, Edinburgh, 1966, 123–6; Wormald, 'Blood Feud'; Wormald, *Community*, London, 1981.

legislators. Though the work of the architects is not immediately apparent, being hidden by the generally sound work of the building contractors, it can be discerned in the structure of the edifice. The do-it-yourself additions are all too obvious.

The establishment of Scots arbitration law

2.5. Extracurial dispute settlement in mediaeval and renaissance Scotland. During most of the second of the three periods mentioned above, law was formally administered in Scotland through two systems of courts — the feudal structure of baronial, burghal and shrieval courts supervised by the royal justiciars and chamberlain and headed by the king's own court, and the ecclesiastical structure of diocesan courts held by the bishop's official and centred on the papal curia.[8] But important as these were in satisfying the demand for the redress of grievances and in strengthening the attachment both of secular vassals and tenants to their lords and ultimately to the king and of Scotland as an outlying province of the Church to the Holy See, they were not the only means that then existed for dealing with conflict. Other, less systematic, procedures for dispute settlement existed within and between kin groups and among neighbours;[9] and the gradual growth of external trade created a role for mercantile arbitration also.[10] Legislation passed in 1427[11] distinguished arbitration in burghs from other secular as well as from ecclesiastical arbitration.

2.6. Far from being regarded with disapproval by the authorities in mediaeval Scotland, extracurial procedures appear to have been accepted and even encouraged. The Church had a long tradition of favour towards procedures that tended to achieve not only justice but reconciliation.[12] Early in the Church's history it became one of

---

[8] Various authors, *An Introduction to Scottish Legal History*, Stair Society, Edinburgh, 1958, Chapters XXIII to XXXI.

[9] Wormald, 'Blood Feud', 66.

[10] See e.g. Wade, T. C. (ed), *Acta Curiae Admirallatus Scotiae 1557–62*, Stair Society, Edinburgh, 1937, xxi–ii. A body of mercantile law clearly existed for the arbiters to apply: Murray, Lord, 'The Law Merchant', in *An Introductory Survey of the Sources and Literature of Scots Law*, Stair Society, Edinburgh, 1936, 240–248.

[11] *APS* 1427 c. 6 (Vol. II, 14).

[12] Julien, *Ev.Hist.*, 187, 201.

the functions of a bishop to reconcile differences between members of the Christian community and even to adjudicate upon them, one of the objects being to prevent their being brought before non-Christian judges to the detriment of the Church's reputation.[13] Though the episcopal jurisdiction became in the period here under discussion as legalistic as any secular court, the Church did not cease to approve of informal methods of dispute settlement so long as they did not result in serious injustice or damage important ecclesiastical interests. In Scotland, a considerable amount of litigation, not only in connection with disputes over questions of status and succession but also in connection with obligations fortified by oaths, was permitted by the Crown to be dealt with in accordance with canon law by ecclesiastical courts. Given that those courts favoured amicable means of settlement, and that an experienced arbiter, arbitrator or amicable compositor could often be found from among the clergy, ecclesiastical attitudes to arbitration must have been particularly influential.

2.7.   The growth of arbitration in Scotland was not simply an indirect result of the Crown's policy of allowing considerable scope to ecclesiastical jurisdiction. A more considered encouragement of arbitration is shown by the fact that the royal courts were very willing, certainly from the fifteenth century onwards and quite probably earlier, to allow even cases which would now be regarded as of a criminal nature to be submitted to an arbiter or arbitrator privately chosen by the parties.[14] Why most kings of Scotland adopted this policy is a matter for speculation. Though in mediaeval constitutional theory one of the primary obligations of royalty was to do justice and redress grievances, there were different ways of discharging it.

> 'Law (standing for learning and the application of rules) and love (standing for commonsense and bonds of affection) can be seen as contrasting styles in the settlement of disputes in the Middle Ages'.[15]

---

[13] *Ibid.*, 189.

[14] See e.g. *Carruthers* v. *Maxwell*, 1471 *ADA* 22; *Inglis* v. *Cunningham*, 1483 *ADA* 134; *Lindsay* v. *Wemyss*, 1489 *ADA* 142, *Malevale* v. *Malevale*, 1493 *ADA* 176; *Hepburn* v. *Wauchope*, 1532, *Acta Sessionis* (Stair), 92; *McLucas* v. *H.M. Advocate*, 1650, *Sel.Just.Cas.*, Vol. III, 838–9.

[15] Clanchy M., 'Law and Love in the Middle Ages', in *Law and Human Relations*, (Past and Present Society) 1980, 3.

Some monarchs, notably the Emperor Frederick II (1215–50) and the Anglo-Norman and Plantagenet kings who laid the foundations of the English system of government, emphasised the rules of law and the courts. Others, such as Louis IX of France (St Louis) (1226–50) laid greater stress on the amicable settlement of disputes, using rather than cutting through the social bonds of kinship and neighbourhood. Though they did not neglect to establish and maintain a system of formal adjudication in courts of law, they permitted and encouraged conciliation and the submission to arbitration of the often complex disputes and vendettas which came to their notice.

2.8.   There are a number of possible reasons for the adoption by Scottish monarchs of the less legalistic policy. Unlike their English counterparts, they did not derive their original authority from conquest, and the Norman elements introduced into the aristocracy between the latter part of the reign of Alexander I (1107–24) and the death of William the Lion (1165–1214) were peacefully absorbed into Scottish society.[16] There was therefore no need to use courts of law as a means of consolidating foreign rule over a native population, though the possession of formal feudal jurisdiction may have helped incomers who had no local family connections to consolidate their power. More importantly perhaps, the relative poverty of the Scottish Crown, frequent royal minorities, and the difficulty of communicating with remote parts of the kingdom must have been a powerful inducement to rely as far as possible upon traditional and local means of bringing warring individuals and groups to agreement or at least to accept a decision reached by respected kin or 'freindis'.

2.9.   The differences between the English and the Scots style of conflict management in this period should not of course be overestimated. Extracurial dispute settlement is now recognised by historians as having had an important part to play in English as well as Scots mediaeval society.[17] Comparisons are made more difficult by reason of the poverty of Scots legal records, and by reason of the fact that economic and social differences between the two countries may have created different patterns of disputes as

[16] Duncan A. A. M., *Scotland: The Making of the Kingdom*, Edinburgh, 1975, 142.
[17] Powell E., 'Arbitration and the Law in England in the late middle ages', (1983) *Transactions of the Royal Historical Society*, 49.

well as of resort to dispute settlement procedures. Nevertheless the broad impression remains that the style of Scottish royal government was much more favourable than English to informal methods.

2.10. In the eyes of contemporary English administrators Scottish justice may have seemed rather unsophisticated, but it is possible that in the late thirteenth and early fourteenth centuries the Scottish preference for traditional forms of dispute settlement and greater reliance upon the exercise of authority by the nobility, small and great, acting as 'arbiters, arbitrators and amicable compositors' in questions involving their 'kin, servandis, tennantis and parttakeris' may have helped to stiffen resistance to English rule and the more legalistic style of government which went with it. It was only towards the end of the sixteenth century, when bonds of kinship had been weakened, partly perhaps by religious division but more obviously because social welfare and discipline were being increasingly taken over from the kin by the kirk and the nobility began to think of their authority as based on the ownership of property rather than personal loyalty, that the management of conflict by means of the rule of law on the English model lost its unattractiveness in the eyes of leading figures on the Scottish political stage, and that an important barrier to incorporating union as a solution to the problem of relations with England could be removed.

2.11. **The forms of extracurial dispute settlement**. Three forms of extracurial dispute settlement appear to have been recognised by the law during this period of Scottish history and were reflected in the common late mediaeval practice of constituting a person 'arbiter, arbitrator and amicable compositor'[18] when appointing him to deal with a dispute. By means of this phrase the draftsman enabled the appointee to act in accordance with any one of three procedural systems. The first two were the legalistic and equitable forms of arbitration: the third was mediation.

2.12. *Legalistic arbitration*. An arbiter was expected to handle proceedings in a relatively formal manner,[19] and to adhere strictly

---

[18] See e.g. *Registrum Episcopatus Moraviensis*, Bannatyne Club, Edinburgh, 1837, 238.
[19] Fowler, *Forms*, 143–4.

to positive law.[20] This is the practice reflected in the first treatise on Scots law to deal in a systematic way with arbitration — *Regiam Majestatem*, a work now believed to have been compiled in the early fourteenth century[21] — and impliedly criticised by the mediaeval makar Robert Henryson in his poem 'The Taill of the Scheip and the Doig'.[22] Many of the rules and principles contained in *Regiam Majestatem* are clearly derived from civilian or canonist sources, and in general the picture of arbitration which it paints is of a system 'framed' as it says,[23] 'on the model of the judicial process'. In particular, the guidance it gives on such matters as what kinds of person can validly submit a dispute to arbitration, who can act as arbiter, what kinds of question can be submitted, what is to be done where there is a submission to two arbiters who cannot agree, and how an award should be issued, can be traced with reasonable certainty to the Corpus Juris or Justinian, the canonist Decretals, or the writings of the civilian jurist Azo.[24]

2.13. This relatively legalistic form of arbitration, which has had a very strong influence upon the modern system of ordinary arbitration, was undertaken by lay and ecclesiastical arbiters, but the civil and canon laws which they respectively applied differed in some respects. The civil law provided that a decree arbitral could be reduced only by means of the '*exceptio doli*'.[25] The '*dolus*' which the challenger of the decree had to prove consisted in 'any guile, chicanery or trickery used to circumvent, defraud or dupe another person'.[26] The canon law on the other hand provided that the decree of an arbiter might be reduced also on grounds of '*laesio enormis*',[27] that is, serious injury or 'enorm lesion' as it came to be called in Scotland. From an early date until the Articles of Regulation 1695 Scots law accepted the canonist rule that enorm lesion as well as *dolus* was a ground of reduction of a decree arbitral.[28] This may have been due to two factors — the large

[20] Julien, *Ev.Hist.*, 214.
[21] Webster, B., *The sources of history: Studies in the uses of historical evidence — Scotland from the 11th century to 1603*, London, 1975, 167.
[22] Wood H. H. (ed), *The Poems and Fables of Robert Henryson*, Edinburgh, 1978, 42 at 44.
[23] Bk. II, Ch. 1, Art. 2, page 105.
[24] *Ibid.*, 105–11.
[25] Fowler, *Forms*, 140: Julien, *Ev.Hist.*, 228.
[26] *D.*4.3.1.2: Thomas, *Text*, 228.
[27] Fowler, *Forms*, 142.
[28] Stair, *Inst.*, IV.1.60.

proportion of ecclesiastics who staffed the central secular courts in Scotland until the Reformation, and the influence from the late thirteenth to the fifteenth centuries of the continental school of jurists known as the 'Post-Glossators' or 'Commentators'. As Rudolph Sohm remarked,[29]

> 'The fact that the Canon Law came to be recognised in the secular as well as in the ecclesiastical courts was due to the way in which the Commentators developed Roman Law in accordance with the principles of the Canonists.'

The Commentators were concerned to reconcile the learned civil and canon law with local law, especially in the field of procedure.[30]

2.14. *Equitable arbitration.* The arbit*rator*, on the other hand, was permitted to handle proceedings more informally and might decide disputes in an equitable manner.[31] This latitude was particularly useful in handling complex disputes among or between members of kindreds, for by this means all the issues in a complex quarrel could be dealt with together. Indeed, the concept of the arbitrator (which is not found in classical Roman law) may have been developed to integrate the traditional dispute-handling procedures of the kindred into the legal systems of the period, though it was also found useful in the context of mercantile and neighbourhood disputes. It appears to have been developed in the twelfth century by the jurist Johannes Bassianus or one of his contemporaries to overcome 'differences between contemporary practice and arbitration as described in the Corpus Juris Civilis'.[32] The decree of an arbitrator might encompass all the particular quarrels between feuding families in a single global decision based on a sense of what was equitable in all the circumstances. An arbitrator could also deal with questions which would not now be regarded even as matters of equity but rather as things determined by agreement or by the market, such as the value or price or amount of something. What later came to be regarded as the completion of 'a bargain not adjusted'[33] would in mediaeval society have been considered to be the decision on grounds of general

[29] Sohm R., *The Institutes — A Textbook of the History and System of Roman Private Law*, Trans. Ledlie J. C., 3rd edn., Oxford, 1907, 143.
[30] Robinson O. F. and others, *Eur. Leg. Hist.*, 116.
[31] Julien, *Ev. Hist.*, 214.
[32] Fowler, *Forms*, 135.
[33] As in *Robertson* v. *Clephan* (1756) 5 Bro.Supp. 852.

principles of justice and custom of a dispute arising out of a relationship.[34] Not surprisingly, given the types of case with which arbitrators dealt, the grounds upon which the decree of an arbitrator could be reduced were different from those available to a person who wished to attack the decree of an arbiter. The former could not only be challenged on grounds of *dolus* or *laesio enormis*; it could also be reviewed and corrected by recourse to the '*arbitrium boni viri*',[35] that is, the judgement of a good man, usually a judge.[36] The important differences between an arbiter and an arbitrator in the mediaeval period were first, that the latter was much more free from restrictions imposed by procedural and substantive law, and could devise a composite equitable solution to a complex quarrel, and second, that his decrees — or hers, for canon lawyers at least agreed that a woman could act in this capacity[37] — were subject to an additional mode of review.

2.15. *Mediation.* An *amicable compositor* appears to have been a person whose function it was to bring disputing parties to agreement. According to the *Epitome of Julian*, an edition of the *Novels* of Justinian,[38] those who acted as amicable compositors were to 'force the litigants to transact rather than themselves judge'.[39] They were, in effect, mediators or conciliators. Among the Scottish examples of the work of persons acting in this capacity is an '*amicabilis compositio*' between the Abbey of Inchaffray and the Hospital of Brackly in the middle of the thirteenth century brought about by the good offices of the bishops of Dunblane and St Andrews.[40] The office was often confused with that of arbitrator, probably because of the frequency with which people were appointed to act in either capacity as they thought fit, and because the effect of a recommendation by a mediator of higher social standing than the parties was not dissimilar in practice to that of a

---

[34] Tawney R. H., *Religion and the Rise of Capitalism*, Pelican edn., 1948, 52; Atiyah P. S., *The Rise and Fall of Freedom of Contract*, Oxford, 1979, 61–3.

[35] Fowler, *Forms*, 139.

[36] *Ibid.*, 140.

[37] Julien, *Ev.Hist.*, 212–3.

[38] Robinson O. F. and others, *Eur.Leg.Hist.*, 40.

[39] Fowler, *Forms*, 135.

[40] '. . . *mediantibus bone memorie Dumblanensi . . . et venerabili fratre nostro Sancti Andree Episcopis*'. Lindsay W. A., Dowden J. and Thomson J. M. (eds.), *Charters of the Abbey of Inchaffray*, Scottish History Society, First Series, Edinburgh, 1908, 78–9.

judgement by an arbitrator, given the weakness of enforcement machinery in the mediaeval state.

2.16.   **The application of arbitration law.** The treatment of arbitration law in mediaeval Scots textbooks, taken by itself, might lead one to think that legalistic arbitration was much more important than the equitable variety, and that the services of an arbiter applying strictly the civil or canon law were more sought after than those of the equitable arbitrator. *Regiam Majestatem* mentions the arbitrator only twice,[41] though on one of those occasions[42] it states that arbit*rators*, unlike arbit*ers*, may determine 'any question between husband and wife, or affecting personal liberty, or any criminal cause'. The *Practicks* of Sir James Balfour of Pittendreich, written in the second half of the sixteenth century, mention the arbitrator only once,[43] and then in a manner which suggests that the term was not being used in the distinct sense which it had acquired in mediaeval jurisprudence. However, surviving submissions to arbitration, court records, and other documents relating to disputes between kindreds, neighbours, and political interest groups suggest that resort to equitable arbitration was not by any means infrequent.

2.17.   The common style in which third parties were appointed to deal with a dispute between or among members of a 'name' — as 'arbiters, arbitrators and amicable compositors' — meant that they could act in any of these three capacities as they thought fit. Disputes within and between 'names' were often complex, with each side raking up all the grievances they could think of, these being collected together in a general submission of 'all debaitis, causis, querelis, actiounis, and controversiis quhatsumever'.[44] In such cases it must frequently have been convenient to act either as arbitrator or as amicable compositor, for a legalistic approach would in many such cases have implied the rejection of claims upon which one or more parties laid great store[45], with the result — given the weakness of official agencies of law enforcement — that

---

[41] II.4.10, page 107; II.6.2., page 108.
[42] II.6.2.
[43] c. III, page 412.
[44] Pitcairn, *Trials*, Vol. I, 167.
[45] Selznick P., *Law, Society and Industrial Justice*, Transaction Books, 1980, 13–4.

the decision was ineffective. Furthermore, the range of matters with which in practice an arbitrator dealt was coextensive with those which could be settled by amicable composition. Assault,[46] kidnapping,[47] and even homicide[48] could be and were dealt with by arbitrators, as well as what would now be regarded as civil questions, such as complex claims and counterclaims concerning land rights[49] and tocher[50] (dowry). One agreement — a bond of friendship between members of the Murray family in 1586 — went so far as to provide that Sir John Murray of Tullibardine and eight others should judge all disputes, civil and criminal, between members of the name.[51] Though the submission of criminal matters was not uncommon elsewhere in mediaeval Europe,[52] it seems to have been accepted as normal much later in Scotland — up to the middle of the seventeenth century[53] — than in most other countries.

2.18. The submission of a dispute to the judgement of an arbitrator or the good offices of an amicable compositor was not always considered to require the concurrence of every person involved. For example, in an agreement between Scott of Branxholm and Ker of Cesfurde in 1564 Scott agreed that if the Laird of Ormstoune (accused of the 'slaughter' of Ker's servant) refused to accept the decree arbitral pronounced by arbitrators chosen by himself and Ker, Scott would 'nowther manteine, fortife nor assist him theireftir in ony time cuming' but would 'tak pairt and fortife, in honest and lesum manner, with the said Lard of Cesfurde, in his contrar'. Scott further agreed that none of his

---

[46] E.g. in the submission between Somervile of Playne and Schaw of Cammysmort concerning the alleged 'hurting and mutilacioune' of the former: Pitcairn, *Trials*, Vol. I, 167.

[47] E.g. *Carruthers* v. *Maxwell*, 1471, *ADA* 22.

[48] E.g. in the submission by Scott of Branxholm and Ker of Cesfurde, 23 March 1564, concerning *inter alia* 'the slaughter of umquhile ... Best, servand to the said Lard of Cesfurde': Pitcairn, *Trials*, Vol. III., 390 ff.

[49] E.g. in a submission between Gilbert Earl of Cassilis and James Gordon of Lochinvar in 1546: *Wigt. Chrs.*, 70–1.

[50] *Wigt. Chrs.*, 247.

[51] Wormald, *Manrent*, 394.

[52] E.g. France: Jeanclos Y., *L'arbitrage en Bourgogne et en Champagne du XII au XV siècle*, Dijon, 1977, 64.

[53] See e.g. *McLucas* v. *H.M. Advocate and Others*, 1650, *Sel.Just.Cas.*, Vol. III, 838–9.

'kynne, freindis, servandis, menne, tennentis, assistaris and pairtakeris' would 'ony way persew the said Lard of Cesfurde, nor na uther comprehendit under this present appointment, criminalie nor civilie, for ony slauchter or blude committit in tyme bipast, and is content to be perpetuallie secludit thairfra, *per pactum de non petendo*'.[54] This was in effect, from the point of view of Scott's inferiors, a form of compulsory arbitration, but such a thing was not regarded as improper, as is indicated by the terms of the Act passed by the Scots Parliament in 1598 'anent removing and extinguishing of deidlie feidis'.[55] This provided that parties in dispute should be required to submit to 'tua or thrie freindis on ather side or to subscryve ane submission formit and sent be his majestie to thame to be subscryvit'. Though some may regard the agreement between Scott and Ker as stretching the concept even of equitable arbitration to its outer limit, it is arguably analogous to modern industrial arbitrations between employers' associations and trade unions which effectively settle the terms of employment of workers who are not directly parties to the submission. Persons of little influence, in the sixteenth century as now, are sometimes willing to have their affairs taken up by influential friends or associates, and understand that if they fail to accept what has been decided on their behalf they are liable to some sanction.

2.19. The number of persons called upon to arbitrate or mediate in such cases was frequently quite large — sixteen was not unknown[56] — the object probably being to ensure that, whether the outcome was an '*amicabilis compositio*' or a decree arbitral, enough people of recognised social authority were involved to guarantee compliance. In such circumstances it was often impossible to achieve agreement, either among the arbitrators on the terms of a decree arbitral or among the parties on the terms of an '*amicabilis compositio*'. The interveners would then, as arbitrators, devolve the matters in issue upon an oversman — or oversmen, for two were not uncommon.[57] Often the oversman was of a higher rank than the arbitrators,[58] to give the decree added force, and indeed

---

[54] Pitcairn, *Trials*, Vol. III, 190.
[55] *APS* 1598 c. 1, Vol. IV, 158.
[56] Pitcairn, *Trials* Vol. I, 167.
[57] E.g. in a submission entered into in 1546, each side chose four arbitrators, and 'in case of discord' two oversmen: *Wigt. Chrs.*, 70–1.
[58] In the above mentioned dispute, the issues were ultimately devolved upon Mary of Guise, the Regent of Scotland: *Wigt. Chrs.*, 75.

the word 'oversman' has — or had at one time — a connotation of social superiority.[59]

2.20. It is not, of course, suggested that disputes were always settled successfully by means of equitable arbitration or amicable composition. Though these procedures may have been no less successful than litigation — it was not unknown for a party who had obtained a decree in his favour from the ordinary courts to have to resort to arbitration or amicable composition to get anything tangible out of his recalcitrant opponent[60] — the same issues were sometimes raised in successive arbitrations, the effect of the last decree arbitral being the subject of litigation between the heirs of the original parties. For example, the effect of one of a set of decrees arbitral pronounced in disputes between the Earl of Cassilis and the Laird of Lochinvar first submitted in 1546 became the subject of litigation in 1583 between the heirs of the original submitters.[61] Furthermore, arbitrators not infrequently took refuge in delay.[62] Yet recourse to this form of dispute settlement by persons of substantial power and influence would not have been so common if it had been regarded with disfavour. It may indeed have been in a sense therapeutic,[63] first, in that it helped to demonstrate the support of kinsmen; second, in the immediacy of the hearing and the unwillingness to exclude on grounds of relevancy grievances which were deeply felt; third in the broadly equitable outcome, from which each party could usually expect to achieve something;[64] and fourth, in that stress was often laid not only on monetary compensation but also on expressions of repentance for wrongs and of forgiveness.[65]

[59] Jameson J., *An Etymological Dictionary of the Scottish Language*, Paisley, 1880, Vol. III, 42; Robinson M. (ed.), *The Concise Scots Dictionary*, Aberdeen, 1985, 465.

[60] Wormald J., 'The Sandlaw dispute 1546', in Davies W. and Fouracre P. (eds), *The Settlement of Dispute in Early Mediaeval Europe*, Cambridge, 1986, Ch. 10. Dr Wormald refers (at p. 194) to the three intervening parties as 'arbitrators' but they must also have acted as amicable compositors (i.e. mediators) since the outcome was a contract between the parties in dispute, not a decree arbitral.

[61] *Laird of Lochinvar* v. *Earl of Cassilis* (1583) Mor. 624.

[62] E.g. in *Forster* v. *McGee*, 1495, *ADC*, 419.

[63] On therapeutic aspects of certain types of procedure for dealing with disputes see Gibbs J. L., 'The Kpelle Moot' in Bohannan P. (ed), *Law and Warfare*, New York, 1967, 277–89.

[64] See e.g. Wormald, 'Blood Feud'.

[65] E.g. *Lundy* v. *Ramsay*, 1495, *ADC* 418.

2.21. Disputes between neighbours in burghs and in landward areas (that is, parts of the country beyond burgh boundaries) were usually over minor matters but the manner of dealing with them was not dissimilar. The number of arbiters or arbitrators involved was greater than is normal in most types of modern arbitration, between four and six being common in burghs,[66] while in landward areas similar numbers of birleymen judged questions of good neighbourhood.[67] There was the same tendency for the oversman — or oversmen, for two were not unknown here also[68] — to be of higher social standing than the other arbiters or arbitrators; in burghs, present or past provosts or bailies, and in landward areas, the laird's bailies, were often appointed.[69] Matters which would now be classed as criminal were sometimes submitted, and it was not unknown for what amounted to a suspended sentence to be pronounced by the arbitrators, as for example when in a dispute between two inhabitants of Dunfermline in 1491/2 the arbitrators ordered that if 'Agnes Bower falt to Will Hart in tym to cum' she is to be 'put on the gowe' (the pillory).[70] Occasionally those making an award were apparently expected to pronounce on the basis of their personal knowledge of the circumstances,[71] as if they were an inquest jury. Within burghs arbitration was also used to deal with disputes between merchants[72] and among members of craft gilds.[73] In all these kinds of arbitration one of the aims seems to have been the reconciliation of the parties. It is easy to be sceptical about the effect of a degree ordering each of the parties to 'tak the other be the hands and ask each others forgiveness ... and in tyme to come to leif and shew charitie ilk ane till another',[74] but if as is probable such a decree had the support of the close-knit community to which the parties belonged its moral force may not have been negligible.

2.22. Occasionally the arbitral form was used in this second period to determine what were essentially political disputes. The proceedings before King Edward I to decide who had right to the

[66] See e.g. *Dunf. Recs.*, 25, 27, 32, 33, 34, 40, 42 etc.
[67] *Carn. Ct. Bk.*, Appendix A.   [68] See e.g. *Dunf. Recs.*, 35.
[69] See e.g. *Dunf. Recs.*, 32, 35, 40, 94; *Carn. Ct. Bk.*, 15, 50.
[70] *Dunf. Recs.*, 32.
[71] *Carmelite Friars* v. *Fauconer*, 1400, *Abdn. Recs.*, 137.
[72] *Williamson* v. *Fynk, a Shipmaster*, 1398, *Abdn. Recs.*, 33; Wade T. C., *Acta Curiae Admirallatus Scotiae 1557–62*, Stair Society, Edinburgh, 1937, xxi–ii.
[73] Smith J., *The Hammermen of Edinburgh*, Edinburgh, 1906, 7.
[74] *Ibid.*, 7.

throne of Scotland after the death of the Maid of Norway in 1290 were not arbitration[75] though Scots afterwards liked to pretend that they were, but other less momentous proceedings did take an arbitral form. For example, when the merchants and craftsmen of Edinburgh fell out over the composition and manner of election of the town council, each side nominated three 'Jugis arbitratouris ... and commissioneris', with King James VI as oversman, 'anent the removing of all questions, differences and contraverseis' between them. The ultimate decree arbitral pronounced by the King was ratified by Parliament and, like many ordinary awards, registered in the Books of Council and Session.[76] And in 1628/29, the settlement of a serious controversy between King Charles I and those who had obtained title to ecclesiastical lands after the Reformation of 1560 — a controversy occasioned by the King's high-handed attempt to invalidate their charters — was achieved by complicated negotiations resulting in a submission by the landowners to the King, who then as arbiter issued a set of decrees arbitral containing the terms of what must in fact have been an agreed solution.[77]

2.23.   Why was the arbitral form adopted for the settlement of these disputes? In cases such as the controversy between the merchants and craftsmen, it reflected the fact that, though the issues involved were of 'public concernment' — a phrase used in a submission in 1675 by 'the whole neighbours of Edinburgh' dealing with the rebuilding of ruinous tenements[78] — the king's intention was to arrive at a solution which would reflect so far as possible the expressed wishes of those most closely affected and thus be most likely to last. Desire for administrative tidiness, which would have required a similar form of government for all town councils, probably did not enter his mind. This kind of arbitration might therefore be described as the sixteenth century Scots equivalent of modern private legislation procedure. The submission of 1628 to Charles I may have been prompted by the need of that 'dread and gracious Soveraign'[79] not to be forced into

---

[75] Stones E. L. G. and Simpson G. G., *Edward I and the throne of Scotland*, Oxford, 1978, 22–3, and Appendix II, 207–8.

[76] *APS* 1584 c. 25, Vol. III, 360.

[77] *APS* 1629, Appendix, Vol. V, 197–207.

[78] *Magistrates of Edinburgh* v. *Anderson*, (1675) 1 Bro. Supp., 732.

[79] The form of address used in the submission to the king by 'certain tacksmen', *APS* Vol. V, 195.

too obvious and ignominious a retraction of his Act of 1625 which had caused all the trouble. By appearing to have the whole matter respectfully and formally submitted to him, and by clothing the settlement in the form of a decree arbitral, the king saved face and the complainers got, in material terms, most of what they wanted. Who it was that conceived this ingenious device appears to be unknown;[80] it was probably not the politically inept Charles,but someone among the commissioners appointed to devise a solution to the disputes which Charles's action had caused.

2.24. As already noted,[81] traditional forms of dispute settlement between and among members of kin groups began to decline from about the end of the sixteenth century. At the beginning of the seventeenth, several factors contributed to the acceleration of that decline. The departure of King James VI for London on his accession to the English throne must have weakened the personal relationship between the monarch and the nobility upon which the traditional style of government had rested, though James has been said to have 'directed affairs no less effectively when he did so through the post'.[82] Furthermore, James's own long-term policy seems to have been to work towards the establishment of a system closer to the English model. Certainly he depended on, and advanced the fortunes of, professional men who served him well in an administrative capacity,[83] and encouraged the emergence of the Faculty of Advocates and the Society of Writers to the Signet.[84] Skilled lawyers were of course nothing new in Scotland — fairly sophisticated points of arbitration law had been pleaded in a Scottish case in the early thirteenth century.[85] and ecclesiastical lawyers especially[86] had played an important role even in the central secular courts since at least the late fifteenth.[87] From the latter part of the sixteenth century onwards however the secular

---

[80] At least, it is not apparent from the best recent study in Lee M., *The Road to Revolution: Scotland under Charles I 1625–37*, Urbana, 1985.

[81] Paragraph 2.10.

[82] Donaldson G., *Scotland: James V to James VII*, Edinburgh, 1971, 215.

[83] Wormald, *Community*, 92.

[84] Smout T. C., *A History of the Scottish People, 1550–1850*, London, 1969, 108.

[85] Cooper, *Sel. Scot. Cas.*, 13–4.

[86] James IV sought and obtained from Pope Alexander VI a Bull giving special permission to ecclesiastics to study civil law at the university of Aberdeen: Innes C., *Fasti Aberdonenses 1494–1854*, Spalding Club, Aberdeen, 1854, 36–8.

[87] Wormald, *Community*, 23–4; MacFarlane L. J., *William Elphinstone and the Kingdom of Scotland 1431–1514*, Aberdeen, 1985, Chap. 3.

legal profession, and especially the advocates and writers to the signet, came to enjoy increasing prestige in its own right and to attract the sons of landed gentry into membership. Though occasionally their enthusiasm for the rule of law might run counter to the king's immediate aims,[88] and though it provided the basis for the revolution of 1689 which ousted his descendant James VII,[89] it was consistent with his ultimate goal of a united kingdom of Great Britain in which the peace was kept by the exercise of power through courts of law, not by fragile agreements to accept the arbitral decision of members of an unreliable and sometimes turbulent nobility whose power was based partly on hereditary feudal jurisdiction and partly on real or assumed kinship. Again, whatever disagreements there might be between King James VI and the Calvinist clergy on other matters, the king's desire to establish the rule of law as a substitute for the arbitrament of the kin was consistent with the reformers' concern to stiffen moral discipline not only through the activities of kirk sessions but also by the exercise of civil authority by the godly magistrate.[90] These policies helped to lay the foundations of eighteenth century economic development and ultimately to produce the professionalisation of the handling of disputes outside the ordinary civil courts which was characteristic of the late nineteenth century. In fact, the traditional system of informal arbitration did not survive the Cromwellian interregnum.

The adaptation of arbitration law to liberal society

2.25. The idea of liberal society. Our third period, running from the middle of the seventeenth century to the last quarter of the twentieth, sees the rise and faltering in Scotland of a society that could almost be described as 'liberal'. By a 'liberal' society is here meant one which has a number of dominant characteristics.

2.26. First, it is a society in which liberty — 'that principle of freedom, that man hath of himself and of other things beside man, to do in relation thereto as he pleaseth, except where he is tied by

[88] As when, in the case of the Rev. Robert Bruce, the judges refused to decide as the King wished: Cooper, *Sel. Pap.*, 116–123.

[89] *Claim of Right*, APS 1689 c. 28, Vol. IX, 37–40.

[90] Cameron, J. K. (ed), *The First Book of Discipline*, Edinburgh, 1972, 62–7, 165–6.

his obedience or engagement'[91] — takes precedence over most kinds of loyalty. Loyalty and obedience are still owed by subjects to their sovereign (or in republics by citizens to the state), by wife to husband, and by children to parents, but this is their fullest extent. Others, such as feudal superiors, heads of 'names', employers, fellow-members of associations, are entitled to obedience only in so far as specified in an agreement. As Stair put it,[92]

'in matters of utility and profit, where the natural liberty is not hemmed in with an obligation, there, unless by his own delinquence or consent, man cannot justly be constrained'.

2.27. Second, it is a society in which contract and perceived interest, rather than kinship, neighbourhood or status or similar vision of what is good, provide the bond which holds society together.[93] Third, it is one in which individuals may and generally do belong to quite a number of significant groups — the nuclear family, work groups or business partnerships, professional and trade organisations and trade unions, political parties and pressure groups, religious societies and clubs, as well as more ephemeral associations. Though an element of benevolent paternalism may continue for some time to influence the dealings of landowners with their tenants and servants, 'as individuals interact more often in impersonal contexts, like markets and bureaucracies ... impersonal respect and formal equality edge out communal solidarity towards some and suspicious hostility towards others'.[94] Fourth, liberal society is one in which members seek to protect their freedom by means of the rule of law rather than by reliance on benevolent discretion.

2.28. There has probably never been an entirely liberal society in the sense in which this phrase is here used, for opposing tendencies normally survive though with reduced influence. In Great Britain, for example, liberalism was challenged at the height of its influence in the nineteenth and early twentieth centuries by trade unionism

---

[91] Stair, *Inst.*, I.2.3.
[92] *Ibid.*, I.2.5.
[93] This passage is based broadly on Unger, R. M., *Law in Modern Society*, New York, 1976, 143–7, 168–81.
[94] *Ibid.*, 143–4.

39

and ideals of solidarity among those who owned little property,[95] and local and family loyalties and the ties which bind ethnic minorities and religious sects have not been extinguished. Yet it may still broadly be asserted that between the seventeenth and the nineteenth centuries Scottish society tended to approximate more and more to the liberal ideal. The world of Scott of Branxholm and Ker of Cesford mentioned earlier,[96] in which power was based on the mutual loyalty of kinsfolk and retainers, gave place to one in which power was based on the ownership of property, even if the change was for a time disguised by the benevolent paternalism of some landowners, as thus presented by an early eighteenth century Professor of Law to his students.[97]

'What more agreeable personage can one form to himself, than that of a country gentleman, living decently and frugally on his fortune, and composing all the differences within the sphere of his activity, giving the law to a whole neighbourhood, and they gratefully submitting to it?'

It was not long before that benevolence gave place to the more calculating spirit which initiated the 'Clearances' in the northern regions of the country.[98] Nevertheless, from about the last quarter of the nineteenth century until the last quarter of the twentieth the influence of liberalism waned in Great Britain because of 'a decline of confidence in the beneficence, and indeed in the possibility, of a freely competitive capitalist market economy.'[99] Though that confidence seemed to revive among those members of the electorate who supported the Conservative (in fact a neo-liberal) party in the early 1980s, they were a minority in Scotland.[100] Since Scotland did not (and at the time of writing does not) have its own

---

[95] Fox, A., *History and Heritage: the social origins of the British industrial relations system*, London, 1985, 172.

[96] Paragraph 2.18.

[97] In 'A Discourse on the Rise and Progress of the Law in Scotland', appended to Bayne's edition of *Hope's Minor Practicks*, Edinburgh, 1726, 187.

[98] Probably the most balanced and scholarly account of this controversial episode is in Richards E., *A History of the Highland Clearances*, London, Vol. I 1982, Vol. II 1985.

[99] MacPherson C. B., *The Rise and Fall of Economic Justice*, Oxford, 1985, 14.

[100] Butler D. and Kavanagh D., *The British General Election of 1983*, London, 1984, Appendix 1, Table A1–3, 301. Since 1945, the Conservative party has only once (1955) obtained a majority of votes cast in Parliamentary general elections in Scotland: Kellas J. G., *The Scottish Political System*, 2nd edn., Cambridge, 1973, 99–100, 105.

legislature the present weakness of the appeal of liberalism in this country is not necessarily reflected in legislation, and in any event the policies of economically weak countries tend to reflect the values of those who control international financial institutions. It is therefore possible that the ideal of a liberal society of the sense in which that phrase is used here may again achieve for an extended period a dominant place in the values underlying the law in Scotland.

2.29. **Dispute settlement in liberal society**. Procedures for handling disputes usually reflect the nature of the society out of which they arise. One would expect therefore to find in a liberal society that formal courts administering positive law are the dominant system, and that legalistic arbitration is preferred to the equitable variety. The ordinary courts are likely to seek to exercise closer supervision over arbitration, emphasising the arbiter's duty to adhere strictly to the law. Emphasis will be placed on the basis of an arbitration in a contract voluntarily entered into, and hence litigation will often turn on such questions as, whether the submission was properly executed or not, or whether the arbiter has exceeded his or her powers or failed to exhaust the remit. In so far as equitable arbitration is tolerated, the awards of arbitrators will not normally be enforceable as such, especially if they are intended to affect individuals who were not directly parties to the arbitration agreement.

2.30. During the period now under discussion arbitration in Scotland does indeed become broadly consistent with the increasingly liberal society in which it is set, though the law, which generally changes only gradually in response to the spirit of a new age, retains — sometimes confusingly — traces of its pre-liberal past. The legalistic arbitration of the pre-industrial society becomes the strongest influence upon the ordinary arbitration of the new age. Though a new form of equitable arbitration arises to deal with disputes between employers and trade unions, the awards of industrial arbitrators generally have no legal effect. Only in special circumstances such as wartime, or allegations of very low pay, are the awards of such arbitral tribunals enforceable in law, and then only in an indirect manner.[101] Statutory regimes which are

---

[101] Wedderburn, Lord, *The Worker and the Law*, 3rd edn., Harmondsworth, 1986, 344–7, 674; Employment Protection Act 1975 s. 21.

given the title of arbitration usually have many of the characteristics of the bodies which used to be called 'administrative tribunals'. Forms of arbitration other than what has in this work been called 'ordinary' arbitration are given little or no space in published textbooks.[102] The turning point for Scots arbitration law appears to have been in the second half of the seventeenth century.

2.31. **Arbitration law in disorder, 1650–1760.** The collapse of traditional equitable arbitration by members of the kin led to an enormous increase in the caseload of the ordinary courts. The central criminal courts, which could no longer assume that many prosecutions would be withdrawn with the agreement of the King's Advocate because the issues between the complainer and alleged wrongdoer had been settled 'at the sicht of freindis',[103] were the first to be reformed. The High Court of Justiciary was established in 1672. Not long after, the attention of the government turned to the problems of the civil court. It was, said Stair, 'very visible how much the weight and toil of the Lords of Session are increased above what they were'.[104] Litigants who were weary of waiting for the Court to determine their cases therefore resorted to arbitration, and the arbiters - or arbitrators or even amicable compositors, for the distinctions were now hardly recognised — issued decisions according to their view of what the situation demanded. To quote Stair again.[105]

'Before the Act of Regulation, it was not known what causes the Lords had upon hand, and were obliged to discuss and finish; for when they called what causes they pleased, and left others uncalled, those who could not get their causes called . . . behoved to leave them, and endeavour by references to bring their pleas to an accord; wherein arbiters must drive the going nail, and advise these, who might worst sustain the present prejudice, to purchase the remedy, by ceding a part of that, which (if they were authoritative judges) they would determine in their favours.'

Such arbitrations did not however necessarily decrease the burden on the courts. They often merely caused further delay and changed

---

[102] See e.g. Bell, *Arb.*; Irons, *Arb.*; Guild, *Arb.*; Russell, *Arb.* 1982.
[103] As in *Ballingall* v. *Sibbett*, 1561, Pitcairn, *Trials*, Vol. I, 426.
[104] *Inst.*, IV.2.18.
[105] *Ibid.*

the nature of the action, for litigants who felt that their arbitrator had given an inequitable decision could raise an action for reduction of the decree arbitral on the ground of enorm lesion.

2.32. Two ways of dealing with this situation were open to the authorities, and they followed both — reform of court procedure and the removal or restriction of certain types of complaint. Actions of reduction of decrees arbitral based on allegations of enorm lesion must have seemed ripe for abolition on two grounds. The proper business of a court, to those imbued with the ideology of the rule of law, is primarily to apply positive law, not to review on merely equitable grounds the decisions of private adjudicators; and in the intensely Protestant atmosphere of seventeenth century Scotland a measure which implied a preference for the secular civil law over canonist opinion must have commanded general approval. The twenty-fifth Article of Regulation, made on 29th April 1695, therefore provided

'That for the cutting off of groundless and expensive pleas and processes in time coming, the Lords of Session sustain no reduction of any decreet arbitral that shall be pronounced hereafter on a subscribed submission at the instance of the parties submitters, upon any cause whatever, unless that of corruption, bribery, or falsehood to be alleged against the judges arbitrators, who pronounced the same.'

Since the main object was to reduce the caseload of the Court of Session, and since the other Articles also dealt with the administration of justice in that Court, it is not perhaps surprising that Article 25 should sometimes have been mistakenly assumed[106] to be an Act of Sederunt, an order made by the Court regulating its own procedure. It was, however, made by royal Commissioners exercising powers granted by Parliament.[107]

2.33. Article 25, which is still in force, effectively brought the law of Scotland concerning the grounds of reduction of a decree arbitral close to the civilian rule that such a decree could be reduced only on grounds of *dolus*, which is defined by Ulpian as 'any guile, chicanery or trickery used to circumvent, defraud or

[106] By Lord Chancellor Eldon in *Sharpe* v. *Bickersdyke* (1815) III Dow App. 102 at 107; and by the compilers of the collection entitled *Acts of Sederunt 1553–1790*, Edinburgh, 1790, 215.
[107] *APS* 1693 c. 72, Vol. IX, 330–1.

dupe another person'.[108] Almost certainly there was no intention to remove the requirement that a valid decree arbitral must be in accordance with the terms of the submission on which it is based, for it had long been accepted that this was a distinct ground upon which a decree might be denied execution,[109] as was recognised shortly after the Article came into force,[110] but the looseness of its drafting was later to give rise to difficulty.

2.34. The distinction between arbiters and arbitrators was a casualty of this intellectually and socially turbulent era. As late as 1603 it had been recognised by Sir Thomas Craig, who had maintained the traditional view that arbiters must decide according to law whereas arbitrators were free to have recourse to equity.[111] By the 1680s, however, as scholarly a lawyer as Sir George Mackenzie could assert, without so much as a mention of arbitrators, that arbit*ers* 'are not tied to the strict Solemnities of Law', and that 'equity is to them [arbiters] a rule, as Law is to other judges'.[112] Stair discussed arbitration hardly at all, but when he did he referred only to arbiters,[113], while the twenty-fifth Article of Regulation used the term 'arbit*rator*' only. Those who drafted deeds of submission in the early eighteenth century used the terms 'arbiter' and 'arbitrator' indiscriminately in the same document.[114] No wonder that Bankton, writing in 1751, remarked[115] that

'the difference between arbiters and arbitrators, whereof notice is taken in the civil law, was observed with us in those days, tho' now these terms are for the most part promiscuously used'.

He also noted,[116] like Sir George Mackenzie had done earlier, that

'arbiters are not tied to the strict rules of law, but may and ought to proceed according to equity and good conscience, and may

---

[108] D. 4.3.1.2.; the translation is that of the late Professor J. A. C. Thomas, *Text.*, 228.

[109] Balfour, *Practicks*, c. xii.

[110] *Crawford* v. *Hamilton* (1707) Mor. 6835.

[111] *Jus Feudale*, (originally published 1655, though written about 1603), Clyde J. A. (trans.), Stair Society, Edinburgh, 1934, III,3.21.

[112] *Inst.*, IV.3.

[113] *Inst.*, IV.1.60, IV.3.18, IV.39.14.

[114] Gouldesbrough P. (Compiler), *Formulary of Old Scots Legal Documents*, Stair Society, Edinburgh, 1985, 13.

[115] *Inst.*, I.23.18.

[116] *Ibid.*, I.23.11.

use any mean of proof sufficient to convince them, tho' not competent in point of law'.

In effect, the concept of the arbiter in Scots law had during the latter part of the seventeenth century expanded so as to include much of what had previously been included in the concept of the arbitrator, so that the latter was by the middle of the eighteenth century almost devoid of content. When it reappeared briefly in 1756[117] it had come to denote merely a person appointed to finalise a 'bargain not adjusted'. The decree of an arbitrator, it was then held, might be reviewed by a court in terms of the *'arbitrium boni viri'*, notwithstanding the twenty-fifth Article of Regulation, while that of an arbiter could be challenged only on the grounds there specified. By the last quarter of the eighteenth century, therefore, the distinction which mediaeval lawyers had sought to draw between the arbiter and the arbitrator had in Scotland all but disappeared[118] with the social structures for which it had been devised.

2.35.   One aspect of the mediaeval tradition — the favour shown by the royal courts towards arbitration — was not yet weakened, however. This is shown by the contemporary attitude to the construction of arbitration agreements. Erskine, writing in 1773, asserted[119] that

'submission, being intended for a most favourable purpose, the amicable composing of differences, ought to receive the most ample interpretation of which the words are capable'.

The judges were still closer to conservative landownership than to the more liberal commerce. Though Lord Braxfield was not typical of the Scottish bench of his time in his outspokenness, and though his attitudes were increasingly distasteful to some young advocates who pleaded before him,[120] his remark at the trial of Thomas Muir in 1793 that British government 'is made of the landed interest, which alone has the right to be represented',[121]

---

[117] *Robertson* v. *Clephan* (1756) 5 Bro. Supp. (Monboddo) 852.
[118] The term was occasionally used later as a mere synonym for man of skill or valuer, as e.g. in *Henderson* v. *Paul* (1867) 5 M 629 per Lord Neaves at 633.
[119] *Inst.*, IV.3.32.
[120] E.g. the future Lord Cockburn, *Memorials of his time*, Edinburgh, 1856, 113.
[121] Quoted in Gray W. F., 'Lord Monboddo and Lord Braxfield', in Blom-Cooper L. (ed.), *The Law as Literature*, London, 1961, 255.

probably commanded the assent of most of his brethren. Though litigation arising out of commercial arbitration did sometimes occupy the Court of Session in the eighteenth century,[122] it was arguments over rights to land, succession, and matrimonial provision that provided the staple judicial diet until the very end of the period.[123]

2.36. Arbitration and the rise of commercial jurisprudence. At the end of the eighteenth century Scottish society was still some way short of its nearest approach to the liberal ideal, but some important milestones had been passed. Workmen were beginning to organise themselves into associations outside the ancient craft gilds, and were coming into conflict with the authorities for so doing.[124] Dissenting churches were becoming quite numerous;[125] new professions such as that of land surveyor were appearing;[126] and new kinds of economic organisations such as chambers of commerce[127] and societies for promoting agricultural improvements[128] were establishing themselves as the old economic structure centred on the royal burghs and their privileges fell into decay. These developments created pressure for the alteration of a number of long-established rules governing what must now begin to be regarded as ordinary arbitration law, in particular the invalidity of submissions to unnamed persons[129] and the gratuitous nature of the office of arbiter.[130] The Court of Session resisted change, but the problem did not go away. And for the first time there appears in the reported cases a type of lawsuit that was eventually to become one of the main sources of income

---

[122] E.g. *Williamson v. Fraser*, (1739) Mor. 665.

[123] Cockburn, *op. cit.*

[124] E.g. in *Procurator Fiscal v. Journeymen Woolcombers of Aberdeen*, (1762) Mor. 1961. See in general Marwick W. H., *A Short History of Labour in Scotland*, Edinburgh, 1967, 4–6.

[125] Smout T. C., *A History of the Scottish People 1550–1850*, London, 1969, 233–5.

[126] Adams I. H. (ed.), *Papers of Peter May, Land Surveyor, 1749–1793*, Scottish History Society, Edinburgh 1979, xvii–xxxix.

[127] In *Buchanan v. Muirhead* (1799) Mor. Appx. I (Arb.) 11.

[128] The 'Society for Improving in the Knowledge of Agriculture' was founded in 1723: Lenman, B., *An Economic History of Modern Scotland 1660–1976*, London, 1977, 80.

[129] *Buchanan v. Muirhead (supra)*.

[130] *Blair v. Gib*, (1738) Mor. 664; *Jack v. Cramond*, (1777) Mor. Appx. I (Arb.), 6; *Montgomery v. Strang, Lennox and Co.*, (1798) Mor. 631.

for professional arbiters in Scotland — the public works contract.[131]

2.37. It was during the nineteenth century that the modern character of Scots arbitration law was established, the most important single influence upon it being probably that of Lord President Inglis. Under his influence and that of a number of other judges such as Lord Fullerton arbitration law was increasingly shaped by the liberal spirit of the age. Though the tradition of judicial respect for arbitration, transmitted from the mediaeval past, was strong enough — given the general indifference of the legislature—to ensure that the supervision of arbitration by the courts was never as close in Scotland as in England[132] or post-revolutionary France,[133] it did increase during this period.

2.38. This manifested itself in a number of ways. Thus, while searching inquiries into the legal rectitude of arbitral decisions were not attempted,[134] the freedom to decide according to equity which arbiters had acquired in the confusion of the seventeenth and early eighteenth centuries was removed by a decision of the House of Lords to the effect that error of law on the face of an award was a ground on which it could be reduced.[135] In the absence at that time of any Scots equivalent of either the English special case[136] or the French 'appel',[137] and in the absence of any requirement that decrees arbitral be accompanied by reasons, the Scottish judges used strict construction of arbitration agreements to facilitate the reduction of decrees arbitral. They laid down a rule, now widely considered to be highly inconvenient in practice, that arbiters have no implied power to award damages;[138] fearful

---

[131] *Milne* v. *Magistrates of Edinburgh* (1770) II Paton App. 209.

[132] Hon. Mr Justice Kerr, 'The English Courts and Arbitration', in Schmitthof C. (ed.), *International Commercial Arbitration*, London, 1974–5, 199.

[133] Robert, *Arb.*, paragraph 2.

[134] See e.g. *Morrison* v. *Robertson* (1825) I. Wilson and Shaw App. 143; *Wauchope* v. *Edinburgh and Dalkeith Railway Co.* (1846) 8 D. 816.

[135] *Clyne's Trs.* v. *Edinburgh Oil and Gas Light Co.* (1835) II Shaw and MacLean App. 243 at 271.

[136] On which see Walton A., *Russell on the Law of Arbitration*, 19th edn., London, 1979, Chapter 15.

[137] On which see Robert, *Arb.*, paragraph 234 ff.

[138] *Aberdeen Railway Co.* v. *Blaikie Brothers* (1852) 15 D. (H.L.) 20, approving the dissenting judgment of Lord Fullerton in the Court of Session (1851) 13 D. 527 at 537.

that members of professions other than that of the law, who were acting as arbiters to an increasing extent,[139] might commit errors of law in their reasoning,[140] they drew a sharp distinction between executorial arbitration clauses and those of an unrestricted character;[141] and justified their decision to uphold the rule against submission to unnamed arbiters on the historically incorrect[142] ground that in a dispute on a matter involving legal rights

'the only proper jurisdiction is a court of law, and the courts of law cannot be ousted of their jurisdiction by an arbitration in which an arbiter is not named'.[143]

The nineteenth century judges did not, however, interfere with the procedural freedom which arbiters had gained from their confusion with arbitrators in the seventeenth and early eighteenth centuries. Though the duty of procedural fairness was continually emphasised,[144] so was the freedom of arbiters to direct proceedings formally or informally as seemed most appropriate given the nature of the issues.[145] And where the desire to emphasise the supervisory jurisdiction of the court was opposed by the desire to uphold freedom of contract, the latter, consistent as it was with the lingering vestiges of the ancient favour towards arbitration,[146] was hardly questioned. When the issue was raised in the present century, the modern framework of the law was well established and the result was a ringing declaration of the absence of any power in the court to override a valid agreement to submit a dispute to arbitration.[147]

2.39. Besides questions arising out of commercial relations and construction contracts, the courts had to deal with disputes arising

[139] The first reported arbitration case involving a utility company, *Forbes* v. *Edinburgh Water Co.* (1830) 8 S. 459, also involved the great civil engineer Telford as the arbiter.

[140] This fear is exemplified in the judgments of Lord Fullerton in *Aberdeen Railway Co.* v. *Blaikie Brothers* (*supra*) and of Lord Deas in *Pearson* v. *Oswald* (1859) 21 D. 419 at 429–30.

[141] *Pearson* v. *Oswald* (*supra*).

[142] Hostiensis, *Comm.*, X.1.43.12. fol. 209: '*compromissum de incerta persona factum non valeat, quia in illa persona assumenda possent dissentire*'.

[143] *Campbell* v. *Shaws Water Co.* (1864) 2 M. 1130 per L. J. C. Inglis at 1131.

[144] See e.g. *Mitchell* v. *Cable* (1848) 10 D. 1297.

[145] See e.g. *Ledingham* v. *Elphinstone* (1859) 22 D. 245.

[146] As expressed in *Tenants of Dennie* v. *Lords Fleming and Sanctjohn*, (1553) Mor. 623.

[147] *Sanderson* v. *Armour and Co.* 1922 S.C. (H.L.) 117 per Lord Dunedin at 126.

out of the affairs of private clubs, dissenting churches and other voluntary societies. These bodies often established domestic tribunals for dealing with members whose conduct was alleged to be detrimental in some way to the interests of the body as a whole. Especially in the case of the churches, the tribunals were modelled on the disciplinary systems operating in bodies established by law, such as the Church of Scotland and the corporate trade gilds, and had a degree of permanence not normally possessed by arbiters. Given this background, they often acted as if they had a statutory rather than a merely contractual basis. The policy of the courts in dealing with disputes arising out of the proceedings or decisions of these tribunals was very similar to their policy in dealing with ordinary arbitration, though it was expressly held that they were not arbiters.[148] The main object was to ensure that they did not act beyond the powers lawfully granted to them under the constitution of the body concerned, and conducted proceedings in a fair and judicious way.[149]

2.40. Between 1760 and the end of the nineteenth century Parliament intervened hardly at all to regulate ordinary arbitration in Scotland. The Arbitration (Scotland) Act 1894, which is still in force, was not a Scottish equivalent of the English Arbitration Act 1889, but merely instituted two useful reforms; the abolition of the rule against submission to unnamed arbiters and the grant to the courts of a power to appoint an arbiter in certain circumstances where a party had failed to act in terms of the arbitration agreement. Numerous enactments[150] did however establish statutory 'arbitration' regimes. Disputes involving public bodies or the operators of utility or railway companies had become very frequent, and Parliament thought it expedient to standardise the procedures by means of which they were disposed of, using the model of ordinary contractual arbitration.[151] Alterations in the legal rights of agricultural tenants and industrial workers were sometimes accompanied by the establishment of statutory machinery for handling certain kinds of questions arising between

---

[148] *McMillan* v. *Free Church* (1859) 22 D. 290.
[149] *Skerret* v. *Oliver* (1896) 23 R. 468.
[150] A convenient source of information on the most important is Irons, *Arb.*, 111–16 and Chapter VIII.
[151] E.g. Lands Clauses (Scotland) Act 1845 s. 23 ff.

them and their landlords or employers,[152] including a form of
equitable arbitration established to handle collective disputes.[153]
Parliament also reintroduced into Scotland a means of obtaining
by stated case the opinion of the court on a matter of law,[154] which
had previously existed in the form of an 'oraculum' under
mediaeval canon law.[155]

Arbitration in a peripheral society

2.41. The twentieth century has witnessed a centralisation of
decisionmaking in both political and economic life. Since the
centre of power even in the United Kingdom could not be situated
in Scotland, many issues affecting or arising in this country have
come to be determined elsewhere.[156] It is natural that those who
draft the contracts entered into by major industrial or commercial
enterprises should frame them in terms of the law of England or of
some other centre of financial or industrial power, and that when
disputes arise it should be found most convenient to sue in English
courts or to submit to arbitration under English law even where the
issues arise in Scotland. Since it was English law rather than Scots
which was exported to most of the territories which now form the
Commonwealth, English arbitration has understandably been
much more familiar than Scots to traders in these countries. There
is now established in England an élite corps of skilled arbiters who
enjoy a world-wide reputation and whose earnings make an
important contribution to the economy of the United kingdom.

2.42. Not surprisingly therefore the development of the
commercial law of Scotland has generally been much more
sluggish than that of the law of England and other foreign
jurisdictions. Nowhere has this been more evident than in the law
relating to ordinary arbitration. This is apparent from the fact that
the standard English textbook on this subject[157] has gone through

---

[152] E.g. in the Combination Act 1800 (39 and 40 Geo III c. 106 ss. 18–22;
Agricultural Holdings (Scotland) Act 1883 s. 9.
[153] Conciliation Act 1896 (59 and 60 Vict. c. 30) s. 2(1)(d).
[154] Excise Act 1827 s. 84.
[155] See e.g. *Cambuskenneth Abbey* v. *Dunfermline Abbey*, 1207, in Cooper, *Sel. Scot. Cas.*, 13.
[156] Lenman B., *An Economic History of Modern Scotland*, London, 1977, 236, 244, 268.
[157] *Russell on the Law of Arbitration.*

twelve editions since 1900, the latest being in 1982, and it now has an equally solid rival.[158] Only two works have been published on Scots arbitration law since 1904, neither of which can seriously bear comparison with their English counterparts. There have been relatively few decisions of note by Scottish courts, most of which occurred in the first quarter of the century, though there has been a recent small flurry of activity, and the legislature has passed only one measure affecting ordinary arbitration, and it consists merely of one section in an Act[159] devoted mainly to other matters. This provision extended to ordinary arbitration proceedings the 'stated case' system by means of which the opinion of the court on a question of law could be obtained. Unlike the previous legislative intervention — the Arbitration (Scotland) Act 1894 — its enactment was widely opposed by the major professional bodies within Scotland. It was believed to have been introduced — in the aftermath of a judgment of the House of Lords[160] which had arisen out of a refusal by an arbiter in Scotland to state a case — to bring Scots law more into line with what was then the law of England.[161] There are indeed some unfortunate obscurities in the law of Scotland relating to the interpretation of decrees arbitral in the context of actions of reduction, as will become apparent below,[162] and it is arguable that some form of review of awards should be substituted for actions of reduction, which rarely lead to a satisfactory outcome. Reform of the Scots law of arbitration should however be the result of thorough study by the Scottish Law Commission, leading perhaps to a codifying statute, not of hasty and piecemeal legislation.

2.43. The ordinary Scots law of arbitration has nevertheless, in spite of a number of inadequacies, served its small world of local businesspeople, landowners, and public authorities reasonably well, providing the basis for a workmanlike arbitration practice carried on by a small number of architects, surveyors, engineers, accountants and other experts. Indeed it could be argued that the

---

[158] Mustill, *Comm. Arb.*
[159] Administration of Justice (Scotland) Act 1972 s. 3, brought into force on 2nd April 1973 by the Administration of Justice (Scotland) Act 1972 (Commencement) Order 1973, SI 1973 No. 339.
[160] *James Miller and Partners* v. *Whitworth Street Estates (Manchester) Ltd.* [1970] A.C. 583.
[161] It has since been altered by the Arbitration Act 1979.
[162] Paragraphs 16.12 ff.

low incidence of litigation relating to arbitration in this country reflects considerable credit on its practitioners, and justifies the tradition — originating probably in mediaeval notarial practice — of appointing solicitors as clerks in all but the simplest proceedings. Some credit may also be due to the mediaeval jurists and practitioners who fashioned many of its basic principles and traditions. Whether it can long continue as an independent system in the context of a commercial world which is increasingly international is however a matter of grave doubt. The likeliest outcome is assimilation to English arbitration law. The remark of King Henry VII of England to his Council during a discussion of the proposed marriage of his eldest daughter Margaret to the King of Scots has on many issues been prophetic:

> 'Some of the table did put the case; that if God should take the King's two sons without issue, that then the Kingdom of England would fall to the Kingdom of Scotland, which might prejudice the monarchy of England. Whereunto the King himself replied; that if that should be, Scotland would be but an accession to England, and not England to Scotland, for that the greater would draw the less.... This passed as an oracle, and silenced those that moved the question.'[163]

However, the United Kingdom as a whole is now, in relation to the European Economic Community as an emerging political entity, in somewhat the same position as Scotland to England. This fact, and intense competition for arbitration business, may bring the arbitration law of the whole of the UK closer to the most highly developed laws of continental countries, even if exact adoption of the uniform law of the European Convention, or the UNCITRAL Model Law (which can be used for domestic as well as international commercial arbitration) is unlikely. Perhaps, therefore, Scots arbitration law will again find itself subject to strong universalistic influences, as in the period between the thirteenth and the fifteenth centuries when its foundations were laid.

2.44.   In the field of equitable arbitration, Scots law has followed a path indistinguishable from that of the law of England. The state has continued to encourage the submission of industrial disputes

---

[163] Bacon F., *History of the Reign of King Henry VII*, London 1622, republished in edition by Lumby J. R., London 1882, 189.

between employers and trade unions to arbitration, by maintaining public institutions such as the former Industrial Court[164] (later reconstituted as the 'Industrial Arbitration Board'[165] and now as the 'Central Arbitration Committee'[166]) and the Advisory, Conciliation and Arbitration Service (ACAS),[167] to which parties could have recourse. The awards of industrial arbitrators have however been enforceable — if at all — only indirectly through the insertion of terms in contracts of employment.[168]

2.45. The main area of legislative activity has been in the creation of statutory régimes providing special procedures referred to as 'arbitration' because of their similarity to or derivation from the ordinary system governed mainly by the common law. One of the most important is the régime which handles disputes arising out of agricultural holdings.[169] These regimes differ from ordinary arbitration in various ways. Many of them are compulsory, and the procedure to be followed is often laid down in considerable detail. The object of the creation of these régimes, which could be said to be almost forms of administrative tribunal, is to lay down standard systems of dealing with types of dispute which arise frequently in certain contexts and which are best determined by persons other than lawyers.

Advantages and disadvantages of arbitration

2.46. Whether arbitration in either its ordinary or equitable form, or indeed any type of adjudication, is the most suitable means of handling a dispute depends on the nature of the issue and on the point of view from which it is considered. Consumers have different attitudes from suppliers, tenants from landlords, the poor from the wealthy, the public at large from those who are actually involved in the controversy. Arbitration, as other forms of adjudication, works best where the parties to a particular dispute

---

[164] Established under the Industrial Courts Act 1919.

[165] Industrial Relations Act 1971 s. 124.

[166] Employment Protection Act 1975 s. 10.

[167] Its present legal basis is the Employment Protection Act 1975 ss. 1–3.

[168] Employment Protection Act 1975 s. 21; see also previous legislation (now repealed) such as the Terms and Conditions of Employment Act 1959 s. 8.

[169] Agricultural Holdings (Scotland) Act 1949 s. 75 and the Sixth Schedule thereto.

are as likely, if and when they are again at odds, to have opposite interests to those they now have; and least well where they always have the same conflicting interests. Thus, in disputes between merchants who are involved both in buying and selling the choice of an arbiter and acceptance of his or her decision is less likely to cause difficulty than in disputes between landlord and tenant or worker and employer, because in the latter situations the general as well as the particular perceptions and values of the parties are likely to be different.

2.47. With regard to ordinary arbitration, it is sometimes said that one of its advantages over litigation is that it is cheaper. Whether this is generally true in fact may be doubted, since in arbitration the parties are responsible for paying the fees of the arbiter and his or her clerk, as well as the hire of accommodation, whereas the salaries of judges and officials in the ordinary courts and the cost of maintaining court buildings are all borne by the taxpayer. Furthermore, there now exists a form of 'summary trial' in the ordinary courts which is cheaper — and speedier — than ordinary civil procedure.[170] Even if arbitration were generally cheaper than litigation, it would not always be preferable from the point of view of both parties. A wealthy individual or corporation faced with a claim by a person of lesser substance may well wish to use the threat of the expense of litigation as a means of discouraging pursuit of the claim.

2.48. Again, privacy is often held to be an advantage of arbitration. Certainly, arbitration proceedings are normally private, whereas civil litigation is conducted in open court. Not everyone, however, has an interest in private proceedings. In a dispute between a supplier and a consumer, the threat of adverse publicity may be a weapon which the latter may be most unwilling — or unwise — to give up. In the United States, it has been remarked that 'diversion of consumer grievances to arbitration . . . [has] muffled public disclosure of consumer fraud'.[171] Arbitration may be speedier, especially where the arbiter possesses technical expertise (for example, as an engineer) which makes detailed explanation of the implications of the evidence unnecessary, but

---

[170] Administration of Justice (Scotland) Act 1933 s. 10. See Maxwell, *Ct. of Sess. Pract.*, 489–90.
[171] Auerbach J. S., *Justice without law?*, New York, 1984, 126.

the most expert arbiters are often in such great demand that it is difficult to secure their services at an early date. The procedure may be more informal than that of an ordinary court, but this may merely change the nature of the injustices that can arise, rather than eradicating injustice altogether. The complex procedures of the courts were devised to ensure for example that each party is made fully aware of the case to be met. Informality on the other hand may facilitate surprise, and may increase the chances of serious delay.[172] Furthermore, there is always the risk that an award may be reduced because of some error on the part of the arbiter, whereupon the whole proceedings may prove a waste of time. In cases with an international dimension, arbitration may provide a neutral forum, but a party who thinks that the courts in a particular country may favour him or her may not always be so virtuous as to disregard that possible advantage.

2.49. The existence of a fashion for ordinary arbitration in relation to any particular type of dispute may therefore indicate nothing more than conservatism, lack of interest in comparative legal study, and lack of awareness of public need, in those who govern the procedure of the ordinary courts, and an unwillingness in governments to finance necessary research. There remains, however, one feature of arbitration which in many cases may be a very great advantage — the opportunity to appoint as arbiter a person whose knowledge and expertise lie not so much in the law — though some knowledge of law is usually important — as in some other field such as engineering, surveying, or agriculture, which is of particular relevance to the subject matter of the dispute. Here the Scots practice of appointing a solicitor as clerk to the arbiter helps to reduce the risk that an arbiter who is not legally qualified will commit an error of law which renders the decree arbitral liable to reduction. It must be admitted, however, that since the Law Society of Scotland has not hitherto laid any emphasis, in its regulations for admission to or continuance in the profession, upon the study of international private law, European Community law, or comparative law, the assistance of a solicitor as clerk is likely to be less of a safeguard in international commercial arbitrations than in the normal domestic type.

---

[172] As in *Allied Marine Transport Ltd.* v. *Vale do Rio Doce Navegaçao S.A.*, [1983] 2 Ll.Rep. 411.

2.50. Finally, the question may be posed whether and to what extent the practice of ordinary arbitration is in the interests of society at large. It does after all often provide a means of avoiding the effect of legislation which is contrary to the interests of both parties. Recently the supranational regulation of economic affairs in the European Economic Communities has created a new official interest in the strict control of arbitration, as may be observed in the cases of *Re the Agreements of the Davidson Rubber Company*[173] and *Re the Agreements of Davide Compari-Milano.*[174] In these cases the Commission of the European Communities approved certain arbitration clauses under Article 85(3) of the Treaty of Rome, but only on conditions which ensured that they could not be used to restrict competition. Perhaps surprisingly the European Court of Justice has ruled[175] that an arbiter is not 'a court or tribunal of a member state' for the purposes of Article 177 of the Treaty of Rome, and therefore cannot make a reference to the European Court. It is apparent from the judgment[176] that the Court assumed that in all member states arbitral awards can always be reviewed by an ordinary court, which can of course make such a reference. No such right exists in Scots law. Error of law by an arbiter, unless it appears on the face of the award[177] does not ground an action of reduction,[178] and there is no requirement that an award be reasoned. The only means of obtaining a reference to the European Court in a Scots arbitration is indirectly by asking the arbiter during the arbitration proceedings to state a case for the opinion of the Court of Session or a sheriff, and parties may contract out of the stated case procedure.[179] Though in a statutory 'arbitration' to which parties are compelled by law to have recourse reference may be made directly to the European Court by the arbiter,[180] the power of the European Court to supervise arbitration in Scotland seems

---

[173] [1972] C.M.L.R. (R.P. Supplement) D52.
[174] [1978] 2 C.M.L.R. 397.
[175] In *Nordsee Deutsche Hochsee Fischerei GmbH* v. *Reederei Mond Hochsee Fischerei Nordstern A.G. and Co. K.G. and Another* (Case 102/81), [1982] E.C.R. 1095.
[176] At 1111.
[177] *Clyne's Trs.* v. *Edinburgh Oil Gas Light Co.* (1835) II Shaw and MacLean App. 243 at 271.
[178] *Mitchell-Gill* v. *Buchan* 1921 S.C. 390 at 395.
[179] Administration of Justice (Scotland) Act 1972 s. 3.
[180] *Vaassen* v. *Beambtenfonds voor het Mijnbedrijf* (Case 61/65) [1966] E.C.R. 261.

effectively to be conditional upon its acceptance by the parties. It is one thing for a mediaeval monarch in close personal contact with his magnates to abstain from close supervision of arbitration proceedings designed to settle local differences; it is perhaps another matter for democratic states to allow international business corporations to resort to private arbitration for the purpose of evading controls designed (for example) to prevent unfair competition.

2.51. There is no intention here of suggesting that ordinary arbitration is of no value to the public at large. It does after all relieve the state of the burden of providing for the adjudication of a large proportion of the commercial caseload, and in its equitable form it may provide a means of settling some otherwise intractable disputes between opposing interest groups. Those countries, such as England, in which there exists a substantial body of skilled arbiters of international repute, are likely to derive considerable economic benefit from the practice of arbitration. Yet only if sufficient supervision is exercised over arbitration to prevent it from becoming a means of evading democratic control will its benefits clearly outweigh its disadvantages.

2.52. The advantages and disadvantages of equitable arbitration are similar but not identical, and the main points of difference are worth at least a brief discussion here. Since in equitable arbitration rules of law may give way to principles of equity as understood by the parties and their arbitrators, there is some reason for it to be distrusted by those committed to the rule of law or the exercise of social control through law. On the other hand, there are some types of dispute, such as those between trade unions and employers, which are so complex and give rise to such strong passions among so many people, that a legalistic framework is quite inappropriate. If arbitrators can be found who possess the confidence of all those concerned, and if it is in the interests of the parties - in the longer term at least — to accept their decisions even if adverse, then equitable arbitration may be able to settle otherwise intractable controversies. Nevertheless, there remains a danger that in such cases the arbitrators will succumb to the temptation to have regard simply to the desire to achieve a settlement, so that their decision reflects the balance of power between the contending parties and has no reference to principles or standards of any kind. This is especially likely to occur when — as is the case in labour disputes -

there is no consensus concerning underlying values. In the long run this practice, inconsistent as it is with the core of the concept of arbitration, must tend to weaken the authority of what purport to be arbitral decisions.

PART B

ORDINARY ARBITRATION CONTRACTS

CHAPTER THREE

THE CONTRACTUAL FRAMEWORK

Introduction

3.1. This part of the work, which deals with submissions to arbitration, arbitration clauses, and the appointment of arbiters, is based on the assumption that in Scots law most of the rights, liberties and powers of those who submit disputes to arbitration in relation to each other and to their arbiter may be expounded in terms of the rules and principles of ordinary Scots contract law. This is not a wholly uncontroversial assumption so far as the relations between the submitters and their arbiter are concerned, for, though it is arguably consistent with existing authoritative textbooks and judicial decisions in Scotland,[1] it has not previously been stated expressly. It must also be acknowledged that in relation to English law it has been authoritatively stated that, while the relations between the parties to an arbitration agreement may be analysed in terms of contract law, to attempt to expound the relations between those parties and an English arbitrator in this way would be 'a mistake' even though 'with a little ingenuity a contract between these two persons could undoubtedly be devised'.[2] The reasons given for this view by such distinguished authors deserve as full a discussion as is possible within the framework of a general work.

3.2. The main reason for the view that, in English law, the relations between those who submit disputes to arbitration on the one hand and the arbitrator on the other should not be dealt with in terms of contractual principles is that to do so 'will not produce a reliable answer unless a contract really exists to be found'.[3] The authors go on to say[4] that

---

[1] See e.g. *McIntyre Brothers* v. *Smith* 1913 S.C. 129 per Lord Kinnear at 132.
[2] Mustill, *Comm. Arb.*, 188.
[3] *Op. cit.* 189.
[4] *Ibid.*

'even in the extreme case of a massive reference, employing a professional arbitrator for a substantial remuneration, we doubt whether a businessman would, if he stopped to think, conceive that he was making a contract when appointing an arbitrator. Such an appointment is not like appointing an accountant, architect, or lawyer. Indeed it is not like anything else at all. We hope that the courts will recognise this, and will not try to force the relationship between arbitrator and party into an uncongenial theoretical framework, but will proceed directly to a consideration of what rights and duties ought, in the public interest, to be regarded as attaching to the status of arbitrator.'

3.3. There are several reasons why this view is not adopted in this work. The first is that in Scots law the relations between submitters and their arbiter have scarcely been regulated by statute at all and have not been much discussed by the judiciary, whereas in English law they have been the subject of quite detailed statutory provisions. This means that there is both more need and more scope for the use of a recognised jurisprudential framework in this area of Scots law than in the corresponding area of English law. Arguably it is generally more pragmatic to approach a somewhat uncharted field in the light of a rational theory than to treat each case on its own, because law which has a theoretical structure is more predictable in its development and more comprehensible than law which is a mass of particular instances. It may well be that in English law, given the extent to which the matter is regulated by statute, a contractual framework would be 'uncongenial'; in Scots law there is no such reason to reject it, at least so long as it is recognised that arbitration has a jurisdictional as well as a contractual nature, and that the judicial duties of an arbiter cannot properly be enforced by remedies appropriate for breach of contract.[5] In older styles of submission in Scotland the submitters and the arbiter all subscribed the same deed,[6] and today it is common practice for the submitters to send the deed of submission to the arbiter who accepts office by endorsing a minute of acceptance thereon. Both these practices are consistent with the existence of a contractual relationship not only between the submitters, but also between the submitters on the one hand and the arbiter on the other. That Scots law is not peculiar in assuming

[5] *Forbes* v. *Underwood* (1886) 13 R. 465.
[6] Dallas, *Stiles*, 814; Carruthers, *Stiles*, 271-3.

a contract between the submitters and their arbiter is indicated by the fact that this is the basis of that relationship both in the law of Sweden[7] (the system with which Scots arbitration law appears to have most in common), and in French law.[8] Finally, though the way in which a business person understands a relationship should not be dismissed out of hand, it should not determine how that relationship is analysed in law, especially when that understanding is merely a matter of conjecture.

Outline of the types of contract involved in arbitration

3.4. Ordinary arbitration[9] proceedings are based on a set of at least two distinguishable agreements. There is first of all the *contract of submission* by which two or more parties — the 'submitters' — resolve that certain questions between them shall be decided by arbitration rather than by litigation. That agreement may exist on its own as an *ad hoc* contract, taking the form of an originating 'deed of submission' or 'minute of reference', or may be attached to some other agreement in the form of an ancillary arbitration clause. The contract of submission, whatever its form, is the primary contract upon which ordinary arbitration is based.

3.5. Having agreed to submit a dispute to arbitration, the submitters must appoint someone to act as arbiter. They therefore enter into a secondary contract with a person who is willing to act in that capacity. This contract has no generally accepted title, and it will in this work be generally given the — admittedly rather infelicitous — title of *contract of appointment*, since the formal deed by which parties to an ancillary submission often appoint an arbiter to determine a particular dispute is usually called a 'deed of appointment'. In the case of an *ad hoc* contract, appointment is usually effected by sending to the nominee the principal copy of the deed of submission with a covering letter containing a request that the recipient will formally agree to act as arbiter in the matter; where the submission is contained in an ancillary arbitration clause, a 'deed of appointment' or implementing deed of

---

[7] Holmbäck, *Arb. Swe.* 1984, 78, but see note 26.
[8] Robert and Carbonneau, *Arb.*, I: 2–24.
[9] The meaning of 'ordinary arbitration', and the distinctions between it and other forms of procedure, are discussed above in paragraphs 1.3. ff.

submission in the traditional form is presented. The nominee indicates acceptance of the office by endorsing a minute to that effect upon the submission or appointment deed. There is however no requirement that the contract be entered into thus formally; it may be effected by letter or telex.

3.6. In addition to the foregoing, there are three types of agreement which, though not essential to arbitration proceedings, are nevertheless often entered into in practice. These are:

(a) a contract by means of which submitters already bound by an ancillary arbitration clause define the issues actually being presented to the arbiter and specify some of the powers which the arbiter may exercise. This agreement, which is often contained in an implementing 'deed of submission',[10] will here be referred to generally as an *'implementing contract'*;
(b) two contracts which will here be referred to generally as *'facilitating contracts'*, namely —
(i) the mandate given by the submitters to a third party to appoint an arbiter; and
(ii) the contract for services entered into between the arbiter and the clerk in the arbitration.

3.7. Sometimes during arbitration proceedings the submitters find it necessary to extend the duration of their original contract of submission or to give the arbiter additional powers. Agreements entered into for such purposes are not so much separate contracts as variations of the original contracts.

The contract of submission

3.8. The primary contract upon which arbitration proceedings are based in Scots law is the contract of submission. A definition of this contract which is generally accepted[11] (except to the extent that it has since been affected by the Arbitration (Scotland) Act 1894[12]) is contained in a judgment of Lord Moncreiff.[13]

---

[10] A deed of submission may either contain an *ad hoc* contract of submission, or implement a contract of submission contained in an ancillary arbitration clause.
[11] E.g. by Irons, *Arb.* 45.
[12] The part of the definition so affected is omitted from the quotation given in this paragraph.
[13] *Brakenrig* v. *Menzies* (1841) 4 D. 274 at 283.

'... A submission to arbiters is a contract by which the parties commit to the entire and exclusive cognisance of the arbiter or arbiters ... the whole matters submitted, and bind themselves to abide by his or their decision in all things.'

A contract of submission may thus be said to be a contract between two or more persons (the submitters) which includes expressly or impliedly agreement to the effect —

(a) that a certain existing dispute between the parties (the submitters) or certain kinds of dispute which the parties believe may arise in the future between them shall be determined by arbitration rather than by litigation in the ordinary courts;
(b) that either —
(i) the person or persons identified in the contract of submission shall act as arbiter or arbiters; or
(ii) the parties will, if and when occasion arises, concur in the appointment of an arbiter or arbiters; or
(iii) the arbiter or arbiters shall be appointed on behalf of the parties by a person or persons identified in the contract; and
(c) that the parties shall be bound by any valid procedural orders and decrees arbitral that the arbiter may make in the arbitration.

3.9.   Not all the essential features of a contract of submission specified in the previous paragraph need to be expressly stated. Some extremely laconic agreements have been upheld by the courts, including one which stated merely —

'Arbitration. Disputes to be settled by arbitration in Glasgow.'[14]

Such brief expressions may in certain circumstances be expanded by implying terms to the extent necessary to give efficacy to the contract.[15] This may be done if the intention of the parties may be presumed from custom (especially custom of trade) or from the nature of the particular agreement which they have apparently sought to enter into.[16]

---

[14] *United Creameries Co. Ltd.* v. *David T. Boyd and Co.* 1912 S.C. 617.
[15] *The Moorcock* (1889) 14 P.D. 64, per Bowen L. J. at 68. Though the remarks of Bowen L. J. have not in all respects found favour, the concept of 'business efficacy' has been accepted as consistent with Scots law by McBryde, *Contract*, 6–14.
[16] *Morton* v. *Muir Brothers* 1907 S.C. 1211, per Lord McLaren at 1224, followed in *Microwave Systems (Scotland) Ltd.* v. *Electro Physiological Instruments Ltd.* 1971 S.C. 140.

3.10. The parties to a contract of submission are in modern practice the submitters only. Though arbiters by accepting office expressly or impliedly agree to decide the matters — and only the matters — which the submitters have agreed to refer to their decision, they are not normally parties to the contract of submission itself. Opinions to the contrary[17] are, it is submitted, based on the practice which was common before ancillary arbitration clauses were normal, under which arbiters and submitters were all parties to *ad hoc* contracts contained in deeds of submission.[18] Contracts of submission do not nowadays effect the actual presentation of a dispute to the arbiters, nor does a deed of submission, whether it contains an *ad hoc* contract or implements a contract contained in an arbitration clause, normally constitute by itself a contract between them and the submitters. The contract of submission might be more accurately entitled a contract 'to submit', but the traditional title, derived from a period in which the arbiter was normally a party to the deed along with the submitters, is too well established to be altered.

3.11. The form of the contract of submission will be discussed in more detail below.[19] At this stage it should be noted that it may be contained in a formal document such as a deed of submission or minute of reference, or in informal business letters,[20] or in an ancillary arbitration clause attached to another contract.[21] At one time the deed of submission was the normal vehicle for the contract. Nowadays that function is often — perhaps normally — performed by the ancillary arbitration clause. The existence of such a clause does not however make a deed of submission necessarily superfluous. It may still be employed to define the issues which are being presented to the arbiter and to specify powers which the arbiter may exercise. In so far as the issues as so defined are within the scope of the arbitration clause, the deed of submission is merely a convenient means of implementing the contract of submission contained in the arbitration clause,[22] and it is open to the submitters to dispense with it altogether. Indeed if, when a dispute has arisen which is within the scope of a contract

---

[17] Bell J. M., *Arb.* paragraph 157; Guild, *Arb.* 10.
[18] *Supra,* note 6.
[19] Chapter 5.
[20] *Dykes* v. *Roy* (1869) 7 M. 357.
[21] Irons, *Arb.* 72.
[22] *Clydebank District Council* v. *Clink* 1977 S.C. 147.

contained in an ancillary arbitration clause, one of the submitters is unwilling to proceed with arbitration, the other may simply address a letter to whoever has been appointed arbiter, stating that differences have arisen and requesting him or her to deal with them.[23] The recalcitrant party who persists in ignoring opportunities given by the arbiter to appear and enter defences risks the pronouncing of a decree arbitral in favour of the party who has initiated the proceedings.[24]

3.12. The term *'agreement to refer to arbitration'* or its shorter form 'agreement to refer' is sometimes used in juristic writing, professional practice, and legislation in connection with submissions to arbitration in Scotland, and it is therefore necessary to consider whether it has a distinct meaning.

3.13. It seems not to have appeared in authoritative juristic writing until after the passing of the Arbitration (Scotland) Act 1894,[25] and may therefore be largely the product of legislation, but the term 'referee' had then for some time been applied to a person appointed to decide matters 'in his professional capacity only'.[26] By this it was apparently meant that the person concerned was expected to deal with the issues put to him by applying his own powers of observation, scientific knowledge, and technical expertise of a non-legal nature, without taking evidence from others. This usage may have developed concurrently with the growth of arbitration by members of new professions applying science-based knowledge.[27] In 1902 Irons and Melville used the term 'reference' to denote cases in which 'a person in whom the parties have confidence' is made responsible for 'settling something necessary to expiscate or liquidate a contract, purify a condition therein, or fulfil some obligation'.[28] It seems that they considered that some, but by no means all, such 'references' were arbitrations. The term 'minute of reference' is frequently used in practice, usually (but not invariably) to indicate that the issues require the exercise of professional knowledge and expertise of a non-legal nature. J. M. Bell uses the phrase 'agreement to submit'

[23] Irons, *Arb.* 88.
[24] *Hunter* v. *Milburn* (1869) 6 S.L.R. 525 per Lord Deas.
[25] In particular, it does not appear in the work of J. M. Bell.
[26] Parker, *Arb.*, 1.
[27] See paragraph 2.36 and footnote 126 above.
[28] *Arb.*, 47.

in connection with arbitration clauses. Apart from legislation, then, the term 'agreement to refer to arbitration' appears not to be a precise term of art, though the use of the words 'refer', 'reference' and 'referee' generally suggests that the person to whom the matter is presented is to deal with it very informally without hearing evidence.

3.14. The purposes of the Arbitration (Scotland) Act 1894 were to abolish the common law rule[29] invalidating submissions to arbiters unnamed and to enable the court to appoint an arbiter where a party had refused to appoint or concur in an appointment. To achieve the first of these ends it provided that

'from and after the passing of this Act, an agreement to refer to arbitration shall not be invalid or ineffectual by reason of the reference being to a person to be named by another person, or to a person merely described as the holder for the time being of any office or appointment.'

The use in this section of the words 'refer' and 'reference' cannot have been intended to imply restriction to cases where technical issues of a non-legal nature are dealt with informally without the hearing of evidence, because this would have had the effect of limiting the scope of the intended reform. The term 'agreement to refer to arbitration' was clearly meant to cover at least all ancillary arbitration clauses. Possibly those who drafted the Act had in mind English usage, which apparently then did and certainly now does[30] distinguish between an 'agreement to refer' contained in an arbitration clause relating to future disputes and a 'submission' of an existing dispute. The Act was however interpreted more widely in Scotland. Irons and Melville subsequently noted[31] that

'any difficulties which might arise when there has been a failure to nominate arbiters have now been obviated by the Arbitration (Scotland) Act 1894; and it is now no bar to the validity of a submission that the reference is to a person not named.'

By then the Act had already been applied in the context of a contract of submission of an existing dispute.[32] Effectively, the

---

[29] Stated e.g. in *Davidson (MacFarlane's Tr.)* v. *Oswald* 28 Feb. 1810 F.C.
[30] Russell, *Arb.* 1982, 44.
[31] *Arb.* 61.
[32] *Cowie* v. *Kiddie* (1897) 5 S.L.T. 259.

term 'agreement to refer to arbitration' in this context was interpreted as applying to all contracts of submission whether contained in an ancillary arbitration clause or an *ad hoc* deed.

3.15. The other statutory provision applicable to Scotland in which the term 'agreement to refer to arbitration' occurs is section 3 of the Administration of Justice (Scotland) Act 1972. The object of this section was to enable a party to ordinary arbitration proceedings in Scotland to require an arbiter to state a case for the opinion of the court on a question of law arising in the arbitration. Probably as a concession to the opponents of the measure, a clause was inserted in subsection 3(1) giving power to submitters to exclude the stated case procedure by 'express provision to the contrary in an agreement to refer to arbitration'. It was also provided in subsection 3(4) that the new procedure would not apply 'in relation to an agreement to refer to arbitration made before the commencement of this Act'.

3.16. The courts have since been called upon to determine the meaning of the phrase 'agreement to refer to arbitration' in the context of subsection 3(4).[33] The facts were that two contracts, each containing arbitration clauses, were entered into by the parties to the action before the commencement of section 3 on 2nd April 1973.[34] Subsequently a deed of submission was executed after that date. After sundry proceedings, the arbiter issued a proposed award, and the Council asked the arbiter to state a case for the opinion of the court. The arbiter replied that since the agreement to refer had been entered into prior to the commencement of the section he had no power or duty to state a case. The Council then applied to the court to order the arbiter to state a case, but the court refused on the ground that the 'agreement to refer to arbitration' had been contained in the arbitration clauses which had been executed prior to the commencement of the section. The deed of submission in that case had not contained an agreement to refer to arbitration; it had simply implemented the contract contained in the arbitration clauses. It was not suggested, however, that a deed of submission standing on its own without prior arbitration clauses would not be

---

[33] *Clydebank District Council* v. *Clink* 1977 S.C. 147; 1977 S.L.T. 190.
[34] Administration of Justice (Scotland) Act 1972 (Commencement) Order 1973, SI 1973 No. 339.

regarded as containing such an agreement. It seems therefore that in the 1972 Act, as in the 1894 Act, all *contracts* of submission are 'agreements to refer to arbitration' whether contained in arbitration clauses or not; but *deeds* of submission only contain arbitration agreements to the extent that they do not merely implement prior contracts.

The arbiter's appointment contract

3.17. Before arbitration proceedings can commence, it is obviously necessary for the submitters to obtain the services of one or more arbiters. Normally the submitters agree upon a single joint nominee, and offer that person appointment. It is competent, though highly undesirable, for the submitters to appoint one of their own number as arbiter.[35] The contract of submission may (and where it is contained in an ancillary arbitration clause it often does) provide that in the event of the parties being unable to agree on the nomination of a single arbiter, a third party may on the request of one of them make an appointment. Sometimes the submitters agree that each of them may nominate one arbiter, and the two arbiters are given power jointly to appoint an oversman to decide any issues which the original arbiters are unable to agree upon. Where a party has failed to nominate or to concur in the nomination of an arbiter, or the arbiters have failed to concur in the nomination of an oversman, the court may be asked to make an appointment in terms of the Arbitration (Scotland) Act 1894.

3.18. The basis of the relationship between the submitters and their arbiter or arbiters and oversman has not been the subject of anything more than isolated comments in judicial decisions or juristic writing in Scotland, though it has been seriously discussed by jurists in other countries.[36] Scottish neglect may be due to the fact that until towards the end of the nineteenth century it was assumed that an arbiter normally acted gratuitously as a favour rather than professionally, and disputes between arbiters and parties hardly ever reached the courts. The means by which arbiters were appointed did however suggest that the relationship

---

[35] *Buchan* v. *Melville* (1902) 4 F. 620.
[36] E.g. France: see Robert J., *Arbitrage Civil et Commercial*, 4th edn., Paris, 1967, 257, 261–2, 331.

was fundamentally one of contract. Either the submitters and the arbiter all executed the deed of submission,[37] or the submitters executed the deed containing their contract of submission which was then presented to the intended arbiter who endorsed a minute of acceptance thereon,[38] or (in informal mercantile arbitrations) the appointment was made by an exchange of letters. Since arbiters now generally act professionally for remuneration, and since in Scotland the question of the immunity of arbiters from liability for negligence is becoming a live issue, the legal basis of the relationship between submitters and arbiters requires clarification.

3.19. When the office of arbiter was gratuitous, it was apparently believed that the submitters granted a form of 'mandate or commission, authorising arbiters to hear and determine'.[39] J.M. Bell remarked that a decree arbitral could 'possess no inherent force beyond that which is derived from the joint mandate of the contracting parties'.[40] Certainly there must then have seemed to be a striking similarity between mandate and the contract between submitters and arbiters. Both were gratuitous; both were commonly construed as either general or special, as indeed they still are;[41] and just as the act of a mandatary who exceeds his or her powers does not bind the mandant, so a decree arbitral which goes beyond the matters submitted does not bind the submitters, a point first decided in a Scottish case in 1208[42] and since periodically reiterated.[43] There are however features of arbitration which have no counterpart in mandate, such as the rules of fairness between the submitters,[44] and the fact that an issue decided by a decree arbitral is '*res judicata*'[45] — a 'juget thing' as an old Scots court

[37] Carruthers, *Stiles, supra*, note 6.
[38] Bell J. M., *Arb.*, Appendix VII.
[39] *Fraser* v. *Williamson* (1773) Mor. 8476. See also the style in Donaldson G. and Smith D. B. (eds), *St Andrews Formulare 1516–46*, Stair Society, Edinburgh, 1942, Vol. I, 99.
[40] *Arb.* paragraph 158.
[41] Walker, *Prin.*, 283; Guild, *Arb.* 27.
[42] Patrick D. (ed.), *Statutes of the Scottish Church*, Scottish History Society, 1st Series, Edinburgh, 1970, 199.
[43] E.g. in *Caledonian Railway Co.* v. *Turcan* (1898) 25 R. (H.L.) 7 per Lord Watson at 17.
[44] *Sharpe* v. *Bickersdyke* (1815) III Dow App. 102, per Lord Chancellor Eldon at 107.
[45] *Fraser* v. *Lord Lovat* (1850) VII Bell App. 171; *Crudens* v. *Tayside Health Board* 1979 S.C. 142 per Lord Kissen at 153.

precisely and pithily put it[46] — precluding the raising of the same matter between the same parties in subsequent litigation. These features have led some foreign courts and jurists to assert that arbitration has a jurisdictional rather than a contractual nature.[47]

3.20. Nevertheless, the partially jurisdictional nature of arbitration does not necessarily mean that the relations between the parties and their arbiter are other than contractual. Since there is no general legal obligation on anyone to act as arbiter when called upon to do so,[48] the office of arbiter and the legal rights, duties, liberties and powers which go with it must be assumed voluntarily. This does not necessarily imply the existence of a contract. It was long doubted whether the relations between the Crown and its servants, who clearly acted voluntarily, were based on contract.[49] Neither does it necessarily imply that, if there is a contract, all these rights, duties and powers may be freely determined by the agreement of the parties. Yet, where legal obligations are assumed voluntarily there must be a heavy burden on anyone who asserts that no contract exists to show why this must be so. Here, though the main duties of an arbiter are defined by law, so that it can be said that arbitration is in a sense a public office, there seems no good reason to deny that a person can be said to undertake those duties, and any others that may be specified, under a contract, which also lays duties upon the submitters.

3.21. The situation may be analysed in one of two ways. First, it may be considered that the submitters offer appointment as arbiter to the person upon whom their choice has fallen, and that person then accepts appointment. The secondary *appointment contract* here entered into between the submitters and the arbiter, is thus theoretically and often also actually separate from the primary contract of submission. Alternatively, it may be considered that the submitters approach the chosen person and ask him or her to indicate willingness to accept appointment as arbiter. That person may then promise to accept office if appointed on certain terms relating for example to remuneration. The subsequent act of

---

[46] *Spottiswod* v. *Mowbra* (1479) *ADC*, 40.

[47] See e.g. Robert, *Arb.*, 257.

[48] *Macanqual* v. *Boswell* (1563) Mor. 636. The decision reflects the civil law rule 'nemo cogitur ab initio in se compromissum suscipere': Odofredus, *Lect.* 1.4.8., Fol. 193 r.

[49] *Gallagher* v. *The Post Office* [1970] 3 All E.R. 712 at 718.

appointment, by fulfilling the condition, brings the set of obligations contained in the unilateral promise into effect. Since unilateral promises are binding in Scots law though provable only by writ or oath,[50] the latter is a possible basis for the imposition of the duties of the office of arbiter, and may indeed be the only basis where the appointment is made by the court.

3.22. It is submitted that, unless the circumstances clearly indicate otherwise, the first approach is generally preferable. The effect in the first case of an offer of appointment is that there is no contract until it has been accepted; in the second case, the appointment is effective as soon as it has been made on the faith of the binding promise to accept. Where a third party has been given a mandate to appoint an arbiter, the power is exhausted in the first case when, and only when, the contract has been completed,[51] and in the second case where, and only where, there is an act of appointment which follows on a binding promise to accept office. The first approach is closer to the normal course of events in modern practice, in which the submitters send to the proposed arbiter either the submission or a deed of appointment, upon which that person then endorses and executes a minute of acceptance of office, and is consistent with former practice under which the arbiter was a party to the deed of submission. The existence of this *contract* between the submitters and the arbiter does not mean that in the performance of judicial functions the arbiter does not exercise a subordinate *jurisdiction*. During the course of arbitration proceedings the arbiter is subject to the control of the court by means of remedies appropriate in the supervision of subordinate judicial bodies;[52] otherwise, the remedies for breach of the respective obligations of submitters and arbiter are the same as for breach of any other contract.[53]

3.23. It is submitted therefore that an arbiter undertakes the office by a contract with the submitters, but that the nature and scope of the powers granted to and assumed by the arbiter are ultimately governed by law, since the enforcement of a decree

---

[50] Stair, *Inst.* 1.10.4.
[51] This is consistent with view of Irons and Melville that the power of two arbiters to appoint an oversman is not exhausted if their nominee declines to accept office: *Arb.* 179.
[52] *Forbes* v. *Underwood* (1886) 13 R. 465.
[53] As in *McIntyre Brothers* v. *Smith* 1913 S.C. 129.

arbitral as a judgment is conditional upon the proceedings having been conducted in a judicial manner.

3.24. Though submissions to a single arbiter are believed now to be commoner than submissions to two arbiters and an oversman or a tribunal of three arbiters, submission to two arbiters with an oversman is not unknown. Here the contract of submission gives each of the submitters (normally there are two) the right and the duty to nominate and appoint an arbiter. A distinction may be drawn between the nomination and the appointment of an arbiter, though the words are often used loosely so that it is necessary to have regard to their context to ascertain their precise significance. *Nomination* ordinarily implies no more than an overt unilateral act of selection; it does not by itself create any rights, duties, powers or liabilities in the nominee, who may indeed be unaware of it, though it must, to be effective, be communicated to someone. *Appointment* on the other hand, normally involves the assent of the appointee, and does grant rights and powers to and impose duties on that person. Where each submitter is to nominate and appoint one of two arbiters, the nomination of an arbiter is a unilateral act communicated by the nominating submitter to the other party, and does not necessarily involve the nominee at all. The appointment of an arbiter necessarily involves the agreement of both the person nominated and one of the submitters on behalf of both. It must be emphasised that even where only one of the submitters is actively involved in making an appointment, it is made on behalf of the other also, for the arbiter is not, as such, in any sense the agent of one party in the arbitration, and has contractual duties to both of them.

3.25. Two arbiters have an implied power to nominate an oversman unless the submitters expressly provide otherwise.[54] It seems to have been generally assumed that the Act did not intend here to draw a distinction between nomination and appointment, so that once a nomination has been properly made, there has been no objection to the arbiters also making the appointment even if they have no express power to do so. This is indeed a commonsense view, even if not fully warranted by the language of the Act. In appointing an oversman the arbiters act on behalf of the submitters, so that the oversman is brought into a contractual

[54] Arbitration (Scotland) Act 1894 s. 4.

relationship with the submitters which is similar to that which binds them to the arbiters

3.26. The terms of an arbiter's contract with the submitters are rarely expressed, and they must therefore often be implied from the nature of the contract and the functions which an arbiter has to perform. It has been authoritatively stated[55] that in England an arbiter has a threefold obligation 'to take care, to proceed diligently, and to act impartially'. It is suggested that as a minimum the terms upon which a person undertakes to act as arbiter or oversman in Scots law are as follows:

(a) the appointee shall perform the functions of arbiter (or oversman) —
(i) fairly;[56];
(ii) with reasonable diligence;[57]
(iii) with reasonable care[57a] and such special skill as he or she professes;
(iv) in accordance with law;[58] and
(v) in accordance with the provisions of the contract of submission and any deed implementing it, in particular ensuring that the issues submitted for decision are exhausted and their limits observed;[59]
(b) the submitters shall vest the arbiter with at least such powers in relation to themselves as are ordinarily necessary to enable the arbiter to conduct the proceedings in an effective manner;[60] and
(c) the submitters shall be liable jointly and severally for the expenses of the arbiter.[61]

Nowadays it will normally be assumed as an implied term that the submitters are liable jointly and severally for the arbiter's fees also, at least where he or she is acting in a professional capacity,[62] though in former times arbitration was assumed to be conducted gratuitously unless the arbiter had before accepting office

---

[55] Mustill, *Comm. Arb.* 190.
[56] *Mitchell* v. *Cable* (1848) 10 D. 1297 per Lord Mackenzie at 1308.
[57] Bell J. M., *Arb.* paragraph 377.
[57a] See paragraph 8.54, 8.58 below.
[58] *Mitchell-Gill* v. *Buchan* 1921 S.C. 390 at 395.
[59] *Mackenzie* v. *Girvan* (1840) 3 D. 318 per Lord Moncreiff at 328, affd. (1843) II Bell App. 43.
[60] Erskine, *Inst.* I.2.8., applied to arbitration by Bell J. M., *Arb.* paragraph 252.
[61] *Dunlop* v. *Ralston* (undated) 5 Bro. Supp. 428.
[62] *Macintyre Brothers* v. *Smith* 1913 S.C. 129.

expressly stipulated for a fee.[63] The old rule, derived from canon law, was justified on the ground that one of the main objects of arbitration was the avoidance of expense to the submitters,[64] but the practical result may frequently have been that the arbiter was out of pocket, and that the office of arbiter was avoided if possible. As an old German proverb put it,

'Wer sich als Schiedmann zwischen Zänker stellt,
Verliert die guten Worte, und sein Gelt.'[65]

Facilitating contracts

3.27. **The mandate to appoint an arbiter.** One of the commonest types of contract which help to facilitate arbitration is that by which the submitters authorise a third party to appoint an arbiter. The nature of this contract has not been the subject of juristic or judicial discussion in Scotland, perhaps because third party appointment has only been competent since 1894[66] and has never apparently been the subject of litigation. However, it is difficult to regard the contract (which is generally gratuitous) otherwise than as a form of mandate. It is common practice to provide in an ancillary arbitration clause for appointment of an arbiter by the holder for the time being of some office, such as that of sheriff principal or president or chair of a relevant professional body such as the Scottish branch of the Chartered Institute of Arbitrators, the Law Society of Scotland,[67] the Royal Institute of British Architects, the Institute of Civil Engineers, or the Royal Institute of Chartered Surveyors. If a dispute arises and the submitters are unable to agree upon a suitable arbiter, the holder of the designated office is approached informally by one of the submitters as mandant and asked to make an appointment. If (as is usual) the person concerned is willing to act as mandatary, he or she then in turn approaches suitable individuals until someone is found who is willing to undertake the office of arbiter. The mandatary then on behalf of the submitters makes an appointment, and in so doing brings the arbiter into a contractual relationship with them.

[63] See e.g. *Jack* v. *Cramond* (1777) Mor. Appx. Arb. 6.
[64] Durandus, *Speculum*, T.1, Fol. 117.
[65] Quoted by Hirst F. W. in *The Arbiter in Council*, London, 1906, 364.
[66] Arbitration (Scotland) Act 1894 s. 1.
[67] See the styles of arbitration clause and of submission in *Arbitration Service*, Law Society of Scotland, Edinburgh, 1986.

3.28.   The mandatary acts gratuitously, but the submitters as joint mandants would presumably be liable jointly and severally for expenses such as telex, telephone or postal charges. Since these have never apparently been claimed, or if claimed, have always been paid without question, the matter of liability for expenses has never come before the courts. The question whether the third party making the appointment owes any duty of care to the submitters has also not yet been raised in Scotland, but it has been judicially suggested in a similar context that the duty of nominating and appointing an arbiter implies 'the duty ... also of taking reasonable care to appoint a proper and fit person'.[68]

3.29.   Where one of the submitters has failed to appoint an arbiter or concur in the appointment of an arbiter in terms of a contract of submission which expressly or impliedly specifies the number of arbiters, and where an arbiter has failed to concur in the appointment of an oversman, the court has power under the Arbitration (Scotland) Act 1894[69] to make an appointment. What normally happens is that a person thought to be appropriate is discreetly approached to discover whether he or she would be prepared to undertake the office. When assurances have been obtained from someone of willingness to act, the court makes the appointment. There is here no direct contract between the submitters and the arbiter, and the court acts by virtue of statutory powers not in terms of a mandate granted by the submitters. The basis of the duties of the arbiter towards the submitters may be found in the nominee's unilateral promise — if given in probative writing, or informal writing followed by homologation or *rei interventus* — to undertake those duties if appointed. The condition is fulfilled when the court makes the appointment. Since no one is obliged to accept the office of arbiter it is very doubtful whether an act of appointment would be effective by itself. Alternatively, if appointment by the court is effective by itself, an appointment of a person who had never intimated willingness to accept office would presumably be liable to reduction on grounds of unreasonableness.[69a]

---

[68] *Sellar* v. *Highland Railway Co.* 1919 S.C. (H.L.) 19 per Lord Buckmaster at 22.

[69] Ss. 2–4.

[69a] *Associated Picture Houses Ltd.* v. *Wednesbury Corporation* [1948] 1 K.B. 223, approved as consistent with Scots Law in so far as relating to substance not

3.30.   **Contract for the services of a clerk.** Except in technical references and cases where the matter in issue is of small value arbiters in Scotland usually as one of their first acts on taking up office appoint a clerk in the arbitration. In practice the clerk is usually a solicitor. The main duties of the clerk are the custody of documents connected with the arbitration and the reception and despatching of communications between the arbiter and the submitters. The clerk is often also asked to assist in the drafting of interlocutors and decrees arbitral, and to give advice to the arbiter on questions of law and practice relating to arbitration procedure. The tendency of arbitrations in Scotland to proceed in a manner very similar to a sheriff court action is probably due to the practice of employing solicitors as clerks.

3.31.   Questions sometimes arise over the nature of the contract under which the clerk is employed, and whether the clerk is employed by the arbiter or by the submitters. There is little doubt but that the contract is a contract for services, which has been defined as a contract by which one party (the client or employer) lets out to another (the contractor) 'the doing, for a fee, of some piece of work . . . in the achievement of which the contractor is required to use his professional or technical skill and knowledge but is not subject to the detailed supervision, direction or control of the client'.[70] Though it is of course the arbiter's responsibility to determine the procedure to be followed in the arbitration and the terms of any decree arbitral, the clerk is not normally a mere secretarial assistant but rather the provider of professional services.

3.32.   The clerk is normally regarded as having been employed by the arbiter rather than the submitters.[71] This means that it is the arbiter, not the submitters, who is primarily responsible for payment of the clerk's fees and outlays, though naturally the arbiter will then include the amount thereof in his or her own charges.[72] In an early nineteenth century case[73] it was held,

---

procedure in *Brown* v. *Hamilton District Council* 1983 S.L.T. 397 *per* Lord Fraser of Tullybelton at 414.
    [70] Walker, *Prin.* 283.
    [71] Irons, *Arb.* 191, cited with approval in *Johnson* v. *Gill* 1978 S.C. 74.
    [72] *Glasgow Corporation Water Works Commissioners* v. *Henry* (1866) 3 S.L.R. 79.
    [73] *McFarlane* v. *Black* (1842) 4 D. 1459.

apparently on equitable principles of recompense,[74] that the clerk had a right of action directly against the submitters. It is doubtful whether this decision would now be followed.

[74] There is a statement of such principles in Bell, *Prin.*, paragraphs 538–9, but N.B. dicta in *Edinburgh Tramways* v. *Courtenay* 1909 S.C. 99.

CHAPTER FOUR

THE VALIDITY OF ARBITRATION CONTRACTS: CAPACITY AND POWER

Introduction

4.1. Contracts of submission and contracts of appointment both depend for their validity upon compliance with the rules of law governing their formation. These rules may be organised for purposes of analysis under the following headings:

(a) the capacity or power of the parties to enter into any type of contract or into these particular types of contract;
(b) the form which the contract has to take;
(c) the content of the contract; and
(d) the circumstances in which the contract is made.

This chapter is concerned with the first of these — capacity or power under Scots law to enter into contracts of submission or of appointment. The remainder are considered in the three subsequent chapters. The law governing the validity of these contracts is not necessarily the law of Scotland even if Scots law governs the arbitration proceedings,[1] and in principle (though rarely in practice in the case of ancillary submissions) even if the law governing the subject of the dispute is different from the law governing the submission and the arbiter's appointment. With the validity of arbitration contracts under other systems of law this work has for obvious reasons nothing to do.

4.2. **Capacity to contract** is the quality of being legally capable in one's own person of entering into, performing and enforcing any kind of contractual obligation other than one to which special rules apply.[2] This general ability is distinguished from the **power to contract**, which is the ability to enter into a contract of a

---

[1] *James Miller & Partners* v. *Whitworth Street Estates (Manchester) Ltd.* [1970] A.C. 583 per Lord Wilberforce at 616–7.
[2] Walker, *Contracts* paragraph 5.2.

particular kind,[3] either in one's own person or as the holder of some office such as that of tutor to a pupil child or trustee in bankruptcy. The special rules of the law of arbitration are concerned with power rather than capacity, but for the convenience of readers who are not professional Scots lawyers the application to arbitration of the rules of capacity is considered here.

Capacity, power, and the contract of submission

4.3. The law of arbitration imposes no special restrictions on the power of individuals to enter into contracts of submission in their own person. Such restrictions as exist are derived from the general rules of law relating to capacity. As J. M. Bell, following the civil law,[4] put it,[5]

'All persons may enter into a contract of submission who are under no disability in adhibiting an obligatory consent to a personal contract.'

It follows that any person who has attained the age of 18 years,[6] is not incapable by reason of unsoundness of mind[7] or physical disability[8] of indicating consent to a contract, and whose control over affairs has not been restricted by sequestration[9] or some other general legal embargo,[10] may enter into a contract of submission. The restrictions on the contractual capacity of married women have long been abolished,[11] and they therefore have a similar

---

[3] *Ibid.* paragraph 5.3.
[4] Citing Voet, *Comm.* IV.8.4. The canon law principle was similar — see Julien, *Ev. Hist.*, 210.
[5] *Arb.* paragraph 158.
[6] Age of Majority (Scotland) Act 1969 s.1.
[7] Stair, *Inst.*, I.10.13.
[8] What kinds of disability now fall into this category is unclear. The traditional rule, derived from Roman law, that persons who were deaf and dumb from birth could not contract (*Hamilton* (1663) Mor. 6300; Bankton, *Inst.*, I.11.66.) seems never to have been fully accepted (Erskine, *Inst.*, III.1.16) and is probably now obsolete (*Kirkpatrick* (1853) 15 D. 734).
[9] On sequestration, the bankrupt person's control over his or her property and affairs is affected by the powers first of the interim and then of the permanent trustee: Bankruptcy (Scotland) Act 1985 ss. 2(1)(a), 18, 31, 39.
[10] Such as that laid upon enemies in wartime — *Daimler Co. Ltd.* v. *Continental Tyre and Rubber Co. Ltd.* [1916] 2 A.C. 307 — though this is better regarded as a matter of illegality than incapacity — McBryde, *Contract*, paragraph 8–03.
[11] By the Married Women's Property (Scotland) Acts 1877, 1881 and 1920.

liberty. A person may be temporarily affected by some such influence as alcohol or a drug[12] or severe pain such as that experienced by a woman in labour[13] or fear[14] so as to be incapable of consent, but the disability here arises from factual circumstances at the time of the transaction rather than status, and these matters are considered in chapter seven.

Particular types of status and the power to submit

4.4. **Pupils and minors.** The contractual capacity of young people is presently under review by the Scottish Law Commission, which has issued a consultative memorandum on the subject.[15] Reform may therefore be expected. The present law so far as relevant to arbitration is summarised below.

4.5. A pupil is a child who has not yet attained the age of 14 (if a boy) or 12 (if a girl),[16] these being the ages fixed for convenience by the civil law as the age when puberty is reached. The law regards pupils as incapable of contracting,[17] and hence of entering into a submission to arbitration.[18] Contracts are made on their behalf by their tutors, whose powers are considered below[19] along with those of other types of trustee. By statute, where necessaries are sold and delivered to a pupil he or she must pay a reasonable price therefor,[20] but this liability is not contractual. Hence, even if a pupil desirous of obtaining some necessary article signs a standard form of contract containing an arbitration clause, the lack of contractual capacity of the pupil will ensure that any dispute arising out of the transaction has to be determined by a court rather than an arbiter.

4.6. Minors are young persons above the age of pupillarity who

---

[12] Stair, *Inst.*, I.10.13; Bankton, *Inst.*, I.11.66; Erskine, *Inst.*, III.1.16.
[13] *Belford* v. *Scot* (1683) Mor. 6297.
[14] Stair, *Inst.*, I.10.13.
[15] Consultative Memorandum No. 65 on Legal Capacity and Responsibility of Minors and Pupils.
[16] Stair, *Inst.* I.10.13.
[17] *Bruce* (1577) Mor. 8979.
[18] Bell, *Arb.*, paragraph 172.
[19] Paragraphs 4.17–19.
[20] Sale of Goods Act 1979 s. 3.

have not yet reached the age of 18.[21] Minors possess contractual capacity but it is limited. The validity and effect of the agreements into which they enter differ according to whether there is, as is usual, a curator, and according to whether the curator (if there is one) has concurred in the transaction. In general, where a minor has a curator, that curator's consent to any contract of submission which the minor may wish to enter into is required.[22] There are however a number of exceptional and doubtful cases.

4.7.   The main clear exception to the rule requiring the curator's consent is a contract entered into in connection with the minor's business, profession or employment.[23] A submission may come into this category. Some doubt exists concerning submissions which are ancillary to contracts under which consideration has been applied 'for the minor's use profitably'. The main contract does not require the curator's consent,[24] but this does not necessarily mean that the same rule applies to a submission which is ancillary thereto, for the latter is in some respects at least a separate transaction,[25] and involves no such consideration. Furthermore, submission to arbitration is a matter upon which the advice of a curator is particularly desirable. It seems therefore that an ancillary submission without the curator's consent is invalid.

4.8.   A contract of submission relating to or permitting an arbiter to ordain a gratuitous alienation of a minor's property is invalid. As J. M. Bell stated,[26] 'that which [the minor] cannot himself do directly, he cannot empower an arbiter to ordain him to do by any award.'[27]

4.9.   Otherwise a submission by a minor is valid, subject to reduction on grounds of enorm lesion if the action is raised before the expiry of four years from the date of the attainment of the age of

[21] Age of Majority (S) Act 1969 s. 1. The age of majority is a matter of law: a parent cannot, for example by trust deed appointing curators, prolong minority and thus limit the contractual powers of their children: *Adams* v. *Adam* (1861) 5 Jo. of Juris. 268.
[22] Bell, *Arb.*, paragraph 187.
[23] Bankton, *Inst.*, I.7.78.
[24] Stair, *Inst.*, I.6.33.
[25] For a discussion of this matter, see chapter 9 below.
[26] *Arb.*, paragraph 189.
[27] A rule probably derived ultimately from a canon law, on which see Julien, *Ev. Hist.*, 209.

majority except where the contract was in connection with the minor's business or employment.[28] What might constitute enorm lesion for this purpose has never been decided, but it is possible that if the minor or his curator had been induced to agree to the appointment as arbiter of a biased or otherwise clearly unsuitable person who then issued an award damaging to the minor's interests this would count as such.

4.10. A submission validly entered into by a tutor on behalf of a pupil is binding on the young person when he or she reaches the age of minority unless and until it is reduced on the ground of enorm lesion. If at the point of transition arbitration proceedings have already begun on the basis of the submission, notice of them must be served on the minor and the curator (if there is one) unless they have voluntarily sisted themselves as parties, which they are entitled to do.[29] The curator is not necessarily the same person as the tutor,[30] but even if he or she is the same intimation should be made. If a dispute has arisen, but no proceedings have yet commenced, the minor's opponent should intimate the existence of the dispute to the minor and curator (if any), and state that unless the matter is settled within a short but reasonable period arbitration proceedings will be initiated in terms of the submission.

4.11. The rule stated at the beginning of the preceding paragraph applies whether the submission stands alone or is ancillary to another contract. However, the position is complicated in the case of an ancillary submission by the fact that it is conceivable that the minor might seek the reduction of the main contract on grounds of enorm lesion without also seeking (or perhaps being able to seek) the reduction of the ancillary submission on that ground. In other words, the question of the separability of the ancillary submission may be raised. That question is considered in chapter nine below.

4.12. When a minor reaches the age of majority a similar situation arises. If arbitration proceedings have been commenced prior to majority the curator simply ceases to participate in any

---

[28] Bell, *Arb.*, paragraph 190.

[29] Bell J. M., *Arb.*, paragraph 185.

[30] Though a person appointed by a parent to be tutor of a child after his or her own death automatically becomes curator unless the appointment otherwise provides: Law Reform (Parent and Child) (Scotland) Act 1986 s. 4.

proceedings that have commenced. No intimation to the former minor is required because he or she was a direct — indeed the true — party even before attaining majority.[31]

4.13. **Insane persons**. It has long been accepted that insane persons have no contractual capacity[32] and thus no power to enter into a contract of submission. Where a *curator bonis* has been appointed by the court, the person subject to the order is deemed to be insane and incapable of contracting even if he or she was lucid at the time when the supposed contract was made.[33] Where there is no curator, contracts made during lucid intervals by someone afflicted by bouts of insanity are valid.[34] Though as in the case of pupils payment must be made for necessaries sold and delivered to a person who is, or is deemed to be, insane,[35] the obligation is not contractual and hence no ancillary submission connected with the sale is valid.

4.14. **Insolvent persons**. The Bankruptcy (Scotland) Act 1985 has made substantial alterations to the law as previously contained in the Bankruptcy Acts of 1621 and 1696 and the Bankruptcy (Scotland) Act 1913. The concept of 'notour bankruptcy' has been replaced by that of 'apparent insolvency', which is constituted by certain specified indications of inability or unwillingness to pay debts.[36] On sequestration, first an interim then a permanent trustee is appointed, and the debtor's estate vests in the latter as at the date of sequestration.[37] In certain specified circumstances, including sequestration, a contract entered into by the debtor which 'has the effect' of creating a gratuitous alienation of the debtor's property within a period specified in the Act (which differs according to whether the alienee is an 'associate' of the debtor or not) or an unfair preference to a particular creditor[38] is voidable and may be reduced.

---

[31] Bell J. M., *Arb.*, paragraph 191.
[32] Balfour, *Practicks*, II.412; Stair, *Inst.*, I.10.13.
[33] Walker, *Contracts*, paragraph 5.14. McBryde, *Contract*, paragraph 8–40, considers that there is merely a rebuttable presumption of insanity.
[34] Stair, *Inst.*, I.10.13.
[35] Sale of Goods Act 1979 s. 3.
[36] Bankruptcy (Scotland) Act 1985 s. 7 and s. 73(1) and Schedule 5 paragraph 8.
[37] S. 31.
[38] 'Gratuitous alienation' and 'unfair preference' are defined respectively in ss. 34 and 36 of the Bankruptcy (Scotland) Act 1985.

4.15. What are the effects of this régime upon contracts of submission? Though persons whose estates have been sequestrated are not deprived of all contractual capacity, they cannot enter into a submission which affects their property because the property is out of their power, and no-one can enter into a submission on a matter over which they have no power of disposal.[39] As to submissions entered into prior to sequestration, the position is more complex. In general, the permanent trustee has power to choose whether or not to adopt 'any contract' entered into by the debtor where he or she considers that its adoption would be beneficial to the debtor's estate.[40] The language of the section is broad enough to include submissions, but this type of contract differs from others because it subjects the parties to the jurisdiction of another. It is suggested therefore that arbitration contracts are not terminated or rendered voidable by sequestration, but the permanent trustee is entitled to be sisted as a party.[41] It is conceivable that circumstances could arise in which a submission entered into prior to sequestration amounted to a gratuitous alienation of the debtor's property or an unfair preference of a particular creditor. If for example the arbiter was, or was a personal friend of, a creditor who was the other party to the submission, it might be said to 'have the effect' of creating a gratuitous alienation or unfair preference, and the submission and any decree arbitral made thereunder could, it is suggested, be reduced on the principle stated by J. M. Bell in another context,[42] that —

'that which a person cannot himself do directly, he cannot empower an arbiter to ordain him to do by any award'.

4.16. **Aliens and enemies.** Those who are aliens[43] have in Scots law virtually[44] the same contractual capacities as British citizens.[45] The situation of persons who are enemies is properly regarded as a matter of the illegality of the contract rather than as a matter of personal incapacity to contract, but it is convenient to deal with the

---

[39] Bell J. M., *Arb.*, paragraph 216.
[40] S. 42.
[41] On the powers of the permanent trustee, see below paragraph 4.18.
[42] *Arb.* paragraph 189.
[43] Defined in the British Nationality Act 1981 s. 50(1).
[44] There are a few things they cannot own and some posts they cannot hold.
[45] Walker, *Contracts*, 5.38.

matter at this point. A person who in time of war[46] lives or carries on business freely in territory occupied by the enemy is regarded as an enemy[47] even if he or she is a British citizen, and all contracts including submissions entered into with such a person are illegal[48] and therefore void. The effect of the outbreak of war upon existing contracts will be considered below.[49]

Fiduciary positions and the power to submit

4.17. **Trustees.** Section 4 of the Trusts (Scotland) Act 1921 provides that those who are trustees within the meaning of the Act have power 'to submit and refer all claims connected with the trust estate' in all cases 'where such acts are not at variance with the terms or purposes of the trust'. This raises two basic questions — what is a 'trustee' and what kinds of acts are 'at variance' with trust purposes?

4.18. The term 'trustee' is very widely defined for the purposes of the 1921 Act. It covers[50] —

'any trustee under any trust whether nominated, appointed judicially or otherwise, or assumed, whether sole or joint, and whether entitled or not to receive any benefit under the trust or any remuneration as trustee for his services, and shall include any trustee *ex officio*, executor nominate, tutor, curator, and judicial factor.'

It includes a trustee appointed under a trust deed for creditors[51] and executors dative.[52] All these have the powers of trustees under the 1921 Act, which include[53] power to 'submit and refer all claims connected with the trust estate' in all cases 'where such acts are not

---

[46] It is not always clear whether an outbreak of international hostilities is in law a war or not: Starke J. G., *Introduction to Public International Law*, 9th edn., 1984, 501.

[47] Trading with the Enemy Act 1939 s. 2; *Sovfracht (V/O)* v. *Van Udens Scheepvaart en Agentuur Maatschappij (N. V. Gebr.)* [1943] A.C. 203; *Vanivakos* v. *Custodian of Enemy Property* [1952] 2 Q.B. 183.

[48] Trading with the Enemy Act 1939 s. 1; *Daimler Co.* v. *Continental Tyre and Rubber Co.* [1916] 2 A.C. 307 per Lord Shaw at 328.

[49] Paragraphs 8.35 and 8.42 below.

[50] S. 2.

[51] *Royal Bank of Scotland, Petitioner* (1893) 20 R. 741.

[52] Succession (Scotland) Act 1964 s. 14.

[53] S. 4.

at variance with the terms or purposes of the trust'. A permanent trustee appointed by the court in a sequestration similarly has power to submit,[54] but if any commissioners have been elected by creditors the trustee must obtain their consent.

4.19.   An act may be 'at variance' with the purposes of a trust even if it is not expressly prohibited.[55] It is hard to envisage circumstances in which a contract of submission entered into honestly by a trustee would come into this category, but it is possible that a submission entered into by a curator independently of the minor might do so. Unlike other persons holding fiduciary positions, a curator to a minor is expected to act *with* the young person concerned rather than merely in his or her interest, and hence for a curator to act alone would seem to be at variance with the implied purposes of the trust.[56]

4.20.   **Receivers.** The receiver of a company has the power 'to refer to arbitration all questions affecting the company' in so far as this is not inconsistent with the instrument creating the floating charge upon which his or her appointment is based.[57] Since there is also power to 'bring or defend any action or other legal proceedings in the name and on behalf of the company',[58] and to 'do all other things incidental to the exercise of the powers mentioned' in the subsection[59] there can be no doubt that a receiver may also carry on any arbitration proceedings in which the company was already involved when it went into receivership. These powers are however subject to the rights of 'any person who has effectually executed diligence on all or any part of the property of the company prior to the appointment of the receiver' and also of 'any person who holds over all or any part of the property of the company a fixed security or floating charge having priority over, or ranking *pari passu* with the floating charge' under which the receiver was appointed.[60] Therefore, though there is generally no need for a receiver to apply to the court under subsection 471(1)(e)

---

[54] Bankruptcy (Scotland) Act 1985 s. 65.
[55] *Tennent's Judicial Factor* v. *Tennent* 1954 S.C. 215 per L. P. Cooper at 225.
[56] This seems consistent with the view of Walker N. M. L., *Judicial Factors*, Edinburgh, 1974, 16.
[57] Companies Act 1985 s. 471(1)(g).
[58] S. 471(1)(f).
[59] S. 471(1)(s).
[60] S. 471(2).

for permission to submit a matter to arbitration, it may be prudent to do so if such persons may be affected and have not given their consent. The receiver of a company incorporated in another part of the United Kingdom which has property in Scotland has the same power over it as over property in that other part unless such powers are inconsistent with the Scottish legislation.[61]

4.21. Administrators. The office of administrator of a company was created by the Insolvency Act 1985 and is now governed by the Insolvency Act 1986. Between an application to the court for the appointment of an administrator and his or her actual appointment by the court no legal proceedings may be commenced without leave of the court except by a receiver already in office.[62] This would appear to mean that, apart from the powers of an existing receiver, no arbitration proceedings may be commenced under an existing submission, and it may possibly also mean that no new *ad hoc* submissions may be entered into. Once appointed, an administrator has power to refer any dispute involving the company to arbitration, and to bring or defend any legal proceedings,[63] including (it is presumed) arbitration proceedings under existing submissions.

4.22. Liquidators. A liquidator (other than a provisional liquidator) of a company incorporated under the Companies Acts may in a winding up by order of the court 'bring or defend any action or other legal proceeding in the name and on behalf of the company' with the sanction of the court or of the committee of inspection if there is one.[64] He or she also has the same powers as a permanent trustee in bankruptcy in Scotland,[65] and these include power to enter into submissions.[66]

Representative positions and the power to submit

4.23. Mandataries and agents. Mandate is a gratuitous,[67] agency an onerous, contract by which one party binds and

[61] Administration of Justice Act 1977 s. 7(1)(2).
[62] Insolvency Act 1986 s. 10(1)(c).
[63] Insolvency Act 1986 s. 15(1)(b) and Schedule 1 paragraphs 5 and 6.
[64] Companies Act 1985 s. 539(1)(a).
[65] *Ibid.* s. 539(5).
[66] Bankruptcy (Scotland) Act 1985 s. 65.
[67] Stair, *Inst.*, I.12.5.

authorises another to act on his or her behalf in some matter. A mandatory or agent may, but does not in all circumstances, have power to enter into a contract of submission which will bind the mandant or principal. In general, the rules on this matter are the same whether the contract is mandate or agency.

4.24. The powers of a mandatary to bind the mandant by a contract of submission depend in the first instance on whether the mandate is a general or special one. A general mandate is one which gives power to act 'in transactions of a particular kind or related to a particular business': a special mandate is one which is confined to a particular transaction.[68] It has always been held in Scotland that 'general mandates extend not to submissions',[69] and that only a special mandate can give power to submit. It is questionable whether a special mandate to enter into a contract to which an ancillary submission happens to be attached also empowers the mandatary to enter into the submission. Given that, as explained below,[70] Scots law appears to incline to the 'solidarity theory' of the relationship between an ancillary submission and the main contract, it is probable that a special mandate to enter into the main contract also gives power to enter into the ancillary submission. This is almost certain to be the case where it is customary for an ancillary submission to be attached to that type of contract, for in cases involving ancillary arbitration clauses no objection has been taken thereto on the ground of lack of separate express authority in the agent or mandatary.[71]

4.25. In general, a special mandate or agency may be express, implied (or ostensible) or presumed. The authority of a mandatary or agent to enter into a contract of submission must, with one possible exception, be express. As Irons and Melville put it,[72]

'an agent has not implied power to submit on behalf of his principal, but any person duly authorised may'.

The law of Scotland on this matter seems to be different from — and it must be said more inconvenient than — the laws of England and France, which appear to permit the authority of the agent in

[68] Stair, *Inst.*, I.12.11; Walker, *Contracts*, 6.19.
[69] Stair, *Inst.*, I.12.15.
[70] Chapter 9.
[71] See e.g. *Ransohoff and Wissler v. Burrell* (1897) 25 R. 284.
[72] *Arb.*, 13.

this situation to be implied, so long as the act is done within the ordinary course of business and in the usual way.[73] The inconvenience is however mitigated by the fact that no objection is taken to the validity of an ancillary submission if the agent or mandatary had express and special authority to enter into the main contract.[74]

4.26. Though an agent or mandatary cannot without express and special authority bind the principal or mandant to a contract of submission, there seems no good reason to extend the scope of this rule to encompass also implementing deeds of submission which commonly follow upon ancillary contracts. The matter has however not yet been the subject of any judicial or authoritative juristic comment, and it is therefore prudent for express authority to be obtained.

4.27. It is consistent with the general rule quoted in paragraphs 4.24 and 4.25 above that a partner has no implied or ostensible authority to bind the firm and the other partners by a contract of submission.[75] The same is true of a solicitor acting for a client[76] and an employee acting for an employer.[77] In very special circumstances, where a consignee of goods in security who had a power of sale was obliged, having made advances, to sell the goods for his own protection on the bankruptcy of the consignor, the court upheld a submission by the consignee as binding on the bankrupt consignor.[78] The court however stated that the decision should be confined to its own facts, and it certainly rested on no clear ground of principle. The only clear exception to the rule is that, within the scope of litigation for which he or she is retained, counsel has implied power to enter into a submission or judicial reference binding on the client unless the client has given express instructions to the contrary.[79]

4.28. Where an agent or mandatary has entered into a submission without authority, the principal or mandant will become bound if

---

[73] Russell, *Arb.* (1982), 34; Robert, *Arb.* 22.
[74] *Ransohoff* (*supra* note 71).
[75] *Lumsden* v. *Gordon* (1728) Mor. 14567.
[76] *Black* v. *Laidlaw* (1844) 6 D. 1254.
[77] *Baird* v. *Officer* (1831) 10 S. 147.
[78] *Douglas* v. *Brunton's Trustees* (1836) 14 S. 843.
[79] *Gilfillan* v. *Brown* (1833) 11 S. 548.

he or she ratifies[80] or homologates it, for example by appearing without objection in the arbitration proceedings.[81] However, a client is not bound if a solicitor, without authority, inserts into the proceedings heads of claim which were not within the scope of the original submission.[82]

4.29. An agent may in some circumstances be liable to implement an award though the principal is not bound. In general this liability is probably based on the principle of breach of warranty of authority,[83] but a contract of submission may sometimes be so framed as to render the agent liable upon it.[84]

Other cases

4.30. **Corporations.** Corporate bodies have the powers granted to them by their incorporating statutes and constitutions. Usually these give a general power to submit disputes between the corporation and outsiders, and power may also be given to submit disputes with its members. In the latter case, the dispute must normally involve the individual in his or her capacity as a member. It has been held in England under a provision corresponding to the present section 14 of the Companies Act 1985 that the memorandum and articles of a company have effect only in relation to a member as member, so that an arbitration clause could not apply to a dispute between the company and a person who happened to be a member where the dispute had no connection with membership rights or liabilities.[85]

4.31. **Heirs of entail.** It has been impossible since 1914 to create new entails[86] but it is just possible that some still exist. It is therefore worth mentioning that an heir of entail in possession generally cannot 'through the instrumentality of a submission,

---

[80] *Baillie* v. *Pollock* (1829) 7 S. 619.
[81] *Fleming* v. *Wilson and McLellan* (1827) 5 S. 906.
[82] *Millar and Son* v. *Oliver and Boyd* (1906) 8 F. 390 per L. P. Dunedin at 401–2.
[83] Guild, *Arb.* 16, Note 9, citing *Livingston* v. *Johnson* (1830) 8 S. 594, an obscure decision.
[84] *Woodside* v. *Cuthbertson* (1868) 10 D. 604.
[85] *Beattie* v. *Beattie Ltd. and Beattie* [1938] Ch. 708; *Hickman's Case*, [1915] 1 Ch. 881 per Astbury J. at 900.
[86] Entail (Scotland) Act 1914 s. 2.

enlarge in any degree his own powers *qua* heir of entail',[87] though in one very unusual case a division of lands over which certain servitude rights existed was achieved by a submission and decree arbitral though the property was subject to an entail.[88] Probably this was permitted only because the likely effect was thought to be a marked increase in the productivity of the land, so that the entailed estate stood to gain more from its share of the divided lands than it had done previously from the whole property as burdened with the servitude.

Capacity and power to act as arbiter

4.32. **Types of disqualification**. The rules which determine who may, and who may not, undertake the functions of an arbiter reflect both the contractual and jurisdictional aspects of arbitration proceedings. On the one hand, since arbitration is undertaken by agreement and is based on a contract of submission the power to act as arbiter is governed both by the general law of contractual capacity and also by the express and implied terms of the submitters' prior agreement. On the other hand, because the decrees of an arbiter are enforced by official agencies in the same manner as the decrees of a court the power to issue such decrees is governed also by rules which reflect the desire of government and community that arbiters should be known to be trustworthy.[89]

4.33. Disqualifications may be either *legal*, that is, imposed by law; or *conventional*, that is, self-imposed by the submitters. Legal disqualifications may be either *compulsory* or *waivable* by the parties; conventional ones may be waived by agreement. Disqualifications imposed by the law may also be either *general*, relating to the capacity of the proposed arbiter; or *particular*, relating to the case, such as an interest in the outcome.

---

[87] Bell J. M., *Arb.*, paragraph 205.

[88] *Magistrates of Dysart* v. *Earl of Rosslyn* (1832) 11 S. 94.

[89] 'Articles of Regulation 1695, art. 25 and the civil law concept of *dolus* which it reflected. Stress was at one time often placed in submissions on the honourable character of the arbiters chosen: see e.g. *Registrum Episcopatus Moraviensis*, Bannatyne Club, Edinburgh, 1837, 236, 246; Pitcairn, *Trials*, Vol. I, 167; Johnston A. W. & A. (eds.) *Orkney & Shetland Records 1056–1634*, Viking Society, London, 1907–13, Vol. I, 117.

4.34. Some systems do not permit submitters to contract out of legal disqualifications to any significant extent.[90] Scots law gives wide powers of waiver,[91] though some disqualifications remain compulsory. Irons and Melville overstate the position only slightly in asserting[92] that —

'the parties themselves having thus the choice of their own judge may waive any objections and therefore, as a general rule, neither natural nor legal disabilities prevent a person from being selected'.

4.35. A person subject to a *compulsory disqualification* cannot validly undertake the functions of an arbiter even if the parties agree to his or her appointment. If therefore such a person is nominated in a contract of submission without any alternative provision having been made, the submission is void and cannot be homologated[93] or set up by *rei interventus*,[94] and no valid award can follow upon it. Where such a person becomes disqualified during the course of proceedings in an arbitration the contract will be terminated by supervening illegality. However, if the name of a disqualified person occurs not in the *contract* of submission but only in a *deed* of submission[95] which has been signed in implementation of a prior contract of submission (including one contained in an ancillary arbitration clause), the contract will be unaffected.

---

[90] E.g. the law of Sweden: Arbitration Act 1929 (as amended) s. 5; see Holmbäck, *Arb. Swe.* 193–4 (trans.), 64–7 (comm); but see 1984 edn., 66.

[91] Not without protest: in *Gordon* v. *Earl of Errol* (1582) Mor. 8915, the unsuccessful party argued that agreement to a minor as arbiter would not be effective '*quia jus commune privatorum pactionibus tolli non potest*' — because the common law cannot be abrogated by private agreement.

[92] *Arb.*, 117.

[93] Homologation is defined in *Mitchell* v. *Stornoway Trustees* 1935 S.C. 558 at 570 as 'implied assent to, or approbation of, a contract entered into but defective in point of form'. For detailed discussion see McBryde, *Contract* 27–53ff.

[94] 'The essence of *rei interventus* is that the party seeking to deny that there is a fully constituted contract is deemed barred from doing so because he has knowingly allowed the other party to proceed to partial performance of the contract': Walker, *Contracts*, 13.33. See also McBryde, *Contract* 27–41ff.

[95] The distinction between an 'agreement to refer' and an implementing deed of submission is drawn in *Clydebank District Council* v. *Clink* 1977 S.C. 147 at 153. All contracts of submission are 'agreements to refer': for a discussion of this see paragraph 3.16 above.

4.36.   A submitter who is aware of circumstances upon which an opponent might base a valid objection to an arbiter or proposed arbiter must disclose them to that opponent.[96] Similarly, as soon as a person who has been asked to act as arbiter, or has accepted appointment, becomes aware of any disqualifying circumstances, he or she must bring them to the notice of the submitters,[97] especially the one who has most ground for objection.

4.37.   A person subject to a *waivable disqualification*, the principal types of which are discussed below,[98] may be appointed arbiter if the submitters were aware when the appointment was made of the facts and circumstances which could have been grounds for objection.[99] A submitter may by homologation or *rei interventus* lose the right to object to the appointment of a person subject to this type of disqualification. This will occur if, for example, the submitter continues without protest to participate in the proceedings or permits the opponent to incur trouble or expense in the reasonable belief that rights of objection have been waived.[100] The waiving of one objection does not of course itself imply that some other objection based on information coming later to light is also waived,[101] but any objection must be stated as soon as the basis for it becomes known. As J. M. Bell stated,[102]

'... justice requires that, if the party considers the arbiter to be disqualified by the objection, he must state the objection without undue delay; otherwise he will be held to have passed from it ...'

Furthermore, if a new objection is very similar to one which has already been waived, it may be held insufficient to justify disqualification.[103] It is probably not open to a person who has accepted appointment as arbiter to resign on the ground of some

[96] Bell J. M., *Arb.*, paragraph 234.
[97] *Ibid.*
[98] Paragraphs 4.48–56 below.
[99] *Crawford Brothers* v. *Commissioners of Northern Lighthouses* 1925 S.C. (H.L.) 22; *Fleming's Trustees* v. *Henderson* 1962 S.L.T. 401.
[100] *Johnson* v. *Lamb* 1981 S.L.T. 300.
[101] *Fleming's Trustees* (*supra* note 99).
[102] *Arb.* paragraph 239, citing *Drew* v. *Drew and Leburn* (1855) II Macq. App. 1.
[103] *Phipps (Fraser's Trustee)* v. *Edinburgh and Glasgow Railway Co.* (1863) 5 D. 1025.

waivable disqualification if the submitters have expressly waived their right to object.[104]

4.38. It is not always clear whether a person who is alleging that a certain arbiter is disqualified was or was not aware at the relevant time of the facts relevant to the objection. To a limited extent — how limited has not been and probably cannot be precisely stated — the court is prepared to hold that a person *must* have had knowledge. In other words, *constructive knowledge* can be sufficient. In *Fleming's Trustees* v. *Henderson*[105] the submitters in a question relating to partnership accounts appointed as arbiters members of a firm of accountants who had drawn up the accounts. Objection was later taken to them on the ground that the accountants were biased in favour of the accounts. Lord Kilbrandon remarked[106] that

'the parties, when they decided to appoint . . . members of their accountants' firm as arbiters, *must be taken to have known* that the subject matter upon which the arbiter might be called upon to adjudicate might be said to be in some degree a matter on which the potential arbiter had made up his mind, at least provisionally.'

4.39. The question whether a waiver may validly be made merely by adhering to a standard form contract[107] has apparently not yet been decided in Scotland. From the report of the decision in *Crawford Brothers* v. *Commissioners of Northern Lighthouses*[108] it is not clear whether such a contract was involved in that case or not. The matter is therefore still open, and consideration should be given to the practice of other countries. In some states legislation has been enacted to prevent the abuse of standard form arbitration clauses,[109] and in others the courts have without legislative assistance refused to uphold such clauses where they appeared oppressive or unconscionable.[110] Though the United Kingdom has

[104] *Commercial Bank* v. *Forsyth* (1866) 1 S.L.R. 175.
[105] 1962 S.L.T. 401.
[106] At 403.
[107] On the meaning of 'standard form contract' see *McCrone* v. *Boots Farm Sales Ltd.* 1981 S.L.T. 103.
[108] 1925 S.C.(H.L.) 22.
[109] E.g. West Germany, Code of Civil Procedure, Art. 1025(2).
[110] E.g. in California: *Player* v. *Geo. M. Brewster and Sons Inc.*, 18 Cal. App. 3d. 526, 96 Cal. Rep. 149 (1971).

not yet ratified the European Convention providing a Uniform Law on Arbitration,[111] the principle contained in Article 3 thereof is persuasive. It provides that —

'an arbitration agreement shall not be valid if it gives one of the parties thereto a privileged position with regard to the appointment of the arbitrator or arbitrators'.

It is submitted that where a standard form contract contains a nomination of an arbiter who is subject to a waivable disqualification, mere adherence to that contract should not constitute an agreement to waive the objection. Nomination by means of a standard form, so that the adhering party has to accept as arbiter a person to whom he or she would apart from agreement have a valid objection, should be regarded as detrimental to the administration of justice and hence as an illegal contract. To avoid any risk of having an arbitration clause struck down on this ground, those who frame standard form arbitration clauses should provide for the appointment of the arbiter by some obviously independent person such as the sheriff principal of the sheriffdom in which the adhering party resides, or the chair for the time being of a relevant institution such as the Scottish Branch of the Chartered Institute of Arbitrators (Arbiters).[112] Appointment by the president of a trade association of which the framing party is a member should *not* be regarded as a sufficient guarantee of impartiality.

4.40.   A person who is subject to a *conventional disqualification* — as for example a qualified solicitor who is asked to act as arbiter in a submission based on a contract which excludes lawyers from acting in that capacity[113] — may nevertheless be validly appointed and may continue to act once appointed if both parties agree to depart from the restriction or homologate the appointment. A person who has been asked to act as arbiter should examine the submission before agreeing, to ensure that it contains no conventional disqualifications which apply.

4.41.   *General disqualifications* are normally compulsory. They

---

[111] *European Treaty Series*, Council of Europe, 1956 No. 56.
[112] Except, obviously, in a dispute involving the Institute itself or one of its members.
[113] As in *Rahcassi Shipping Co. S.A.* v. *Blue Star Line Ltd.* [1967] 3 All E.R. 301.

certainly include pupils,[114] insane persons,[115] and those who by statute are regarded as enemies.[116]

4.42. Whether *minors* may accept appointment as arbiters is a matter of some doubt. For centuries Scots law held to a rule that 'na man beand within the age of xxi zeires may be judge arbiter',[117] but in 1582 the Court of Session decided, by the narrowest possible majority, that a minor could act.[118] It is possible that the case concerned a person of between eighteen and twenty-one, and that the division of opinion among the judges reflected a continuing controversy among civil lawyers, some of whom, then and later, took the view that a minor of eighteen or older could act if the submitters were aware of his age.[119] Unfortunately, since the age of the minor is not stated in the brief report of the case in Morison's Dictionary, and since the original papers are not now available in Register House, the basis of the decision cannot now be discovered. All that can be said is that it would be unsafe to regard it as authority for the view that a minor under the age of eighteen can act as arbiter.

4.43. J. M. Bell, writing at a time when the age of majority was still twenty one, remarked[120] —

'It seems practically impossible that any rational men shall ever submit a question to the arbitration of a youth, so far within the years of majority as to be plainly quite incapable of apprehending and performing his duty. Short of that point, it would seem to be within the power of the parties to bind themselves to abide by his award, if they choose to undertake such an obligation. Beyond that point, if ever such a case shall arise, it will then be time to observe whether the Court will class such a proceeding with a *sponsio ludicra* — a mere agreement to play at pitch and toss for settling a question, — an agreement which the Courts of Scotland decline to consider or enforce; or whether the view should be followed ... of holding parties bound by the award even of such an arbiter.'

[114] Balfour, *Practicks*, 412.
[115] *Regiam Maj.* II.4.3.
[116] Trading with the Enemy Act 1939 ss. 1, 2, 15(1).
[117] *Regiam Maj.* II.4.4.; Balfour, *Practicks*, 412.
[118] *Gordon* v. *Earl of Errol* (1582) Mor. 8915.
[119] Voet, *Comm.* IV.8.2., citing *D.* xlii.1.57.
[120] *Arb.* paragraph 232.

It is submitted that the reduction of the age of majority to eighteen[121] provides a convenient point, and moreover one consistent with some civilian opinion, below which a person may not validly be appointed arbiter, and that a person below the present age of majority should be regarded as compulsorily disqualified from so acting. In view of the current review by the Scottish Law Commission of the legal capacity and responsibility of minors and pupils[122] the matter may in due course be determined by statute.

4.44. In modern times the question whether an *'infamous person'* — that is, one convicted of a crime inferring disregard of an oath or involving acceptance or concealment of the offer of a bribe[123] — is disqualified from acting as an arbiter has not been the subject of any reported decision in Scotland, and has not been discussed by any Scottish writer since before the time of Bankton. Previously it was held that such persons were disqualified.[124] Though that opinion may have been related to practices which have since become obsolete,[125] the absence of recent Scottish juristic comment has probably been due simply to the absence of reported cases drawing attention to it. In England it appears[126] that an equivalent status is a disqualification, and infamy may still have this effect in Scotland.

4.45. Some general disqualifications formerly imposed by law have clearly become obsolete. The old rule excluding a *woman* from acting as arbiter[127] (but not as arbitrator) is now clearly in desuetude even in so far as it has not been abolished by the Sex Disqualification (Removal) Act 1919. At one time Scots law accepted the civil law[128] rule that a *public judge* could not act as

---

[121] Age of Majority (Scotland) Act 1969.
[122] Consultative Memorandum No. 65.
[123] Erskine, *Inst.*, IV.2.23.
[124] *Regiam Maj.*, II.3.3.; Balfour, *Practicks*, 412.
[125] It was formerly customary for arbiters to take an oath when giving their decree: see e.g. Clouston J. S. (ed.) *Records of the Earldom of Orkney 1299–1614*, Scottish History Society (Second Series) Edinburgh, 1914, 131. Styles of decree arbitral contained a clause indicating that the arbiters made their decisions 'having God and a good conscience before our eyes': Carruthers, *Stiles* 274.
[126] From Russell, *Arb.* 1982, 106.
[127] *Regiam Maj.*, II.4.2.; Balfour, *Practicks*, 412.
[128] See e.g. Odofredus, *Lectura super Digesto Veteri*, repub. Bologna 1967, I.4.8.7., fol. 194.

arbiter.[129] It was however considered that he might act as arbitrator, and this fact, together with the confusion between the concepts of arbiter and arbitrator in the seventeenth and eighteenth centuries, led to the disappearance of the rule against his acting as arbiter.[130] No objection has been taken to a sheriff acting as arbiter in a case which has come before his court,[131] and special provision has been made for Court of Session judges to act as arbiters where the dispute is 'of a commercial character'.[132] Elevation to the bench does not terminate a person's appointment as arbiter, though it has been suggested that in general judges should confine themselves to the performance of the public duties.[133]

4.46. It has been judicially decided that some features which were once thought to disqualify do not have this effect in Scots law. A submission to an *unincorporated society* with a fluctuating membership has been held by the House of Lords to be valid.[134] This decision, in which the judges ignored or belittled the practical difficulties inherent in such a submission, was almost certainly motivated by a desire to limit the inconvenient effect of the rule which then existed by which reference to unnamed arbiters was invalid. Notwithstanding the subsequent removal of the inconvenient rule by the Arbitration (Scotland) Act 1894, it has continued to be accepted that a submission to an unincorporated society is valid.[135] What such a submission means in a particular case has to be determined from the terms of the submission and the rules of the society and it is possible that these might give rise to such practical difficulty as to lead to the submission being held invalid, and it is wise to avoid it altogether. The purposes for which this type of submission was used prior to 1894 can now be attained by the simpler and safer method of giving a mandate to the president of a society to nominate an arbiter or arbitral tribunal from among its members. Similar considerations apply to submission to a *partnership* which also was held valid[136] before the

[129] *Regiam Maj.* II.4.1., Balfour, *Practicks*, 412.
[130] Bankton, *Inst.*, I.23.14.
[131] *James Finlay and Co.* v. *Campbell* (1834) 12 S. 792; *Gordon* v. *John Bruce and Co.* (1897) 24 R. 844. N.B. now Sheriff Courts (Scotland) Act 1971 s. 6.
[132] Law Reform (Miscellaneous Provisions) (Scotland) Act 1980 s. 17(1).
[133] *Fisher* v. *Colquhoun* (1844) 6 D. 1286.
[134] *Bremner and Elder* v. *Elgin Lunacy Board* (1875) 2 R. (H.L.) 136.
[135] See e.g. Irons, *Arb.*, 118; Guild, *Arb*, 48.
[136] In *William Dixon Ltd.* v. *Jones, Heard and Ingram* (1884) 11 R. 739.

1894 Act came into force in a decision which is still accepted as law.[137]

4.47. It was formerly considered that *deaf and dumb persons* could not act as arbiters,[138] but the assumption on which the rule was based, that such persons were incapable of complex communication and even of understanding what went on around them, is now discarded. Though the likelihood of any submission being made to such a person except by others similarly afflicted is small, the principle 'where the reason which gave rise to a common law rule no longer exists, the rule itself should be discarded' — '*cessante ratione legis, cessat lex ipsa*'[139] — must surely be applied to abolish it. The ancient civil law rule disqualifying *slaves* from acting as arbiters, which was once part of our law[140] though not known ever to have been given practical effect, was impliedly abolished when slavery was judicially disapproved.[141]

4.48. **Particular disqualifications** are normally waivable by the submitters, for they are normally imposed only to protect their interests. The grounds of disqualification, which are similar to those which form the basis for declinature of jurisdiction by a public judge, reflect the principle stated by Lord Kilbrandon in *Fleming's Trustees* v. *Henderson.*[142] An arbiter, said his Lordship,

'may be disqualified by any circumstance which has a plain practical tendency to bias him in favour of one of the parties'.

Given such a broad principle, it cannot be stated precisely what circumstances will, and what will not, disqualify. All that can be done is to indicate the circumstances which the courts have so far identified as having this effect. They include those mentioned in the succeeding paragraphs.

4.49. In Scotland *kinship* has been regarded as a ground of disqualification of public judges at least since the latter part of the sixteenth century when legislation on this matter was first

---

[137] Guild, *Arb.* 48.
[138] *Regiam Maj.*, II.4.3.; Balfour, *Practicks*, 412.
[139] *Beith's Trustees* v. *Beith* 1950 S.C. 66; Smith T.B., *Sh. Comm.*, 40.
[140] *Regiam Maj.* II.4.1.; Balfour, *Practicks*, 412.
[141] *Knight* v. *Wedderburn* (1778) Mor. 14545.
[142] 1962 S.L.T. 401.

enacted.[143] By statute a judge is disqualified if either pursuer or defender is his father (including grandfather), brother, son, father-in-law, brother-in-law, or son-in-law.[144] It may be assumed that nowadays female relationships of an equivalent degree of propinquity will also disqualify. In the unlikely event of the judge being equally closely related to both parties there would seem to be no objection.[145] By analogy arbiters are bound by the same rules as judges.[146]

4.50. *Financial interest* or prior involvement in the circumstances of the dispute seem to lie behind most other grounds of objection which have hitherto been upheld. For example, in holding a person disqualified from hearing as arbiter a case in which his business partner was involved, the court considered that the objection was valid because he (the arbiter) 'has or may have a material interest in the issue'.[147] The notary of a party was disqualified becaue he had acted (albeit only minimally) for that party in the cause,[148] though it has been considered that in commercial cases it is no objection that the arbiter has acted as agent for one of the submitters.[149] A person who had been a member of a town council which was a party was disqualified because as such he 'might ... acquire information or become imbued with views as to th[e] contract' which was the subject of the dispute.[150]

4.51. These decisions seem consistent with a number of others in which objections have been rejected. Being an agent or consultant of a party in another matter does not disqualify.[151] Where the arbiter was the engineer employed on the project out of which the dispute had arisen, it was indicated that he would have been disqualified if the objector had not been aware at the time of the

---

[143] The legislation arguably indicates a weakening of traditional bonds of loyalty, an aspect of the movement of Scotland towards becoming a liberal society as defined in paragraphs 2.25–27 above.

[144] *A.P.S..* 1594 c. 22 (Vol. IV. 67); *A.P.S..* 1681 c. 79 (Vol. VIII. 350); *McKenzie* v. *Clark* (1828) 7 S. 215.

[145] Stair, *Inst.*, IV.39.14.

[146] Bankton, *Inst.*, I.23.14.

[147] *Tennent* v. *MacDonald* (1836) 14 S. 979.

[148] *Gormock* v. *Gormock* (1583) Mor. 16874.

[149] *Scorrier Steamship Coasters* v. *Milne* 1928 S.N. 109.

[150] *Magistrates of Edinburgh* v. *Lownie* (1903) 5 F. 711.

[151] *Caledonian Railway Co.* v. *Corporation of Glasgow* (1897) 5 S.L.T. 200; *Addie and Sons* v. *Henderson and Dimmock* (1879) 7 R. 79.

arbiter's selection of his relationship with his opponent.[152] The fact that a person acted as broker in the transaction giving rise to the dispute is not a valid ground of objection, but if the broker had identified himself with a party in the subsequent proceedings he would have been precluded from conducting them as arbiter.[153] Membership of a body which was federated with a society which was a party has been held not to be sufficient by itself to disqualify.[154] The evidence which such a connection provides that the arbiter shares similar values or interests with a party is not regarded as a sufficient ground of objection.[154a] It is not clear whether a person is disqualified from acting as arbiter if he or she and one of the submitters are both members of a society whose rules or practices are secret and whose members are generally believed to be obliged to favour the interests of members against outsiders.[155] No doubt one of the reasons why the matter has never arisen for judicial decision is that the membership lists of such societies are normally also secret, and the opponent therefore never discovers whether he or she has a possible ground of objection. It is submitted that, if the obligations of members of a society to each other are secret so that it cannot be discovered whether or not they are likely to create bias, and the arbiter and one of the submitters are both members, the arbiter should be held disqualified.

4.52. It has long been recognised that an arbiter, like other persons acting in a judicial capacity, must have no significant personal interest in the outcome of the proceedings.[156] Sometimes this principle is expressed in terms of the principle of natural justice that no-one should be 'judge in his own cause', though the original basis of that maxim seems to have been that a judge should not be expected to command himself to perform something or prohibit himself from doing it.[157] The amount of interest that is

---

[152] *Crawford Brothers* v. *Commissioners of Northern Lighthouses* 1925 S.C.(H.L.) 22.

[153] *Leary and Co.* v. *Briggs and Co.* (1904) 6 F. 857.

[154] *Hook* v. *Lodge Colinton and Currie* (1931) 47 Sh. Ct. Rep. 144.

[154a] *Goodall* v. *Bilsland* 1909 S.C. 1152 *per* L.P. Dunedin at 1178.

[155] Whether the Freemasons are such a society which affects the administration of justice is disputed. For opposing views see Knight S., *The Brotherhood*, London, 1983, 1 and 182–6; Hamill J., *The craft: a history of English Freemasonry*, Aquarius Press, 1986, 155.

[156] Stair, *Inst.*, IV.39.14.

[157] *D.* 4.8.51.

sufficient to disqualify cannot be precisely determined. Each case has to be considered in the light of the principle enunciated by Lord Kilbrandon quoted above.[158] It appears however, that, where interest is allied to a relationship such as membership of a body which is a party to the dispute, the amount of the interest which is sufficient to disqualify is very small. In one case,[159] in which the arbiter was a shareholder in a company which was a party, and could have been benefited or injured by the outcome of the case only to the extent of 'a few shillings', he was held disqualified. On the other hand, in an older case[160] (which should perhaps be treated with caution) a partner in a firm which was a creditor of one of the parties to the extent of £20 was held not to be disqualified.

4.53.   A person who has been personally *involved in the events* out of which the dispute arises cannot properly act as arbiter because of the difficulty that inevitably exists in such circumstances of approaching the case with an open mind. Such involvement may be as an actor in [161] or commentator on[162] the events. Comments which suggest that the arbiter has, however innocently, taken sides[163] or formed an opinion on the subject of the dispute[164] will disqualify unless objection is waived. However, comments or actions which are no more than normal in a person holding the position of the employer's architect or engineer in a construction project cannot be objected to if the right to object on the ground of the arbiter's being in that position has been waived.[165] The fact that a person has previously acted as arbiter in a very similar case and arrived then at a decision which is likely to be used in argument by one of the parties in the current dispute is not as such sufficient to disqualify.[166] It has been remarked[167] that —

[158] Paragraph 4.48.
[159] *Smith* v. *Liverpool, London and Globe Insurance Co.* (1887) 14 R. 931.
[160] *McKessock* v. *Drew* (1822) 2 S. 13.
[161] *McKenzie* v. *Clark* (1828) 7 S. 215.
[162] *McLauchlan and Brown* v. *Morrison* (1900) 8 S.L.T. 279.
[163] *Pekholtz and Co.* v. *Russell* (1899) 7 S.L.T. 135.
[164] *Aviemore Station Hotel Co. Ltd.* v. *James Scott and Son* (1904) 12 S.L.T. 494.
[165] *Halliday* v. *Duke of Hamilton's Trustees* (1903) 5 F. 800; *Trowsdale and Son* v. *N.B. Railway Co.* (1864) 2 M. 1334; *Low and Thomas* v. *Western District Committee of the County Council of Dumbarton* (1905) 13 S.L.T. 620; *Scott* v. *Gerrard* 1916 S.C. 793; *Scott* v. *Parochial Board of Carluke* (1879) 6 R. 616.
[166] *Grahame House Investments Ltd.* v. *Secretary of State for the Environment* 1985 S.L.T. 502; *Mackenzie* v. *Inverness and Ross-shire Railway Co.* (1861) 24 D. 251.
[167] Stuart S. L., *The Arbiter's Mind — open or closed?* 1986 S.L.T. (News) 27 at 29.

'in the course of a reparation action in respect of personal injuries an Outer House judge may often be referred to a previous decision of his awarding solatium for what may have been a very similar injury and be invited to follow or not follow his earlier award. It has never been suggested that this prevents a judge dealing with such a case with an open mind. Is there any reason, then, to cast doubt on an arbiter's capacity to act judicially in similar circumstances?'

4.54. Though involvement in *events* leading up to a dispute may simply mean that a person can, as arbiter, deal with the matter 'in a summary way, often without any other evidence than his own knowledge',[168] involvement in *proceedings* as a *witness* has been considered 'utterly inconsistent with the subsistence of the reference to him'.[169] The language of the judgement is strong, and could be interpreted as suggesting that once a person has been called as a witness, he or she cannot act as arbiter in any proceedings arising out of the same matter, even if the parties are willing to waive the objection. Probably, however, the judge did not intend to go so far.

4.55. Since there can be no closer involvement with a dispute than as a *party* to it, this is obviously a ground of disqualification from acting as arbiter in it, but by the same token the opponent cannot but be aware of the fact, and by agreeing to the appointment must be taken to have intended to waive the objection. Regrettably, it has long been accepted in Scotland,[170] as formerly elsewhere in some civil law countries[171] and apparently in England today,[172] that this ground of objection may be waived, at least in a submission which is not in standard form and where there is no apparent inequality in bargaining power.

4.56. **Disqualification of an oversman**. The rules governing the disqualification of arbiters apply equally to an oversman. The rules relating to waiver also may apply, but the circumstances are unlikely to bring them into operation except where the submitters

---

[168] *Trowsdale and Son* v. *North British Railway Co.* (1864) 2 M. 1334.
[169] *Dickson* v. *Grant* (1870) 8 M. 566 per Lord Cowan at 568.
[170] *Buchan* v. *Melville* (1902) 4 F. 620; *Earl of Montrose* v. *Scot* (1639) Mor. 14155.
[171] Voet, *Comm.*, IV.8.9.
[172] Russell, *Arb.* (1982), 106.

themselves make the appointment. Where the arbiters themselves appoint the oversman, they must take care to select a person who is not disqualified unless the submitters have previously waived any relevant objection in express terms.[173]

Power to appoint arbiters and oversmen

4.57. **In third parties.** Where a contract of submission does not nominate an arbiter[174] it usually provides for the nomination and appointment to be made, failing agreement, by a specified third party, such as a sheriff or the president of a professional or trade association. If the submitters subsequently fail to agree on a nomination, either of them may then on behalf of both ask the specified third party to act. If the third party agrees, there is a mandate between him or her and the submitters. The ordinary general rules of law apply to the capacity to act as mandatary in such a situation. It is unlikely that a minor or bankrupt person would be asked to make an appointment, but since their property would not be affected there would seem to be no legal reason why they should not do so. It has never been suggested that the widespread practice of giving a mandate to an association or corporate body such as the Court of Arbitration of the International Chamber of Commerce is invalid. It is possible, given the international nature of commerce, that the third party might be or become an enemy. Though the mandate, being gratuitous, could not be of direct benefit to the enemy it would probably involve some intercourse between residents in combatant countries, and would therefore[175] arguably be abrogated on the outbreak of war as an illegal contract, though it might fall into the rather vaguely defined class of contracts[176] which are merely suspended.

4.58. **In arbiters.** Where a submission has been made to two arbiters, they may be given power in the submission to nominate and appoint an oversman to determine any aspect of the dispute which the arbiters are unable to agree upon. If no such power is given expressly, it is implied unless the parties specifically provide

---

[173] Bell J. M., *Arb.*, paragraph 250.
[174] This practice has been valid since the Arbitration (Scotland) Act 1894 s. 1.
[175] Bell, *Comm.* I.323; Walker, *Contracts*, 11.10.
[176] Walker, *Contracts*, 11.10.

otherwise.[177] Since the 1894 Act requires any such prohibition to be made in the 'agreement to refer', it is not competent to make it in an implementing deed of submission following on a contract contained in an ancillary arbitration clause.[178] Where the submitters have expressly given power to the arbiters to appoint an oversman, it is clear that this may be done before any difference between the arbiters has actually arisen,[179] and the language of section 4 of the 1894 Act does not suggest that the position is any different when the arbiters act under implied powers. The arbiters must take as much care in selecting the oversman as the submitters in appointing the arbiters. To draw lots to determine who shall be nominated is not permitted unless there has been prior agreement that all the persons whose names go into the hat are suitable.[180]

4.59. **In the court.** Where the submitters have failed to agree upon the nomination of an arbiter and any provision they have competently made to break the deadlock has failed, or where the arbiters have failed to agree on the appointment of an oversman, either party may apply to the court to make an appointment. There are however a number of conditions which must be satisfied before the court can exercise this power.

4.60. *First*, in relation to arbiters, the submitters must at least have made provision in the agreement to refer[181] as to the number of arbiters to be appointed.[182] *Second*, the submission must not have provided for the appointment of more than two arbiters (not counting any oversman for this purpose), for the statute does not appear to envisage references to three or more arbiters. However, the number need not be expressly specified in the agreement to refer. It has been held sufficient to provide for 'arbitration in the customary manner in the timber trade' in a case where evidence was available that the custom of that trade was for submission to two arbiters, one to be appointed by each party.[183] *Third*, there must be evidence that the parties have failed to concur or that one of them, in a submission to two arbiters, has failed to make a

---

[177] Arbitration (Scotland) Act 1894 s. 4.
[178] *Clydebank District Council* v. *Clink* 1977 S.C. 147.
[179] *Brysson* v. *Mitchell* (1823) 2 S. 382; Bell J. M., *Arb.*, paragraph 346.
[180] *Smith* v. *Liverpool, London and Globe Insurance Co.* (1887) 14 R. 931.
[181] On the meaning of this, see paragraphs 3.12–16.
[182] *McMillan and Son Ltd.* v. *Rowan and Co.* (1903) 5 F. 317.
[183] *Douglas and Co.* v. *Stiven* (1900) 2 F. 575.

nomination, for the Act makes no provision for a case where they have concurred or each made a nomination but the nominee (or one of the nominees in a submission to two arbiters) has died before accepting office[184] or has refused to act.[185] However, failure to concur includes the stipulation of a condition by one party which is unacceptable to the other,[186] and probably a reference to a specified person, 'whom failing to an arbiter to be appointed by the parties' would come within the terms of the Act if the nomination of the specified person failed. Where both the original submitters have agreed, but the judicial assignee of the rights of one of them has failed to concur or make a nomination, this is sufficient to enable the court to make an appointment.[187] *Fourth*, if provision has been made for carrying out the reference in spite of the failure of one of the submitters to act, then an attempt must have been made to put that provision into operation and it must have failed.[188]

4.61.   In the case of the appointment of an oversman, there is only one condition to be satisfied before the court can act, and it is that the arbiters must have failed to agree on a nomination. It seems that it is not legally necessary for them to have failed to agree on any matter connected with the merits of the dispute.[189] Though the expense involved will normally deter a party from making an application to the court until it is clear that it is necessary, there may be cases in which great inconvenience could arise if the oversman did not hear the evidence along with the arbiters.

4.62.   For the purposes of making application under the 1894 Act for the appointment of an arbiter or oversman, 'the court' is normally 'any sheriff having jurisdiction or any Lord Ordinary of the Court of Session',[190] but a Senator of the College of Justice cannot be appointed arbiter or oversman by a court other than the Inner House of the Court of Session.[191]

---

[184] *Bryson and Manson* v. *Picken* (1896) 12 Sh. Ct. Rep. 26.
[185] *British Westinghouse Electric and Manufacturing Co. Ltd.* v. *Provost etc. of Aberdeen.* (1906) 14 S.L.T. 391.
[186] *Hugh Highgate and Co.* v. *British Oil and Guano Co. Ltd.* (1914) 2 S.L.T. 241.
[187] *Rutherford* v. *Licences etc. Insurance Co.* 1934 S.L.T. 31.
[188] *Thom and Sons* v. *Burrell* (1929) 45 Sh. Ct. Rep. 187.
[189] *Glasgow Parish Council* v. *United Collieries Ltd.* (1907) 15 S.L.T. 232.
[190] S. 6.
[191] Law Reform (Miscellaneous Provisions) (Scotland) Act 1980 s. 17(4).

4.63. If all that the court is being asked to do is to make an appointment the procedure is relatively simple as indicated in the succeeding paragraph, but if there are substantial other questions to be determined before the appointment can be made, such as whether there is a subsisting contract between the parties at all, the court may sist the application until that matter has been dealt with in a more formal process.[192] No very precise line can be drawn between matters which can and matters which cannot properly be dealt with in a petition of this kind, and incidental questions such as one relating to the construction of an arbitration clause have been entertained.[193]

4.64. Where application simply to make an appointment is made to the sheriff it takes the form of a summary application under section 50 of the Sheriff Courts (Scotland) Act 1907. The phrase 'any sheriff having jurisdiction' occurring in section 6 of the 1894 Act means a sheriff to whose jurisdiction the defender is subject. The grounds of a sheriff's jurisdiction are, from 1st January 1987,[194] contained primarily in Part III of the Civil Jurisdiction and Judgments Act 1982 and Schedules 3 and 8 thereto. Normally the application should be made in the sheriff court of the district in which the defender is domiciled.[195] Application to the Court of Session is made by way of petition in the Outer House, unless the arbiter is or must be a judge, when it is in the Inner House.

4.65. The act of nomination or appointment by either sheriff or Lord Ordinary is a 'ministerial' rather than a 'judicial' act[196] and is not subject to appeal, though it may be nullified by action of reduction in the Court of Session. The determination of other matters such as the construction of an arbitration clause is however judicial and appealable, and in sheriff court proceedings it is partly for this reason that it is best dealt with by ordinary action so that provision will be made for the recording of evidence.

[192] *United Creameries Co. Ltd.* v. *David T. Boyd and Co.* 1912 S.C. 617; *Cooper and Co.* v. *Jessop Brothers* (1906) 8 F. 714; *Lilley and Co. Petitioners* (1896) 6 S.L.T. 224.

[193] *McMillan and Son Ltd.* v. *Rowan and Co.* (1903) 5 F. 317.

[194] Civil Jurisdiction and Judgments Act 1982 (Commencement No. 3) Order 1986 (SI 1986 No. 2044 (C. 78)). Under s. 20(1)(3) of the 1982 Act, s. 6 of the Sheriff Courts (Scotland) Act 1907 ceased from that date to have effect to the extent that it determines jurisdiction in relation to any matter to which Schedule 8 of the 1982 Act applies.

[195] 1982 Act, Sch., 8, para. 1.

[196] *Cooper and Co.* v. *Jessop Brothers* (1906) 8 F. 714.

CHAPTER FIVE

THE VALIDITY OF ARBITRATION CONTRACTS: FORM

Introduction

5.1. Rules governing the formal validity of obligations must be based on considerations of policy and convenience rather than simply on principles of justice. For this reason they are best established by legislation rather than by judicial decision or juristic pronouncement. Unfortunately neither the pre-Union Scots Parliament nor the post-Union Parliament of the United Kingdom have made any provision for this aspect of Scots arbitration law (though there has been general legislation concerning the authentication of deeds[1]) and the reported decisions of the Scottish Courts on this subject are mostly old, often unclear, and to some extent conflicting. The situation has moved the learned authors of one standard text to observe[2] that it is difficult to deduce general principles concerning the constitution or proof of contracts of submission, and the same could equally well be said of the arbiter's appointment contract and even the decree arbitral itself. The Scottish Law Commission have recently produced a consultative memorandum on this field of law,[3] and reform may therefore be expected in the not too distant future.

5.2. This chapter deals for convenience not only with the formal validity of arbitration contracts — their constitution — but also with proof of their existence, since the two matters are closely connected.

Constitution of contracts of submission

5.3. The principal modern statement of the law on this matter

[1] Listed in Halliday, *Conveyancing*, Vol. I, paragraph 3-03 note 8.
[2] Walkers, *Evidence*, 101.
[3] Memorandum No. 66 on the Constitution and Proof of Voluntary Obligations and the Authentication of Writings, July 1985.

was made in *Millar and Sons* v *Oliver and Boyd*[4] by Lord President Dunedin, who said that —

'... the only foundation of submission must always be the consent of the parties, the submitters. That consent is appropriately shewn by a formally tested contract of submission or, as here, by a clause of submission contained in a contract relating to other things, and it may be shewn in other ways, for whenever you have got something that will shew a consent between two parties to a submission that is enough. There is no technical rule of law which says that it must be done with any certain formality, but none the less you must show consent of the parties.'

This indicates that in general — there are exceptions[5] — a contract of submission may be *constituted* (as distinct from *proved*) by any means whatever so long as there is an expression of consent.[6] Writing — let alone formally executed or holograph writing — is not in general required for constitution. There are of course, as will be explained below,[7] also requirements of *proof*, so that the formal validity of a submission is not always sufficient to ensure that it has legal effect. Furthermore, if there is likely to be a need to enforce the eventual award abroad, the arbitration agreement on which the award is based should be in writing, since it is on this basis that enforcement is required to be granted by the main international agreement for the enforcement of arbitral awards.[8]

5.4.   At first sight Lord President Dunedin appears to contradict and overrule the opinions of J. M. Bell and Irons and Melville on this subject. Bell states[9] that —

'the written Contract of Submission, unless executed with all the formalities of a probative[10] instrument, remains *per se* an invalid deed, so long as nothing has followed upon it.'

---

[4] (1906) 8 F. 390 at 401.
[5] See paragraphs 5.4–5.6.
[6] This rule is the same as, and was probably derived originally from, the civil and canon laws on this topic, on which see Julien, *Ev. hist.* 206.
[7] Paragraphs 5.14–5.18.
[8] New York Convention on the Recognition and Enforcement of Foreign Arbitral Awards, 1958, Article II, in *UN Treaty Series*, 1959, Vol. 330, 38 ff.
[9] *Arb.* paragraph 62.
[10] 'The word "probative" is frequently used in judicial pronouncements and in textbooks to describe a writing which has been properly executed in accordance

Irons and Melville write to the same effect[11] that —

'the proper mode of constituting a submission is by written contract or deed, subscribed by the parties and properly completed as a probative deed. The submission if not so duly completed, remains invalid, but may be validated by homologation or *rei interventus*.'

These statements, and the similar, though more cautiously expressed, recent opinion of Professor Halliday,[12] can however be reconciled with Lord President Dunedin's dictum, though only on one assumption, namely that the parties to a contract of submission normally intend that they shall not be bound until a formal deed of submission has been executed. On this basis they simply reflect the operation of the rule that —

'when the parties to a contract, which may be constituted orally, agree expressly or by implication that they will not be bound until a written contract has been executed, the resulting obligations are to be regarded as *obligationes literis*, with all the consequences flowing therefrom. The authentication statutes[13] apply to the writing unless it is holograph, the contract can be founded on only if the writing is produced, and a judicial admission or reference to oath cannot take the place of its production.'[14]

The case in which the submitters intend not to be bound until a formal deed has been executed may be regarded as an exception — though a very important one — to the general rule as laid down by Lord President Dunedin. If the parties intend to include in their submission a clause of consent to registration for preservation and execution — and this is normal — it may reasonably be presumed that they also intend not to be bound except by a formal probative deed, because only probative deeds can be registered.[15]

---

with the statutory solemnities or is the equivalent of such a writing ... [T]he better practice is to use the word ... as applying only to the kind of writing which affords proof of its own authenticity.' Walkers, *Evidence*, 182.

[11] *Arb.* 53.

[12] *Conveyancing*, Vol. I, paragraph 14.07, citing *Telfer* v. *Hamilton* 1735 Mor. 5657 and *Brown and Colvill* v. *Gardner* 1739 Mor. 5659.

[13] See paragraph 5.1 and note 1 above.

[14] Walkers, *Evidence*, 91.

[15] *Carnoway* v. *Ewing* 1611 Mor. 14988.

5.5. A second exception to Lord President Dunedin's general rule is that submissions of disputes relating to heritable property require, apart from unimportant exceptions,[16] to be formally executed.[17] A verbal submission concerning a heritable subject is not binding and no effective decree arbitral can follow upon it.[18]

5.6. It is arguable that the two exceptions mentioned in the two preceding paragraphs may be based on a more general rule that a contract of submission which is or relates to an *obligatio literis* — an obligation which requires writing for its constitution and for which probative or privileged writings are necessary[19] — must be formally constituted. If this be so — and it has to be admitted that judicial confirmation is lacking — contracts of submission relating to certain other transactions should also be in probative form. Two types of transaction other than those mentioned above are certainly within the category of *obligationes literis*. These are[20] —

(1) contracts establishing an obligation of service or apprenticeship for more than a year; and
(2) acts establishing a unilateral obligation.

Three further types of transaction have been said to be, but are not now usually regarded as being, in this category.[21] These are —

(a) those creating insurance obligations;
(b) those creating cautionary obligations; and
(c) assignations of incorporeal rights.

In view of the uncertainty of the law on this matter, it is safer to have a formal deed of submission executed when the matter in issue falls into any of the categories abovementioned.

5.7. The requirements of formal execution are exhaustively discussed by Professor Halliday and do not require elaboration here. For present purposes the following summary taken from his work[22] should be sufficient.

[16] See below, paragraph 5.12.
[17] *Gairdner of Northtary* v. *Brown and Colvil*, 1738 Mor. 8474. See also Bell J. M., *Arb.*, paragraph 62; Irons, *Arb.*, 53; Guild, *Arb.*, 19; Halliday, *Conveyancing*, Vol. I, 14-07.
[18] *A* v. *B*, 1584 Mor. 12448; *Gairdner* (*supra* note 17).
[19] Halliday, *Conveyancing*, Vol. I, paragraph 3-01.
[20] Walker, *Contracts*, 13.23.
[21] For further discussion see Walkers, *Evidence* Chap. IX; Smith T. B., *Sh. Comm.* 803–7.
[22] *Conveyancing*, Vol. I, paragraph 3-04.

'(1) The deed must be subscribed and (where appropriate) sealed by the granter or granters and any consenting parties, personally or vicariously by other persons duly authorised, on the last page ...

(2) The granter or granters and any consenting parties must sign in the presence of, or acknowledge his or their signature to, at least two competent witnesses who must subscribe on the last page.

(3) The witnesses must be designed in the deed (normally in the testing clause) or by the addition of their designations after their signatures.'

A contract of submission which falls into one of the excepted categories mentioned in the three preceding paragraphs must be executed in accordance with these rules, or must be holograph (in the handwriting) of or adopted as holograph by each party. Clearly a contract of submission cannot be holograph of both parties, and if no witnesses are available at least one of the parties must adopt the deed as if it had been handwritten by him or her by writing the words 'adopted as holograph' immediately above his or her own signature.[23]

5.8.   The main rules concerning the constitution of contracts of submission can therefore be summarised as follows. Subject to the exceptions connected with *obligationes literis*, contracts of submission may be *constituted* by any means, including word of mouth. The main exceptions, in which probative writing is required, are —

(1) contracts of submission in which it has been agreed that a formal deed of submission is essential; and

(2) contracts submitting a dispute concerning heritable rights.

These exceptions are however themselves subject to a qualification and exceptions which are discussed in the immediately following paragraphs.

5.9.   The qualification is, that a contract of submission which falls within one of the categories requiring formal execution but which has not been executed in accordance with the required formalities and is not holograph or adopted as holograph of the parties may be

[23] Halliday, *Conveyancing*, Vol. I, paragraph 3.64.

validated retrospectively by homologation[24] or *rei interventus*.[25] Probably this is so even if the submission was verbal.[26] Thus if a party who has a ground of objection to the validity of a submission appears in arbitration proceedings following thereon without indicating that the appearance is under reservation of the objection, he or she will be held to have homologated it,[27] there being no compulsion to elect between standing on the objection and declining to appear on the one hand and departing from the objection on the other.[28] Also, if trouble or expense is incurred by one party in connection with the arbitration, and this is known to and permitted by the other as if a ground of objection known only to that other did not exist, the latter will be barred from making a subsequent objection on that ground.[29] It has been suggested in a context other than arbitration that *rei interventus* may even complete a contract, at least where one party has delivered a probative writ and has been allowed to act on it as if the contract were completed,[30] but this decision has been energetically attacked as unsound.[31]

5.10.   There are at least three exceptions to the rule that where parties have agreed not to be bound except by a writing the submission must be formally executed or at least holograph or adopted as holograph. The first and most important of these relates to transactions not involving heritable property entered into for business purposes — '*in re mercatoria*' in traditional legal parlance. Mercantile dealings include 'all the varieties of engagements ... which the infinite occasions of trade may require',[32] though 'contracts between private parties not engaged in any trade or even between landlords and tenants are not *in re mercatoria*',[33] and it has been suggested[34] that a contract of service cannot be a mercantile transaction either. A submission if it is between persons engaged in

---

[24] Defined above: paragraph 4.35 note 93.
[25] Halliday, *Conveyancing*, Vol. I, paragraph 14.07. The concept of *rei interventus* is defined above, paragraph 4.35 note 94.
[26] *Gairdner* v. *Brown and Colvil* 1738 Mor. 8474.
[27] *Ibid.*
[28] *Johnson* v. *Lamb* 1981 S.L.T 300 at 304.
[29] *Ibid.*
[30] *Errol* v. *Walker* 1966 S.C. 93.
[31] Walker, *Contracts*, 13.36.
[32] Bell, *Comm.* I 342.
[33] Gloag, *Contract*, 186.
[34] Smith T. B., *Sh. Comm.* 804.

trade and is not related to heritable property but to any other aspect of their business can thus be a transaction *in re mercatoria*.[35]

5.11. The other clear exceptions are agricultural submissions relating to the valuation of moveable objects, such as growing crops or manure or implements,[36] and joint memorials to counsel for a binding opinion.[37] In all these types of submission only informal writing is required.

5.12. There are also at least two exceptions to the rule that a submission relating to heritable property must be probative. These again include joint memorials to counsel for a binding opinion, along with submissions relating to the siting of boundary stones[38] (a practice now obsolete), and submissions between agricultural landlords and tenants relating to property such as buildings and fences.[39]

5.13. As, despite the exceptions, the fundamental rule is that submissions generally do not require formality for their constitution, ancillary submissions do not do so except where the subject matter of the main contract (and thus also of any arbitration proceedings arising out of it) falls into a category requiring formality, or unless it is the intention of the parties not to be bound except by writing. Even then, it may fall into one of the privileged types such as that of mercantile transactions.

5.14. **Stamp duty.** A submission which falls within a category of instruments requiring to be stamped and which does not bear the stamp required by the law in force when it was first executed is 'not ... available for any purpose whatever'.[40] Only those submissions which contain a clause of consent to registration require a stamp.[41]

---

[35] *Dykes* v. *Roy* (1869) 7 M. 357.

[36] *Cameron* v. *Nicol* 1930 S.C. 1; *Gibson* v. *Fotheringham* 1914 S.C. 987; *Davidson* v. *Logan* 1908 S.C. 350; *Nivison* v. *Howat* (1883) 11 R. 182.

[37] *Fraser* v. *Lord Lovat* (1850) 7 Bell's App. 171; Bell J. M., *Arb.* paragraph 69 page 48.

[38] *Livingstone* v. *Feuars of Fauldhouse* 1662 Mor. 2200; *Procurator Fiscal of Roxburgh* v. *Ker* 1672 Mor. 12410; *Otto* v. *Weir* (1871) 9 M. 660.

[39] *McGregor* v. *Stevenson* (1847) 9 D. 1056.

[40] Stamp Act 1891 s. 14(4).

[41] Finance Act 1949 ss. 35, 52(10) and Schedule 8.

Proof of contracts of submission

5.15. With certain unimportant exceptions, the existence of a contract of submission can be proved only by the writ or oath of the party disputing it[42] even where it may be constituted by any means capable of indicating consent. Proof by witnesses ('parole' evidence) is excluded.

5.16. For the purposes of proof as distinct from constitution, a writ need not be formally executed or holograph. If it is not admitted that a signature is genuine, parole evidence is competent to show whether it is or not,[43] but if a document bears no signature or there is no document at all, the only competent mode of proof is reference to oath. Though submissions to arbitration are not included among Stair's examples[44] of the operation of the rule excluding proof by witnesses, the list is clearly not intended to be exhaustive.

5.17. Only the oath of a submitter is competent to prove a contract of submission, and oath is not competent at all to prove a decree arbitral.[45] The reason for this lies in the justification of oaths of verity generally. Stair[46] states that such an oath is —

'a stronger confirmation than the testimonies of witnesses; because parties' oaths are commonly against themselves, whereas witnesses swear not against themselves.'

When an arbiter issues a decree, that decree relates not to his or her own affairs but to those of the submitters. If therefore an arbiter were to be asked to state on oath that a decree had been issued in certain terms, the oath would not be against the swearer; and submitters cannot be asked to give an oath of verity concerning the decree arbitral for the opposite reason, that though it relates to their affairs it is not the deed of either of them.

5.18. The reasons for the exclusion of proof by witnesses are obscure. It may be connected with the practice, apparently common except in judicial references where parties often took an

[42] *Fraser* v. *Williamson* 24 June 1773 Mor. 8476.
[43] *Christie's Trustees* v. *Muirhead* (1870) 8 M. 461.
[44] IV.43.4.
[45] *Ferrie* v. *Mitchell, Ewing and Others* (1824) 3 S. 113.
[46] *Inst.* IV.44.1.

oath to abide by the arbiter's decision,[47] of constituting a submission in writing. Stair noted[48] that

'our law and custom hath in many things refused the testimony of witnesses, how many soever they be, where writ may, and uses to be adhibited; or where it is agreed to be adhibited.'

Once writing had become established as an important means of recording important legal acts, it acquired, in spite of the possibility of forgery, a mystique of its own.[49] Yet though that mystique was apparently powerful, it could not blot out all recognition of the possibility of forgery or the desire to prevent it from defeating the ends of justice. Though oral testimony was held insufficient, reference to oath, which was believed to call supernatural forces into play, could do so. This was therefore retained, and it was subsequently considered that —

'as all men are obliged to remove the ground of strife, so they are obliged to give their oaths when these are necessary, for removing it . . .'[50]

In practice proof by oath is now almost unknown, because most people nowadays, unlike Stair,[51] do not consider it

'convincing reason that oaths of parties should end all strife; because God is called as a witness of the truth, and is acknowledged as a just judge, who will punish the perjurer.'

5.19. There are two exceptions to the rule requiring proof by writ or oath: submissions of disputes relating to matters of small importance,[52] and submissions of questions relating to land boundaries, in which the decision of the arbiter was expressed by his placing large stones where he held the march between two

---

[47] For instances of this practice see e.g. Dickinson W. Croft (ed.) *The Sheriff Court Book of Fife 1515–22*, Scottish History Society, Edinburgh, (3rd Series) 1928, 75 and 91; Clyde J. A. (ed.) *Acta Dominorum Concilii 1501–3* (Stair Society) Edinburgh, 1943, 378.

[48] *Inst.* IV.43.4.

[49] Clanchy M. T., *From Memory to Written Record*, London, 1979, 257.

[50] Stair, *Inst.* IV.44.1.

[51] *Ibid.*

[52] *A* v. *B*, 1746 Mor. 8475; *Hutton* v. *Adams* (1843) 8 S. 591 (ownership of a greyhound). But see *Barcklay* v. *Foord* 1666 1 Bro. Supp. 533.

estates to be.[53] The latter procedure has been rendered obsolete by modern surveying and cartography, and the former by general acceptance of the opinion that the upper limit of 'small importance' is £100 Scots (£8.33),[54] with no allowance for inflation.

Incorporation of ancillary submissions

5.20. A contract of submission may be contained in an arbitration clause which is physically part of another contract or which is, or is alleged to be, incorporated into it by reference. The rules which apply to the incorporation of arbitration clauses by reference are generally the same as those which apply to that of other types of clause. The incorporation must be made when the main contract is entered into and not later: thus an invoice note sent with goods previously contracted for cannot as such create new obligations.[55] Also, the party objecting to the incorporation must have had reasonable notice of their existence. In one case[56] the main contract was constituted in a sale note on which was printed the words —

'Any dispute under this contract to be settled according to the rules of the Glasgow Flour Trade Association.'

The rules of the association provided for reference to arbitration. The defender, who was not a member of the association, refused to accept the decision of arbiters appointed under its rules, and it was not averred by the pursuer that he was aware of them or that a copy had been brought to his notice. Upholding the defence to an action based on the arbiters' award, Lord Dundas said[57] —

'I think it requires clear and distinct language to oust the ordinary jurisdiction of the courts and substitute procedure by way of arbitration ... A mere reference to the rules is ... quite insufficient to import such a condition into the contract ... The

[53] *Livingstone* v. *Feuars of Fauldhouse* 1662 Mor. 2200; *Otto* v. *Weir* (1871) 9 M. 660.
[54] Guild, *Arb.* 21. Not even the most unsuccessful greyhound could now come within this figure.
[55] *Rutherford* v. *Miln* 1941 S.C. 125.
[56] *McConnell and Reid* v. *Smith* 1911 S.C. 635; contrast *Stewart, Brown & Co* v. *Grime* (1897) 24 R. 414.
[57] At 638.

question may, I think, be put thus: did those who found upon the condition take reasonable means to give the other party notice that it was a condition of the contract? I cannot hold that the pursuers [in this case] took reasonable means to give the defender such notice.'

5.21. It might be argued that an incorporation of the 'conditions' of another contractual document is not sufficient to incorporate an arbitration clause in that document, because the word 'condition' is properly used in Scots law to mean —

'a qualification of a particular obligation, as where a debt instantly payable is contrasted with one which will become payable on the occurrence of a certain event.'[58]

The word is also given a restricted meaning in certain trades and professions and in the contractual documents which they use, as for example in the charterparties and bills of lading in the shipping trade.[59] However, Scots lawyers also use the word 'condition' more loosely to mean 'an independent obligation, term or stipulation in a contract'.[60] Accordingly, it is likely that, except where the context or the usage of the trade indicates otherwise, the use of the word 'condition' will not itself exclude the incorporation by reference of an arbitration clause.

5.22. Where an arbitration clause has been incorporated actually or by reference into another contract, it seems that the rules relating to proof by writ or oath may be relaxed so that the submission may be proved by the same means as are sufficient to prove the main contract. This seems to be suggested, though not clearly established, by dicta in *Ransohoff and Wissler* v. *Burrell.*[61]

Constitution and proof of arbiter's appointment

5.23. There has been no statutory provision and almost no litigation on the constitution and proof of the contract between the

---

[58] Gloag, *Contract*, 270. See also Gow J. J., *The Mercantile and Industrial Law of Scotland*, Edinburgh, 1964, 201–14; Walker, *Contracts*, 19.3.

[59] *Skips A/S Nordheim* v. *Syrian Petroleum and Petrofina SA* (1982) (Unreported). The case is discussed in Parris J., *Arbitration: Principles and Practice*, London, 1983, 34–5.

[60] Gloag, *Contract*, 270.

[61] (1897) 25 R. 284.

submitters and their arbiter. Probably it can generally be constituted by any means which imply consent. The only exception is the case where the parties expressly or impliedly intend that they will not be bound until a written contract is executed. In that case, unless the transaction is *in re mercatoria*, formal execution or holograph writing would seem to be required. In practice it appears to be customary where the parties present to the arbiter a formally executed deed of submission for the arbiter to execute thereon a minute of acceptance in an equally formal manner.[62] In informal mercantile transactions the offer and acceptance of appointment as arbiter are generally made in informal letters or even telexes, and though the validity of this practice has not been tested in Scotland it is unlikely that it would be disapproved. In a case in which the arbiter had not expressly accepted but had taken certain steps in the arbitration it was considered that no acceptance was necessary,[63] and it seems therefore that acceptance may be implied, and that no special mode of proof is necessary unless the parties expressly or impliedly indicate otherwise.

Constitution and proof of facilitating contracts

5.24. A mandate to appoint an arbiter and the contract between an arbiter and his or her clerk may, like any other types of mandate[64] and contract for services, be constituted in any manner which implies consent and may be proved by oral or written evidence or inferred from facts and circumstances.

[62] Irons, *Arb.* 431.
[63] *Sheriff* v. *Christie* (1953) 69 Sh. Ct. Rep. 88.
[64] Walker, *Contracts*, 13.52.

CHAPTER SIX

THE VALIDITY OF ARBITRATION CONTRACTS: CONTENT

Introduction

6.1. Submissions may, like other contracts, be invalid by reason of illegality, uncertainty or impossibility of performance of the obligations they contain. The rules governing these matters are considered in this chapter.

The subject of the submission

6.2. **Disputes and questions.** Since arbitration is a form of adjudication,[1] it follows that what is referred to the decision of the third party must be genuinely at issue between the submitters: that is, it must at least be in doubt between them if not in dispute.

6.3. A dispute requires disagreement — the rejection of a claim or the denial of a proposition of fact[2] — and disagreement will not readily be implied. Thus where one party to a contract rejected machinery manufactured by the other, it was considered[3] that —

'there was no dispute until the pursuers wrote . . . saying they could not accept the defenders' right to reject.'

A disagreement must be able to be apprehended by a third party. Where a contract required the use of 'sharp fresh water sand' and the contractor's practice of using 'shivers sand' was objected to by the employer, the Court sustained a suspension and interdict of the arbitration because the contractor had not asserted that 'shivers sand' was 'sharp fresh water sand'.[4] Lord President Inglis said[5] —

[1] See paragraph 1.7 above.
[2] Paragraphs 1.9–1.10 above.
[3] *James Howden and Co. Ltd.* v. *Powell Duffryn and Co. Ltd.* 1912 S.C. 920 per Lord Mackenzie at 932.
[4] *Parochial Board of Greenock* v. *Coghill* (1878) 5 R. 732.
[5] At 734.

122

'I do not apprehend that there can be any dispute or difference of opinion as to the meaning of that clause, unless the term "sharp fresh water sand" is open to construction. It is not said by either party that it is, and even if the parties contended that it was the Court knows that it is not.'

6.4. It is competent for parties to submit to arbitration a matter affecting their relations which is not in dispute but merely uncertain,[6] such as the value of articles being taken over by one from the other. A valuation therefore may also be an arbitration, though not all valuations come into this category.

6.5. There must, however, be a matter in issue. An agreement cannot be fortified by going through the motions of submitting it to arbitration and having the terms of the agreement expressed as an award. Thus where two parties to a lawsuit, whose counsel had agreed a compromise on their behalf, purported to submit the matter to those counsel as arbiters, the House of Lords held that both the award and the submission were invalid.[7] Lord Chancellor Eldon remarked,[8]

'I cannot represent the transaction to my own mind ... in any other light than as an agreement executed under the colour of a decreet arbitral; and I can, therefore, look upon this neither as a valid submission nor a valid decree arbitral.'

This decision raises a question whether it is competent for an arbiter to issue an award in terms of an agreement between the parties arrived at after the commencement of the arbitration. The point is considered below.[9]

6.6. A matter is regarded as being no longer in issue if it has been determined by a court or other legal tribunal domestic or foreign whose judgments are recognised and enforced in Scotland[10] — in other words, if it is *res judicata*.

6.7. The fact that the time allowed by a limitation (but not a prescription) statute for making a claim has expired does not

[6] *Smith* v. *Wharton Duff* (1843) 5 D. 749 per Lord Mackenzie at 752.
[7] *Maule* v. *Maule* (1816) IV Dow 363.
[8] At 389.
[9] Paragraph 8.31.
[10] *Hamilton* v. *Dutch East India Co.* (1732) 1 Paton 69.

necessarily prevent the claim from being submitted to arbitration because, unless the statute otherwise provides, the time bar may be waived.[11] If however the bar has not been waived and its existence is not disputed, there would be no question which the arbiter could be asked to determine. The absence of an issue might of course not become apparent until the detailed claims and defences had been presented in the arbitration. The mere execution of a contract or deed of submission after the claim had become time barred would not, it is thought, as such constitute a waiver.

6.8. The validity of a submission of future disputes depends on whether the scope of the submission is expressly or impliedly restricted. No objection has ever been taken to ancillary submissions of disputes arising out of the main contract.[12] A submission of every aspect of the parties' relations in the future would however probably not be permitted, because this would involve an ousting of the jurisdiction of the courts to an extent now[13] unacceptable. In some countries whose legal systems are comparable with that of Scotland[14] such a provision is invalidated by statute, and though the point has not been directly decided in Scotland an equivalent rule would be consistent with juristic opinion on the construction of the language of general submissions of 'all disputes and differences'. Erskine considered that such submissions 'ought not to be so stretched as to include rights that cannot be presumed to have fallen under the view of the submitters',[15] and Irons and Melville that they had to be construed as embracing only 'questions subsisting and undetermined at the date of the submission'.[16] It may also be observed that creditors on a sequestrated estate have been held unable to decide that all disputes thereafter arising in the sequestration shall be submitted to arbitration.[17]

---

[11] *Burns* v. *Glasgow Corporation* (1917) 1 S.L.T. 301.
[12] Even before such submissions were facilitated by the Arbitration (Scotland) Act 1894: see e.g. *Mackay and Sons* v. *Police Commissioners of Leven* (1893) 20 R. 1093.
[13] This was at one time not uncommon, though evidence of judicial approval is lacking. For an example see the bond of friendship between Patrick Lord Drummond and other kinsmen, 10 July 1588, quoted in Wormald, *Manrent*, 395.
[14] E.g. Sweden, whose Arbitration Act 1929 s. 1 provides (as translated in Holmbäck, *Arb. Swe.* 191) that 'an arbitration agreement ... may ... have reference to future disputes arising from a particular legal relationship specified in the agreement.'   [15] *Inst.* IV.3.32.
[16] *Arb.* 57.   [17] *Cook* v. *Mowbray* (1829) 7 S. 778.

6.9. **The nature of the issue**. Only questions which the parties could if they wished determine for themselves by a legally binding contract may be submitted to ordinary arbitration. As Bankton put it[18] —

'Whatever can be transacted, may be determined by arbitrament.'

6.10. This rule, which like many of those lying at the root of the Scots law of arbitration is consistent with and probably derived from civil or canon law,[19] has positive as well as negative implications. Since people may transact concerning not only rights but also matters of fact or value underlying such rights, they may submit to arbitration questions of law[20] or fact[21] or value.[22] There are no matters of purely private right, not even matters as important traditionally as rights to heritable property,[23] which cannot be submitted to arbitration, though some matters which to ordinary citizens may seem private such as divorce[24] cannot. When an arbiter determines a matter of fact or value, it matters not if he or she has not been asked to order anything to be paid or performed as a result of the decision, but probably a binding award on such a question cannot be made if it has no legal implications for the relations between the submitters.[25] Arbitration may be used as a means of completing a contract,[26] though rules or criteria capable of objective expression must be applied in arriving at the award [27] for otherwise the proceedings would not retain their obligatory[28] character as a form of adjudication.

6.11. It follows from the abovementioned principle stated by Bankton that parties cannot empower a private arbiter to perform

---

[18] *Inst.* I.23.17.

[19] *D.4.8.32.6–7;* Julien, *Ev. Hist.* 216 citing *Decretals* c.X.1.41.

[20] *North British Railway Co.* v. *Newburgh and North Fife Railway Co.* 1911 S.C. 710.

[21] See e.g. *Cochrane* v. *Guthrie* (1859) 21 D. 369.

[22] See e.g. *Morrison* v. *Aberdeen Market Co.* (1847) 9 D. 910.

[23] Irons, *Arb.* 21; and see e.g. *Walker, Grant and Co.* v. *Grant* (1838) 1 D. 38, affd. (1840) 1 Rob. 154.   [24] Bell J. M., *Arb.* paragraph 22c

[25] This seems to be the position in the legal system closest in character to the law of Scotland: Holmbäck, *Arb. Swe.,* 34.

[26] As in *Morrison, (supra* note 22).   [27] See paragraph 1.11 above.

[28] *Maule* v. *Maule* (1816) IV Dow 363 per Eldon L. C. at 380; *Mitchell-Gill* v. *Buchan* 1921 S.C. 390 per L.P. Clyde at 395; Bell J. M., *Arb.* paragraph 13 page 23.

an act which can only be performed by a public officer, such as the grant of a divorce;[29] nor can they authorise him or her to determine a question which necessarily affects the public interest, such as whether a marriage has been lawfully constituted,[30] or whether one of the submitters has committed a crime[31] or is liable for payment of a tax such as rates.[32]

6.12. This does not however mean that questions affecting the public interest cannot be raised and dealt with during arbitration proceedings on another matter, for views arrived at thus incidentally do not even purport to be decisive as between the parties — they do not make the questions *res judicata* in subsequent legal proceedings between the parties. It has been held that as part of the process of reasoning which has to be undertaken to reach a conclusion on the question submitted it is competent for an arbiter to form an opinion on whether a party has committed a crime[33] or is the spouse[34] or child[35] of a certain person. In a case in which an arbiter was asked to determine the amount of certain debts payable by one of the submitters, it was alleged that a certain debt was not due 'by means of its being founded in fraud'. It was considered by Lord Chelmsford in the House of Lords[36] that —

'there is no more reason why the jurisdiction of the arbiter should be excluded from the consideration of that particular ground of invalidity than from the consideration of any other ground upon which the debt cannot be claimed against the estate. Therefore I think it perfectly clear that the question of fraud is a question which is open to the arbiter under this deed.'

6.13. It also follows from the principle stated by Bankton that submission to arbitration is invalid where the transaction out of which the dispute arises is illegal or contrary to public policy or

[29] Bell J. M., *Arb.* paragraph 220.
[30] Irons, *Arb.*, 22.
[31] *Ibid.* 44; Bell J. M., *Arb.* paragraph 219.
[32] *Motion* v. *McIntosh* (1883), Guthrie W. (ed), *Select Cases decided in the Sheriff Courts of Scotland*, (2nd Series), Edinburgh, 1894, 329.
[33] *Hong Kong Fire Insurance Co. Ltd.* v. *The Financier Ltd.* (1895) 3 S.L.T. 197.
[34] *Turnbull* v. *Wilson and Clyde Coal Co.* 1935 S.C. 580.
[35] *Johnstone* v. *Spencer & Co.* 1908 S.C. 1015.
[36] *Earl of Kintore* v. *Union Bank of Scotland* (1863) IV Macq. 465 at 467.

good moral standards ('*contra bonos mores*') or is not serious (in other words, is a '*sponsio ludicra*'). Scots examples of the operation of this consequential rule are wanting, but it can confidently be stated that a dispute over, say, the submitters' respective shares in the profits of the drug smuggling, or a claim for a sum due as the price of prostitution[37] could not be submitted to arbitration.

6.14. Where arbitration is demanded on the basis of an arbitration clause in a contract which is claimed to be illegal a question is likely to arise whether or not the arbitration clause shares the same defect. This matter will be considered in chapter nine below.

6.15. It is conceivable that a submission could be void from the outset (*ab initio*) because it was and had always been impossible to carry it out. 'Contracts of absolute impossibilities' said Stair,[38] 'are void', and arbitration contracts are no exception. If for example the question between the parties was the value of a certain antique object to be sold by one to the other, and that value could only be ascertained by an expert's examination of it, the submission would be void if unbeknown to the parties the object had been destroyed before the submission was entered into.

6.16 **Selection of arbiters.** A contract of submission may be invalid by reason of illegality, uncertainty or impossibility in relation to the selection of arbiters also.

6.17. As to *illegality*, it is clear that an agreement to select as arbiter someone who was compulsorily disqualified[39] from exercising the function, such as an insane person, would be void if no means of nominating an alternative had been provided. It is not illegal, though it may be unwise, to agree to the appointment of an even number of arbiters with a prohibition on their appointing an oversman to decide matters upon which agreement is found to be impossible. The statute of 1427[40] which forbade submission to an even number of arbiters fell long ago into desuetude.

6.18. Since the enactment of the Arbitration (Scotland) Act 1894

[37] Bell J. M., *Arb.* paragraph 223.
[38] *Inst.* I.10.13(3).
[39] On compulsory disqualification see paragraphs 4.35 and 4.41 above.
[40] *APS* 1427 c. 6, (Vol. II.14).

the circumstances in which a submission could be void for *uncertainty* relating to the identity of the arbiter have been reduced but probably not eliminated. The Act does not enable the Court to act where the parties have not indicated expressly or impliedly how many arbiters they agreed to appoint,[41] and a question could thus arise whether, in the event of such a failure, the submission is void for uncertainty. There is some authority for the view that it is not. In a case in the Outer House of the Court of Session[42] an action was raised for payment of a sum alleged to be due under an insurance policy. The insurance company pleaded in defence an arbitration clause in the policy which provided that 'any difference or dispute' arising in respect of the policy 'shall be referred to arbitration in accordance with the provisions of ... the Arbitration Act (Scotland) 1894' [sic]. Wylies refused to concur in the nomination of an arbiter because they considered that there was no dispute, but also argued that the arbitration clause was ineffectual because it did not state the number of arbiters. The Lord Ordinary (Low) sustaining the defences and dismissing the action, said[43] —

'I cannot accept the view that the reference clause is altogether ineffectual and must be disregarded ... There is no impossibility in carrying out the contract ... The defenders offer upon record to concur in the appointment of an arbiter or arbiters. That offer shows that the defenders are willing to fulfil the contract, and if the pursuers are willing to fulfil the contract, and if the pursuers render an arbitration impossible by refusing to concur in the appointment of an arbiter or arbiters they must take the consequences.'

It is respectfully submitted that this aspect of the judgement must be wrong. The problem was not the impossibility of performance, but the uncertainty in a vital point of what was to be performed. Since in this case it was the pursuers who were declining to concur in making a nomination, the effect of the court's decision was simply to put pressure on them to do so if they wished to proceed with their claim, but if it had been the defenders who had refused to concur, the consequence would have been to exclude the

[41] *McMillan & Son* v. *Rowan & Co.* (1903) 5 F. 317.
[42] *Wylie Hill and Co. Ltd.* v. *The Profits and Income Insurance Co. Ltd.* (1904) 12 S.L.T. 407.
[43] At 409.

pursuers from justice. The effect of a failure to indicate in the submission how many arbiters are to be appointed must, since the court is unable to break the deadlock, mean that the submission is void for uncertainty, and that the parties are free to pursue their claims or defences in the courts.

6.19. It is possible for a contract of submission to be void for *impossibility* in relation to the selection of the arbiter. The obvious example is an agreement to appoint as arbiter a person who is dead or a body which has ceased to exist.[44] This may arise inadvertently as a result of the uncritical re-use of old contracts as styles.

6.20. **Other provisions**. Other provisions in a contract of submission may be such as to raise a question whether the contract as a whole or a separable part of it is void by reason of illegality, uncertainty or impossibility.

6.21. A procedural provision which required an arbiter to act in a manner in *disconformity to fundamental principles of natural justice* would, it is submitted, be void for illegality, as it would destroy the character of the proceedings as a form of adjudication and make the award which was their outcome inappropriate for enforcement as a judicial act. However, one which merely made it possible for the arbiter to act unfairly, or required unfairness in circumstances which might not arise in the proceedings, would probably not render the submission void.

6.22. A question may arise whether a submission may validly provide that only one of the parties has the option to require arbitration in the event of a dispute of a specified kind — in other words, whether an agreement for unilateral arbitration is lawful. This is sometimes called the question of *lack of mutuality* in an arbitration agreement. The matter has not yet come before the Scottish courts and is not provided for in legislation, so that here again it is necessary to have regard to the solutions adopted in foreign systems.

6.23. In some countries, such as Sweden,[45] it appears to be laid

---

[44] *Paton* v. *Abernethy Co-operative Society Ltd.* (1923) 39 Sh. Ct. Rep. 283.
[45] Section 11 of the Arbitration Act (as translated in Holmbäck, *Arb. Swe.* 195) provides that 'each party may call for the application of an arbitration agreement', and it appears that this provision is non-excludable.

down that a unilateral arbitration agreement is unlawful. In England, recent judicial[46] and juristic[47] authorities indicate that in English law unilateral arbitration is valid. Russell argues that some arbitration agreements which appear to be mutual are actually unilateral, an example being one which provides that disputes as to short delivery only shall be arbitrated, which in effect means that the buyer only has the right to initiate the steps that lead to arbitration.[48] This being so, it is difficult to see why agreements which are thus tacitly unilateral should be acceptable but those which are expressly so should not. Russell's view that unilateral arbitration agreements should be held valid is supported by Domke[49] writing on the law of the United States of America, though the latter accepts that there are some decisions which conflict with his opinion.[50]

6.24.　On this matter what may be termed the Anglo-American view held by Russell and Domke seems marginally preferable to what appears to be the Swedish view, at least if one starts from the assumption that the onus is on those who wish to restrict freedom of contract to show that a particular restriction is desirable. In some types of case a provision for unilateral arbitration might be desirable as a means of protecting a weaker party. For example, in contracts between a consumer and a business organisation it may sometimes suit the consumer to have the choice of litigation or arbitration, with the business organisation bound to arbitration if the consumer wishes, but without the option of preventing the latter having access to the courts. The principal argument for the view that unilateral arbitration clauses should be illegal is that where there is any advantage in them that advantage will generally be gained by the stronger, not the weaker party to the contract. It is submitted that such disadvantages as there are in permitting such clauses can be obviated by other means than making them illegal, such as strict judicial control of the terms of standard form contracts between trader and consumer, and that therefore they should be upheld in Scots law.

---

[46] *Pittalis* v. *Sherefettin*, The Times, 11 March 1986, (CA).
[47] Russell, *Arb.*, 1982, 38–43; Mustill, *Comm. Arb.*, 89.
[48] *Arb.* 1982, 41.
[49] Domke, *Comm. Arb.*, 5.04.
[50] *Deutsch* v. *Long Island Carpet Cleaning* 5 Misc. 2d. 684 (1958); *Kaye Knitting Mills* v. *Prime Yarn Co.* 37 App. Div. 2d. 951 (1971).

6.25. Cases can be envisaged in which there is uncertainty about the nature of the proceedings that the parties had in mind. It is suggested that if it cannot be determined from the express or implied terms of the contract whether it was arbitration or some other form of procedure that was agreed upon, then the provision should be held void for uncertainty or at least that there is no binding agreement for arbitration. The matter seems not to have been decided in Scotland, but a Spanish court has held that a clause providing simply for the 'intervention of good men' in the event of a dispute was not an arbitration agreement and that the court was not thereby deprived of jurisdiction.[51]

6.26. Also, if the procedural provisions of a contract of submission are so unclear or conflicting that it is impossible for an arbiter to determine how he or she is supposed to conduct the case, the contract should be held void for uncertainty. Again, the matter does not seem to have been considered directly in Scotland, though in one case[52] involving two closely related contracts Lord Shaw of Dunfermline remarked[53] that they were

'so closely interlinked and intermixed as to make it most difficult, and in all likelihood impossible, to extricate by separate arbitration the rights emerging under the respective contracts'

and that the courts of law were not bound by an arbitration clause

'to place the parties in a situation not only embarrassing but unworkable'.

Cases have arisen in England[54] and the Netherlands[55] in which an arbitration agreement has been held void on the ground of uncertainty, and it is submitted that these are highly persuasive.

---

[51] *H.O.* v. *T.G.* [1979] Eur. Law Digest 459.
[52] *Municipal Council of Johannesburg* v. *D. Stewart & Co.* 1909 S.C. (H.L.) 53.
[53] At 57.
[54] See e.g. *Lovelock Ltd.* v. *Exportles* [1968] 1 Ll.Rep. 163.
[55] *Caroline* v. *Dröge* [1982] Eur. Law Digest 461.

CHAPTER SEVEN

THE VALIDITY OF ARBITRATION CONTRACTS: CIRCUMSTANCES OF FORMATION

Introduction

7.1. The circumstances in which a submission is entered into may affect its validity as a contract if they are such as are regarded by the law as vitiating consent. The reported occasions on which the Scottish courts have been called upon to apply the rules of this branch of contract law to arbitration contracts are few and far between, but the rules are nevertheless not without importance, especially as Scottish courts do not have a discretion not to sist (*anglicé* 'stay') proceedings in litigation where there exists a valid arbitration agreement, and do not have extensive powers to set aside or quash arbitral awards. This chapter is concerned with the application to arbitration contracts of the rules relating to what are sometimes called the 'vices of consent'[1] — forgery, error and extortion — and also with some special problems arising from the incorporation of arbitration clauses by reference. As this work is intended for the use not only of lawyers but also of arbiters who practice other professions it has been thought appropriate to preface the sections dealing with the more complex topics with a brief outline of the general legal context.

Forgery

7.2. A contract which is a forgery is void and may be reduced.[2] Submissions are no exception to this rule and furthermore an award which proceeds upon a forged submission may be reduced on grounds of 'falsehood' in terms of section 25 of the Articles of Regulation 1695.[3] Assuming that the view taken in this work of the

[1] Smith, *Sh. Comm.*, 285.
[2] *Scottish Provident Insurance Co.* v. *Pringle* (1858) 20 D. 465.
[3] *Hardie* v. *Hardie* 18 Dec. 1724, Mor. 664.

arbiter's appointment[4] is correct, forgery nullifies that contract also, and the same goes for any mandate empowering a third party to make an appointment.

Error

7.3. **General rules.** The general rules of law relating to the reduction of contracts on the ground of error are complex and require some elucidation before their application to the law of arbitration can be considered. Error has been said to consist in 'a misapprehension as to or mistaken understanding of some element of the contract'.[5] The law classifies error in a number of ways.

7.4. First, a distinction is drawn on the basis of *subject matter* between error of law and error of fact. As to the former, error amounting to ignorance of or erroneous belief concerning the existence, meaning or application of some principle or rule of the general law of the land cannot affect the validity of the contract.[6] However, if it amounts to erroneous belief as to the correct legal interpretation of a provision in a contract, it will do so if it is essential. What constitutes essential error of law is a matter of great difficulty. It has been judicially stated[7] that —

'no one who has made a written contract can escape from its obligations by the mere allegation of his own failure to understand the meaning or effect of the terms to which he has expressly assented.'

Professor Walker has 'tentatively suggested' that[8] —

'an essential error in law is a mistaken belief as to the existence, nature, substance or effect of the legal rights involved, being acquired or surrendered by the contract, not merely as to the extent or value of those rights.'

In the present state of the judicial authorities probably no clearer or more precise statement than this can be made.

---

[4] Paragraphs 3.18–3.19 above.
[5] Walker, *Contracts*, 14.1.
[6] *Ibid.* 14.7.
[7] *Laing* v. *The Provincial Homes Investment Co. Ltd.* 1909 S.C. 812 per Lord Kinnear at 826.
[8] *Contracts*, 14.18.

133

7.5. Error of fact may, but does not necessarily, affect the validity of a contract if it is essential,[9] that is, if it relates to one or more of the facts which the law considers must be agreed in the class of contract concerned.[10] Whether it does so depends on the effect of certain other factors mentioned in the two following paragraphs.

7.6. Second, error may also be classified on the basis of its *effect on the minds of the parties*. Thus it may be either

(a) *common*: where both parties make the same mistake;
(b) *mutual*: where one party is mistaken as to the other's intentions; or
(c) *unilateral*: where one party is mistaken and the other realises he is mistaken or is presumed by the law so to do.[11]

7.7. Third, error may be classified on the basis of the *manner of occurrence*. Thus it may be *induced* in one party by the representations of the other, or it may not. For the purposes of determining the effect of error on the validity of a contract it appears not to matter whether a representation be fraudulent, negligent, or innocent, since innocent representation inducing essential error has been held to be a ground for reduction of a contract.[12]

7.8. The effect of error on contracts generally may be summarised as follows. Erroneous belief as to the correct legal interpretation of a contract nullifies it only if the error is not only essential but also unilateral and induced by the other party. Neither common[13] nor mutual[14] error of law, even of this limited kind, will generally[15] make it void or even voidable.

7.9. Error of fact must also be essential, but its effect differs

[9] *Ibid.* 14.22.
[10] *Ibid.* 14.11.
[11] *Ibid.* 14.25.
[12] *Ferguson* v. *Wilson* (1904) 6 F. 779.
[13] *Manclark* v. *Thomson's Trustees* 1958 S.C. 147. The error was referred to in this decision as 'mutual' but in the nomenclature adopted in this work it counts as 'common'.
[14] Walker, *Contracts*, 14.39.
[15] There appears to be at least one exception — see *Mercer* v. *Anstruther's Trustees* (1871) 9 M. 618 — but this is not important for present purposes.

according to whether it is common, mutual or unilateral. If it is common, nullity follows only if the error relates to the existence of something essential to the contract[16]; if it is mutual, only if —

'the parties agreed in words which concealed such ambiguity that the agreement was only an apparent one and the dissensus related to an essential part of the bargain.'[17]

If the error is unilateral, the contract is reducible only if it was induced by the other party[18] and if otherwise the mistaken party would not have contracted.[19]

7.10. **Effect of error on contracts of submission.** In principle a contract of submission or a contract of appointment of an arbiter may be invalidated on grounds of error of law to the same very limited extent as other contracts, but there appears to have been no successful action of reduction on this ground. There is one case[20] which could be regarded as involving error of law though the judgments are not explicit. An outgoing farm tenant alleged that he had entered into a reference with the incoming tenant concerning the price of dung on the farm, induced (he said) by a representation made by the landlord's factor, that the effect of an award in the reference would be to fix an element in the mutual obligations of himself and the landlord in the waygoing. The court refused to allow proof of this averment. The error was not induced by the other party to the reference or anyone acting for him.

7.11. No decisions of the Scottish courts appear to have been reported concerning the effect on arbitration contracts of common error of fact, but a case has occurred in England[21] which, if it had occurred in Scotland, would have come into this category.[22] One party acted as the other's commodity brokers under a written 'customer's agreement' which did not contain any arbitration clause. Disputes arose, and the parties, who mistakenly believed that the contract did oblige them to refer the matter to arbitration,

---

[16] *Sibson and Kerr* v. *Barcraig Co.* (1896) 24 R. 91.
[17] Walker, *Contracts*, 14.37.
[18] *Stewart* v. *Kennedy* (1890) 17 R. (H.L.) 25 per Lord Watson at 29.
[19] *Irvine* v. *Kirkpatrick* (1850) 13 D. (H.L.) 17.
[20] *Marquis of Tweeddale* v. *Hume* (1848) 10 D. 1053.
[21] *Altco Ltd.* v. *Sutherland* [1971] 2 Ll. Rep. 515.
[22] The report refers to the mistaken belief as 'mutual', but in Scotland it would be regarded as 'common'.

submitted them to arbitrators. The arbitrators issued an award, and the losing party moved the court to set it aside on a number of grounds, one being that there had been no original arbitration agreement. The court set the award aside. An English court has much wider power to set an award aside than does a court in Scotland, but it would seem likely that a Scottish court would come to the same conclusion.

7.12. It is also possible to envisage a case in which the parties to an *ad hoc* submission both mistakenly believe, at the time of entering into the contract, that the person whom they agree should be appointed arbiter has certain qualifications which they regard as essential for the arbitration. It is submitted that the submission would be void on the ground of essential common error of fact.

7.13. Such an error of fact on the part of the submitters may also affect the arbiter's contract of appointment. Here, however, the submitters act together as one party to the contract with their common nominee, the prospective arbiter, as the other. The error of the submitters as to the qualifications of the arbiter is in this context unilateral (the nominee being presumed to be aware of his own qualifications), and the contract is therefore only reducible on this ground[23] if it was induced by the nominee. However, if the contract of submission itself is void, there is from the outset no basis upon which the arbiter can act, and the contract of appointment is impossible for the arbiter to perform and therefore also void.

7.14. It may also happen that the prospective arbiter is mistaken as to the nature of the dispute being referred to him or her for decision, and that if the mistake had not occurred he or she would not have accepted the appointment. Here again the error is unilateral, and the arbiter is free from the obligation to act only if the mistake was induced by the submitters. In practice the submitters, if they are wise, will be willing to release an arbiter who feels in such circumstances that the case is inappropriate for a person of his or her qualifications.

7.15. There has been at least one reported decision in Scotland as to the effect of mutual error of fact. In *Gillespie* v. *Paisley Road*

[23] It may be ineffective on other grounds.

136

Trust and Burgh Commissioners[24] the defenders in an action for decree conform to an arbitral award pleaded, amongst other things, that the submission and award both proceeded on the basis of mutual essential error as to the area of ground whose value was to be determined. The court allowed proof of the defenders' averments.

7.16.   Mutual essential error of fact may arise not only in relation to the subject matter of the dispute as in *Gillespie* but also in relation to the person of the arbiter. This may occur if, for example, A proposes to B that the arbiter in their dispute should be 'Mr. Joseph Smith', meaning a local surveyor of that name, and B agrees in the reasonable belief that A means the Mr. Joseph Smith who is currently president of the national trade association of builders.

7.17.   There do not seem to have been any reported decisions of the Scottish courts relating to unilateral error of fact in arbitration contracts. It has, however, been remarked, *obiter*, in an English appeal to the House of Lords[25] that an injunction could in that country be granted to stop arbitration proceedings upon a claim by one party that the agreement upon which they were based was void or voidable for mistake. Circumstances can be envisaged in which a submission might be invalidated by unilateral error of fact concerning, say, the terms of the procedural rules of an arbitration body which were incorporated into the contract by reference, where the error had been induced by the representations of the opposing party.

7.18.   It should be noted, however, that a submission or other arbitration contract which is vitiated by error may become binding by adoption if the mistaken party, on discovering the error, continues to participate in the proceedings without objection.

Extortion

7.19.   **General rules**. The term 'extortion' covers in Scots law several grounds on which a contract may be reduced, namely force

---

[24] (1900) 7 S.L.T. 350.
[25] *Bremer Vulkan Schiffbau und Maschinenfabrik* v. *South India Shipping Corporation* [1981] 1 Ll. Rep. 253 per Lord Diplock at 260.

and fear, facility fraud and circumvention, and undue influence, which each involve some imposition or constraint upon free consent.

7.20. Force and fear implies violence or other unlawful acts or omissions or threats thereof such as would overcome the resistance of a person of ordinary strength of mind.[26] It probably includes what in English[27] and American[28] law is coming to be known as 'economic duress', for Erskine states[29] that —

> 'all bargains which from their very appearance discover oppression, or an intention in any of the contractors to catch some undue advantage from his neighbour's necessities, lie open to reduction on the head of dole or extortion, without the necessity of proving any special circumstance of fraud or circumvention on the part of that contractor.'

However, the continued[30] use of the strength of mind of a physical individual as a criterion in judging whether the force exerted was unlawful and the fear sufficient and reasonable makes the law difficult to apply in the context of corporate persons, given that the power of a small company owning, say, a small shop or local contracting business differs enormously from that of a large corporation whose shares are quoted on a stock exchange or a public body funded largely from taxation, and this may account for the sparsity of authority on this subject in Scotland.

7.21. A contract may be reduced on the ground of facility fraud and circumvention where one party, being in a state of mental or physical weakness, is induced to consent by the fraudulent practices of the other.[31] Undue influence involves abuse of a relationship or position of trust, such as that of trustee in relation to a beneficiary[32] or solicitor in relation to a client.[33]

---

[26] Stair, *Inst.* I.9.8.
[27] *Universe Tankships Inc. of Monrovia* v. *International Transport Workers' Federation* [1982] 2 All E.R. 67 (H.L.).
[28] For a survey of American decisions see Dawson J. P., 'Economic Duress, an Essay in Perspective' in 45 *Mich. L.R.* 253.
[29] *Inst.* IV.1.2.7.
[30] See e.g. Walker, *Contracts*, 15.10.
[31] Stair, *Inst.* I.9.8.
[32] *Murray* v. *Murray's Trustee* (1826) 4 S. 374.
[33] *Anstruther* v. *Wilkie* (1856) 18 D. 405.

7.22. Effect of extortion on contracts of submission.
Reported decisions of the Scottish courts concerning the reduction
of arbitration contracts on the ground of extortion are very sparse.
There seems however no reason to doubt the opinion of Lord
Kames[34] that a submission obtained by force and fear is void and
may be reduced. Thus perhaps if a threat by one party not to
complete an important contract[35] or to 'black' the victim's
operations or a part of them[36] was what induced the other, an
individual or corporate person of average size and capacity or
relative weakness, to enter into the submission the contract would
be void.

7.23. There is at least one reported decision in Scotland which
appears to have involved the application to arbitration of the rules
relating to facility fraud and circumvention. In *Dalgleish* v.
Johnson[37] a submission by a 'poor old countryman' which was
'brought about by trickery' was reduced. There is also an
unreported decision[38] in a petition for reduction of the
appointment of a certain church minister as oversman, the arbiters
having already, by the appointment of someone else, 'exauctorated
themselves by a regular and solemn deed'. A subsidiary argument
for the petitioner was that the minister had used improper means
to persuade the arbiters to revoke the original deed and appoint
him instead. The minister (Mr. Leslie) had invited the arbiters to
dinner where (according to the petitioner) 'a pretty free circulation
of the glass took place, and Mr. Leslie having seized the
opportunity to persuade the arbiters that he would make a better
oversman than Mr. Tod, the arbiters wrote out a new minute
appointing him.' The petition was refused, possibly — the
decision is not accompanied by reasons — because the defence of
homologation was upheld. It is arguable that apart from
homologation the appointment would have been void on the

---

[34] *Elucidations respecting the law of Scotland*, Edinburgh, 1777, Art. XL.
[35] As occurred in the English case of *North Ocean Shipping Co. Ltd.* v. *Hyundai Construction Co. Ltd.* [1978] 3 All E.R. 1170.
[36] As occurred in *Sutherland* v. *Montrose Fishing Co. Ltd.* (1921) 37 Sh. Ct. Rep. 239. See also the House of Lords decision in an English appeal, *Universe Tankships* (*supra* note 27).
[37] 1742 Mor. Appx. II, (Elchies), Arb. 7.
[38] *Hepburn* v. *Roy and Leslie* 1795. The pleadings may be found in the Signet Library, Session Papers 199:6, and the decision in the Scottish Record Office, CS 236 H7/1.

ground that the minister had acted fraudulently in taking advantage of the arbiters' facility induced by intoxication.

7.24. It is suggested that wherever one party to a submission has agreed to constitute the other as arbiter the circumstances should be very carefully scrutinised to discover whether or not the arbiter obtained that position by any form of extortion. It is undoubtedly (while very regrettably) competent in Scots law for a party to be appointed arbiter,[39] but if there is a marked imbalance of power between the parties and any threat of the use of that power has been made the contract would seem to come within the scope of the rule laid down by Erskine quoted above.[40]

[39] *Buchan* v. *Melville* (1902) 4 F. 620.
[40] Paragraph 7.20.

CHAPTER EIGHT

TERMINATION OF ARBITRATION CONTRACTS AND PROCEEDINGS

Introduction

8.1. Most writing in Scotland on this topic has concentrated attention on the duration of proceedings under a submission, almost to the point of identifying this with the duration of the contract of submission itself.[1] Before arbitration clauses came into general use and arbitration became professionalised there was some reason to adopt this approach, but now it is necessary to conceive the topic in broader terms.

8.2. As is indicated above[2] the legal framework within which arbitration proceedings take place is based primarily on a number of contracts, two of which — the contract of submission and the appointment contract — are essential. A further contract implementing the submission is common, at least where the submission consists of an ancillary arbitration clause, and in addition there are certain facilitating contracts. Each of these contracts may be brought to an end on much the same grounds as other contracts governed by Scots law, except where this is incompatible with the concept of an arbiter as a private judge exercising a subordinate jurisdiction under the control of the Court of Session. Performance, lapse of time, the death of a party, agreement, frustration or impossibility of performance, and material breach followed by rescission, are all events which may in principle bring one of these contracts to an end, and this chapter is concerned mainly to explain the working out of the rules relating to these concepts in the context of arbitration.

8.3. Some specialities relating to ancillary submissions should be mentioned at the outset. First, an implementing deed of submission and the arbitration proceedings following thereon may

[1] See e.g. Irons, *Arb.* Chapter III.
[2] Paragraphs 3.4–3.6.

be brought to an end without affecting the ancillary contract of submission which underlies them. Even in England, where there is less stress placed on the existence of a contractual framework, this appears to be recognised. As Mustill J. put it,[3] when a dispute arises under an arbitration clause, and one party invokes the clause and an arbiter is appointed,

> 'there comes into existence a series of mutual contractual relationships between the parties *inter se,* and between each party and the arbitrator. I will for convenience refer to the group of relationships as "the reference" . . . The reference may be terminated by consent, leaving the arbitration agreement intact.'

Second, an ancillary submission is often so intimately connected with the main contract that in certain circumstances the termination of the latter may lead to the termination of the former also. This matter is dealt with in the next chapter.

Termination by performance

8.4. Contracts of submission. When parties submit to arbitration a matter which is in question between them, they commit

> 'to the entire and exclusive cognisance of the arbiter or arbiters . . . the whole matters submitted, and bind themselves to abide by his or their decision in all things.'[4]

It follows that an *ad hoc* submission, which by its very nature relates to a defined set of existing disputes, comes to an end when the parties have performed their several obligations under the arbiter's final decree. It is of course not always clear in practice whether a particular decree arbitral is or is not final, but this does not detract from the force of the general rule.

8.5. An *ancillary* submission of future disputes, however, is a different case. Until the time arrives when all the claims or questions which could possibly arise under it out of the main

---

[3] In *Allied Marine Transport Ltd.* v. *Vale do Rio Doce Navegaçao S.A.* (*The 'Leonidas D'*) [1983] 2 Ll. Rep. 411 at 414.
[4] *Brakenrig* v. *Menzies* (1841) 4 D. 274 per Lord Moncreiff at 283.

contract have prescribed,[5] it is still conceivable that one party might bring the contract of submission into operation. It follows that only a submission which is narrowly executorial of the contract to which it is ancillary can terminate simply by performance.

8.6. Arbiter's appointment. Where an arbiter or oversman is appointed to determine a particular dispute or set of disputes, the appointment contract will terminate by performance when both arbiter and submitters have fulfilled their obligations to each other. This will occur when the arbiter has performed the judicial and administrative tasks required in connection with the proceedings, and the parties have paid the arbiter whatever fees and expenses may be due. An arbiter's duties under the appointment contract do not necessarily terminate with the issue of a final award or the devolution of the arbitration upon an oversman. They may end earlier, as for example where the submitters settle their dispute by agreement and no award is required; or later, if there are administrative tasks, such as the payment of the clerk or the return of documents to the parties, to be performed or supervised. This does not detract from the rule that, as far as judicial duties in the arbitration are concerned, an arbiter is '*functus officio*' (that is, has discharged the duties of the appointment in relation to a particular issue when he or she has issued a final reward upon it.[6] The reason is that the final award is the last judicial act of the arbiter on that issue with which the submitters are obliged, as between each other, to comply under the agreement contained in the contract or deed of submission.

8.7. Where an arbiter is appointed to determine all disputes, or all disputes of a particular kind, which may arise under a contract to which a certain submission is ancillary, the appointment contract is no more likely than the ancillary submission itself to terminate simply by performance. One must however distinguish carefully between on the one hand the case where the arbiter has

---

[5] An *ad hoc* submission, and probably also the initiation of proceedings under an ancillary clause, interrupts prescription: *Vans* v. *Murray* June 14 1816 F.C.; *Dunn* v. *Lamb* (1854) 16 D. 944; Bankton, *Inst.* II.12.62; Bell J.M., *Arb.* paragraph 613.

[6] *Miller and Son* v. *Oliver and Boyd* (1906) 8 F. 390 per Lord McLaren at 403; *Mackenzie* v. *Inverness and Aberdeen Junction Railway Co.* (1866) 38 Sc. Jur. 429 per Lord Deas at 432.

been appointed to determine all disputes of the prescribed kind that may arise under the main contract, and on the other the case where the arbiter has been appointed to determine a particular dispute that has actually arisen under it. It is only in the former that termination by performance is virtually inconceivable.

Termination by lapse of time

8.8. **Contracts of submission.** Provision has long been made in *ad hoc* contracts[7] and in implementing deeds of submission, and sometimes also in ancillary contracts, to the effect that the final award in all the matters actually in dispute which have been presented to an arbiter for determination must be pronounced within a *specified time* from the commencement of proceedings. In the case of an *ad hoc* submission or an implementing deed, the execution of the deed counts as the commencement of proceedings. Nowadays it is not uncommon for an ancillary contract to incorporate the procedural rules of an arbitration institution, and these may prescribe a time limit.[8] Where this is done it is as if the provision had been contained in the contract of submission itself. Though the parties may of course vary that agreement in an implementing deed of submission, it is questionable whether the traditional practice of framing a deed of submission with the duration provisions left blank would be sufficient to achieve this effect. It is also competent, though nowadays extremely rare if not unknown, for the parties to an *ad hoc* contract to designate a particular day on which the decree must be pronounced,[9] or to prohibit the arbiter from issuing the decree before a specified date.[10] It is for obvious reasons rare if not unknown for any provisions to be inserted in ancillary submissions which limit the duration of the submission itself as distinct from arbitration proceedings initiated in terms of it.

8.9. Formal deeds of submission are in Scotland often drafted leaving the day and month of the stipulated time of *expiry blank*, so that the submitters agree to be bound by a decree arbitral issued

[7] *Cunninghame* v. *Drummond* 17 May 1491, Mor. 635.
[8] See e.g. Article 18(1) of the Rules for the International Chamber of Commerce Court of Arbitration: in Lee, *Int. Comm. Arb.*, paragraph 435.
[9] *Bonar* v. *Balfour* 7 Mar. 1505, Mor. 637.
[10] *Campbell* v. *Calder* 31 Jan. 1612, Mor. 637.

'between this and the _____ day of _____ next to come'. The blanks may not be filled up either by the arbiter[11] or by one of the submitters acting alone. This curious practice probably arose because the courts, having been presented with the problem of determining the effect of a deed in which the dates had been left blank by inadvertence, gave the incomplete clause a precise meaning instead of striking down the whole deed. Practitioners who thereafter wished to give the duration clause in a deed of submission that same meaning simply drafted the deed with blanks instead of entering a precise date.

8.10. What is the effect of leaving blanks in the duration clause in the manner just described? Where the deed in which the clause appears is itself the contract of submission and not merely an implementing deed, the effect is not in doubt. Unless there has been a valid prorogation — that is, extension — of the duration of the submission the primary obligations[12] under the contract expire at the end of a year and a day.[13] After that period the submitters are not bound by any directions or decisions of the arbiter, and are free to have recourse to the ordinary courts on any matter left undetermined by a final award.

8.11. Where the deed of submission merely implements a prior ancillary contract the effect of a blank expiry date is unclear, the matter not having been the subject of any judicial decision. It is submitted that there can be little doubt on one aspect of the matter. Arbitration proceedings under the deed of submission terminate (unless the time has been prorogated) on the expiry of a year and a day, and the authority of an arbiter who has been appointed merely to deal with the issues mentioned in that deed ceases at that point. There remains, however, a question whether by presenting the dispute to an arbiter the submitters have done all that is required of them in relation to that matter and are free, if the arbitration

---

[11] *Wallace* v. *Wallace* 23 Feb. 1672, Mor. 639.

[12] 'Breaches of primary obligations give rise to substituted secondary obligations on the part of the party in default. . . . The contract, however, is just as much the source of secondary obligations as it is of primary obligations.' *Photo Productions Ltd.* v. *Securicor Transport Ltd.* [1980] 1 All E.R. 556 per Lord Diplock at 566. Though this was an English appeal, these views seem consistent with the best Scots doctrine, on which see McBryde W. W., 'Breach of Contract' 1979 J.R. 116 at 124–6.

[13] *Earl of Dunmore* v. *McInturner* (1829) 7 S. 595.

proceedings are abortive, to have recourse to the ordinary courts, or whether they remain bound by their ancillary contract of submission to enter into new arbitration proceedings. The espousal of the latter view would prevent an arbitration from being brought to an end because of a procedural oversight, and would often lead to less waste of time and money. On the other hand it could lead in some cases to a multiplication of arbitrations. Since arbitration contracts are normally interpreted so that the jurisdiction of the courts is not ousted except to the extent that the parties clearly intended, the former view is more likely to be correct.

8.12. It may happen that *no provision relating to the duration* of the arbitration proceedings has been made in the contract of submission or any subsequent implementing agreement. This situation was considered in relation to an *ad hoc* submission *in re mercatoria* by a Full Bench of fifteen judges in *Fleming v. Wilson and McLellan*.[14] The parties had entered into a submission by joint missive dated 2nd September 1818, but no decree arbitral was pronounced until 29th March 1822. An action of reduction of the decree was brought on the ground that the decree had been granted after the expiry of the submission. The Court dismissed the action. Lord President Hope said,[15]

'As the letter of reference between these parties is not limited to any determinate time, within which the arbiters or oversman were to give their award, and does not contain the usual blank, as applicable to the duration of the power of the arbiters, we are of the opinion that the powers of the arbiters and oversman did not expire at the lapse of the year from the date of the letter of reference and that the parties were bound by the award, at whatever time pronounced.'

The use of the phrase 'at whatever time pronounced' suggests that, as regards *ad hoc* contracts and deeds of submission, the obligation to abide by the award in a particular dispute does not in such a case terminate at all by mere lapse of time. This view seems consistent with the opinion of at least some civil and canon lawyers,[16] but

[14] (1827) 5 S. 906. See also *Hili v. Dundee and Perth Railway* (1852) 14 D. 1034.
[15] At 907, expressing the views of six other judges.
[16] See e.g. Baldus, *In Primum Digesti Veteris Partem Commentaria*, Venice, 1616, 4.8.15. fol. 259: 'Compromissum factum sine temporio praefinitione, censetur perpetuum ... nisi sit tempus statutum ab arbitro de consensu partuum

Erskine[17] was of the opinion that a submission ceases to be obligatory after the expiry of the period of the long negative prescription. That period is now twenty years.[18] Since the lapse of time in *Fleming* was only just under four years, the dictum of Lord President Hope need not be regarded as contradicting Erskine. It can therefore be said that where is no agreement concerning the duration of an agreement, the obligations contained in *ad hoc* contracts and implementing deeds of submissions prescribe after twenty years if not earlier abandoned.

8.13. Ancillary contracts of submission are a different case. They do not terminate at the end of a single year,[19] and are probably not affected by prescription, though of course the claims made under the main contract may be. They do not require to be prorogated[20] and if of an executorial nature will endure at least until work under the main contract is completed.

8.14 The submitters are only bound by the arbiter's decree arbitral if it is pronounced within the period specified in the contract or implementing deed of submission unless that period has been validly *prorogated* — that is, extended — before the time originally fixed has expired.[21] The prorogation may be performed by agreement of the submitters, or by the arbiter if the necessary power has been granted. The arbiter has no implied power of prorogation: if power is not expressly granted by the submitters, the arbiter cannot prorogate.[22] If there are more arbiters than one, the act of prorogation must be executed by all or, if power has been given to act by a majority,[23] by a sufficient number. There seems to be no limit to the number of times that the powers of an arbiter may be prorogated[24] unless the submitters have agreed otherwise.

... Credo quod compromissum sit perpetuum, donec vivit arbitrator.' For the view of canonists see Julien, *Ev. Hist.* 230.

[17] *Inst.* IV.3.29.
[18] Prescription and Limitation (Scotland) Act 1973 s. 7.
[19] *Brysson* v. *Mitchell* (1823) 2 S. 382.
[20] *Halket* v. *Earl of Elgin* (1826) 5 S. 154; Bell J. M., *Arb.* paragraph 324 page 177.
[21] *Earl of Linlithgow* v. *Hamilton* 12 Jan. 1610, Mor. 636.
[22] Bell J. M., *Arb.* paragraph 325; Irons, *Arb.* 135. This rule is probably derived from civil law: see *D.* 4.8.32.21.
[23] *Love* v. *Love* (1825) 4 S. 53.
[24] *Maitland* v. *Representatives of William Mitchell* 18 May 1796, Mor. 631.

8.15. Prorogation must be in writing and should be dated as well as signed, so that it is clear from its own terms whether or not it was enacted before the expiry of the original time. When performed by the arbiter it does not, being a procedural act, require formal execution.[25] It has been said that prorogation by the submitters must be formally authenticated,[26] but the decision upon which this opinion rests related to an agreement made after the expiry of the original deed, so that the act was in effect, as Lord Justice Clerk Hope said, 'a new and substantive submission',[27] and it is questionable whether in any event this could be required where the original submission did not require to be formally executed. It is suggested that a minute of prorogation by the submitters should be executed in the same manner as the original submission.

8.16. Where proceedings have been devolved upon an oversman, the arbiters cease to have power of prorogation even in relation to matters not devolved, and the oversman has such power[28] only in relation to what has been devolved.[29] The existence of this inconvenient rule means that if arbiters are agreed upon any aspect of a dispute submitted to them they must take care to issue a part award on that matter before the original expiry date. (A part award, unlike an interim award, is final,[30] and will stand if the oversman makes a valid award dealing with the remaining issues.) Alternatively the arbiters should prorogate the submission before proceedings are devolved upon the oversman.

8.17. Unless the submitters specify otherwise, there seems to be no limit to the number of occasions on which an arbitration may be prorogated, but it has been suggested that apart from specific authority an arbiter may not prorogate for more than a year at a time as 'an act of prorogation for a longer period at once could scarcely be supposed to be fairly within the contemplation of the parties in such a submission'.[31]

[25] *Stewart* v. *Watherstone* 8 Mar. 1804 F. C., impliedly overruling *Sutherland of Cambusnavie, Suspender*, 1744 Mor. 652.
[26] Irons, *Arb.* 135–6.
[27] *Hill* v. *Dundee and Perth and Aberdeen Railway Junction Co.* (1852) 14 D. 1034.
[28] *MacBryde and Logan* v. *MacRae's Executors* 21 Jul. 1748, Mor. 657.
[29] *Lang* v. *Brown and Ferguson* (1852) 15 D. 38.
[30] Bell J. M., *Arb.* paragraph 502; Guild, *Arb.* 81.
[31] Bell J. M., *Arb.* paragraphs 337–9.

8.18. A submitter may be *personally barred* from alleging that a submission has expired.[32] This may happen, for example, where he or she has continued to plead after the specified date of termination. This is sometimes said to be an instance of homologation,[33] but it must surely be adoption since there is no inchoate or informal contract to be set up, but rather an expired contract to be renewed. The courts are most unwilling to entertain a suggestion that the actings of a submitter were performed without knowledge of the expiry of the time limit because 'such knowledge cannot but be inferred in the circumstances'.[34] The duration of an extension effected by adoption is unclear, but from the length of time involved in this case — 13 months from the date of the last act by the parties before the issue of the award — it would appear to be such as the parties must be taken in the circumstances to have contemplated.

8.19. The *effect of these rules* may be indicated by the following hypothetical examples.

(a) The submitters enter into an *ad hoc* contract of submission, the last signature being appended on 5th February 1985. In the duration clause they have left the day and month of expiry blank. A final decree arbitral given on 6th February 1986 would be valid,[35] but one given on 7th February 1986 or thereafter would be invalid.

(b) The submitters enter into an *ad hoc* contract of submission, as above, and the arbiter executes on 6th February 1986 a minute prorogating the submission for 'a year'. An award issued on 6th February 1987 is valid, but one issued on 7th February would not be.

(c) The submitters enter into an *ad hoc* contract of submission, as above. There is no prorogation but both of them continue without protest to appear and plead before the arbiter after the expiry date. An award issued 13 months after the last appearance by the parties is valid.[36]

8.20. **Arbiter's appointment**. Though the duration of the powers of an arbiter to bind the submitters by orders and decrees arbitral, and the duties of an arbiter in connection with the conduct

---

[32] *Paul v. Henderson* (1867) 5 M. 613.
[33] *Ibid.* at 622.
[34] *Ibid.* per Lord Cowan.
[35] *Earl of Dunmore v. McInturner* (1829) 7 S. 595.
[36] *Paul v. Henderson* (*supra* note 32).

of proceedings is limited by the terms of the contract or implementing deed of submission, there are usually a number of administrative duties to be attended to or supervised by the arbiter, and the submitters must pay the arbiter's fees and expenses. The contract between the arbiter and the submitters is therefore not terminated by the expiry of any time limits laid down in any deed of submission. This has been recognised judicially by implication if not expressly. In *McIntyre Brothers* v. *Smith*[37] an arbiter conducted proceedings under a deed of submission which made no reference to the arbiter's remuneration, and a final decree arbitral was pronounced which was also silent on the matter. A fee was however later paid by one of the submitters to the arbiter, but the other party refused to contribute. In a question between the submitters, the court held that the remuneration actually paid had been due, and granted decree for payment against the objector. Lord Kinnear remarked[38] that there was 'an implied term of the contract between an arbiter and the parties' relating to the remuneration of the former.

8.21.   Where the proceedings have been extended by an act of prorogation by the submitters, it appears to be generally assumed that the arbiter is obliged to continue to act. The matter has not been judicially determined, and it may well be that when an arbiter accepts office he or she does so in the knowledge that the submitters have power to extend the duration of proceedings. However, if the submitters' act of prorogation was not performed until after the expiry of the original date, so that there is in effect a 'new submission',[39] it is suggested that an arbiter appointed under an *ad hoc* or implementing deed of submission is only obliged to continue if a new appointment contract is expressly or impliedly entered into, or if the arbiter becomes personally barred from asserting that this has not occurred.

Termination by death of submitter or arbiter

8.22.   **Contracts of submission.** Normally the death of a submitter terminates a contract of submission and any

[37] 1913 S.C. 129.
[38] At 132.
[39] *Hill* (*supra* note 27).

implementing agreement between the submitters. As Erskine put it,[40]

> 'Submissions, like mandates, expire by the death of one of the submitters.'

The death of a submitter therefore normally brings to an end any ongoing arbitration proceedings. Though the arbiter is not a party to these agreements, his or her death will terminate an *ad hoc* contract or an implementing agreement in most cases, because unless the submitters have provided against this eventuality it frustrates the contract.

8.23.   There are however a number of exceptions or apparent exceptions to the rule stated by Erskine.

(1) The parties may if they think fit specifically provide in the contract of submission that it shall continue to subsist, notwithstanding the death of either of them.[41] This rule is certainly of great antiquity in Scots law.[42]

(2) Where the submission is ancillary to another contract it does not fall by the death of a submitter, at least if its purpose was to explicate a term of the main contract,[43] or if it is clearly provided that a representative is bound.[44]

(3) The death of one of a group of trustees does not terminate a contract of submission to which they are parties,[45] at least if there is a quorum of trustees remaining.

8.24.   It is not clear what the legal position is if there is no such quorum remaining or, where no quorum has been specified, the last surviving trustee has died. Given the power of the court to appoint new trustees in a lapsed trust,[46] and the normal power of existing trustees to assume new trustees to bring numbers up to a

---

[40] *Inst.* IV.3.29. See also *Macanquhal* v. *Boswell* 14 May 1563, Mor. 636.

[41] Bell J. M., *Arb.* paragraph 594; *Ewing & Co* v. *Dewar* 19 Dec. 1820 F. C.

[42] *Regiam Maj.* II.10.4. It was probably derived from civil or canon law: see *D.* IV.8.27.1; *Decretals* c. 14.X.1.43.

[43] *Caledonian Railway Co.* v. *Lockhart* (1860) 3 Macq. 808; *Orrell* v. *Orrell* (1859) 21 D. 554.

[44] *Smith* v. *Smith* (1953) 69 Sh. Ct. Rep. 237. The widow of a deceased partner would have been bound as his 'representative' under an arbitration clause in the partnership deed if she had sued as such.

[45] *Alexander's Trustees* v. *Dymock's Trustees* (1883) 10 R. 1189.

[46] Trusts (Scotland) Act 1921 s. 22; Wilson, *Trusts*, 270, 282–3.

quorum,[47] and in view of the expense and delay which results from the termination of arbitration proceedings by events beyond the control of the parties, the preferable view would seem to be that the contract subsists. The trust estate is in a sense the true party, and as long as it continues to exist, and there is a means of appointing new trustees, arbitration proceedings involving the trust should not be terminated. It is however stated by Bell,[48] discussing the position of tutors, that —

'If ... by death or otherwise, the number of surviving tutors should be reduced below a quorum, it seems difficult to avoid the conclusion, that the submission itself would then fall, just as in the case of the death of an ordinary party-submitter, or the death of a sole tutor. The legal effect of the extinction of a quorum, seems, *quoad hoc*, the same as the extinction of the whole tutors.'

It is submitted that Bell's opinion, expressed before the enactment of legislation giving the court powers of appointment, is now no longer authoritative, but the matter can be resolved only by legislation or judicial decision.

8.25. Arbiter's appointment. The contract between the submitters and an arbiter falls on the death of the arbiter.[49] It will also fall on the death of one of the submitters, unless that event does not terminate the submission itself, in which case presumably the responsibilities of the original submitter, including the obligation to pay the arbiter's fees and expenses, will devolve upon the successor.

Termination by agreement

8.26. Contracts of submission. A contract of submission may be brought to an end by the agreement of the submitters. As Bell puts it[50] —

'As it depended entirely on the will of the parties to enter into the contract at first, so it is within their power, by joint consent,

---

[47] Wilson, *Trusts*, 303.
[48] *Arb.* paragraph 182 page 106.
[49] *Macanquhal* v. *Boswell* 14 May 1563, Mor. 636.
[50] *Arb.* paragraph 603.

to bring it to a termination when they please. But the contract of submission cannot be recalled, more than any other onerous contract, at the pleasure of one of the parties, without the consent of the other.'

This rule, which is consistent with and probably derived from canon law,[51] is uncontroversial, but it now requires some elaboration.

8.27. An *ad hoc* submission, or an implementing contract following upon an ancillary submission, may be brought to an end by agreement. In the latter case this will not normally affect the ancillary submission itself,[52] which continues to subsist for the purpose of requiring arbitration in future disputes.

8.28. The agreement to terminate may be express, or it may be implied, and it appears that though the implied *abandonment* of a submission or of particular proceedings under it has not been judicially considered in Scotland it is not inconsistent with general rules of Scots contract law. Professer Walker has suggested[53] that —

'a contract may be held discharged by abandonment if both parties ... act in such a way as clearly to evidence disregard of their contractual obligations.'

The authority for this proposition[54] provides some indirect support for the view that *ad hoc* submissions and the arbitration of particular disputes under ancillary submissions may be abandoned by implied agreement.

8.29. The matter has been the subject of consideration by the House of Lords in an English appeal.[55] The case arose out of arbitration proceedings which had not been concluded seven years after their commencement. Ultimately one of the parties issued a writ seeking a declaration that the arbitration agreement had been terminated by repudiation or by frustration or by agreement to

---

[51] On which see Julien, *Ev. hist.* 231.
[52] So, at least, it has been held in England: *Allied Marine Transport Ltd.* v. *Vale do Rio Doce Navegaçao S. A.*, (The 'Leonidas D') [1983] 2 Ll. Rep. 411 at 414.
[53] Walker, *Contracts*, 34.3.
[54] *Smail* v. *Potts* (1847) 9 D. 1043 per L. P. Boyle at 1045–6.
[55] *Paal Wilson & Co. A/S* v. *Partenreederei Hannah Blumenthal* (*The 'Hannah Blumenthal'*) [1983] 1 All E. R. 34.

abandon it. The concept of implied abandonment of a contract was stated by Lord Brandon[56] to be well established in English law, and though on the evidence it was held that there had been no implied agreement to abandon that particular arbitration, a subsequent case[57] has shown that implied agreement to abandon can in some circumstances be established.

8.30.   The grounds upon which an agreement to abandon may be established were set out by two of the judges in similar though not identical terms. Lord Diplock said[58] that —

'where the inference that a reasonable man would draw from the prolonged failure by the claimant in an arbitration procedure is that the claimant is willing to consent to the abandonment of the agreement to submit to arbitration and the respondent did in fact draw such inferences and by his own inaction thereafter indicated his own consent to its abandonment in a similar fashion to the claimant and was so understood by the claimant, the court would be right in treating the arbitration agreement as having been terminated by agreement.'

Lord Brandon considered[59] that —

'Where A seeks to prove that he and B have abandoned a contract in this way, there are two ways in which A can prove his case. The first way is by showing that the conduct of each party, as evinced to the other party and acted on by him, leads necessarily to the inference of an implied agreement between them to abandon the contract. The second method is by showing that the conduct of B, as evinced towards A, has been such as to lead A reasonably to believe that B has abandoned the contract, even though it has not in fact been B's intention to do so, and that A has significantly altered his position in reliance on that belief.'

These *dicta*, it is submitted, are highly persuasive in Scotland. Nevertheless, it is unlikely that many cases would come within the

---

[56] At 47.
[57] *Excomm Ltd.* v. *Guan Guan Shipping (Pte.) Ltd.* (*The 'Golden Bear'*) The Times, November 18 1986.
[58] *Paal Wilson and Co. A/S* v. *Partenreederei Hannah Blumenthal* [1983] 1 All E.R. 34 at 49.
[59] At 47.

rules thus laid down, because of the difficulty of proving that the respondent's inaction implied consent to abandonment.

8.31. If the parties have agreed to settle the whole issue, or whole remaining issue, which has been the subject of an *ad hoc* contract of submission or of a deed of submission executed in implement of an ancillary arbitration agreement, those contracts will be impliedly brought to an end by agreement. The arbiter's powers then cease, because if there is no longer any dispute there is nothing for the arbiter to decide and no judicial function to exercise. (Ordinary courts commonly issue a decree of consent of parties, but in so doing they are, strictly speaking, not acting judicially but giving the agreement effect by an exercise of sovereign power.) In Scots, unlike English,[60] law it is apparently not competent for an arbiter to issue an award in terms of a settlement agreed between the parties.[61] This may give rise to some difficulty in practice, because under the rules of certain international arbitration bodies which may be incorporated into a submission it is provided that where submitters come to an agreement in the presence of the arbiter, the agreement may — in the case of agreements covered by rule 17 of the Rules of the Court of Arbitration of the International Chamber of Commerce, 'shall'[62] — be recorded in the form of an arbitral award. However, enforcement of a 'Convention award' made in pursuance of an arbitration agreement in the territory of a state other than the United Kingdom would not be able to be refused on the ground that it merely recorded the agreement of the submitters.[63]

8.32. Where the parties relations are governed by an ancillary submission rather than one which relates to a particular existing dispute, they should make it quite clear whether they intend to terminate the ancillary submission or merely certain proceedings.

8.33. **Arbiter's appointment**. The arbiter may by agreement of the submitters be released from office, and the judicial duties of an arbiter in any event cease if the parties settle the dispute or agree to abandon the arbitration proceedings in which he or she is

---

[60] See on this Mustill, *Comm. Arb.* 96; Russell, *Arb.* 1982, 143. Neither source gives any judicial authority for the opinion.
[61] *Maule* v. *Maule* (1816) IV Dow 367.
[62] In Lee, *Int. Comm. Arb.*, 434.
[63] Arbitration Act 1975 s. 5.

involved. It should be noted, however, that the termination of the submission by agreement does not of itself imply the termination of the whole duties of an arbiter under the contract between the submitters and the arbiter, because there may be administrative matters still to be attended to. Furthermore, the arbiter will often be entitled to certain fees and expenses even if there has been no hearing or decision, and the amount thereof will require to be determined and paid.

Termination by supervening impossibility etc.

8.34. Most discussion of this topic in Scotland[64] has hitherto concentrated upon the effect which frustration of the main contract has upon an ancillary submission. That matter is discussed in chapter nine below. This chapter is concerned with the direct effect on arbitration contracts of supervening impossibility, illegality of performance, and frustration.

8.35. **Contracts of submission.** There are few circumstances affecting a submitter, apart from death, which result in the termination of the submission by supervening impossibility, illegality or frustration. It is conceivable, however, that a submitter might become an enemy alien, and if that happened the submission would be terminated by supervening illegality.

8.36. Though an ancillary submission is unlikely to be affected by an arbiter's practical or legal inability to act since it usually does not contain the nomination of the arbiter or make provision for the failure of any nomination, an *ad hoc* submission or a contract implementing an ancillary submission may be. It is therefore wise for submitters involved in proceedings likely to be of some length to insure against this eventuality.

8.37. A contract is frustrated if, after it has been made,

'an unforeseen turn of events takes place which renders performance impossible or, if possible at all, so delayed or changed that it would not be at all what the parties had contemplated . . .'[65]

[64] See e.g. Guild, *Arb.* 44–6; Marshall, *Merc.* 621–3.
[65] Walker, *Contracts*, 31.52.

156

Termination of Arbitration Contracts

An *ad hoc* submission or implementing contract may be frustrated if the arbiter dies, or becomes mentally or physically incapable of acting, if no provision has been made for the substitution of another person. Though where the arbiter has become affected by bias or has committed misconduct an aggrieved party may waive the right of objection which then accrues,[66] supervening bias has been regarded as a frustrating event[67] and the same principle would seem to apply to misconduct.

8.38. It is conceivable, though in practice unlikely, that a submission might be terminated because it had become illegal, for a reason which the submitters could not waive, for the arbiter to continue to act.

8.39. Whether a submission may be frustrated because the physical object upon which the dispute is centred has ceased to exist probably depends on the kinds of arbitration which the submitters had in mind. In an English appeal to the House of Lords, Lord Diplock remarked[68] that —

'the subject matter of an arbitration agreement is not a thing that is susceptible of physical destruction. It is an agreement by the parties (1) to embark on and follow a joint course of action ... for the purpose of obtaining from a third party ... a decision of the dispute, and (2) to abide by that decision.'

Thus, if the dispute concerns the price to be paid by A to B for certain goods, the property in which has already passed, the destruction of the goods does not remove the cause of difference or make the arbitration impossible to conduct. However, if the article was unique, and the parties had in mind arbitration by a skilled valuer who would require an opportunity to inspect the thing in question, the destruction of the thing would make the arbitration something very different from what the parties had contemplated, and would frustrate the submission.[69]

---

[66] *Drew* v. *Drew* (1855) 2 Macq. 1 at 9.
[67] So, at least, it has been considered in an English appeal to the House of Lords: *Bremer Vulkan Schiffbau und Maschinenfabrik* v. *South India Shipping Corporation* [1981] 1 Ll. Rep.253 per Lord Diplock at 259.
[68] *Paal Wilson and Co. A/S* v. *Partenreederei Hannah Blumenthal* [1983] 1 All E.R. 34 at 50.
[69] *Graham* v. *Mill* (1904) 6 F. 886.

8.40. Some kinds of situations almost certainly do not result in the frustration of a submission. In '*The Hannah Blumenthal*' Lord Diplock observed[70] that —

'inability to obtain a "satisfactory trial" because of the difficulty which the arbitral tribunal will encounter in ascertaining the true facts, even if caused by delay in the proceedings, is not capable in law of bringing an arbitration agreement to an end by frustration.'

Two main reasons were adduced for this opinion. First, the submitters must have had in mind at the time of contracting that 'witnesses may die or disappear, documents or physical evidence may be lost or be destroyed even before or at any time, however short, after' an arbitration agreement has been entered into. Second, in some cases at least the problem of ascertaining the facts is due to the dilatoriness of one of the submitters, and 'the essence of frustration is that it should not be due to the act ... of a party'.[71] The principles of frustration here applied to arbitration are in harmony with the doctrines of Scots contract law, and the observations must therefore be regarded as highly persuasive.

8.41. Delay caused by the dilatoriness of the arbiter can not frustrate the submission either. Though a Scottish court does not possess the power exerciseable by a High Court judge in England[72] to remove an arbitrator for failing to use all reasonable dispatch, a submitter may petition the Court of Session to order an arbiter to perform the duties of the office.[73] Only if the arbiter failed to obey the court's order and was imprisoned for contempt of court would the submission (to which the arbiter is not a party) be frustrated.

8.42. **Arbiter's appointment.** This may also be terminated by reasons of illegality, impossibility of performance, or frustration. As to illegality, if either of the submitters, or the arbiter, becomes an enemy alien, performance becomes unlawful and the contract is abrogated. It may become impossible for the arbiter to continue to conduct the proceedings because of the onset of some incapacitating disease, or because the particular article which it was the chief task of the arbiter to appraise has been destroyed

---

[70] [1983] 1 All E.R. 34 at 51.
[71] *Ibid.*, at 57.
[72] Under the Arbitration Act 1950 s. 13(3).
[73] *Forbes* v. *Underwood* (1886) 13 R. 465.

otherwise than due to the fault either of the arbiter or of a submitter.

8.43. Neither supervening impossibility nor frustration of the contract between the arbiter and the submitters relieves the latter of their obligation to pay the arbiter any expenses already incurred and any fees that have already been earned. Payments made in advance by the submitters to the arbiter for performance not rendered by reason of frustration or impossibility are, unless the contract otherwise provides, recoverable on the quasi-contractual principle of the *condictio causa data, causa non secuta*.[74] In the event of the termination of the contract by supervening illegality no further performance by either party is required.[75]

Termination by rescission following breach of contract

8.44. Scottish texts on the law of arbitration have not hitherto discussed the effect of material breach of contract upon the contract of submission and the contract between the submitters and the arbiter, except in connection with the effect on an ancillary arbitration clause of the repudiation of the main contract.[76] The matter has however been considered in an English appeal to the House of Lords.[77] The principal speech in that case was made by Lord Diplock, who said[78] —

'I would accept that the unperformed primary obligations on the parties under an arbitration agreement, like other contracts, may be brought to an end ... at the election of one party where there has been a repudiatory breach of that agreement by the other party ... I would also accept that when, upon the commission of such a breach, the party to an arbitration agreement who is not in default has lawfully elected to bring to an end the unperformed primary obligations of both parties to continue with the arbitration up to the issue of an award, the

[74] Walker, *Contracts*, 32.9; *Cantiere San Rocco* v. *Clyde Shipbuilding Co.* 1923 S.C.(H.L.) 105.
[75] Walker, *Contracts*, 31.51; *Fraser* v. *Denny, Mott & Dickson* 1944 S.C.(H.L.) 35.
[76] Guild, *Arb.* 45.
[77] *Bremer Vulkan Schiffbau und Maschinenfabrik* v. *South India Shipping Corporation* [1981] 2 Ll. Rep. 253.
[78] At 259–60.

High Court has jurisdiction, in protection of that party's legal right to do so, to grant him an injunction to restrain the other party from proceeding further with the arbitration.'

Though Lord Diplock went on to hold that the facts in that case were not such as to make the grant of an injunction appropriate, it is clear that he regarded repudiation as a ground upon which an arbitration agreement — or rather, strictly speaking, the primary obligations under it — could be rescinded. This judgment, which applies principles also accepted in Scots law, must be regarded as highly persuasive.

8.45. **Contract of submission.** There is little doubt but that an *ad hoc* submission and an agreement implementing an ancillary submission may be terminated by rescission following material breach. It is possible also to envisage circumstances in which an ancillary submission itself might be terminated on this ground. This would, however, raise questions of the separability of that submission from the main contract, and these questions are dealt with in the next chapter.

8.46. An *ad hoc* contract of submission or an implementing agreement may be repudiated by any conduct which constitutes a material breach of the party's obligations under it. This may include the appointment of a biased or otherwise unqualified arbiter,[79] where each party appoints an arbiter. It must also be material breach of contract to present to an arbiter a demonstrably concocted case[80] or to induce a witness to commit perjury.[81] There seems no good reason to hold that damages may not be claimed for losses consequent upon a contractual breach of this kind. Where in a sale of goods the determination of their price has been submitted to an arbiter, and the arbiter has been prevented by the fault of a party from making the valuation the innocent party has by statute[82] an action for damages against the party at fault.

---

[79] *Sellar* v. *Highland Railway Co.* 1919 S.C.(H.L.) 19 per Lord Buckmaster at 22, and 1918 S.C. 838 per Lord Mackenzie at 855. See also *Bremer Vulkan Schiffbau und Maschinenfabrik* v. *South India Shipping Corporation* [1981] 1 Ll. Rep. 253 per Lord Diplock at 260.
[80] *Logan* v. *Lang* 15 Nov. 1798 Mor. Appx. 1 (Arb.) 6; Guild, *Arb.* 92.
[81] Guild, *Arb.* 92.
[82] Sale of Goods Act 1979 s. 9(2).

8.47. Whether delay in presenting a claim or defences or in producing material or documentary evidence amounts to repudiation is very doubtful. It has been decided that in English law it does not,[83] because both submitters have an equal obligation to keep proceedings moving, and a party who is aggrieved by delay caused by an opponent may obtain a remedy by seeking directions from the arbitrator or ultimately the assistance of the court. As Lord Diplock remarked,[84]

'Respondents in private arbitrations are not entitled to let sleeping dogs lie and then complain that they did not bark.'

This opinion has been strongly criticised in England both by academic lawyers[85] and by judges,[86] though it has been followed, however reluctantly, by the latter. The main ground of criticism has been that it is

'wholly divorced from reality and the expectations of commercial men that those facing claims should be under the same obligation to keep those claims moving against them as was imposed upon those who made the claim.'

It is certainly doubtful if such an obligation could be regarded on ordinary principles as an implied term of the contract of submission. The matter has not been the subject of judicial decision in Scotland, perhaps because the practice of including in deeds of submission provision for a time limit has restricted the opportunities for dilatory conduct. The question whether inordinate delay by a claimant amounts to repudiation therefore remains open. Even if inordinate delay does amount to repudiation, however, a submission could not be terminated by the repudiatory conduct alone: the innocent party would have to have taken action to rescind the contract (or, as it is sometimes put, 'accept the repudiation'). The jurisdiction of the arbiter would remain in existence until that had been done, and it might be difficult to argue that rescission could be effected after the claimant has begun to prosecute the claim, though an arbiter may issue an award without having heard one of the parties if that party has been

---

[83] *Bremer Vulkan (supra).*
[84] At 264.
[85] B.J.D., 'Stale arbitrations: The Leonidas D', (1985) *Lloyd's Maritime and Commercial Law* 293–305.
[86] Griffiths L.J. in *Paal Wilson & Co. A/S v. Partenreederei Hannah Blumenthal* [1983] 1 A.C. 854 at 879 (CA).

guilty of unreasonable delay in presenting his or her case.[87] Since the arbiter has no general legal power to dismiss a claim for want of prosecution there are only two solutions to the problem of delay: the traditional one of specifying a time limit in the submission with power in the arbiter to prorogate, or that of granting power to the arbiter to dismiss a claim for want of prosecution. The effect of the former is well known, and is therefore generally preferable.

8.48.   Where the delay is caused partly or wholly by the arbiter the position is a little more complex than in England because the court in Scotland does not have any power comparable to that of the High Court in England under section 13(3) of the Arbitration Act 1950 to remove an arbiter for 'failing to use all reasonable dispatch'. There have been a number of cases in which the dilatoriness of an arbiter[88] or of a party[89] has been regarded as a ground for setting an award aside or refusing to accede to a request for arbitration, but these have been brought under statutory arbitration régimes. If one party to the submission takes refuge in delay, and the arbiter has been asked to take appropriate action but has failed to do so within a reasonable time, the other party may petition the Court of Session to order the arbiter to perform the duties of the office on pain of imprisonment,[90] but that does not necessarily get proceedings moving. Arguably, since the effective cause of the failure of the arbitration is the conduct of the arbiter rather than that of the other submitter, the submission is terminated by frustration, and neither need nor can be terminated by rescission following material breach. Where an ancillary submission arises out of an agreement to sell goods on the terms that the price is to be fixed by the valuation of a third party, and that party fails to act, the submission is rendered void by statute.[91]

8.49.   **Arbiter's appointment.** If there is indeed a contract between the submitters and the arbiter, there can be little doubt but that either party may commit a material breach of that contract, the submitters by failing to pay the arbiter the fees due and the expenses properly incurred, and the arbiter by failing to

---

[87] *Low* v. *Banks* (1836) 14 S. 869.
[88] *Halliday* v. *Semple* 1960 S.L.T. (Sh. Ct.) 11.
[89] *Shewan* v. *Johnston* (1933) 49 Sh. Ct. Rep. 285.
[90] *Forbes* v. *Underwood* (1886) 13 R. 465.
[91] Sale of Goods Act 1979 s. 9(1).

perform important judicial[92] and administrative duties. There is also little doubt but that the arbiter has a remedy against the submitters.[93] What is controversial is the immunity of the arbiter from suit. It is widely assumed that the arbiter is immune where the ground of action relates to an alleged breach of the judicial as distinct from the administrative duties connected with the office, but doubts about the correctness of this assumption grow with the professionalisation of arbitration and the increase in value of the losses which can be caused by arbitral misconduct.

8.50. Up to 1986 the Scottish courts had not been required directly to determine the extent of an *arbiter's immunity from suit*. There are some judicial observations which are relevant but they are not of great weight. Two of them[94] arose in cases decided before the payment of remuneration to arbiters became generally accepted[95] and concerned the disciplinary proceedings of courts of non-established churches, proceedings which have been held not to amount to arbitration[96]; the third[97] was an Outer House decision in an action by an arbiter for payment of fees.

8.51. In *Auchincloss*,[98] a minister who had been deposed by a presbytery on grounds of fornication raised an action of defamation and damages against the presbytery as well as against certain women who had testified against him. The Lord Ordinary assoilzied all the defenders, and the Court of Session on a reclaiming motion adhered to the Lord Ordinary's interlocutor. The judgments were laconic, as was common in those days, and it is not entirely clear what the grounds of the decision were, but the report contains a suggestion that the pursuer might have had a relevant case if he had alleged malice.

8.52. In *McMillan*,[99] the pursuer was again a deposed minister, and the action was for reduction of a sentence of the General

---

[92] Set out in paragraph 3.22 above.
[93] *McIntyre Brothers* v. *Smith* 1913 S.C. 129.
[94] *Auchincloss* v. *Black* 1793, Hume's *Decisions*, 595; *McMillan* v. *Free Church of Scotland* (1862) 24 D. 1282.
[95] *McIntyre Brothers* v. *Smith* 1913 S.C. 129.
[96] *McMillan* v. *Free Church* (1859) 22 D. 290 at 324.
[97] *Rutherford* v. *Magistrates of Findochty* 1929 S.N. 130.
[98] *Supra* note 94.
[99] *Supra* note 94.

Assembly of the Free Church and for damages. There was again no allegation of malice except against three individuals, and that was not insisted in. The court held that the General Assembly as such could not be sued. For present purposes the main interest of the case lies in an additional ground of dismissal of the action stated by Lord Curriehill, who considered that persons exercising judicial functions were, unless malice be proved, immune from liability for error. He said[100] that —

'parties upon whom judicial functions are lawfully conferred, and who in the *bona fide* exercise of these functions over parties subject to their authority, fall into errors of judgment, are not liable in damages to their parties in consequence of such errors. *Humanum est errare.* Infallibility of judgment is attainable by no man, however laboriously and conscientiously he may exert his powers to do what is right; and if, notwithstanding a judge's best and *bona fide* endeavours to do so, he should be liable in damages for errors into which he might fall, such offices would be shunned by those best qualified for performing their functions. But such functionaries have an immunity from liability for errors in judgment, unless their errors arise from corruption or malice. The law unquestionably confers such an immunity upon judges officiating in the public judicial institutions of the country, whether civil, criminal, or ecclesiastical, upon whom jurisdiction is conferred by the state. It also extends such immunity to private persons, upon whom parties, by voluntary agreement, confer authority to adjudicate in certain matters among themselves; it being the policy of our law to encourage and support the settlement of disputes by such private arrangements. . . . Such arbitrators [*sic*] are not liable in damages to the contracting parties for errors of judgment into which they may happen to fall in the *bona fide* exercise of the functions so conferred upon them.'

These remarks, which are strictly *obiter*, provide some authority for the view that in Scots law arbiters are immune unless malice is proved from liability at least for errors of judgment contained in their awards. The legal policy lying behind the rule as thus stated was that it was necessary in the encouragement of private settlement of disputes. At that time that policy was clearly sound, since arbiters were generally unpaid.

[100] At 1295.

8.53. In *Rutherford*,[101] an arbiter sued one of the submitters for half the amount of his fee. The defenders, who had been unsuccessful in the arbitration, averring that the arbiter's decision had gone beyond the matters referred to him and that they intended to bring an action of reduction, contended that in the circumstances the arbiter was not entitled to payment. The Lord Ordinary (Moncreiff) rejected these defences. He was not convinced that the arbiter had indeed exceeded his powers, but in any event, he said,

> 'the fact that an arbiter had gone wrong and given an inept legal decision afforded no ground for depriving him of his remuneration, unless it could be shown that he had acted corruptly.'

This decision is consistent with that of Lord Curriehill quoted above.

8.54. With some exceptions, opinion in other jurisdictions seems to be similar. It appears from a comparative survey carried out by Professor Domke[102] that the legal systems of many countries[103] recognise that an arbiter has at least some immunity from suit. In some cases the immunity appears to rest on an implied term in the contract between the submitters and the arbiter. Domke quotes[104] a decision of a German Federal Tribunal[105] as stating that —

> 'the parties to an arbitration, if the question of the restriction of liability of the arbitrator would be put before them, would in principle agree to a custom which is considered usual by participants in such matters.'

The immunity is however generally not complete. Domke continues[106] —

> 'the arbitrator is not immune from court action for damages resulting from his misconduct in the arbitration and negligence in the performance of his duties, outside the (final) rendering of

[101] *Supra* note 97.
[102] 'The Arbitrator's Immunity from Liability: A Comparative Survey' (1971) *University of Toledo Law Review*, 99–105.
[103] Including in particular England, France, Germany, Switzerland, Austria, India and the United States.
[104] At 101–2.
[105] 15 Bundesgerichtshof 12 at 16 (1959).
[106] At 102.

an award. Indeed, the arbitrator's unwillingness to proceed with the arbitration and thus delaying the resolution of the controversy ... may cause damage to the parties for which the arbitrator is responsible. Also, the premature withdrawal of an arbitrator, more often a party-appointed one, may sometimes cause new arbitration proceedings with new expenses to the parties for which no immunity from liability exists.'

Under Swedish law, not apparently considered by Domke in this survey, it seems to be accepted[107] that an arbiter may be liable in damages at least for refusal to act, failure to observe mandatory procedural rules, and criminal conduct, though misinterpretation of the evidence or misapplication of the law, neither of which are grounds in Sweden for setting the award aside, cannot ground an action, however negligent the arbiter's behaviour may have been.

8.55. The matter was considered in 1975 in an English appeal to the House of Lords.[108] The speeches of their Lordships on this point are strictly *obiter*, because it was decided that the person who made the decision which was under attack had acted as a valuer not as an arbitrator, there being a distinction in English law between these two concepts. The case is nevertheless of particular interest to Scots lawyers because three Scottish law lords took part in the decision, two of them expressing difficulty in conceiving how arbiters but not valuers could be regarded as immune, while the third was content to assume that (as had been conceded by counsel) arbiters were generally immune. Both Lord Kilbrandon and Lord Fraser accepted that public judges were immune from suit but Lord Kilbrandon did so in terms which drew a clear distinction for this purpose between public judges and arbiters. 'The state' he said,[109]

'sets up a judicial system, which includes not only the courts of justice but also the numerous tribunals, statutory arbitrations, commissioners and so on, who give decisions, whether final or not, on matters in which the state has given them competence. To these tribunals the citizen is bound to go.... The citizen does not select the judges in this system, nor does he remunerate them otherwise than as a contributor to the cost of government.

---

[107] Holmbäck, *Arb. Swe. 1984*, 79.
[108] *Arenson v. Casson Beckman Rutley & Co.* [1975] 3 W.L.R. 815.
[109] At 832.

The judge has no bargain with the parties before him. He pledges them no skill. His duties are to the state ... and if it be necessary to state the matter in terms of the law of tort, litigants are not persons to whom judges owe a legal duty of care.'

On the immunity of arbiters, he noted that it had been conceded that aside from fraud this was (in England) the law,

'But why? I find it impossible to put weight on such considerations as that in the case of an arbitrator (a) there is a dispute between the parties; (b) he hears evidence; (c) he hears submissions from the parties, and that therefore he, unlike the valuer, is acting in a judicial capacity. As regards (a), I cannot see any juridical distinction between a dispute which has actually arisen and a situation where persons have opposed interests, if in either case an impartial person has had to be called in to make a decision which the interested parties will accept. As regards (b) and (c), these are certainly not necessary activities of an arbiter ... I have come to be of opinion that ... an arbitrator ... is indeed a person selected by the parties for his expertise, whether technical or intellectual, that he pledges skill in the exercise thereof, and that if he is negligent in that exercise he will be liable in damages.'

8.56. The contrary argument had been put earlier, again strictly *obiter*, by another Scottish law lord in a previous English appeal to the House of Lords.[110] In that case it was also decided that the person whose decision was under attack had not been acting as an arbitrator, and it was again assumed by a majority that arbitrators were immune from suit on grounds of negligence. Lord Reid said[111] —

'I think that the immunity of arbitrators from liability for negligence must be based on the belief — probably well founded — that without such immunity arbitrators would be harassed by actions which would have very little chance of success. And it may also have been thought that an arbitrator might be influenced by the thought that he was more likely to be sued if his decision went one way than if it went the other way, or that in

[110] *Sutcliffe* v. *Thakrah* [1974] 1 All E.R. 859.
[111] At 862g.

167

some way the immunity put him in a more independent position to reach the decision which he thought right.'

This opinion is widely held. Professor Domke has noted[112] that in the United States it is generally considered that —

'inasmuch as the function of arbitration tribunals is similar to the courts: and the duties of the arbitrator require the exercise of independent judgment, arbitrators enjoy immunity from court actions for their activities in arriving at their award. Were the law otherwise, the losing party could in every case expose an arbitrator to the vexation and hazards of a lawsuit.'

8.57. The arguments in favour of arbitral immunity have to be strong to be convincing now that arbiters are generally paid (often very handsomely) for voluntarily providing their services to people who have no general legal obligation to resort to them. It could be argued that if a particularly high risk of liability for negligence is attached to the profession of arbitration, higher fees can be charged to compensate for this, insurance cover can be obtained, and express provision made in contracts with the submitters restricting the extent of such liability. Yet the fact that one of the submitters will almost inevitably be seriously out of pocket as a result of an arbiter's decision means that the risk of litigation would, if there was no immunity rule at all, be higher than most insurance companies would be prepared to contemplate, and the fees that would then have to be charged would be such as to frighten off most clients. Therein lies the real problem: if there were no immunity for arbiters under the laws of the various parts of the United Kingdom, the arbiters whose services were most in demand in international commercial arbitration would simply go where they enjoyed that privilege, with resultant economic loss to the country. Arbitral immunity must therefore be regarded as required by public policy to the extent that it is allowed by other developed legal systems.

8.58. The rule stated by Lord Curriehill in *McMillan*[113] and Lord Moncreiff in *Rutherford*,[114] to the effect that apart from malice arbiters enjoy immunity from suit arising out of their

---

[112] In *Comm. Arb.*, 23.01.
[113] *Supra*, paragraph 8.52.
[114] *Supra*, paragraph 8.53.

awards, is in accordance with the limited immunity granted by other legal systems, notably that of Sweden. It is therefore submitted these decisions should be followed, but that immunity should not be extended further to cover conduct connected with the general conduct of the proceedings or purely administrative functions. It follows that, though during the proceedings the conduct of the arbiter can in general only be controlled by the court by a petition to the Court of Session requesting it to exercise the supervisory power which it possesses in relation to subordinate jurisdictions,[115] the submitters may agree not only to terminate the submission but also to rescind the arbiter's appointment on the ground of his or her material breach of contract, and either of them may on completion of the arbitration sue for damages arising out of any breach of contract or negligence not connected with the award, and refuse to pay any fees demanded by the arbiter. It should perhaps be added that, as the distinction which apparently exists in English law between arbitrator and valuer has no counterpart in the law of Scotland,[116] the actual decisions as distinct from particular *dicta* in *Sutcliffe* v. *Thakrah*[117] and *Arenson* v. *Casson Beckman Rutley & Co.*[118] do not have even persuasive authority in Scotland.

[115] *Forbes* v. *Underwood* (1886) 13 R. 465.
[116] See on this paragraph 1.21 above.
[117] [1974] 1 All E.R. 859.
[118] [1975] 3 W.L.R. 815.

CHAPTER NINE

ANCILLARY SUBMISSIONS: THEIR RELATIONSHIP TO MAIN CONTRACTS

Introduction

9.1. It is not certain when the practice of attaching an ancillary arbitration clause to other contracts first arose in Scotland, but by the middle of the nineteenth century it was not uncommon. Informal adjudication was particularly favoured in connection with disputes relating to the quality of merchandise sold and delivered and to the performance of obligations under building and engineering contracts, for it was (and still is) generally believed that these are usually best handled by persons of relevant practical knowledge and experience. It was increasingly accepted that an obligation to submit to arbitration any disputes that might arise out of such contracts should be entered into at the outset, even though at that point it was not always appropriate or even possible to nominate an arbiter. Until the commencement of the Arbitration (Scotland) Act 1894, however, the use of ancillary clauses was discouraged by the existence of a rule that a submission which did not name the arbiter was invalid, no distinction being drawn for this purpose between an ancillary agreement to submit future disputes to arbitration and a contract submitting an existing dispute. The 1894 Act abolished the rule against submission to unnamed arbiters and provided a means by which deadlock could be prevented in case of subsequent failure to nominate or agree on the nomination of an arbiter, and in so doing removed an important obstacle to the use of ancillary arbitration clauses.

9.2. Not all the practical and legal problems associated with ancillary arbitration clauses were removed by the 1894 Act. As already indicated,[1] an ancillary submission is in Scots law a contract of submission,[2] not a mere exchange of promises to enter

---

[1] Paragraph 3.11 above.
[2] *Charles Mauritzen Ltd. v. Baltic Shipping Co.* 1948 S.C. 646 at 650.

into a contract of submission, as the 'clause compromissoire' appears to be in French law.[3] Furthermore, as an arbitration clause is concerned with disputes arising out of the main contract it has a rather different character from other contractual clauses. For these reasons questions concerning the extent to which a question of the validity of a particular contractual provision can be separated from the validity of the whole contract are particularly acute where an arbitration clause is concerned. It is the purpose of this chapter to address this problem.

The relation of arbitration clauses to main contracts

9.3. An ancillary submission is an agreement that any dispute, or any dispute of a stated type, arising out of a specified contract or contracts, shall be determined by arbitration. It is convenient to refer to the contract to which a submission is thus ancillary as the 'main' or 'principal' contract. Though an ancillary submission need not necessarily be expressed in a clause which forms part of the same document as the main contract, it commonly does so, and indeed ancillary submissions which are not arbitration clauses are rare if not unknown in practice.

9.4. An arbitration clause is contained in the same document or set of documents as the main contract.[4] To all outward appearances an arbitration clause is no different from the other provisions in the main contract. Even if it is merely incorporated into the main contract by reference, such incorporation does not set it apart from but rather emphasises its inclusion among, the ordinary provisions of the main contract. Materially, therefore, an arbitration clause is as closely identified with the main contract as it is possible to be.

9.5. In its non-material features, however, an arbitration clause is very different from the other clauses in the main contract. It can be attached to almost any contract whatever, and the obligations constituted by it can, if the parties so wish, be made the subject of a separate agreement. An agreement to submit to arbitration is in no sense a consideration for an obligation in a clause of the main contract, and indeed an arbitration clause normally imposes the same obligations on both parties. Most significant of all, an

---

[3] Robert and Carbonneau, *Arb.*, I: 2-2.
[4] Verbal arbitration clauses are apparently unknown.

arbitration clause sets up a special tribunal to judge disputes arising out of the terms of the main contract, and is only called into operation if any such disputes arise.

9.6. The question of the severability of an arbitration clause is posed where a dispute covered by the terms of the clause arises out of the main contract, but the latter is actually or allegedly void or voidable from the outset, or terminated subsequently by force of law or the act of one or both of the parties. Does an arbiter have jurisdiction to entertain a dispute arising out of the main contract if that contract (1) was never entered into; (2) was legally void and thus from the outset never had any existence in law at all; (3) was voidable and has been nullified; or (4) did have an existence but has been frustrated or rescinded by one party following material breach by the other?

Approaches to the problem of severability

9.7. There are two main approaches to the solution of this problem. One emphasises the material association or 'solidarity' of the arbitration clause with the main contract; the other stresses the 'autonomy' of the clause and its non-material dissociation from the main contract. Those who emphasise the 'solidarity' of the arbitration clause with the main contract consider that in at least the first three of the four situations mentioned in paragraph 9.6 above the arbiter can have no jurisdiction. Some go further and argue that the arbiter has no jurisdiction even in the fourth situation, except where the dispute arose while the main contract was still in existence. If the submitters are at issue over the validity or continued subsistence of the main contract, an arbiter who holds that he or she has jurisdiction by virtue of an arbitration clause attached to that contract and who then issues a decree arbitral finding the main contract invalid is guilty of self contradiction. Those who stress the 'autonomy' of the arbitration clause consider that if the main contract was never entered into or is legally void or voidable or has been terminated by frustration or rescission it is not necessarily true that the arbitration clause falls also, since a fact which invalidates the former may have no effect on the latter. Though it is likely that if the main contract was never entered into the same will be true of the arbitration clause, and though circumstances which render the main contract void or voidable may well have a similar effect on the arbitration clause so that the two fall together, nevertheless the validity or continued effect of the main contract and of the arbitration clause have to be judged separately.

9.8. **Scots authorities**. Due to the disparity and sparsity of authority it is not entirely certain which of these approaches is taken by the law of Scotland, though as explained below the authorities appear to lean towards the 'solidarity' approach.

9.9. In general, the Scots law of contract lays particular stress on the *unity of contracts*.[5] Lord Neaves once went so far as to say[6] that —

'it is a general principle that all the material stipulations in a contract forming a *unum quid* are mutual causes.'

It has been suggested, however, that this is best taken merely as an emphatic statement of a presumption in favour of unity.[7] The law recognises that what in purely material terms appears to be a single contract —

'may really be a congeries of contracts undertaken at one time, but independent of each other.'[8]

There is thus no reason in principle why the notion of the independence of an arbitration clause should be rejected in Scots law, though the onus of proof lies initially on those who uphold it.

9.10. There are a number of *decisions* of the Scottish courts which are at least *consistent with the 'solidarity' approach*. The earliest appears to be *Pearson* v. *Oswald*,[9] which concerned an arbitration clause in a mineral lease. After the lease had expired, a dispute arose and the landlord lodged a claim with the arbiter nominated in the lease. The former tenant brought an action of declarator and interdict to stop the arbitration from proceeding, and pleaded that as the lease had expired the arbiter had no jurisdiction. The court granted interdict, and Lord Ivory remarked[10] in the course of his judgment that —

---

[5] *Somerville* v. *B. P. Goodrich Co.* (1904) 12 S.L.T. 188 per Lord Low at 190.
[6] In *Turnbull* v. *McLean & Co.* (1875) 1 R. 730 at 739.
[7] Gloag, *Contract*, 594.
[8] *Ibid.*
[9] (1859) 21 D. 419.
[10] At 426.

'this clause of reference ... is a subordinate contract entirely, ancillary to the primary contract with which it is connected, and, except in so far as it is ancillary to the execution of that contract, I do not think it has any legal existence whatever.'

These observations could be regarded as emphasising the solidarity of the arbitration clause with the main contract, but Lord Ivory does appear to recognise the arbitration clause as a distinct, even if subordinate, contract, and the judgment could be interpreted as meaning no more than that the arbitration clause had terminated with the main contract because, being merely executorial, this was required by its own terms.

9.11. In the following year the court decided the case of *Robertson* v. *Robertson's Trustees*,[11] which concerned articles of roup containing a clause submitting questions between exposers and offerers, or between offerers, to arbitration, but the decision appears — there are no detailed reasons — to have turned upon whether an arbiter could be given power to grant a decree of reduction of a deed.

9.12. More to the point is *Ransohoff and Wissler* v. *Burrell*.[12] Here Ransohoffs raised an action for damages for breach of a contract for the delivery of a quantity of sugar. The contract note, signed by brokers on behalf of Ransohoffs, contained an arbitration clause. The defenders pleaded that there was no contract with the pursuers because the latter had not themselves signed certain confirmation slips as provided for in the contract. Ransohoffs then moved that their action should be sisted pending arbitration, but the sheriff substitute rejected their plea and, having found that there was no contract, dismissed the action. This judgment was upheld by the Court of Session. Lord Justice-Clerk MacDonald said[13] —

'If there is a contract ... then all disputes under it are ... referred to the association, but if there is no binding contract, then there can be no reference of disputes under it. What they [the pursuers] found on as a contract confers no rights on them as principals, they not having signed the same, or the confirmation slip.'

[11] (1860) 22 D. 1145.
[12] (1897) 25 R. 284.
[13] At 289–90.

Lord Moncreiff agreed, and remarked[14] that —

'one who alleges that he is not a party to the contract is not bound to submit the question whether he is a party to it to a referee to whom *ex hypothesi* he has never agreed to submit any dispute. In short, the reference clause does not come into operation until the existence of a contractual relation is either admitted or established by a Court of Law.'

This decision is clear authority for the uncontroversial proposition that a question whether there has ever been a contractual tie of any kind between the parties cannot be required to be submitted to arbitration which itself has never been agreed to. The *dicta* go further, however, and contain a suggestion, which is strictly *obiter*, that where there is a principal contract but it is alleged to be legally void, a dispute over whether it is indeed void cannot be governed by an arbitration clause attached to that contract. This proposition is consistent with observations of Viscount Simon and Lord Macmillan in *Heyman* v. *Darwins*,[15] an English appeal to the House of Lords, but it is highly controversial,[16] and should therefore not be accepted too readily as being the law of Scotland.

9.13.   There are two further Scottish decisions containing *dicta* supporting the 'solidarity' view. In the first, *Thomson's Trustees* v. *The Accident Insurance Co. Ltd.*,[17] the arbitration clause in an insurance policy provided that if any dispute arose respecting the liability of the company to make compensation or as to the amount to be paid, or as to the liability of the company to make any payment at all, the matter should be referred to arbitration. It was also provided — in a type of clause developed in England known as a 'Scott v. Avery clause'[18] — that no action might be brought until the liability of the company had been ascertained by arbitrators. The pursuers raised an action for payment of £1000 which they alleged was due under the policy. The defenders averred on the merits that as certain statements in the proposal had been untrue they should be assoilzied, but also pleaded that the case should be

---

[14] At 297.
[15] [1942] 1 All E.R. (H.L. (E)) 337 at 343–5.
[16] Sanders, *Aut. cl. comp.*, 34–7.
[17] (1898) 6 S.L.T. 180 (O.H.).
[18] Because of its use there to circumvent a rule of English law, enunciated in a case of that name reported at (1856) 25 L.J. Ex. 308, that parties cannot agree to oust the jurisdiction of the courts: see Russell, *Arb.* 1982, 199.

sisted pending arbitration. Arbitration was denied. Lord Pearson remarked that though arbitration was clearly a condition precedent to suing on the policy as regards all matters falling within the scope of the clause, a dispute in which a party averred that the policy was void was not covered. He went on —

'It might be that the parties to a contract containing a clause of reference could so frame it as to submit the original validity of the contract to the decision of the arbiter. But that would be an independent and collateral contract to refer a question antecedent to the policy; and . . . it would require express words or a plain implication to extend an arbiter's power so far as to enable him to pronounce on the original validity of the contract of which his reference clause formed part.'

Lord Pearson's actual decision avoids the question of severability by finding that the arbitration clause did not cover the dispute presented, and his remarks do not altogether rule out the possibility of an autonomous arbitration clause, but the thrust of his remarks favour the 'solidarity' approach to the problem.

9.14. The case of *Hegarty and Kelly* v. *Cosmopolitan Insurance Corporation Ltd.*[19] also involved an arbitration clause in an insurance policy. In response to an action for damages for breach of contract, the company pleaded that the case should be sisted pending arbitration, and here the plea was successful. The court sisted the action on the ground that though the main contract was alleged to have been broken, it had not been rescinded. Lord Mackenzie however, expressly following *Municipal Council of Johannesburg* v. *D. Stewart & Co.*,[20] said that —

'if one party to a contract is in breach of it as regards a stipulation which goes to the root of the contract, the other party has the option of rescinding the contract. If he does, then the contract with all its clauses goes, and amongst them the clause providing for a reference to arbitration.'

Though the decision in this case upheld the validity and continuing effect of the particular arbitration clause as being annexed to a subsisting contract, the *obiter dicta* are clearly

[19] 1913 S.C. 377.
[20] 1909 S.C. (H.L.) 53. Though this appeal arose out of litigation in the Scottish courts, it was considered that the contract was governed by English law.

unsympathetic to the notion of the autonomy of arbitration clauses generally.

9.15. There are also some *neutral authorities*. The earliest case in Scots law dealing with an ancillary arbitration clause appears to be *Shand* v. *Shand*, decided in 1832.[21] This arose out of a deed of separation between spouses, which included a clause submitting to two advocates the determination of the amount of aliment to be paid by the husband during the separation. Before the arbiters could complete their task, the husband revoked the separation, as he was entitled to do. The arbiters nevertheless proceeded at the instance of the wife to issue a decree arbitral. The husband brought an action of reduction, but this failed, though it was remarked that once the deed of separation had been revoked the practical effect of the decree was very limited. There were no *dicta* indicating support for the opinion that the ancillary arbitration clause was to any extent autonomous, and the submission occurred before the revocation of the main contract, so that the decision[22] is essentially neutral as between the contending opinions.

9.16. Finally, there are *authorities consistent with the 'autonomy' approach*. The earliest — and it is more recent than any of those mentioned as being on the other side — is *Scott* v. *Gerrard*,[23] which involved an action for damages for breach of a building contract to which there was annexed an arbitration clause providing that —

'all disputes and differences whatsoever that may arise between the parties, from the date of the subscription of this contract by the parties, until the whole work shall be fully completed, the last instalment paid to the contractors, and the work taken off their hands, shall be and are hereby referred to the decision of'

a certain person as arbiter. The pursuers argued that as the main contract had, albeit unjustifiably, been rescinded by the defenders, the arbitration clause was no longer binding. The court nevertheless sisted the cause pending arbitration. Lord Dundas remarked,[24]

---

[21] 10 S. 384.
[22] As also *Paterson* v. *United Scottish Herring Drift Insurance Co.* 1927 S.N. 75, 141; *Dryburgh* v. *Caledonian Insurance Co.* 1933 S.N. 85.
[23] 1916 S.C. 793.
[24] At 802.

'The clause . . . seems to me to make it clear that, if the contract is declared at an end . . . it is not thereby ended to all intents and purposes: for the latter part of the clause expressly provides for what is to follow upon such a declaration, and that term of the contract at least must necessarily survive the 'ending' of the contract.'

Though the decision rests on features of the particular arbitration clause, it is difficult to reconcile the remarks of Lord Dundas with those of Lord Mackenzie in *Hegarty*, and indicates that an arbitration clause may, if it is expressed in appropriate terms, continue in effect in spite of the rescission of the main contract. This view was impliedly supported by the House of Lords in *Sanderson* v. *Armour & Co.*,[25] in which the buyers of certain goods had rescinded the main contract and sued for damages. The court upheld the defenders' plea that in view of the width of the arbitration clause which was of a 'universal' rather than a merely executory character the dispute had to be referred to arbitration.

9.17. The question whether the arbitration clause is separable where it is alleged that the main contract has been frustrated was avoided in *James Scott and Sons Ltd.* v. *Del Sel*[26] but has since been considered by a judge in the Outer House in *Charles Mauritzen Ltd.* v. *Baltic Shipping Co.*[27] The pursuers, a firm of merchants in Leith, chartered a ship owned by the defenders to proceed to a port in Spanish territory (the Balearic Islands) and there load a cargo of salt for the Faroes. On the arrival of the ship in the Balearics the port authorities refused to allow her to be loaded without a certificate that she was running in British service. This difficulty was intimated to the defenders' agents, and although the pursuers took the matter up with the Spanish authorities who eventually gave permission to load, the ship sailed without loading before the permission was issued. The pursuers brought an action for damages for breach of contract, and the defenders in reply averred that the contract had been frustrated, and also pleaded that the dispute should go to arbitration. The charterparty contained an arbitration clause which provided that —

'any dispute arising under this charter shall be referred to the arbitration of two persons at London.'

[25] 1922 S.C. (H.L.) 117.
[26] 1923 S.C. (H.L.) 37 per Lord Shand at 42.
[27] 1948 S.C. 646.

The Lord Ordinary sisted the cause pending arbitration, declining to follow the decision of the Judicial Committee of the Privy Council in *Hirji Mulji* v. *Cheong Yue S.S. Co.*,[28] and instead adopting and applying the remarks of Viscount Simon in the English case of *Heyman* v. *Darwins*[29] that —

> 'in a situation where the parties are at one in asserting that they entered into a binding contract, but a difference has arisen between them whether there has been a breach by one side or the other, or whether circumstances have arisen which have discharged one or both parties from further performance, such differences shall be regarded as differences which have arisen "in respect of" or "with regard to" or "under" the contract, and an arbitration clause which uses these, or similar, expressions should be construed accordingly.'

9.18. **Comparative survey**. Given the sparsity of Scots authority it is necessary to have regard to the solutions adopted in other legal systems. It appears that in modern times there has been a growing tendency to favour the independence of the arbitration clause. This is particularly apparent in international commercial arbitration,[30] but it can be observed also in the domestic arbitration laws of many countries.[31] It has for example been noted[32] that in the legal systems of the United States, while —

> 'the arbitration clause, whatever its form and scope, has traditionally been considered an integral part of the commercial contract . . ., there has been a fundamental change in the courts' attitude . . . Federal law seems to be evolving the doctrine . . . under which the arbitration clause is considered an agreement apart from the principal contract.'

Section 4 of the Federal Arbitration Act 1925 provides that a court must order arbitration to proceed once it is satisfied that

> 'the making of the agreement for arbitration or the failure to comply therewith is not in issue.'

[28] [1926] A.C. 497.
[29] [1942] 1 All E.R. (H.L. (E)) 337 at 343–4.
[30] Sanders, *Aut. cl. comp.*, 39–41.
[31] Lalive, P. A., 'L'arbitrage international privé', in 120(I) *Recueil des Cours*, Académie de Droit International, 1967, 574 at 592.
[32] Domke, *Comm. Arb.*, 8.01.

179

This has been interpreted by the Supreme Court[33] to mean that —

'if the claim is fraud in the inducement of the arbitration clause itself— an issue which goes to the "making" of the agreement to arbitrate — the federal court may proceed to adjudicate it. But the statutory language does not permit the federal court to consider claims of fraud in the inducement of the contract generally.'

Where the dispute is over whether any contract — including a contract to have disputes determined by arbitration — exists at all, it is of course recognised that the matter must be determined by a court.[34]

9.19. Not all the states of the USA have followed the federal lead in this matter, but some of the greatest commercial states, such as New York, have done so.[35] The Swedish courts many years ago allowed substantial autonomy to the arbitration clause,[36] and have since reaffirmed this stance.[37] The highest courts in the Netherlands,[38] and the Federal German Republic[39] have adopted a similar view, and the European Convention providing a uniform law of arbitration[40] states in Article 18(2) that —

'a ruling that the contract is invalid shall not entail *ipso jure* the nullity of the arbitration agreement contained in it.'

9.20. In France the position is more complex, for French law distinguishes between international and domestic arbitration. In connection with the former, the supreme civil court, the Cour de Cassation, has held[41] that —

---

[33] *Prima Paint Corporation* v. *Flood and Conklin Manufacturing Co.*, 388 US 395, 18 L.Edn. (2d.) 1770 (1967).
[34] *Kulukundis Shipping Co. SA* v. *Amtorg Trading Corporation*, (1942) 126 Fed. 2d. 978.
[35] Holtzmann, H. M., Report on arbitration in the United States, in *Yearbook on Commercial Arbitration* II, 1977, 123.
[36] *AB Norrköpings Trikåfabrik* v. *AB Per Persson* NJA 1936 521.
[37] *Hermansson* v. *AB Asfaltbeläggningar* NJA 1976 125.
[38] H.R. 27 Dec. 1935, NJ 1936 442.
[39] Bundesgerichtshof 27 Feb. 1970, BGHZ 253, 315.
[40] European Treaty Series, Council of Europe, No. 56. The treaty has not yet been ratified by the United Kingdom.
[41] *Ets. Gosset* v. *Carapelli*, Cass. (Civ) 7 Mai 1963; quoted in Robert and Carbonneau, *Arb.*, II.2–20.

'the arbitration agreement, whether a separate agreement or included in the juridical act to which it refers, always presents, save in exceptional circumstances ... a complete juridical autonomy excluding the possibility of its being affected by the eventual invalidity of this act.'

This rule has however not yet been applied in French domestic arbitration law.[42]

9.21. In England the law still stresses the solidarity of the arbitration clause with the main contract, though not so strongly as it once did. The leading case is *Heyman* v. *Darwins*.[43] Here the facts were that Heyman, alleging that Darwins had repudiated the contract which admittedly had existed between them, rescinded the contract and issued a writ claiming damages. Darwins pleaded that the action should be stayed pending arbitration in terms of an arbitration clause attached to the main contract, to which Heyman replied that as Darwins had repudiated the contract and he had accepted this repudiation, the arbitration clause had been terminated along with the main contract. The House of Lords held that the action should be stayed as requested by the defendants, but the speeches of their Lordships reveal strong support for the view that in general the arbitration clause has to be regarded as part of the main contract.

9.22. Viscount Simon appears to distinguish three main situations, according to whether there is dispute over whether the main contract (1) was ever entered into at all, (2) purported to be entered into but was legally void from the outset, or (3) was originally binding but has since been brought to an end in the sense that one or both parties are discharged from further performance. On the question of whether an arbitration clause remains in force in any of these situations, he said —

'If the dispute is as to whether the contract which contains the clause has ever been entered into at all, that issue cannot go to arbitration under the clause, for the party who denies that he has ever entered into the contract is thereby denying that he ever joined in the submission. Similarly, if one party to the alleged contract is contending that it is void *ab initio*, (because, for

---

[42] Sanders, *Aut. cl. comp.*, 39–41.
[43] [1942] 1 All E.R. (H.L. (E)) 337.

example, the making of such a contract is illegal) the arbitration clause cannot operate, for on this view the clause itself is also void. If, however, the parties are at one in asserting that they entered into a binding contract, but a difference has arisen between them as to whether there has been a breach by one side or the other, or as to whether circumstances have arisen which have discharged one or both parties from further performance, such differences should be regarded as differences which have arisen "in respect of" or "with regard to" or "under" the contract, and an arbitration clause which uses these or similar expressions should be construed accordingly ... I do not agree that an arbitration clause expressed in such terms as above ceases to have any possible application merely because the contract has 'come to an end' as, for example, by frustration. In such cases it is the performance of the contract which has come to an end ... If ... circumstances arise before the performance of the contract is completed which, in the view of one party, bring the contract to an end by frustration ... but the other party does not agree, this is a difference about the applicability of the implied term, and is just as much within the arbitration clause as if it were a difference about an express term of the contract.'

It seems from these remarks, most of which are technically *obiter*, that in English law an arbitration clause remains in force in cases of frustration, supervening impossibility or illegality of performance and rescission following material breach of contract, because here only the *primary* obligations under the main contract have come to an end; the *secondary* obligations, of which the obligation to have disputes determined by arbitration is one, continue in effect. Otherwise, however, the arbitration clause is tainted with the same objections as the main contract.

9.23. The speech of Lord Macmillan is broadly consistent with that of Viscount Simon. He said that —

'if it appears that the dispute is as to whether there has ever been a binding contract between the parties, such a dispute cannot be covered by an arbitration clause in the challenged contract. If there has never been a contract at all, there has never been as part of it an agreement to arbitrate; the greater includes the less. Further, a claim to set aside a contract on such grounds as fraud, duress, or essential error cannot be the subject matter of a reference under an arbitration clause in the contract sought to be set aside. Again, an admittedly binding contract containing a general arbitration clause may stipulate that in certain events the contract shall come to an end. If a question arises whether the contract has for any reason come to an end. I can see no reason why the arbitrator should not decide that question. It is clear, too, that the parties to a contract may agree to bring it to an end to all intents and purposes and to treat it as if it had never existed. In such a case, if there be an arbitration clause in the contract, it perishes with the contract.'

Lord Macmillan here adds allegedly voidable contracts and contracts which the parties have agreed to treat as void from the outset to the cases in which there can be no obligation to have disputes determined by arbitration.

9.24. This reasoning has the appearance of logical rigour, but it possesses this quality only on the assumption that the arbitration clause is an integral part of the main contract. Those who are unwilling to make this assumption remain unconvinced. As Professor Pieter Sanders has argued,[44] one can well imagine that —

'error or fraud [dol] may invalidate only the principal contract. The nullity of the contract due to violation of the rules of public policy [ordre public] will not necessarily affect the arbitration clause either.'

Public policy

9.25. Treating the arbitration clause as an integral part of the main contract has the effect of strengthening the control of the ordinary courts over the determination of disputes. This is not necessarily undesirable, for arbitration may be used as a means of escaping from rigorous application of the law, and a desire to achieve this effect may be shared even by parties otherwise in dispute. Of certain kinds of stock-jobbing transactions in prewar Germany it has been remarked[45] that —

'the frequency of arbitration clauses ... was not accidental: it constituted an organised effort of brokers and affiliated financial

[44] *Aut. cl. comp.*, 34.
[45] Nussbaum A., 'The separability doctrine in American and Foreign Arbitration', 17 *New York Univ. L.Q. Rev.* (1940) 609 at 613.

183

groups to make an adverse law ineffective. That law may have been objectionable, but arbitration is not the proper tool to do away with an undesirable law.'

It is not surprising, therefore, that in England an arbitration clause was held void along with the betting transaction to which it was annexed.[46] Yet taken by itself this approach has a rather haphazard effect. Though it brings more disputes concerning the validity of contracts within the purview of the courts, evidence is wanting that this prevents parties who are united in seeking to avoid the application of a particular law from succeeding in their attempt.

Conclusions

9.26. The brief comparative survey in the preceding paragraphs indicates that during this century the legal systems of other countries have increasingly come to recognise the autonomy of the arbitration clause. Given the sparsity of authority in Scotland it remains open for the courts in this country to do likewise. It must be admitted, however, that the tendency of modern Scots law to follow the lead of English law without further inquiry makes it probable that this will not happen. The law of this country may therefore be summarised as follows:-

(a) Where what purports to be the main contract was allegedly never in fact entered into by the parties, an arbitration clause which was physically part of that contract is of no effect.[47]

(b) Where what purports to be the main contract was apparently agreed to by the parties but is nevertheless alleged to have been legally void from the outset, it is almost certain that the Scottish courts would follow *Heyman* v. *Darwins*[48] and refuse to enforce arbitration under an ancillary clause, though very clear language in the clause might in some cases lead to a different conclusion.[49]

(c) Where the main contract is alleged to be voidable, the probability is scarcely less high that a Scottish court would refuse to enforce an ancillary clause.

(d) Where the main contract has been terminated by frustration or rescission following material breach, then disputes arising out of

---

[46] *Joe Lee Ltd.* v. *Lord Dalmeny* [1927] 1 Ch. 300.
[47] *Ransohoff and Wissler* v. *Burrell* (1897) 25 R. 284.
[48] [1942] 1 All E.R. (H.L. (E)) 337.
[49] *Thomson's Trustees* v. *The Accident Insurance Co. Ltd.*, (1898) 6 S.L.T. 180.

it will be required to be determined by arbitration,[50] assuming of course that the language of the arbitration clause is sufficiently wide.

[50] *Scott* v. *Gerrard* 1916 S.C. 793; *Sanderson* v. *Armour & Co.* 1922 S.C.(HL) 117; *Charles Mauritzen Ltd.* v. *Baltic Shipping Co.* 1948 S.C. 646.

CHAPTER TEN

THE TERMS OF ARBITRATION CONTRACTS: THEIR INTERPRETATION AND EFFECT

Introduction

10.1. Submissions to arbitration are subject to the same basic canons of interpretation as other contracts. Thus for example, in seeking to discover the meaning of an ancillary arbitration clause one must endeavour —

'to discover what was truly the purpose and intention of the parties',[1]

taking ordinary words —

'in their ordinary meaning, if there is nothing in the context or in the rest of the contract to imply the contrary'.[2]

In so doing one must normally look only to the written text itself, for —

'as a general rule it is incompetent to contradict, modify, or explain writings by parole or other extrinsic evidence'.[3]

10.2. As with other contracts, if there is an interpretation which makes sense of a provision in an *ad hoc* submission or in an arbitration clause it should be preferred.[4] There is a special readiness to give a meaning to commercial documents not framed by lawyers but by business people in the course of their affairs,[5] though sometimes an arbitration clause has to be held to be void because it is so impenetrably vague or internally inconsistent that it is impossible to discover what the parties could have intended.[6]

[1] *Pearson* v. *Oswald* (1859) 21 D. 419 at 424–5.
[2] Gloag, *Contract*, 399.
[3] Walkers, *Evidence*, paragraph 240.
[4] *Muir* v. *City of Glasgow Bank* (1879) 6 R. (H.L.) 21.
[5] Walker, *Contracts*, 24.6; for an example see e.g. *United Creameries Co. Ltd.* v. *David T. Boyd & Co.* 1912 S.C. 617.
[6] As in *Lovelock Ltd.* v. *Exportles* [1968] 1 Ll. Rep. 163.

10.3. Where a contract has been framed by a dominant party and the other has little option but to accept the terms offered, ambiguous expressions are construed against the interests of the dominant party.[7] This is known as construction '*contra proferentem*'. The rule can affect the interpretation of standard form contracts (also known as 'contracts of adhesion') and the arbitration clauses which they often contain. Standard form contracts can be divided into two main types.[8] There are first of all —

'those which set out the terms on which mercantile transactions of common occurrence are to be carried out.'

Their terms have normally —

'been settled over the years by negotiation by representatives of the commercial interests involved.'

The *contra proferentem* rule has little application to the dealings of business people using such contracts. There are however also contracts —

'which have been dictated by that party whose bargaining power, either exercised alone or in conjunction with others providing similar goods or services, enables him to say: 'If you want these goods or services at all, these are the only terms on which they are available. Take it or leave it'.

An example of the latter type is a form of contract drafted by a trade association for the use of its members in their dealings with the public. Many of these contain arbitration clauses the terms of which, if they are ambiguous, should normally be construed against the interests of the member of the trade, unless they have been approved by some person or body acting in the interests of the public, such as the Office of Fair Trading.

10.4. Some rules of construction used in the interpretation of submissions do not however appear to have exact counterparts in other fields of law. The task of determining whether a particular issue does or does not fall within the scope of a particular ancillary or *ad hoc* submission has, for the reasons of judicial policy

---

[7] Walker, *Contracts*, 24.12; Stair, *Inst.* IV.42.21.
[8] So, at least, it has been held by the House of Lords in an English appeal: *Schroder Music Publishing Co. Ltd.* v. *Macaulay* [1974] 1 W.L.R. 1308 per Lord Diplock at 1316.

discussed below, given rise to a number of broad categories — those of 'general', 'special' and 'general-special' or 'mixed' submissions, and 'restricted' or 'executorial' and 'ample' arbitration clauses.[9] The effect of these categories is that the scope of a submission or clause is governed by the rules attaching to the category into which it falls.

Legal policy in the interpretation of submissions

10.5. The interpretation of arbitration contracts, far from being merely a matter of 'the rules of grammar and logic' as has been judicially claimed,[10] has been strongly affected by judicial policy concerning the extent to which arbitration should be free from the supervision of the ordinary courts. When arbitration has been unpaid or has concerned itself with types of case which are of little importance or which could not readily be handled by ordinary courts, and when ordinary judges have been overburdened with cases which were readily determinable by arbiters, and the courts have not been jealous of their jurisdiction or fearful that arbitration was being used as a means of escaping from the rules of national positive law, the rules governing the interpretation of submissions have tended to be relatively liberal. To the extent that these conditions have been absent, the courts have tended to interpret submissions in a relatively restrictive manner.

10.6. Most of these conditions existed in Scotland up to the first quarter of the nineteenth century. Up to that time it was considered that, as successive editions of Erskine's Institutes put it,[11]

'submissions, being intended for a most favourable purpose, the amicable composing of differences, ought to receive the most ample interpretation of which the words are capable.'

These words, published in 1773, remained influential until about 1850. The last reported nineteenth century decision on the scope of an arbitration clause to reflect this attitude was that reached by a

[9] Guild, *Arb.* 27, 32.
[10] In *Robertson* v. *Brandes Schönwald & Co.* (1906) 8 F. 815 per Lord McLaren at 821.
[11] IV.3.32.

majority in *Watt and Anderson* v. *Shaw*[12] over the dissenting voice of Lord Fullerton, who subsequently played an important role in changing the approach of the courts towards the construction of arbitration contracts.

10.7. Between about 1850 and 1892 the Court of Session and the House of Lords departed emphatically from what may be described as the 'Erskine' view of the interpretation of arbitration contracts. It is clear that one of the main reasons was what the judges of this period saw as the incapacity of legally unqualified arbiters for dealing with the complex issues of law or mixed fact and law that were often presented to them, especially in disputes arising out of substantial construction contracts. It may also be that the Court of Session was becoming more concerned for its own standing and thus more inclined to assert its own jurisdiction. Faced with the very ancient[13] tradition of official favour towards arbitration, the Court could not go so far as to hold that an agreement to oust its jurisdiction was contrary to public policy or that it had an inherent jurisdiction whether or not to enforce an arbitration agreement. Nevertheless it could and did insist upon strict interpretation of the scope of arbiters' powers, choosing to assume that parties would normally prefer to have recourse to judges rather than arbiters, and restricting lay arbiters where possible to the determination of matters of fact. As Lord Justice Clerk Inglis (as he then was) put it in *Calder* v. *Mackay*,[14] references should be construed

> 'carefully and strictly, because it would be highly inexpedient to allow a reference of value to tradesmen to be converted into a submission of a dispute; yet that is what is attempted to be done here in ... maintaining that these tradesmen were entrusted with the duty of construing this contract — that is, of determining a question of law.'

Referring to the then recent case of *Aberdeen Railway Co.* v. *Blaikie Brothers*,[15] in which the House of Lords had approved a dissenting judgment of Lord Fullerton in the Court of Session[16] to

---

[12] (1849) 11 D. 970.
[13] See paragraphs 2.6–2.8 above.
[14] (1860) 22 D. 741 at 743.
[15] (1852) 15 D. (H.L.) 20, disapproving by implication this aspect of the decision in *Montgomerie* v. *Carrick & Napier* (1848) 10 D. 1387.
[16] (1851) 13 D. 527 at 537ff.

the effect that an arbiter may not award damages unless explicitly empowered by the parties to do so, Lord Justice Clerk Inglis went on to say[17] that this rule had been laid down

'because an arbiter cannot be allowed to oust the jurisdiction of the courts of law, nor can parties be considered as intending to do so, except to the extent that they have expressly specified.'

A category of 'executorial' or 'restricted' arbitration clauses was developed[18] containing those which were thought to be concerned only with questions arising out of and during the performance of work under the contract and which were thought likely to be appropriate for arbiters who were engineers, surveyors or architects. Between such clauses and those of more 'ample' scope an emphatic distinction was drawn,[19] and a presumption stated in favour of holding a clause as 'restricted'.[20] This led to some quite surprising decisions in lower courts. For example, it was held by a sheriff substitute in *Murdoch* v. *Ayr Shipping Co.*[21] that a clause providing simply that

'should any dispute arise between the contracting parties, the same to be settled by arbitration in Glasgow'

was of the restricted type and thus did not cover questions arising after the termination of the contract works.

10.8.   The policy of the court dominated by Inglis from 1858 to 1891 first as Lord Justice Clerk and later as Lord President has had a deep and lasting effect on the interpretation of arbitration clauses in Scots law, the more so because this was also the period of the consolidation of the doctrine of binding precedent,[22] and because, from about the turn of the century, the flow of litigation concerning arbitration dwindled to a trickle due to the centralisation of mercantile and industrial management in south Britain and the establishment of London as one of the main centres of arbitral expertise in the world. The main canons of interpretation were laid down — usually though not always with restrictive effect — in a series of fourteen cases between 1852 and

---

[17] At 744.
[18] *Pearson* v. *Oswald* (1859) 21 D. 419 per L. P. McNeill at 429.
[19] *Beattie* v. *MacGregor* (1883) 10 R. 1094 per L. J. C. Inglis at 1096.
[20] Beattie (*supra*) per Lord Shand at 1097.
[21] (1892) 8 Sh. Ct. Rep. 193.
[22] Smith T. B., *Doctrines of Judicial Precedent in Scots Law*, London, 1952, 10–17.

1889.[23] In eight of these[24] Inglis delivered the leading judgment. Since then it has been very difficult for the Court to retreat from what may be called the 'Inglis policy' and to develop rules more suited to an age when lay arbiters are generally very knowledgeable about the law, or at least those aspects of the law relating to the practice of their own trades and professions.

10.9. There were nevertheless some signs that during the first quarter of the twentieth century the Scottish courts retreated slightly from the position taken up by Inglis in the nineteenth. This retreat seems to have been most marked during the period 1905-1929 when Lord Dunedin, first as Lord President and then as a Lord of Appeal in the House of Lords, was the outstanding intellectual figure among the Scottish judiciary — 'the greatest master of the principles of Scots law in our time'.[25] Lord Shand's suggestion in *Beattie*[26] that there is a presumption that arbitration clauses are of the restricted type was impliedly disapproved in *McCosh* v. *Moore*,[27] and the principle that the Scottish courts, unlike those in England, have no ultimate discretion whether or not to enforce a valid and subsisting arbitration clause was very strongly reaffirmed in two cases in which Lord Dunedin gave the leading judgment.[28] Most striking of all was the difference between the interpretations given by Inglis and Dunedin respectively to the arbitration clauses concerned in the cases of *McCord* v. *Adams*[29] and *North British Railway Co.* v. *Newburgh & North Fife Railway Co.*[30] In the former, the clause provided that —

[23] *Lauder* v. *Wingate* (1852) 14 D. 633; *Aberdeen Railway Co.* v. *Blaikie Brothers* (1852) 15 D. (H.L.) 20; *Pearson* v. *Oswald* (1859) 21 D. 419; *Calder* v. *Mackay* (1860) 22 D. 741; *McCord* v. *Adams* (1861) 24 D. 75; *Mungle* v. *Young* (1872) 10 M. 901; *Kirkwood* v. *Morrison* (1877) 5 R. 79; *Howden & Co.* v. *Dobie & Co.* (1862) 9 R. 758; *Savile Street Foundry Co.* v. *Rothesay Tramways Co. Ltd.* (1883) 10 R. 821; *Mackay* v. *Parochial Board of Barry* (1883) 10 R. 1046; *Beattie* v. *MacGregor* (1883) 10 R. 1094; *Levy & Co.* v. *Thomson* (1883) 10 R. 1134; *Gerry* v. *Caithness Flagstones Quarrying Co.* (1885) 12 R. 543; *McAlpine* v. *Lanarkshire and Ayrshire Railway Co.* (1889) 17 R. 113.
[24] *Calder*, *McCord*, *Kirkwood*, *Howden & Co.*, *Savile Street Foundry Co.*, *Beattie*, *Levy & Co.*, and *McAlpine*.
[25] *Stewart* v. *L. M. S. Railway* 1943 S.C. (H.L.) 19 per Lord Macmillan at 38.
[26] *Supra* note 19.
[27] (1905) 8 F. 31 per Lord McLaren at 41.
[28] *North British Railway Co.* v. *Newburgh & North Fife Railway Co.* 1911 S.C. 710; *Sanderson* v. *Armour & Co.* 1922 S.C. (H.L.) 117.
[29] *Supra* note 23.
[30] *Supra* note 28.

'should any dispute connected with the contract arise at any time, either previous to the commencement, during the progress, or after the completion of the contract, the same shall be referred to the decision of the architects.'

Lord Justice Clerk Inglis (as he then was) went so far as to deny that this was an arbitration clause at all,[31] while Lord Neaves[32] considered that it was executorial. In the latter case the clause provided that —

'all questions which may arise between the parties hereto in relation to this agreement or to the import or meaning thereof or to the carrying out of the same shall be referred to arbitration.'

This was held by Lord President Dunedin[33] to fall within the 'ample' category. The phrase 'in relation to' occurring in *North British Railway* cannot seriously be said to have in common parlance a wider meaning than 'connected with', the phrase used in *McCord*; and the submission of the 'import or meaning' of the contract in *North British Railway* cannot be regarded as weighing the balance towards the ample category because those words had generally been construed during the Inglis era as requiring the allocation of the clause to the restricted category.[34] Given the eminence of the judges involved in *McCord* and *N.B. Railway*, neither of the decisions can be regarded as merely careless. The only rational explanation for the difference between them is a change in judicial policy.

10.10. The extent of the change must not however be exaggerated. Such is still the authority of Lord President Inglis and the strength in the twentieth century of the doctrine of judicial precedent that the judicial policies enshrined in the decisions of the Inglis court are still generally followed and referred to with deference.[35] Furthermore, most of the conditions which influenced that court still exist. Arguably the only relevant change has been an improvement in the legal knowledge of members of non-legal professions, and it may have been this that influenced the slight retreat by the Dunedin court from the policies of its predecessor.

[31] At 81.
[32] At 83.
[33] At 718.
[34] See e.g. *Pearson v. Oswald* (1859) 21 D. 419 per Lord Ivory at 428.
[35] E.g. in *Crudens v. Tayside Health Board* 1979 S.C. 142 per Lord Allanbridge at 146.

Thus, though the rule laid down in *Blaikie*[36] that an arbiter has no implied power to award damages is widely regarded as inconvenient, and as capable of leading to 'futile proceedings'[37] in which an arbiter determines questions of breach of contract leaving damages to be assessed by the court,[38] it remains settled law[39] and has not been restricted in its effect. The English doctrine of the 'sufficiently close connection',[40] which helps to obviate the inconvenience of separate proceedings before arbiter and court dealing with the same facts but slightly different grounds of claim, has no parallel in Scots law.[41] And the categories of 'restricted' and 'ample' arbitration clauses, with the restrictions they impose on the freedom of judges to discover the intentions of the parties from the language they have used, continue to be fully recognised.

10.11. Though the construction of contractual terms governing the extent of an arbiter's jurisdiction — in other words the scope of a submission — is of particular importance and is therefore given pride of place in this chapter, terms relating to the identification of the parties to the contract, the appointment of an arbiter, the law applicable to arbitration proceedings, the exclusion of the stated case, and conditional arbitration also require consideration.

The scope of submissions

10.12. The language of provisions relating to the scope or extent of an arbiter's jurisdiction is extremely varied. To assist them in the task of consistent interpretation in line with current judicial policy the courts have established a number of categories to which submissions can be assigned. A submission is interpreted in the

---

[36] *Supra* note 23.
[37] *Gilmour* v. *Drysdale* (*No. 2*) (1905) 13 S.L.T. 505 per Lord Salvesen at 506.
[38] As occurred in *Sanderson* v. *Armour & Co.* 1922 S.C. (H.L.) 117.
[39] *Mackay & Son* v. *Police Commissioners of Leven* (1893) 20 R. 1093 per Lord Adam at 1100; *Gilmour* v. *Drysdale* (*No. 2*) 1905 13 S.L.T. 505; *North British Railway Co.* (*supra* note 28); *Scott & Sons* v. *Del Sel* 1922 S.C. 592 per Lord Ormidale at 602, affd. 1923 S.C. (H.L.) 37.
[40] *Woolf* v. *Collis Removal Service* [1947] 2 All E.R. 260 per Asquith L.J. at 263; *Government of Gibraltar* v. *Kenney* [1956] 2 Q.B. 410 at 422–3; *Astro Vencedor S.A.* v. *Mabanaft* (*The 'Damianos'*) [1971] 2 Q.B. 588.
[41] The decisions in *Governors of Daniel Stewart's Hospital* v. *Waddell* (1890) 17 R. 1072 and *Dewar* v. *Hallpenny* (1898) 6 S.L.T. 30 do not go far enough to have this effect.

first instance according to the rules relating to the relevant category, and only then —

'according to its language and in the light of the circumstances in which it is made.'[42]

10.13. **Ad hoc submissions**. The oldest classification of submissions, established long before ancillary arbitration clauses became common, divides them into 'special', 'general', and 'mixed' or (inelegantly) 'general-special'.[43] Some writers have recognised only the first two of these categories,[44] but the threefold classification is more widely accepted.[45] It is generally applied to *ad hoc* contracts and implementing deeds of submission, rather than ancillary submissions. Probably the categories owe their application in this context to a perceived likeness between *ad hoc* submissions and mandates, for the latter are also regarded as being either special or general.[46]

10.14. A '*special*' submission is one in which the jurisdiction of the arbiter is limited to one or more specific issues.[47] The arbiter is obliged not to go beyond the precise matters specified,[48] though all of them must of course be fully exhausted.

10.15. A '*general*' submission[49] has been described by J. M. Bell[50] as one which —

'purports in the following, or some similar, terms, to submit to the arbiter's judgment "all demands, claims, and disputes, questions and differences, depending and subsisting between the parties, upon any account, occasion, or transaction whatsoever." '

A number of rules of interpretation have been applied to general

---

[42] *Charles Mauritzen Ltd.* v. *Baltic Shipping Co.* 1948 S.C. 646 at 650.

[43] *Lovat* v. *Fraser of Phopachy* June 22 1738, Mor. 625.

[44] See e.g. Bankton, *Inst.* I.23.7.

[45] See e.g. Bell J. M., *Arb.*, paragraph 101; Irons, *Arb.*, 128–32; Guild, *Arb.* 27–30; Weir, *Arb.*, 26–8.

[46] Stair, *Inst.*, I.12.11.

[47] Bell J. M., *Arb.* paragraph 102; *Crudens* v. *Tayside Health Board* 1979 S.C. 142 per Lord Kissen at 154. Styles may be found in Halliday, *Conveyancing*, Vol. I, 14.37–8.

[48] *McEwan* v. *Middleton* (1866) 5 M. 159 per L. J .C. Inglis at 163.

[49] Styles may be found in Halliday, *Conveyancing*, Vol. I, 14.36, 14.39.

[50] *Arb.* paragraph 103.

submissions, with the general purpose of ensuring that they are not —

'so stretched as to include rights that cannot be presumed to have fallen under the view of the submitters.'[51]

First, they are said to cover only those questions which at the time of the contract were being actively pursued between the parties. They therefore do not include either disputes which have arisen since the date of the contract[52] or disputes which have long been dormant.[53] Second, they probably do not include questions of heritable right. There is some conflict of authority on this point, the greater weight being on the side of this more restrictive opinion.[54] This is not surprising, when one considers that most of the authorities are derived from a period between the beginning of the seventeenth and the middle of the eighteenth centuries, when heritable property was the principal source of social and economic power, and disputes concerning it were legally among the most complex to come before the Court of Session, which regarded itself as especially competent to deal with them. Today, when heritable property is of relatively less importance, and when equally complex disputes may arise out of commercial contracts, the rule is an anachronism.

10.16.   The use of general words in an *ad hoc* submission may make it very difficult for an arbiter or a court to determine when the submission has been exhausted. The courts have been willing, as an exception from the normal rule, to entertain extrinsic evidence to explain the scope of a general submission,[55] but arbiters may find it helpful to follow the suggestion of J. M. Bell[56] that a distinct and agreed statement should be placed on record specifying the whole matters that are to be determined by the award.

---

[51] Erskine, *Inst.*, IV.3.32.

[52] *Mackenzie* v. *Calder* June 11 1751, Mor. Appx. (Elchies) Arb. 9. The rule is probably derived from civil law, on which see e.g. Voet, *Comm.* IV.8.18.

[53] *Hood* v. *Baillie* (1832) 11 S. 207 at 209.

[54] The authorities are not unanimous. In favour of the more restricted view are Bankton, *Inst.* I.23.7.; *Paterson* v. *Laird of Forret*, 4 Mar. 1612, Mor. 5064; *Maxwell* v. *Maxwell* 27 Feb. 1624, I Bro. Supp. 15 (Durie): in favour of the more liberal view is *Kincaid* v. *Aitkenhead* 15 Dec. 1631, Mor. 5064. Erskine, *Inst.* IV.3.32 is equivocal.

[55] *Maxwell* v. *Maxwell* 27 Feb 1624, I Bro. Supp. 15 (Durie); *Steele* v. *Steele* 22 June 1809 F.C.; *James Finlay & Co.* v. *Campbell* (1834) 12 S. 792.

[56] *Arb.*, paragraph 108.

10.17. A '*mixed*' or '*general-special*' submission[57] has been described by J. M. Bell[58] as one —

'in which there is a general clause, submitting all disputes between the parties, coupled with a particular specification of some subject or subjects of dispute which are precisely set forth'.

Here the general clause is construed as covering only such matters as are of the same kind ('*ejusdem generis*') as the matters particularly specified.[59] It is of no significance whether the general words precede or follow the specification of particular issues.

10.18. **Ancillary submissions.** The construction of arbitration clauses annexed to other contracts is based on a presumption that the parties must have intended them to require only matters relating to the main contract to be determined by arbitration, even if their language, taken out of context, might indicate a wider interpretation.[60] This is sometimes[61] known as construction '*secundum subjectam materiem*'. Nineteenth century authority[62] has also bequeathed to the modern law a twofold classification of ancillary submissions into —

(a) 'restricted' or 'executorial'; and
(b) 'ample' or 'universal',

and this classification has not since been departed from.[63] It seems to have been generally assumed that all ancillary submissions are assignable to one or other of these categories,[64] but it is arguable that arbitration clauses in mercantile contracts[65] and perhaps also in partnership agreements[66] may not be treated as rigidly as those which appear in construction contracts.

---

[57] Of which a style may be found in Halliday, *Conveyancing*, Vol. I, 14.35.
[58] *Arb.* paragraph 117.
[59] Erskine, *Inst.* III.4.9.
[60] *Graham v. Pollock and Gibson* (1848) 10 D. 646.
[61] As in Guild, *Arb.*, 30.
[62] *Beattie v. MacGregor* (1993) 10 R. 1094 per L.P. Inglis at 1096.
[63] *Sanderson v.Armour & Co.*, 1922 S.C.(H.L.) 117 per Lord Dunedin at 125.
[64] Irons, *Arb.*, 75–6; Guild, *Arb.*, 32.
[65] *Charles Mauritzen & Co. Ltd. v. Baltic Shipping Co.* 1948 S.C. 646.
[66] The authorities here appear to ignore the two categories mentioned: see e.g. *Landale v. Goodall* (1879) 16 S.L.R. 434; *Gerry v. Caithness Flagstone Quarrying Co.* (1885) 12 R. 543; *Jones Trustees v. Smith* (1893) 1 S.L.T. 45; *Gilmour v. Drysdale* (1905) 13 S.L.T. 433, 505; *Muir v. Muir* (1906) 8 F. 365; *MacGregor v.*

10.19. In those types of contracts in which this twofold system of classification is appropriate, the category to which an ancillary submission belongs is determined —

'on a sound construction of the whole deed, and the circumstances in which it was executed, sometimes even of the position and profession of the arbiters named'.[67]

There is now no presumption that a clause is of the restricted variety.[68] Contracts which fall into the first category are so construed that only matters arising during the execution of the work required to be done under the main contract and which require to be quickly disposed of to prevent delay will be regarded as required to be determined by arbitration.[69] Those which fall into the second category are not thus restricted,[70] but they are not normally interpreted as carrying claims or questions not governed by the terms of the contract,[71] though a phrase such as 'all disputes arising out of the contract' has been held to include questions of law regarding the construction of the contract.[72] There have been cases in which claims not based on the main contract have been held within the scope of a very broad arbitration clause,[73] and on occasion the concept of what is a claim based on the contract has been stretched quite far.[74] Nevertheless, no doctrine equivalent to

---

Leith & Granton Boatmen's Association 1916 2 S.L.T. 69, 1917 1 S.L.T. 13; *Hackston* v. *Hackston* 1956 S.L.T. (Notes) 38; *Fleming's Trustees* v. *Henderson* 1962 S.L.T. 401.

[67] *Caledonian Railway Co.* v. *Greenock & Wemyss Bay Railway Co.* (1872) 10 M. 892 per Lord Kinloch at 898.

[68] *McCosh* v. *Moore* (1905) 8 F. 31 per Lord McLaren at 41.

[69] *Pearson* v.*Oswald* (1859) 21 D. 419 per L. P. McNeill at 425; *Mungle* v. *Young* (1872) 10 M. 901 per Lord Kinloch at 906; *Kirkwood* v. *Morrison* (1877) 5 R. 79 per L. P. Inglis at 81; *Savile Street Foundry Co. Ltd.* v. *Rothesay Tramways Co. Ltd.* (1883) 10 R. 821 per L. P. Inglis at 823.

[70] *Mackay* v. *Parochial Board of Barry* (1883) 10 R. 1046; *Levy & Co.* v. *Thomson* (1883) 10 R. 1134; *Wright* v. *Greenock and Port Glasgow Tramways Board* (1891) 29 S.L.R. 53; *Sanderson* v. *Armour & Co.* 1922 S.C. (H.L.) 117 per Lord Dunedin at 125; *Scott & Sons Ltd.* v. *Del Sel* 1923 S.C. (H.L.) 37; *Charles Mauritzen Ltd.* v. *Baltic Shipping Co.* 1948 S.C. 646; *Hackston* v. *Hackston* 1956 S.L.T. (Notes) 38.

[71] *Gerry* v. *Caithness Flagstone Quarrying Co.* (1885) 12 R. 543; *Gilmour* v. *Drysdale (No. 2)* (1905) 13 S.L.T. 505.

[72] *North British Railway Co.* v. *Newburgh & North Fife Railway Co.* 1911 S.C. 710.

[73] *Governors of Daniel Stewart's Hospital* v. *Waddell* (1890) 17 R. 1077; *Dewar* v. *Hallpenny* (1898) 6 S.L.T. 30.

[74] As in *Bain* v. *Alliance Assurance Co. Ltd.* 1956 S.L.T. (Sh. Ct.) 2.

the English doctrine of the 'sufficiently close connection'[75] has been developed in Scots law to sweep up incidental claims (for example, those based on the law of delict) which the parties would probably have wished originally to include.

10.20. It is impossible to comment on the meaning of all types of clause that have come before the Scottish courts, let alone all those that might do so. The following observations must be taken with the caution that where the meaning placed upon a phrase by the 'Inglis Court' appears very different from that which would generally be placed upon it today by people in the position or trade of the parties to a contract under discussion, the judicial interpretation should be confined very strictly to its own facts and historical circumstances, and should not be regarded as binding. The object of a court in interpreting a contract must after all be to discover from the words and phrases used what the particular parties concerned must be taken to have meant at the time when they entered into the contract.

(a) A submission of the 'meaning or execution'[76] or the 'true import'[77] or the 'true meaning'[78] or the 'true intent and meaning'[79] of the main contract have been taken to mean that general legal questions, such as arise in claims based on breach of contract, can not be decided by the arbiter unless other expressions in the clause provide a clear indication that this is so. In two cases[80] the scope of the submission was indicated only by words such as those quoted above, and there the submission was held to be of the restricted variety, so that the arbiter had it in his power to construe the contract only for the purposes of giving effect to its execution.

(b) Phrases of generality, such as 'any matter arising thereout or connected therewith' occurring after or before references to 'the meaning of the plans' or 'the manner in which the work is to be executed' have been construed as not extending the scope of the submission beyond matters which are of the same kind (*'ejusdem generis'*) as those indicated in the more specific provisions of the

[75] *Woolf* v. *Collis Removal Service* [1947] 2 All E.R. 260 per Asquith L.J. at 263; *Government of Gibraltar* v. *Kenney* [1956] 2 Q.B. 410 at 422–3; *Astro Vencedor S.A.* v. *Mabanaft (The 'Damianos')* [1971] 2 Q.B. 588.

[76] *Pearson* v. *Oswald* (1859) 21 D. 419.

[77] *Mungle* v. *Young* (1872) 10 M. 901.

[78] *Beattie* v. *MacGregor* (1883) 10 R. 1094.

[79] *Savile Street Foundry Co. Ltd.* v. *Rothesay Tramways Co. Ltd.* (1883) 10 R. 821.

[80] *Pearson* and *Mungle.*

clause, so that the arbiter's jurisdiction remains confined to matters connected with the execution of the contract and does not extend to general claims of breach of contract.[81]

(c) Where a clause nominates as arbiter a person who either is actually in charge of the execution of the contract or is of the same profession as the person who is or might be in charge of the work the balance is weighted in favour of classifying the clause as being of the restricted variety.[82]

(d) If it is desired to take an arbitration clause clearly into the ample category, it is appropriate expressly to give the arbiter power to determine questions of legal obligation, as was done in *Levy & Co.* v. *Thomson*[83] and *Mackay* v. *Parochial Board of Barry*.[84] Alternatively, words of generality may be included without any specific mention of the execution of the contract, or with an emphasis upon the extension of the arbiter's jurisdiction beyond the completion of the contract.[85]

10.21.   A question whether a proposed new business venture is within the terms of a relevant *partnership agreement* has been accepted[86] as within the scope of an ancillary submission of —

'any disputes that may arise between the partners ... in any way relating hereto'

and the arbitrability under an arbitration clause of disputes over balances struck at dissolution,[87] including claims of incorrect[88] or fraudulent[89] preparation of accounts has been readily upheld. There is nevertheless a tendency to construe general words in arbitration clauses in partnership agreements as excluding questions not relating to the partnership or the business it carried on[90] or to the parties in their capacities as partners.[91] Where a partnership deed contained a clause providing that

[81] *Beattie* v. *MacGregor* (1883) 10 R. 1094.
[82] *McCord* v. *Adams* (1861) 24 D. 75 per L.P. Inglis at 82; *McAlpine* v. *Lanarkshire and Ayrshire Railway Co.* (1889) 17 R. 113.
[83] (1883) 10 R. 1134.
[84] (1883) 10 R. 1046; see also *Hackston* v. *Hackston* 1956 S.L.T. (Notes) 38.
[85] As in *Scott* v. *Gerrard* 1916 S.C. 793.
[86] *Muir* v. *Muir* (1906) 8 F. 365.
[87] *Gilmour* v. *Drysdale (No. 1)* (1905) 13 S.L.T. 433.
[88] *Fleming's Trustees* v. *Henderson* 1962 S.L.T. 401.
[89] *Jones' Trustees* v. *Smith* (1893) 1 S.L.T. 45.
[90] *Gilmour* v. *Drysdale (No. 2)* (1905) 13 S.L.T. 505.
[91] *Gerry* v. *Caithness Flagstone Quarrying Co.* (1885) 12 R. 543.

'if any differences shall arise between the partners, or in the event of death or bankruptcy between the surviving and solvent partner and the representatives or creditors of the other, all such are hereby submitted to'

two arbiters, this was held not to cover a claim for damages based on an alleged collusive action by a partner and a creditor to bring the business to an end by sequestration.[92] A reluctance to allow parties to place before an arbiter a disagreement on partnership policy, such as the replacement of an employee, is also apparent.[93]

10.22. A general submission of 'all disputes' is insufficient to carry the submission of a question whether a partnership should be dissolved, or of a question relating to competition between the parties after dissolution. In one case[94] an attempt was made to have a petition, brought under section 35(f) of the Partnership Act 1890 and under common law for the dissolution of a partnership, sisted pending arbitration. The plea for a sist was based on a clause in the partnership agreement submitting 'any question, dispute or difference between the parties arising out of this agreement or relating to the partnership business' to the decision of a named arbiter. The court held that the clause was not wide enough to confer jurisdiction on an arbiter to dissolve the partnership on the ground that dissolution was 'just and equitable'. In another case a partnership had been dissolved, and some of the former partners continued the business together while another sought to set up on his own. A dispute then arose over whether the latter was entitled to compete with the new partnership. This was held not to be a matter 'relating to' the partnership or the meaning of the contract of copartnery or the rights and liabilities arising therefrom.[95] However, a question whether or not a partnership should be dissolved by reason of the alleged violation by one of the partners of his obligations under the contract was held to be within a clause submitting disputes —

'... as to the meaning of these presents or [the partners'] rights or liabilities hereunder or in the winding up of the partnership

[92] *Lauder* v. *Wingate* (1852) 14 D. 633.
[93] *Landale* v. *Goodall* (1879) 16 S.L.R. 434.
[94] *Roxburgh* v. *Dinardo* 1981 S.L.T. 291.
[95] *MacGregor* v. *Leith and Granton Boatmen's Association* 1916 2 S.L.T. 69, 1917 1 S.L.T. 13.

or in any other matter, thing or claim relating to or arising out of the partnership or the affairs thereof'.

It was considered that it could be referred to an arbiter notwithstanding the power of the court under section 35 of the Partnership Act 1890 to order dissolution.[96]

10.23. In clauses annexed to *other mercantile contracts* the main general question of interpretation often concerns whether the parties have agreed to submit to arbitration questions of the quality or value of goods, or some other matter which can be determined mainly by appraisal, or have submitted wider questions such as liability for breach of contract. It would seem that the courts are in modern times willing to adopt a relatively liberal approach in such cases.[97]

10.24. The *relationship* of an *ancillary clause with an implementing deed* deserves to be mentioned in this context. The submitters may, by a deed of submission executed in implementation of a contract of submission contained in an arbitration clause, agree to include in the deed matters which are not required by the clause to be determined by arbitration. If they do so, the deed itself to that extent becomes the contract of submission. It is also possible for them to abandon altogether the contract in the ancillary clause and enter upon a deed which, though it covers matters required by the terms of the clause to be determined by arbitration, does not in any way depend upon it. It has however been emphatically stated[98] that—

'it would require very clear evidence in the deed of submission to convince us that the parties intended thereby to change course completely, to abandon all that had gone before for no explicable or stated reason, and to enter into a completely fresh and independent agreement to refer to arbitration.'

Effect of arbitration agreements

10.25. The main effect of a valid and binding agreement that the issues contained therein shall be determined by arbitration is to

[96] *Hackston* v. *Hackston* 1956 S.L.T. (Notes) 38.
[97] See e.g. *Charles Mauritzen Ltd.* v. *Baltic Shipping Co.* 1948 S.C. 646.
[98] In *Clydebank District Council* v. *Clink* 1977 S.C. 142 at 154.

remove the determination of those matters from the jurisdiction of the ordinary courts. As Lord Dunedin put it in a remark which has become famous,[99]

'The English common law doctrine — eventually swept away by the Arbitration Act of 1889 — that a contract to oust the jurisdiction of the courts was against public policy and invalid, never obtained in Scotland. In the same way, the right which in England pertains to the Court under that Act to apply or not to apply the arbitration clause in its discretion never was the right of the Court in Scotland. If the parties have contracted to arbitrate, to arbitration they must go.'

This does not mean that the jurisdiction of the court is wholly ousted. It merely —

'deprives the Court of jurisdiction to inquire into the merits of the case, while it leaves the court free to entertain the suit and to pronounce a decree in conformity with the award of the arbiter. Should the arbitration from any cause prove abortive the full jurisdiction of the Court will revive, to the effect of enabling it to hear and determine the action upon its merits.'[100]

Where an arbitration agreement is between a state and a body which is not a state, it is binding upon the state (unless it otherwise provides) for the purposes of 'proceedings in the courts of the United Kingdom which relate to the arbitration',[101] but a decree arbitral cannot be enforced against a state without its consent by such measures as interdict, or order for specific performance or arrestment.[102]

10.26. The scope of the matters on which the submitters are obliged to accept the decision of an arbiter is established expressly or impliedly by their agreement in the contract of submission. If that contract is contained in an ancillary arbitration clause, issues which have actually arisen are normally specified and identified in an implementing deed of submission. If the arbiter has contracted to determine the issues in the implementing deed, the submitters will not for their part be able to compel him or her to decide any

[99] *Sanderson* v. *Armour & Co.* 1922 S.C. (H.L.) 117 at 126.
[100] *Hamlyn & Co.* v. *Talisker Distillery Co.* (1894) 21 R. (H.L.) 21 per Lord Watson at 25, applied in *Motordrift A/S* v. *Trachem Co.* (O.H.) 1982 S.L.T. 127.
[101] State Immunity Act 1978 s. 9.
[102] 1978 Act s. 13.

others, even if they have agreed between themselves that additional matters come within the original arbitration clause, for as Lord McLaren said in *Miller & Son* v. *Oliver & Boyd*,[103]

'No arbitration can be enlarged without the consent of the arbitrator [*sic*]'.

The extension of the scope of the issues to be determined by a particular arbiter thus requires tripartite consent — in other words the express or implied agreement of the arbiter as well as that of the submitters.

Other provisions

10.27. **Relating to the parties.** In modern times changes of company name and alterations to the corporate structure of groups of companies have become commonplace. For the purposes of arbitration proceedings there is an obvious difference between a mere change of name and a change of legal personality. Where a change of corporate name occurs there is no change in the rights or obligations of the company concerned, though if proceedings are taking place a minute should be lodged intimating the change, for the arbiter probably has no jurisdiction to give a different designation to a party in the award or other document from that which that party had in the originating documents.[104] Where there has been a change of legal personality caused, for example, by a change in the corporate structure of the enterprise, the new company is not a party to the submission unless there has been an assignation of the old company's rights and obligations. It is proper for a joint minute to be lodged in the arbitration by the old and new companies and their opponent narrating the assignation and agreeing that the new company should be sisted as a party in place of the old.

10.28. Provision may be made in a submission for the sisting of a successor to a deceased party and rights under a submission which is ancillary to another contract or disposition of property may be assigned. Thus the obligations under an arbitration clause in a

[103] (1906) 8 F. 390 at 404.
[104] So it has been held in England, at least: *Phoenician Express SARL* v. *Garware Shipping Corporation Ltd.*, The Times, Nov. 23rd 1983, (Q.B.D.).

lease[105] or a feu charter[106] transmit with the lease or feu concerned. A person may become entitled, as the judicial assignee of rights under a contract, to replace the cedent as a party to arbitration proceedings connected with that contract[107]; and the assignation to a third party of a contractor's rights and obligations in relation to an employer under a construction contract normally carries with it any rights and obligations under any arbitration clause annexed thereto.[108] The rationale appears to be the solidarity of the arbitration clause with the main contract. As Lord Mackenzie said in *Montgomerie v. Carrick & Napier*,[109]

> 'the condition of a lease is binding upon singular successors, and a clause of this sort [the arbitration clause] is just such a condition of the lease, and as binding as any other condition.'

Whether or not that rationale is objectively sound, there is no reason to believe that the decisions influenced thereby would not be followed.

10.29.   It appears that the transmission of obligations under an arbitration clause is not restricted to those relating to the execution of a contract. A suggestion by Lord Fullerton, whose attitude to arbitration foreshadowed that of Lord President Inglis, that it was so restricted,[110] did not receive majority support at the time and the opportunity for asserting such a restriction does not seem to have arisen again until well after the Inglis era (1858–91) was over, when it was not taken.[111]

10.30.   **Multilateral disputes** often arise out of construction works involving a number of contractors and the transmission through several hands of the property in goods while in transit or in store, and it is often convenient at least to some of the parties concerned to draw together the arbitration proceedings that may arise as a result. This cannot be done in a construction project merely by providing in the contract of each of the subcontractors

---

[105] *Montgomerie v. Carrick & Napier* (1848) 10 D. 1387.
[106] *Holburn v. Buchanan* (1915) 31 Sh. Ct. Rep. 178.
[107] *Rutherford v. Licences & General Insurance Co. Ltd.* 1934 S.L.T. 31; *Cant v. Eagle Star and British Dominions Insurance Co. Ltd.* 1937 S.L.T. 444.
[108] *Whately v. Ardrossan Harbour Co.* (1893) 1 S.L.T. 382.
[109] *Supra* note 105.
[110] *Montgomerie* (*supra* note 105).
[111] *Rutherford* (*supra* note 107).

that the work is to be executed according to the 'drawings, specifications and general conditions' contained in the main contract, even though those 'specifications and general conditions' include an arbitration clause. It was held in *Goodwins, Jardine and Co. Ltd.* v. *Brand & Son*[112] that the effect of such a provision in a subcontract is merely to make the order of the arbiter in a question between the employer and the main contractor binding in any subsequent question between the main contractor and any subcontractor. Thus, if an arbiter holds in a dispute between employer and main contractor that certain materials are below the standard required by the specifications, a subcontractor cannot be heard to assert that they are satisfactory, though in a question with the main contractor a subcontractor may allege (for example) that the offending materials had been tampered with by someone else after having been supplied.

10.31. An attempt to overcome the problem of the unification of disputes arising out of construction works has been made in the 1980 edition of the Scottish Building Contract.[113] Clause 4.2 of this standard form contract provides that —

'If the dispute or difference is substantially the same as or is connected with a dispute or difference between —

4.2.1. the Employer and a Nominated Subcontractor ... or
4.2.2. the Contractor and any Subcontractor,

the Employer and the Contractor hereby agree that such dispute or difference shall be referred to an Arbiter appointed or to be appointed to determine the related dispute or difference: Provided that either party may require the appointment of a different Arbiter if he reasonably considers the Arbiter appointed in the related dispute is not suitably qualified to determine the dispute or difference under this Contract.'

The Contract goes on in clause 4.3.5. to enable the Arbiter to —

'award compensation or damages and expenses to or against any of the parties to the arbitration.'

In effect these provisions appear to unify the proceedings in related

---

[112] (1905) 7 F. 995; followed in *Haskins (Shutters) Ltd.* v. *David J. Ogilvie (Builders) Ltd.* 1978 S.L.T. (Sh. Ct.) 64.
[113] Published by the Scottish Building Contract Committee, Edinburgh.

disputes by combining those between the employer and main contractor with any already in progress between either the employer and a nominated subcontractor or the main contractor and any subcontractor. They are fortified by the provision giving the arbiter power to order damages to be paid to any one of the parties by any other.

10.32. A solution to the problem of contracts in a 'string' has been devised by the Grain and Feed Trade Association (GAFTA). The arbitration rules of that body[114] provide that —

'in the event of a contract forming part of a string of contracts which are in all material points identical in terms except as to price, any arbitration for quality and/or condition shall be held between the first seller and the last buyer in the string as though they were contracting parties'

provided that every party against whom arbitration is claimed and who claims to be in a string shall have supplied his or her contracts and all relevant information to the arbiter. If all the parties in the string contract under GAFTA rules and are known to have done so, the handling of disputes is greatly simplified.

10.33. In Scots law the parties to a contract may confer on a third party a right to enforce an obligation under the contract against either or both of them[115] — the so-called '*jus quaesitum tertio*'. This legal power could be of some use in the context of multilateral disputes under contracts all of which were governed by Scots law or a legal system which permitted the granting of similar rights to third parties. For example, a subcontract (or a contract likely to be one of several in a 'string') might provide that the parties thereto conferred on the employer under a building contract or the last buyer in a string of contracts (the third party in this context) a right to have any disputes under it heard and determined by the same arbiter as had been appointed to determine disputes under the main or last contract. This would amount to a unilateral right to demand arbitration, and therefore the validity in this context of the *jus quaesitum tertio* would seem to depend on lack of mutuality in an arbitration agreement being acceptable in Scots law. As is indicated above,[116] this question has not yet been decided in this

---

[114] Art. 5, quoted in Lee, *Int. Comm. Arb.* 366.
[115] Stair, *Inst.*, I.10.5.
[116] Paragraphs 6.22–6.24 above.

country, and all that can be said is that the balance of the argument seems to be in favour of accepting it.

10.34. **Number of arbiters.** There is in Scotland no requirement that there shall be an uneven number of arbiters, since the statute of 1427[117] to this effect has long been in desuetude and thus of no force or effect. It was at one time common practice to provide in submissions for the appointment of two arbiters, one nominated by each party, the risk of deadlock being obviated by the appointment of an oversman. Unless the submission otherwise provides, the arbiters have power in terms of section 4 of the Arbitration (Scotland) Act 1894 to appoint an oversman, but the submitters sometimes make the appointment themselves at the outset. Nowadays the appointment of a single arbiter is said to be more usual than two arbiters with an oversman. A tribunal of three arbiters is said to be relatively uncommon in Scotland, though it is frequent in continental countries.

10.35. It is highly desirable that the number of arbiters to be appointed is made clear in the contract of submission, for if this is not done and no term can be implied from custom of trade[118] or otherwise the court will be unable to break a deadlock by making use of its powers of appointment under sections 2 and 3 of the 1894 Act.[119]

10.36. **Nomination of arbiters.** Though in an *ad hoc* submission the arbiter is usually named, nomination is unusual and often inconvenient in an ancillary submission. Failure to make a nomination in the contract does not render it void because of section 1 of the 1948 Act, but for practical reasons provision should be made for nomination and appointment by a third party should the parties fail to agree or one of them fail to nominate as envisaged in the contract.

10.37. It is (regrettably) permissible in Scots law for an agreement to nominate as arbiter one of the parties[120] or his or her

---

[117] *APS* c. 6 (Vol. II.14). Reference to an uneven number of arbiters was in civil and canon law considered undesirable, but it did not render the submission void: Julien, *Ev. Hist.* 214–15.
[118] *Douglas & Co.* v. *Stiven* (1900) 2 F. 575.
[119] *McMillan and Son* v. *Rowan and Co.* (1903) 5 F. 317.
[120] *Buchan* v. *Melville* (1902) 4 F. 620.

agent,[121] and there is no power in a court — as there would seem to be in England under section 24 of the Arbitration Act 1950[122] — to substitute an independent person.

10.38.   The practice of appointing a party or his or her agent has apparently not wholly died out.[123] Under a form of contract[124] used by departments of Her Majesty's Government, as well as by some local authorities, the employing body is designated arbiter in the certain kinds of dispute, namely those dealing with allegations of bribery and corruption[125] and questions as to the contractor's right to a certificate.[126] These provisions are valid in Scots law except in the unlikely event that circumstances could be proved amounting to extortion.

10.39.   In view of the absence of any power in a Scottish court to revoke such an appointment, it is possible that an aggrieved contractor might have an indirect remedy by means of a petition to the European Commission of Human Rights under Article 25 of the European Convention on Human Rights.[127] Article 6 of that Convention provides that —

'In the determination of his civil rights and obligations ... everyone is entitled to a fair and public hearing within a reasonable time by an independent and impartial tribunal established by law.'

It is suggested that there is a breach of this Article of the Convention where a government department or other public body refuses to enter into contracts of a certain type except in terms of a standard form under which that department or body itself is appointed judge of certain questions which may arise under the contract. The rights of employees of public bodies under their contracts of employment have (in England at least) been held to be 'civil rights and obligations',[128] and the same could equally be said

---

[121] *Crawford Brothers* v. *Commissioners of Northern Light-houses* 1925 S.C. (H.L.) 22.
[122] Parris J., *Arbitration: Principles and Practice*, London, 1983, 52.
[123] *Ibid.*
[124] GC/Works/1.
[125] Clause 55(3).
[126] Clause 42(3).
[127] The text may be found in Brownlie I (ed.), *Basic Documents on Human Rights*, 2nd edn. Oxford, 1981, 249.
[128] *R* v. *East Berkshire Health Authority, ex parte Walsh* [1984] I.R.L.R. 278.

of the rights of contractors under public works contracts, and it could hardly be maintained that the officials of a public body determining a dispute involving that body in terms of a contract of adhesion constitute an 'independent and impartial tribunal established by law'.

10.40. **Competence-competence**. In Scots law, the scope of the matters which the parties have agreed shall be determined by arbitration cannot be determined, though it may be considered, by the arbiter.[129] As Lord Kinloch said, delivering the decision of a court of seven judges in *Caledonian Railway Co. v. Greenock and Wemyss Bay Railway Co.*[130] —

'Each arbiter will, of course, proceed in the submission according to his own best views. But his decision on this point will not be binding upon the parties. To hold that an arbiter was entitled not merely to decide the question actually submitted to him, but conclusively to determine what questions were within his determination — in other words, to determine the extent of his own jurisdiction — would be as unwarrantable in principle as I think it would be inexpedient in practice.'

Probably the submitters cannot by agreement give an arbiter power to determine his or her own jurisdiction. The Scottish courts have not yet had to decide this point directly, but in view of the language of Lord Kinloch here quoted it seems almost certain that like the English courts[131] they would refuse to uphold such an agreement. In view of the absence of any appeal against a Scottish decree arbitral and the difficulties which the law places in the way of a party seeking to attack such a decree by way of an action of reduction, Lord Kinloch's view seems reasonable,[132] though a

[129] It appears that not all legal systems take this view: see e.g. Robert and Carbonneau, *Arb.*, 3.01, commenting on Article 1466 of the 1981 French Code of Civil Procedure. N.B. however that under Articles 1482-3 of the Code of Civil procedure French law makes provision for an appeal against an award, unless parties have agreed otherwise.
[130] (1872) 10 M. 892 at 898, affd. (1874) 1 R. (H.L.) 8; See also *Mackay and Son v. Police Commissioners of Leven* (1893) 20 R. 1093 per Lord Kinnear at 1103; *McCosh v. Moore* (1905) 8 F. 31 per L.P. Dunedin at 40; *Crudens v. Tayside Health Board* 1979 S.C. 142 at 146.
[131] *Dalmia Dairy Industries v. National Bank of Pakistan* [1978] 2 Ll. Rep. 223 (C.A.).
[132] Bell J. M., *Arb.* paragraph 97.

Federal court in the USA where the grounds of challenge of an award are quite narrow[133] has come to a different view.[134]

10.41. **Power to award damages.** No provisions in an *ad hoc* submission, or in any arbitration clause however ample, will give an arbiter power to award damages unless that power is mentioned expressly. However inconvenient that rule may be, it is clearly the law[135] and practically beyond reform by judicial means. It should be noted that even if an arbiter has been given a general power to award damages, this will not be effective if in a special submission the precise issues put to the arbiter do not include a question of liability for payment of damages.[136]

10.42. **Incorporation of procedural rules.** It is common practice to provide in an arbitration clause for the arbitration proceedings to be conducted in accordance with the rules of a specified trade association or arbitration body. If this is not done expressly an equivalent term may be implied from custom of trade, but for obvious reasons an express provision is preferable.

10.43. **Exclusion of stated case.** Under the Administration of Justice (Scotland) Act 1972 subsection 3(1) an arbiter may be requested by either party or required by the court to state a case for the opinion of the court on any question of law arising in the arbitration, but only 'subject to express provision to the contrary in an agreement to refer to arbitration'. If the submitters wish to deny themselves the power to obtain a stated case they must include a provision to this effect in the arbitration clause if there is one, and in any event in whatever is the original agreement under which they are required to accept the arbiter's decision on the issue in question. If they omit to conclude an agreement to this effect in the original agreement to refer — usually the arbitration clause — they cannot retrieve the position by inserting a provision in an

---

[133] Domke, *Comm. Arb.*, Chapter 34.
[134] *Ibid.* 12.01, citing *Necchi* v. *Necchi Sewing Machine Sales Corp.*, 348 Fed. 2d. 693 at 696 (1965) cert. den. 383 US 909, 15 L. Ed. 2d. 664 (1966).
[135] *Aberdeen Railway Co.* v. *Blaikie Brothers* (1852) 15 D. (H.L.) 20; *Mackay & Son* v. *Police Commissioners of Leven* (1893) 20 R. 1093 per Lord Adam at 1100; *Gilmour* v. *Drysdale (No. 2)* (1905) 13 S.L.T. 505; *North British Railway Co.* v. *Newburgh & North Fife Railway Co.* 1911 S.C. 710; *Scott & Sons* v. *Del Sel* 1922 S.C. 592, affd. 1923 S.C. (H.L.) 37.
[136] *Crudens* v. *Tayside Health Board* 1979 S.C. 142 per Lord Kissen at 154.

implementing deed,[137] though possibly they may do so by amending the original agreement.

10.44. **Conditional arbitration**. The operation of an ancillary arbitration clause may be made subject to a suspensive or resolutive condition. An example of the former is a provision in the rules of an association to the effect that —

> 'any differences between any member and the executive council ... must be submitted to the decision of the arbitration committee, on the condition that both parties bind themselves in writing to agree to the decision of the arbitration committee'.

If a suspensive condition is not satisfied, the arbitration clause is ineffective.[138] It is difficult to see what advantage there might be in having an arbitration clause at all if it is to be hedged about with such a condition.

10.45. Of more practical use is the type of clause which provides that if an arbitration under it is not commenced within a certain time of the occurrence of a stated event (such as the arrival of a ship) it may not be commenced at all, and the parties must seek their remedy in the ordinary courts. The clause may be combined with a provision requiring arbitration as a condition precedent to the enforcement of an obligation under the main contract, so that failure to present a claim timeously to arbitration means that the claim can no longer be presented in any forum whatever. A common form is as follows —

> 'It is further agreed that any claim hereunder must be made in writing and the claimant's arbiter must be appointed within [a specified time after a specified event] and that any claim not so made shall be deemed to be waived and absolutely barred.'

This type of clause has been the subject of considerable litigation in England,[139] where it is commonly known as an 'Atlantic Shipping' clause, from the name of a party to an early case in which it was considered,[140] but it does not appear to have been the subject

[137] *Clydebank District Council* v. *Clink* 1977 S.C. 147.
[138] *Drennan* v. *Associated Ironmoulders of Scotland* 1921 S.C. 151.
[139] English law on this matter is discussed in detail in Mustill, *Comm. Arb.* 166–180.
[140] *Atlantic Shipping and Trading Co. Ltd.* v. *Louis Dreyfus & Co.* [1922] 2 A.C. 250.

of any reported decision in Scotland. The English courts have held that a time bar is lawful, even if short,[141] and that a claim may be barred even though it did not exist when the time limit expired.[142] It appears to be permitted to frame a clause so that it affects only one of the parties.[143] Clauses containing a time bar are however strictly construed.[144] It may be pointed out that in Scotland the courts have no power equivalent to that possessed by the High Court in England under section 27 of the Arbitration Act 1950 to extend the time fixed for commencing an arbitration.

10.46. **Choice of procedural law.** The law governing arbitration proceedings may be different from the law governing the substantive issues which the arbiter has to decide. This has been clearly established by the House of Lords in a case which, though it arose in an appeal from a decision of an English court, involved arbitration proceedings in Scotland.[145] In general the law of the place where arbitration proceedings are held governs those proceedings. Lord Wilberforce stated in that case[146] —

'It is a matter of experience that numerous arbitrations are conducted by English Arbitrators in England on matters governed by contracts whose proper law is or may be that of another country, and I should be surprised if it had ever been held that such arbitrations were not governed by the English Arbitration Act in procedural matters ... The principle must surely be the same as that which applies to court proceedings brought in one country concerning a contract governed by the law of another, and that such proceedings as regards all matters which the law regards as procedural are governed by the *lex fori*'.

What is less clear is whether it is open to the submitters to agree that the law governing the arbitration procedure shall be different from the law of the place where the arbitration is held (the '*lex fori*' or '*lex loci arbitri*'). Dicta in *Bank Mellet* v. *Helleniki Techniki*

---

[141] *Ayscough* v. *Sheed, Thomson & Co. Ltd.* (1924) 19 Ll. L. Rep. 104 (3 days).
[142] '*The 'Himmerland'* [1965] 2 Ll. Rep. 353.
[143] *W. J. Alan & Co. Ltd.* v. *El Nasr Export and Import Co.* [1971] 1 Ll. Rep. 401.
[144] *Board of Trade* v. *Steel Brothers & Co. Ltd.* [1952] 1 Ll. Rep. 87.
[145] *James Miller and Partners Ltd.* v. *Whitworth Street Estates (Manchester) Ltd.* [1970] A.C. 583.
[146] At 616.

SA[147] suggest that this is permissible, though without countenancing the notion that proceedings might be free from subjection to any system of law. There are weighty juristic authorities on either side of the main question.[148] It has been strongly argued that freedom to select a procedural law other than that of the law of the place where the arbitration is held can be exercised only so far as that law allows[149] and there may be some rules, such as the rules of natural justice or public policy, which national legal systems would be unwilling to allow to be excluded. The extent of the uncertainty on these matters lends additional force to the view that in the context of international commercial arbitration an ancillary clause is defective if it does not specify the place of the arbitration,[150] and that the law governing the proceedings shall be that of the place of the arbitration.

10.47. **Registration for execution.** The enforcement of a decree arbitral may be facilitated by including, in the *ad hoc* submission or implementing deed on which it is based, a clause containing a consent to the registration of the decree along with the submission or deed in the Books of Council and Session for preservation and execution.[151] The deed containing the consent must be in probative form,[152] and the order contained in the decree arbitral — whether for payment of a sum of money or the performance of some act — must be as definite as a decree of a court upon which diligence[153] could be carried out.

---

[147] [1983] 3 W.L.R. 783.

[148] In favour of the validity of such an agreement there is Mustill, *Comm. Arb.* 61–2: against are Mann F. A. 'English Procedural Law and Foreign Arbitration' [1969] *International and Comparative Law Quarterly* 997; Parris, *Arb.*, 109. Thomas D. R., 'The curial law of arbitration proceedings', in [1984] *Lloyds Maritime and Commercial Law Quarterly* 491 at 498, appears to consider that practical consideration favour tying the curial law to the law of the place of the arbitration proceedings, but recognises that parties may be able to agree to the contrary.

[149] Mann F. A., 'England rejects "delocalised" contracts and arbitration' [1984] *ICLQ* 193 at 198.

[150] Schmitthoff C. M., 'Defective Arbitration Clauses', in Schmitthoff. *Comm. Arb.*, Vol. I, Part I, 45 at 57.

[151] For a style of clause, see Halliday, *Conveyancing*, Vol. I, 14–35, 14.37.

[152] *Carnoway* v. *Ewing* 1611 Mor. 14988.

[153] 'Diligence' is the technical name in Scotland for the procedures by which court orders are enforced by messengers-at-arms and sheriff officers.

PART C

ARBITRATION PROCEEDINGS
AND THE DECREE ARBITRAL

CHAPTER ELEVEN

THE COMMENCEMENT OF PROCEEDINGS

Introduction

11.1. This and the following chapters are concerned with arbitration proceedings under the law of Scotland. The sparsity of reported cases in Scotland in which a question has been raised as to the law applicable to proceedings in this country[1] suggests that the parties are usually in no doubt on the matter. It should be emphasised, however, that the law applicable to arbitration proceedings (the 'curial law of the arbitration') is not necessarily the same as the proper law of the arbitration agreement or the law applicable to the subject matter of the dispute or the law governing the formal validity of the decree arbitral. It is therefore appropriate to outline briefly the apparent rules of Scots private international law on the law governing arbitration proceedings.

11.2. On the basis of the decision of the House of Lords in *James Miller and Partners*[2] it is usually considered that the curial law of an arbitration is the law of the place where the arbitration proceedings are held, unless the parties specify otherwise, which they are permitted to do.[3] If in addition the proceedings take the form which is usual under the law of that place and no protest against this practice is made to the arbiter, this will be taken as a clear sign that the parties have agreed to the choice of that law[4] or at least are personally barred from denying such agreement. Whether the submitters are permitted to choose a curial law different from the

[1] The leading case, *James Miller & Partners Ltd* v. *Whitworth Street Estates (Manchester) Ltd* [1970] A.C. 583, arose out of arbitration proceedings in Scotland, though the action was raised in the English courts.
[2] *Supra* note 1; see also *dicta* of Lord Morris and Lord Diplock in *Compagnie d'Armement Maritime S.A.* v. *Compagnie Tunisienne de Navigation S.A.* [1971] A.C. 572 at 588 and 604.
[3] Anton A. E., 'Arbitration: International Aspects', 1986 S.L.T. (News) 45 at 48.
[4] *James Miller & Partners* (*supra* note 1) per Lord Guest at 609.

law of the place where the proceedings take place is however controversial in English law[5] and is technically open in Scotland.

11.3. Whether a Scottish court has jurisdiction to control proceedings is a separate question. If the proceedings in an arbitration take place in Scotland, it follows that the arbiter at least must be in Scotland and it might therefore be thought that the Scottish civil courts must therefore have jurisdiction to control what he or she does. However, mere presence of a person within Scotland is not, under the common law of Scotland, a sufficient ground of jurisdiction; substantially continuous residence for at least forty days is required,[6] apart from express or tacit consent to submit to, or arrestment to found,[7] jurisdiction. Under Schedule 8 of the Civil Jurisdiction and Judgments Act 1982, which was brought into force on 1st January 1987,[8] the Scottish courts have jurisdiction 'in proceedings concerning an arbitration which is conducted in Scotland or in which the procedure is governed by Scots law'.

Modes of commencement of proceedings

11.4. In Scots law no particular mode of commencing arbitration proceedings is generally required, though contracts of submission may lay down special rules, for example by adopting the procedure laid down by an institution[9] or under the standard form of conditions of contract of a professional body[10] or trade association.[11] The phrase 'commencement of proceedings' is not in Scots law a technical term, and is generally used merely to refer to

[5] The view that they can is espoused in Mustill, *Arb.* 65; doubts are expressed by Thomas D. R. 'The curial law of arbitration proceedings', (1984) LMCL 491 at 497.

[6] Anton A. E., *Private International Law*, Edinburgh, 1967 93, 95–6.

[7] *Motordrift A/S* v. *Trachem Co. Ltd.* 1982 S.L.T. 127.

[8] Civil Jurisdiction and Judgments Act 1982 (Commencement No. 3) Order 1986, S.I. 1986 No. 2044 (C. 78).

[9] E.g. the Law Society of Scotland, whose Model Rules are contained in *Arbitration Service*, Law Society of Scotland, Edinburgh, 1986.

[10] E.g. the Arbitration Procedure for Scotland under the Conditions of Contract formulated by the Institute of Civil Engineers, Rule 1, printed in Hawker and Ors., *I.C.E. Arb.*, Chapter 12.

[11] E.g. The Rules of Arbitration and Appeal of the Federation of Oils, Seeds and Fats Association Ltd. Rules 1–3, printed in Lee, *Int. Comm. Arb.* paragraphs 315–17.

the acts which must in practice be performed to get an arbitration under way, though in ancillary submissions the parties may designate a particular event as constituting under their contract the commencement of an arbitration.[12] This may be helpful as a means of determining the point at which periods of prescription and limitation cease to run.

11.5. Where proceedings are based on an ancillary submission an arbitration is normally commenced by —

(a) invoking the arbitration contract by intimating a demand for arbitration of a particular claim or other matter in issue;
(b) nominating and appointing arbiters (if this has not already been done in the submission); and
(c) presenting to the arbiter a statement of the claim or other matter in issue.

The last two may be effected by drawing up an implementing deed of submission and presenting it to the person nominated therein as arbiter, but it is not necessary to adopt this formal method. Where proceedings are based on an *ad hoc* submission there is obviously no initial demand for arbitration since there has *ex hypothesi* been no prior contract. The commencement of arbitration proceedings may therefore be distinguished from the commencement of a contract of submission which takes place when the last signature is appended thereto,[13] though where proceedings are based on an *ad hoc* rather than an ancillary contract proceedings and contract begin simultaneously.

The existence of a dispute

11.6. Before invoking an arbitration agreement a claimant should consider whether or not there is a real dispute or question for an arbiter to decide. Some rules contain a definition of what is deemed to be a dispute.[14] If nothing that can in terms of the submission be regarded as a dispute has arisen, and the opponent is simply

---

[12] As was done in the ancillary submission which was considered in *Clydebank County Council* v. *Clink* 1977 S.C. 147.
[13] *Taylor* v. *Grieve* 25 Nov. 1800 Mor. Appx. I Arb. 11. (Here the last signature was that of a cautioner.)
[14] See e.g. the ICE Arbitration Procedure for Scotland, Rule 1.1., in Hawker and Ors, *ICE Arb.*, 113–14.

refusing or delaying to fulfil his or her obligations, arbitration is inappropriate.[15]

11.7. If it is not clear whether there is a real dispute, the claimant has to decide whether to raise an action or to commence arbitration proceedings. If it is probable that there is a real dispute, the immediate commencement of arbitration proceedings may be appropriate, for there would be a risk that a court might regard the raising of the action as unnecessary and find the pursuer liable in the expenses connected therewith. If a court action is raised and the opponent has a real defence, the latter should, before the closing of the record in the action,[16] move the court to sist (*anglicé* 'stay') the case pending the outcome of the arbitration. Such a motion would be granted — always assuming that the matter in dispute was within the scope of the arbitration clause and was arbitrable in law — for in Scotland the courts have no discretion not to enforce a valid arbitration agreement.[17] If on the other hand arbitration proceedings are commenced and the opponent does not participate, the arbiter may properly proceed to hear and determine the matter in that party's absence,[18] provided that proper intimation is made to him or her of all documents and interlocutors, especially those prescribing the date, time and place of hearings. The assistance of the court may if necessary be invoked to appoint an arbiter,[19] and the commencement of the arbitration proceedings will interrupt the running of prescription.[20]

11.8. Raising an action is nevertheless sometimes appropriate even where the case may well be sisted pending arbitration. This does not of itself imply waiver of the right to arbitration.[21] Where

---

[15] *Albyn Housing Society Ltd.* v. *Taylor Woodrow Homes Ltd* 1985 S.L.T. 309 at 311; *Brodie* v. *Ker*; *McCallum* v. *MacNair* 1952 S.C. 216; *Allied Airways (Gandar Dower) Ltd.* v. *Secretary of State for Air* 1950 S.C. 249; *Parochial Board of Greenock* v. *Coghill & Son* (1878) 5 R. 732; *Woods* v. *Co-operative Insurance Society Ltd.* 1924 S.C. 692.

[16] *Halliburton Manufacturing and Service Ltd.* v. *Bingham Blades and Partners* 1984 S.L.T. 388, *Robertson and Co.* v. *Robertson* 1987 S.C.L.R. 329.

[17] *Sanderson & Son* v. *Armour & Co* 1922 S.C. (H.L.) 117 per Lord Dunedin at 126.

[18] *McIntyre* v. *Wolski* (1865) IV S.L.M. (Sh. Ct.) 29; *Hunter* v. *Milburn* (1869) 6 S.L.R. 525.

[19] Arbitration (Scotland) Act 1894 ss. 2–3.

[20] See on this paragraph 11.15 below.

[21] *McDougall* v. *Argyll & Bute District Council* (O.H.) 1987 S.L.T. 7.

the dispute relates to the ownership of, or rights to possession in, moveable goods, and there is doubt about the defender's ability to pay the amount claimed along with any interest and expenses that may become due, the raising of an action may be prudent — and accepted as reasonable by the court[22] — because there are in Scots law no interim security measures comparable with subsections 12(6)(a) and (e) to (g) of the English Arbitration Act 1950 available to preserve the effectiveness of unsecured claims pending the outcome of arbitration proceedings. Even with the assistance of the court, a claimant in Scotland would appear to be in a weaker position than his or her counterpart in England,[23] France,[24] or Sweden,[25] to name but three comparable countries, unless provision has been made in the submission or rules incorporated therein enabling the arbiter to order the deposit of money or the provision of security.[26] In Scotland the only interim security measures available for the preservation of the effectiveness of unsecured claims pending the outcome of litigation are (1) arrestment of corporeal and incorporeal moveable 'on the dependence' (of the action) in the hands of third parties; (2) inhibition 'on the dependence' against the defender attempting to dispose of or burden with secured debt his or her heritable property (3) Admiralty actions *in rem* against a ship or its cargo. There is no Scots procedure fully equivalent to the French '*saisie conservatoire*' under Article 48 of the Code of Civil Procedure, or of the provisional attachment which may in Sweden be granted by the competent District Court.[27]

Invoking the arbitration contract

11.9.   An ancillary submission is commonly invoked by an intimation by one party to the other requiring that one or more specified matters in dispute be referred to arbitration. In some

---

[22] In *Motordrift A/S* v. *Trachem Co. Ltd.* 1982 S.L.T. 127, the court sustained arrestments to found jurisdiction, though accepting that the action was likely to be sisted pending arbitration in England.
[23] See on this Mustill, *Comm. Arb.* 295–301.
[24] See Robert and Carbonneau, *Arb.*, II.7.–6.
[25] See Holmbäck, *Arb. Swe. 1984*, 99.
[26] As e.g. in Rules 2(5) and (6) of the Model Rules of the Law Society of Scotland, in *Arbitration Service*, Law Society of Scotland, Edinburgh, 1986.
[27] Holmbäck, *supra* note 25.

contracts this is known as a 'notice to refer'.[28] The rules of trade associations which provide for two arbiters sometimes require the nomination of the claimant's arbiter to be intimated to the respondent at the same time.[29] Where the rules of an arbitration institution are incorporated into the submission, it is commonly required that a 'request for arbitration' be presented to the secretary of the institution.[30] A time limit for invoking the submission is often prescribed.[31]

11.10. Even where the submission does not incorporate institutional rules, prudent practice[32] demands that a notice requiring arbitration should be in unequivocal terms and should contain a clear statement of the claim or question which the arbiter will be asked to determine. The latter is particularly important where the expiry of a period of prescription or limitation[33] or a period prescribed by contract is imminent: here the claim must be stated with some precision, though not necessarily in such full detail as the arbiter will require during the proceedings.[34]

11.11. Some legal systems[35] lay down a general rule that the invocation of an ancillary submission must be in writing. There is no such general rule in Scots law, but it is obviously desirable that the act should be performed in such a way that it can be readily proved, and some institutional rules expressly require writing for this purpose.[36] Notice is best intimated by recorded delivery, where the other party resides or has a place of business within the

[28] E.g. in the ICE Conditions, Rule 2.
[29] E.g. under the Rules of FOSFA, rule 2, printed in Lee, *Int. Comm. Arb.,* paragraph 316.
[30] E.g. in the Rules for the ICC Court of Arbitration, Article 3.
[31] E.g. in Rule 2 of the FOSFA Rules; and in Rule 2 of the Arbitration Rules of the Grain and Feed Trade Association Ltd., printed in Lee, *Int. Comm. Arb.,* paragraphs 358–60.
[32] The Scottish courts have not yet had to determine whether this is legally necessary. It is required in some systems — for example by the law of Sweden: see Holmbäck, *Arb. Swe. 1984,* 56.
[33] On arbitration and the interruption of prescription, see paragraphs 11.13–11.17 below.
[34] *British Railways Board* v. *Strathclyde Regional Council & Others* 1982 S.L.T. 55.
[35] E.g. that of Sweden: Arbitration Act 1929 s. 11; Eng. trans. in Holmbäck, *Arb. Swe.* 195–6, and *1984,* 175.
[36] E.g. the Rules of the London Court of International Arbitration 1985, Article 1, printed in Lee, *Int. Comm. Arb.,* paragraph 516.

United Kingdom, but in mercantile arbitrations with an international dimension telex is apparently now often used, and this has been accepted in England.[37]

11.12. Though a general agent or mandatary has no power to bind a principal to a contract of submission,[38] there seems no good reason to suppose that a person acting in that capacity is equally powerless to invoke an existing ancillary submission, though the matter seems not to have been the subject of judicial comment in Scotland.

Arbitration and the interruption of time limits

11.13 **Prescription.** It has been doubted by some writers whether, prior to the Prescription and Limitation (Scotland) Act 1973, the commencement of arbitration proceedings could interrupt the running of prescriptive periods.[39] A general submission of all claims clearly could not have had this effect,[40] but there is substantial authority that a special submission, or the presentation of particular claims to an arbiter in terms of a general submission, could have done so.[41]

11.14. The principal rules governing the effect of arbitration upon the running of periods of prescription are now contained in sections 4 and 9 of the 1973 Act. Section 4 is concerned with positive, section 9 with negative, prescription, but the latter incorporates the most important rules contained in the former.

11.15. Subsection (1) of section 4 provides that the running of periods of positive prescription may be interrupted by —

'the making in appropriate proceedings, by any person having an interest to do so, of a claim which challenges the possession in question.'

[37] In *N.v. Stoomv Maats 'De Maas'* v. *Nippon Yusen Kaisha* (*The 'Pendrecht'*) [1980] 2 Ll. Rep. 56 at 66.
[38] See paragraph 4.24. above.
[39] See the general note to section 4 of the Act in the Scottish Current Law Statutes edition.
[40] Bankton, *Inst.* II.12.62; *Garden* v. *Rigg* Nov. 26 1743, Mor. 11274, and Kilkerran, Prescription, 11; Bell J. M., *Arb.*, paragraph 615.
[41] *Vans* v. *Murray* June 14 1816 FC; *Eddie* v. *Monklands Railway Co.* (1855) 17 D. 1041 per Lord Wood at 1046; Bell J. M., *Arb.*, paragraph 614.

Subsection (2) defines 'appropriate proceedings' as including —

'... (b) any arbitration in Scotland; [and]
(c) any arbitration in a country other than Scotland, being an arbitration an award in which would be enforceable in Scotland.'

By virtue of sections 6–8 of the Act the running of periods of negative prescription is interrupted by a 'relevant claim', which is defined in subsections (1) and (2) of section 9 as including a claim made in 'appropriate proceedings'. By subsection (4) of that section, this expression has the same meaning as in subsection (2) of section 4. It is therefore clear that the running of both positive and negative prescription may be interrupted by arbitration in any country, provided that the award which might be made therein is enforceable in Scotland.

11.16. The point at which a 'claim' is made is prescribed for this purpose by subsections (3) and (4) of section 4 of the Act. Subsection (3) provides that —

'the date of a judicial interruption [of prescription] shall be taken to be —
(a) where the claim has been made in an arbitration and the nature of the claim has been stated in a preliminary notice relating to that arbitration, the date on which the preliminary notice was served; [and]
(b) in any other case, the date when the claim was made.

The term 'preliminary notice' is defined in subsection (4) for the purpose of both section 4 and section 9[42] as —

'a notice served by one party to the arbitration on the other party or parties requiring him or them to appoint an arbiter or to agree to the appointment of any arbiter, or where the arbitration agreement or any relevant enactment provides that the reference shall be to a person therein named or designated, a notice requiring him or them to submit the dispute to the person so named or designated.'

Subsections (3) and (4) of section 4 thus make clear provision for claims made within the scope and in terms of ancillary submissions, where the nature of the claim is stated in the

[42] S. 9(4).

'preliminary notice': here prescription stops running on the day that the notice is sent. The effect of these provisions — in particular of subsection 4(3)(b) — is not so obvious in other cases. The context suggests that the phrase 'the date when the claim was made' means the date when it was first made in arbitration proceedings. In proceedings following upon an ancillary submission where the claim has been specified in a 'preliminary notice', the phrase presumably means the date upon which it is intimated to the opponent in such terms or in such circumstances that it must be regarded as having been done in the context of an existing arbitration. Where a special or mixed *ad hoc* submission has been entered into which clearly includes a disputed claim, it is at least arguable that the date on which the final necessary signature is appended to the deed is the date on which that claim was 'made'. This would appear to be the interpretation which best accords with practical commonsense, for otherwise the 1973 Act would produce a less satisfactory solution than the previous law. Where the claim is not clearly included in the submission, the date on which it is 'made' must be the date on which it has become clear not only that it has been intimated to the opponent but also that it is within the scope of the arbitration. If a claim not within the original scope of the submission has been included in the pleadings of one party, it probably cannot be regarded as having been 'made' in the arbitration unless and until the other party has either agreed that it shall be determined by the arbiter or — as is possible[43] — has become personally barred from objecting to its inclusion in the proceedings. Since the scope of an arbitration cannot be enlarged without the consent of the arbiter,[44] it must presumably be clear also that the arbiter has no objection to its inclusion.

11.17. Prescription does not run during the currency of arbitration proceedings.[45] It often happens, however, that for one reason or another no award is pronounced: the arbiter may die, or a claim may be formally withdrawn, or the claimant may cease from prosecuting it. A question may then arise whether or not the prescriptive period must begin again from whatever date arbitration on the claim can be said to have come to an end. The

---

[43] *North British Railway Co.* v. *Barr & Co.* (1855) 18 D. 102 per Lord Deas at 107; *Miller & Son* v. *Oliver & Boyd* (1906) 8 F. 390 per Lord President Dunedin at 401.
[44] *Miller & Son* v. *Oliver & Boyd* (1906) 8 F 390 per Lord McLaren at 404.
[45] *Dunn* v. *Lamb* (1854) 16 D. 944.

matter has not been determined by the courts in Scotland, but on the basis of analogy with the rule governing similar circumstances in litigation[46] it is suggested that prescription starts again from scratch on the day after the last date of any proceedings in the arbitration relating to the claim in any way.

11.18. **Limitation.** The effect of limitation is to remove the power to enforce a right by legal action, whereas that of prescription is to extinguish the right altogether. The plea of limitation may moreover be waived, whereas a judge may take notice of prescription even if not pleaded as a defence.[47] It is probable, but not certain, that prior to the commencement of the 1973 Act arbitration proceedings interrupted the running of periods of limitation.[48] J. M. Bell advised a creditor to insist on the insertion, in any submission of a claim which could be affected by limitation, of an express declaration that in the event of the proceedings terminating without an award he (the creditor) would be as free to raise an action as he had been when the submission was entered into.[49]

11.19. The modern law on limitation of actions in Scotland is contained mainly in Part II of the 1973 Act, though there are numerous other statutes which contain limitation provisions. Part II contains no mention of arbitration apart from three subsections of marginal importance.[50] In particular it does not attempt for the purposes of section 17 (which contains the main provisions on limitation of actions for damages or solatium for personal injuries) to define an 'action' as including claims in arbitration proceedings. The effect of Part II of the 1973 Act appears to be that on the one hand a claim in an arbitration concerned with damages or solatium for personal injuries does not interrupt the running of the limitation period, but on the other hand a claim can still be made in arbitration proceedings even after the expiry of the relevant limitation period. Thus, if a special submission of a claim for reparation is entered into after the expiry of the three year limitation period but before the expiry of the five year prescriptive

---

[46] *George A. Hood & Co v. Dumbarton District Council* 1983 S.L.T. 238.
[47] Walker D. M., *The Law of Prescription and Limitation of Actions in Scotland*, Edinburgh, 2nd edn. 1976, 4.
[48] *Dudgeon v. Robertson* (1859) 21 D. 351 at 360.
[49] *Arb.* paragraph 626.
[50] Subsections 20(3) and (4) and 21(2).

period, the claim may be entertained by the arbiter and an award upholding the claim would be valid. The contract of submission would in effect be an implied waiver of the limitation if a waiver were required. An award upholding the claim would (other things being equal) be valid and an action to enforce it, being an action not for damages but for decree conform to the award, would be sustainable.

11.20. **Contractual time bar.** Clauses barring claims not made in writing within a specified period of a particular kind of event such as the discharge of a ship are not infrequently included in mercantile contracts, especially those which incorporate the arbitration rules of a trade association.[51] The Scottish courts do not seem to have been called upon in any reported case to interpret or decide the validity of such clauses, but it seems likely that English decisions[52] upholding their validity[53] subject to strict construction[54] would be found to be persuasive. In England a time bar as short as three days has been upheld,[55] though longer periods are more commonly prescribed; and a claim for an indemnity was judged to be time-barred under a limitation clause in a charterparty though the basis for an action on the claim had not arisen before the expiry of the specified period.[56]

11.21. A distinction is drawn by the English courts between contractual time-bar clauses which extinguish claims and those which merely extinguish the right to have them determined by arbitration.[57] In the former case the effect is that the issue may be submitted to arbitration but the arbiter will dismiss the claim; in the latter case the claim remains enforceable in law through the ordinary courts but disputes relating thereto cannot be determined by arbitration.

11.22. A contractual time bar may be waived by the person entitled to enforce it, who may also become personally barred from

[51] See e.g. the GAFTA arbitration rules, rule 2:7; printed in Lee, *Int. Comm. Arb.*, paragraph 361.
[52] For a lucid and detailed account of which see Mustill, *Comm. Arb.* 166–180.
[53] *Atlantic Shipping and Trading Co. Ltd.* v. *Louis Dreyfus & Co.* [1922] 2 A.C. 250.
[54] *Board of Trade* v. *Steel Brothers and Co. Ltd.* [1952] 1 Ll. Rep. 87; *Bunge* v. *Deutsche Conti-Handelgesellschaft mbH (No. 2)* [1980] 1 Ll. Rep. 352.
[55] *Ayscough* v. *Sheed, Thomson & Co. Ltd* (1924) 19 Ll. L. Rep. 104.
[56] *The 'Himmerland'* [1965] 2 Ll. Rep. 353.
[57] See on this Mustill, *Comm. Arb.* 168–170.

founding upon it. It may be that such time bars may be affected by the Unfair Contract Terms Act 1977. Mustill and Boyd, commenting upon the sections of that Act applicable to England, suggest that subsection 13(2) (which provides for the exclusion from the operation of sections 3 and 7 of agreements to submit present or future differences to arbitration) does not apply to clauses barring claims which are not submitted within a specified time, because such clauses are entirely distinct from the agreements to which they relate.[58] The equivalent Scottish provision is subsection 25(3), which states that —

'any reference to excluding or restricting any liability ... does not include an agreement to submit any question to arbitration'.

It is submitted that Mustill and Boyd's comment may equally well apply to this provision.

11.23. Some arbitration rules commonly incorporated into contracts provide that the arbiter has a discretion to extend a contractual time limit.[59] Where this discretion is exercised in a proper judicial manner the arbiter's decision is final.

Nomination and appointment of arbiters

11.24. Distinction between nomination and appointment. These terms have no technical meaning in law, and in contracts parties often use them loosely, but a distinction may be drawn between types of act which may conveniently be referred to respectively as nomination and appointment. Nomination is the overt act of choosing a particular person by name with a view to his or her appointment; appointment is an act, or the last in a series of acts, by which a person is legally established in a particular post. Nomination does not necessarily involve the nominee, who may be entirely unaware of it, though it is customary to make informal soundings to discover whether the person concerned would, if nominated, be willing to accept appointment; appointment must involve the appointee, because he or she cannot be compelled by any private person to undertake any onerous position.

---

[58] *Comm. Arb.* 175.
[59] See e.g. the GAFTA Arbitration Rules, Rule 2.7, printed in Lee, *Int. Comm. Arb.*, paragraph 361.

11.25. **Nomination**. Though nomination is an act of choice it is not something purely mental. Where the terms of a submission require each party to nominate an arbiter, the act of nomination is not complete until it has been intimated to the other party.[60] As Lord Denman put it in an English case,[61]

'neither party can be said to have chosen an arbitrator until he lets the other party know the object of his choice. "Nomination" implies notice.'

Once intimated a nomination cannot be unilaterally withdrawn.[62] Where parties considering entering upon a contract of submission intend their agreement to contain the nomination of the arbiters, as is usual in *ad hoc* submissions, it is particularly important for them to make preliminary approaches to the proposed nominee or nominees or to make provision for the failure of the initial nomination, because otherwise a nominee's refusal to accept office will frustrate the contract. Such approaches will not, if their preliminary nature is clear, constitute either nomination or an offer of appointment.[63] Where the nomination is made by a third party it is probably incomplete until it has been intimated to both the submitters. The grant of a mandate to 'appoint' an arbiter may be taken as including the power to nominate, but in the normal case where the mandate is given by both the submitters the stage of nomination may be superfluous.

11.26. The nomination of an arbiter has to be taken very seriously, not only because a poor choice resulting in the appointment of a person who is disqualified or unsuitable for the type of arbitration concerned may make the whole proceedings abortive, but also because nominators have a legal duty to take care to choose a fit and proper person.[64] A submitter is not entitled arbitrarily to increase the cost of an arbitration by nominating a person whose known or expected fee would be extravagant in the circumstances.[65] In an English appeal it has been observed that the

[60] *Hugh Highgate & Co.* v. *British Oil & Guano Co. Ltd* 1914 2 S.L.T. 241.
[61] *Thomas* v. *Fredericks* (1847) 10 Q.B. 775. See also *Tew* v. *Harris* (1848) 11 Q.B. 7.
[62] *Landale* v. *Ritchie* (1859) 1 S.L.J. (Sh. Ct.) 102.
[63] *Hugh Highgate & Co.* (*supra* note 60).
[64] *Sellar* v. *Highland Railway Co.* 1919 S.C. (H.L.) 19 per Lord Buckmaster at 22.
[65] *MacAndrew, Wright and Murray* v. *North British Railway Co.* (1893) 1 S.L.T. 142.

choice by a submitter of a biased person as one of two arbitrators would be a material breach of the submission,[66] and this seems highly persuasive. It has been observed in Scotland that a submitter ought not to suggest the appointment as arbiter of a person who was his own architect without disclosing this fact to the other party,[67] and it may be that a negligent or fraudulent nomination by a third party mandatary would constitute a material breach of the mandate. A nominator should therefore take proper steps to discover whether at the time of the proposed appointment the proposed nominee is or may be disqualified or is otherwise unsuitable for the kind of arbitration being envisaged, for failure to do so might give rise to liability in damages if the arbitration was abortive as a consequence.

11.27. It is possible that a negligent or fraudulent misrepresentation by one of the submitters or a professional body, causing the nomination and appointment of a person who was at the material time either disqualified or clearly unsuitable for the type of arbitration concerned, might be actionable at the instance of the party imposed upon if the arbitration was abortive causing financial loss. What is sometimes called the '*Hedley Byrne*' principle imposes liability for financial loss caused by negligent statements made in the context of relationships —

'where it is plain that the party seeking information or advice was trusting the other to exercise such a degree of care as the circumstances required, where it was reasonable for him to do that, and where the other gave the information or advice when he knew or ought to have known that the inquirer was relying on him.'[68]

The full scope of that principle, which is consistent with previous Scottish authority,[69] is not yet certain, but it is arguable that it applies in this context to create liability in certain circumstances where a name is suggested by someone who is not formally making a nomination.

[66] *Bremer Vulkan Schiffbau und Maschinenfabrik* v. *South India Shipping Corporation* [1981] 1 Ll. Rep. 253 per Lord Diplock at 260.
[67] *Blythe Building Co. Ltd.* v. *Mason's Executrix* (1937) 53 Sh. Ct. Rep. 180.
[68] *Hedley Byrne & Co.* v. *Heller and Partners* [1964] A.C. 465, per Lord Reid at 486.
[69] *Robinson* v. *National Bank of Scotland* 1916 S.C. (H.L.) 154.

11.28. **Appointment**. As already indicated,[70] appointment involves a contract between the submitters and the arbiter, and is effected when either the nominee, following an approach by or on behalf of the submitters, offers his or her services as arbiter and the offer is accepted, or when the submitters have offered appointment and the offer is accepted by the nominee. An offer of appointment may be made, or an offer of service accepted, either —

(1) jointly by both submitters; or
(2) by one of them on behalf of both; or
(3) by a third party as the mandatary of both.

Where the submission provides that each party shall nominate an arbiter, appointment is generally effected after intimation of the nomination, but probably the order may be reversed.[71] Where the parties have failed to nominate or to concur in a nomination in terms of the submission, and where any supplementary provision for appointment has failed, the court may appoint in terms of sections 2–3 of the Arbitration (Scotland) Act 1894.

11.29. The principles underlying the appointment of arbiters have already been discussed.[72] Essentially the same principles apply to the appointment of an oversman by the submitters and the arbiters, the power of the court being here based on section 4 of the 1894 Act. The court does not have power to appoint a third arbiter as distinct from an oversman.[73]

11.30. Once nominations have been made, it is improper for a submitter to attempt to persuade a nominee not to accept appointment. In a case in which it was alleged that the defender had written to a person he had nominated in a deed of submission, pressing him to refuse to accept appointment, it was observed[74] that though an action to ordain him to withdraw the letter was incompetent, the allegation might perhaps, if true,

'found an action of damages for depriving the pursuer of any advantage he could instruct by the arbitration proceedings.'

---

[70] Paragraph 3.17 above.
[71] So, at least, it has been held in England: *Bunge, S. A.* v. *Kruse* [1979] 1 Ll.Rep. 279 at 295.
[72] Paragraphs 3.1–3.3, and 3.17–3.26 above.
[73] *Twibill* v. *Niven & Co.* (1897) 13 Sh. Ct. Rep. 313.
[74] *Landale* (*supra* note 62).

11.31. It is common practice for parties to present a deed of submission to the person nominated therein as arbiter, and for the arbiter then to execute a minute of acceptance upon it. Where this is normal it may be understood by both the submitters and their nominee that the appointment contract will not be completed until the minute of acceptance has been executed. It may happen in such a case that the submitters were originally unable to agree who should act as arbiter, and it has been necessary to call upon the services of a third party to break the deadlock. The third party strictly speaking does not then appoint but merely nominates the arbiter unless he or she also has to present the deed of submission to the arbiter.

11.32. From the point of view of a nominee there are advantages in the rather formal practice of appointment through the acceptance of a deed of submission. The deed generally provides clear and sufficient evidence of matters upon which the nominee must be satisfied before accepting office — namely the identities of the submitters, the nature of the questions in issue and the main powers being granted to and duties being imposed upon the arbiter. Other matters which should be settled, perhaps in a collateral agreement, before the arbitration contract is entered into, are the scale of fees to be paid to the arbiter and the rates of expenses the submitters are prepared to entertain, for example in connection with the hire of rooms and the arbiter's personal travelling and subsistence. Fees may conveniently be determined by incorporating the rates approved by a body such as the Chartered Institute of Arbitrators. Though formerly the payment of fees to arbiters was generally disallowed[75] on the ground — so some writers[76] said — of avoidance of expense to the submitters, this rule is no longer applied,[77] and there is no objection to a nominee stipulating for a fee as a condition of accepting office.[78] The rules of some trade associations, professional bodies, and arbitration institutions make provision for the method of nomination or appointment,[79] and even for the rates of fees and

[75] *Kennedy* v. *Kennedy* 20 Jan. 1819 F.C.
[76] E.g. Durandus, *Speculum*, t.I, fol. 117, section 7.74.
[77] *Macintyre Brothers* v. *Smith* 1913 S.C. 129 per Lord Kinnear at 132.
[78] *Fraser* v. *Wright and Others* (1838) 16 S. 1049 per Lord Medwyn at 1057.
[79] See the arbitration rules of e.g. FOSFA (Rule 1), GAFTA (Rule 3), the ICC Court of Arbitration (Article 2) and the London Court of International Arbitration (Article 3), all in Lee, *Int. Comm. Arb.*, at paragraphs 315, 362–4, 419, and 518 respectively.

expenses,[80] and these may be incorporated into the submission and the contract between the submitters and the arbiter.

11.33. Once the third party has effectively made a nomination or appointment, his or her power is exhausted unless the mandate — which normally incorporates appropriate terms from the submission — otherwise provides. It should be noted, however, that where the third party is expected to make an appointment, the power to do so is not exhausted until either the mandate is withdrawn or a contract between the submitters and a nominee has been brought into existence: if what purports to be a letter of appointment of a certain nominee has been issued, but the nominee has not accepted office, the mandatary may approach someone else. This has admittedly never been the subject of any judicial pronouncement in Scotland, but the views here expressed seem to be consistent with those of respected writers,[81] and to follow from the fact that the relationship between an arbiter and the submitters is contractual, and from the nature of the mandate which must exist between the third party and the submitters.

11.34. The arbitration rules of some bodies such as the Grain and Feed Trade Association[82] require a claimant to 'appoint' an arbiter within a certain time. The meaning of this word has to be discovered from the context, interpreted in accordance with the rules of the legal system under which the rules are intended to operate. In view of the provision requiring arbitration to take place in London unless the parties otherwise agree, and under the English arbitration legislation, it is probable that the GAFTA rules have been drafted on the assumption that English law will apply to the submission. Since English law apparently does not conceive the relationship between the submitters and the arbitrator in terms of contract,[83] the assumption that might have been made in Scotland, that since the GAFTA rules go on to provide for the case where the proposed arbiter declines office the

---

[80] See e.g. the rules of the ICC Court of Arbitration, Article 20, Appendix II paragraph 23 and Appendix III; and of the London Court of International Arbitration Article 18 and Schedule; both in Lee, *Int. Comm. Arb.*, paragraphs 437, 463, and 465–9, and paragraphs 533 and 536–8.
[81] Halliday, *Conveyancing*, Vol. I, 14.05; Burns J., *Conveyancing Practice according to the Law of Scotland*, 4th edn., Edinburgh, 1957, 71.
[82] Rules 3:1 and 3:3, in Lee, *Int.Comm.Arb.*, paragraphs 362–3.
[83] Mustill, *Comm. Arb.* 188–9.

word 'appoint' in this context means 'offer appointment', may well not be correct.

11.35.   In ordinary arbitration the *power of the court to appoint* an arbiter or oversman exists only by virtue of the Arbitration (Scotland) Act 1894: there is no power under the common law to this effect.[84] Normally 'the court' means in this context any sheriff having jurisdiction[85] or any Lord Ordinary of the Court of Session,[86] but where the arbiter or oversman to be appointed is a Senator of the College of Justice, the appointment must be made by the Inner House of the Court of Session.[87] Though it is always an important factor to be taken into account, the mere choice of Scots law as the proper law governing the arbitration agreement (which has to be distinguished from the law governing the arbitration procedure[88]) probably does not necessarily imply prorogation of the jurisdiction of the Scottish courts for the purposes of supervising the implementation of the agreement.[89] Nevertheless a person who clearly has entered into an agreement to refer a matter to arbitration in Scotland thereby prorogates the jurisdiction of the Court of Session as far as is necessary to render the agreement effective, so that the Court of Session has jurisdiction to entertain a petition for the appointment of an arbiter to conduct proceedings in Scotland although the respondent lives in London.[90] A court in Scotland, unlike the District Court in Sweden,[91] has no power to remove and replace an arbiter not named in the submission, though the submitters may under the submission or rules incorporated therein, which are expressly or

[84] *Bryson & Manson* v. *Picken* (1896) 12 Sh. Ct. Rep. 26; *Thom & Sons* v. *Burrell* (1929) 45 Sh. Ct. Rep. 187.
[85] Under the Civil Jurisdiction and Judgments Act 1982 s. 20 and Schedule 8 paragraph 1, which came into force on 1st January 1987 by virtue of the Civil Jurisdiction and Judgments Act 1982 (Commencement No. 3) Order 1986 (S.I. 1986 No. 2044 (C.78)), the principal ground of jurisdiction is the place where the defender or respondent is domiciled, domicile being defined in Part V of the Act. The application of the Sheriff Courts (Scotland) Act 1907 s. 6 is now limited to cases outwith the scope of Schedule 8.
[86] Arbitration (Scotland) Act 1894 s. 6.
[87] Law Reform (Miscellaneous Provisions) (Scotland) Act 1980 s. 17.
[88] *James Miller & Partners* v. *Whitworth Street Estates (Manchester) Ltd.* [1907] 1 All E.R. 796; and see paragraphs 13.10.–13.12 below.
[89] Anton, A. E., 'Arbitration, International Aspects', 1986 S.L.T. 45 at 46.
[90] *Lawrence* v. *Taylor* 1934 S.L.T. 76; Civil Jurisdiction and Judgments Act 1982 s. 20 and Schedule 8 paragraph 5.
[91] Arbitration Act 1929 ss. 9(2), 10(3); Holmbäck, *Arb. Swe. 1984*, 122.

impliedly agreed to by the arbiter on appointment, give to a third party the power to remove an arbiter.[92] Furthermore, since the exercise of discretion whether or not to make an appointment and whom to appoint is considered to be a ministerial rather than a judicial act it is not normally subject to appeal or review by a higher court.[93] An appeal to the Court of Session from a decision of a sheriff has been entertained in a case in which the application for appointment was irregularly made in the form of an ordinary action,[94] but this was highly unusual. However, if a sheriff or Lord Ordinary in making or refusing to make an appointment misconstrued or exceeded the jurisdiction granted by the 1894 Act, it is probable that an application might be made under Rule of Court 206B.[95]

11.36. A number of conditions must be satisfied before the court may entertain an application for the appointment of an arbiter under the 1894 Act.

(1) The 'agreement to refer' — that is, the contract of submission[96] — must provide either expressly or impliedly for the disputes or questions to be determined either by one or by two arbiters. If it cannot be discovered even by reference to custom of trade[97] how many arbiters the parties had in mind when they entered into the contract,[98] or if they then agreed upon more than two arbiters[99] (not counting the oversman for this purpose as an arbiter) the court cannot act.

(2) One of the parties to the agreement to refer must have refused either to concur in the nomination of a single arbiter or to nominate one of two arbiters in terms of the contract. If the submitters themselves were not to have made the appointment, but delegated this under the contract to one or more other persons who failed to

---

[92] As in rules 1.2 and 1.3 of the Model Rules of the Law Society of Scotland, in *Arbitration Service*, Law Society of Scotland, Edinburgh, 1986.

[93] *Magistrates of Glasgow* v. *Glasgow District Subway Co.* (1893) 21 R. 52; *Mackenzie* v. *Inverness & Ross-shire Railway Co.* (1861) 24 D. 251.

[94] *Ross* v. *Ross* 1920 S.C. 530.

[95] Inserted by the Act of Sederunt (Rules of Court Amendment No. 2) (Judicial Review) 1985 (S.I. 1985 No. 500 (S. 48)).

[96] See on this paragraphs 3.12–3.16 above.

[97] *Douglas & Co.* v. *Stiven* (1900) 2 F. 575; *United Creameries Co. Ltd.* v. *David T. Boyd & Co.* 1912 S.C. 617.

[98] *McMillan & Son Ltd.* v. *Rowan & Co.* (1907) 5 F. 317.

[99] *Twibill* v. *Niven & Co.* (1897) 13 Sh. Ct. Rep. 313.

act, the court has no power to supply the deficiency.[100] This is also the outcome if the submitters have each made or agreed upon a nomination in terms of the submission, but the nominee has refused to accept office[101] or has died,[102] and the submitters cannot agree on a replacement. The Act and its interpretation are not wholly unreasonable however. Where a party expresses willingness to nominate only on certain conditions not provided for in the agreement to refer — for example that proceedings must be conducted in a formal manner — this will be regarded as equivalent to refusal to nominate, and the court will entertain an application for an appointment.[103]

(3) If any provision has been made in the contract for carrying out the reference in the event of a refusal by a submitter to act, that provision must have been tried and must have failed.[104]

11.37. The court may appoint an oversman under the 1894 Act if and only if the arbiters have failed to agree on a nomination, but it is immaterial whether or not they have also failed to agree on the terms of an award.[105] (It is common practice for the nomination and appointment of an oversman to be made, or at least attempted, shortly after the arbiters themselves have taken up office.) Oddly, it appears not to matter in this case if provision has been made for the arbiters' failure to agree on a nomination and that provision has not been put into effect, though probably the court would decline to act in those circumstances. If the implied power to appoint an oversman which the arbiters have under section 4 of the Act has been excluded by the submission, which has confined the power to the submitters themselves or to some other party, and the persons who had to exercise that power have failed to use it, the court appears to be unable to act.

11.38. The 1894 Act empowers the court to 'appoint' an arbiter or oversman where the parties or their arbiters have failed to make a 'nomination' or to 'name' a person. It thus suggests that a distinction is being drawn between nomination and appointment,

[100] *Cowie* v. *Kiddie* (1897) 5 S.L.T. 259.
[101] *British Westinghouse Electric and Manufacturing Co. Ltd.* v. *Provost etc. of Aberdeen* (1906) 14 S.L.T. 391.
[102] *Bryson & Manson* v. *Picken* (1896) 12 Sh. Ct. Rep. 26.
[103] *Hugh Highgate & Co.* v. *British Oil & Guano Co Ltd.* 1914 2 S.L.T. 241.
[104] *Thom & Sons* v. *Burrell* (1929) 45 Sh. Ct. Rep. 187.
[105] *Glasgow Parish Council* v. *United Collieries Ltd* (1907) 15 S.L.T. 232.

but without indicating what are the consequences of a failure by a party or the arbiters to appoint. It is unusual for a party to nominate but to refuse to assist in making an appointment, but it has happened.[106] It would seem that once nomination has been performed, appointment has been assumed to be secure. It may have been considered that each party has an implied power to appoint a person who has been properly nominated in terms of the submission, whoever had the power to make the nomination.

11.39.   Where the court makes an appointment, there appears to be no contractual relationship between the submitters and the arbiter concerned, but the Act provides that —

'the arbiter so appointed shall have the same powers as if he had been duly nominated by the party so refusing.'

The Act does not say anything about the duties of the arbiter, but it must be assumed that the arbiter has been appointed to carry out the express and implied terms of the submission, and that he or she has a right to fees and to reimbursement of expense not on the basis of contract but recompense.[107] For prudential reasons soundings are made to discover whether a proposed appointee is willing to act, but it is not clear what legal consequences would follow from a refusal by a person appointed by the court to undertake an arbitration.

11.40.   The procedure for appointment of an arbiter or oversman by the court is normally by way of petition. However, this may be inappropriate where there is more to decide than merely whether there has been a failure to nominate in terms of the submission, as for example where there is a question whether the agreement to refer specifies a definite number of arbiters. It has been considered[108] that —

'there may ... be questions which it is necessary to determine before an arbiter can be appointed, such as questions of the competency of the application.'

The court has some power to consider such questions in the context of a petition, but only with limits, on the ground —

---

[106] *Landale* v. *Ritchie* (1859) 1 S.L.J. (Sh. Ct.) 102.
[107] Bell, *Prin.* 538.
[108] In *Cooper & Co.* v. *Jessop Brothers* (1906) 8 F. 714 per Lord Low at 723.

'that the procedure authorised by the Act was intended to be of a summary nature, and that it was not contemplated that an application under the Act should be used for the determination of questions requiring investigation and procedure appropriate to an action in the ordinary courts, but not appropriate to an application to a special tribunal constituted for a special purpose, and whose statutory functions are ministerial rather than judicial.'

No precise line is drawn, however, between what will be entertained in a petition of this kind and what will not,[109] since this is a matter not simply of the legal nature of the question but of its complexity and the extent to which averments are disputed. It is in practice therefore usually best to proceed first with a petition, which will be sisted (*anglicé* 'stayed') pending the raising of a separate action if the court finds the petitionary form to some extent unsuitable.

[109] *United Creameries Co. Ltd.* v. *David T. Boyd & Co.* 1912 S.C. 617.

CHAPTER TWELVE

THE CONDUCT OF ARBITRATION PROCEEDINGS: 1 BASIC RULES AND PRINCIPLES

Introduction

12.1. This chapter is concerned with the basic rules and principles governing the conduct of an arbitration. In the following chapter the law is expounded in more detail, so far as possible in the order which proceedings normally take.

12.2. The conduct of ordinary arbitration proceedings in Scotland is regulated publicly by the general law and privately by contract. Some of the rules contained in the general law are compulsory (*jus cogens*) reflecting the jurisdictional element in arbitration, and the need to preserve its character as adjudication. As Lord Watson put it in a Scottish appeal to the House of Lords,[1] an arbiter must —

'conform to all those rules for securing the proper administration of justice which the law implies in the case of every proceeding before an arbiter as well as in the case of every proceeding before a Court of Justice.'

Legal rules which are not essential for the administration of justice are generally excludable by contract (*jus dispositivum*). For example, section 3 of the Administration of Justice (Scotland) Act 1972 provides not only that an arbiter may, and shall if the Court of Session on the application of either party so directs, at any stage in the arbitration state a case for its opinion on a question of law, but also that the submitters may renounce this power by contract in the agreement to refer. Rules established by contract may be express — framed by one or both of the parties or incorporated from codes framed by institutions such as the Institution of Civil Engineers[2] — or implied from custom. It is for example —

[1] *Holmes Oil Co. Ltd.* v. *Pumpherston Oil Co. Ltd.* (1891) 18 R. (H.L.) 52 at 55.
[2] The ICE Arbitration Procedure for Scotland, with commentary, is contained in Hawker and Ors., *ICE Arb.*, Chapter 12.

'an implied condition of the contract [in a formal submission], imported by universal practice, that the parties have a right to make representations upon the [proposed] findings of the arbiter.'[3]

12.3. **Legislation.** Scots law differs from the law of most other European countries in that public legal regulation of arbitration proceedings is effected mainly by means of judicial precedent with some assistance from juristic writing.[4] There is little legislation, and certainly no Scottish equivalent of the Swedish Arbitration Act 1929, or of Part I of the English Arbitration Act 1950.[5] Only three statutory provisions, each consisting of one section, are applicable and in force. They are —

(i) article 25 of the Articles of Regulation 1695;
(ii) section 4 of the Arbitration (Scotland) Act 1894; and
(iii) section 3 of the Administration of Justice (Scotland) Act 1972.

With the exception of a similarly brief statute enacted in 1427[6] which long ago fell into desuetude, these three provisions represent the whole of the legislation which has ever affected the conduct of ordinary arbitration proceedings in Scotland. Article 25 of the 1695 legislation lays down the main grounds upon which the validity of awards may be challenged;[7] section 4 of the 1894 Act is concerned with the power of arbiters to appoint an oversman, and section 3 of the 1972 Act impinges directly upon the proceedings by providing an opportunity to obtain the opinion of the court on a question of law. However useful these provisions may be, they hardly add up to a comprehensive code.

12.4. **Precedent.** The precedents which contain most of the law governing arbitration procedure in Scotland span some four hundred years. During this time judicial attitudes to arbitration generally, to the interpretation of statutory and contractual provisions, and to rules enshrined in the civil and canon laws have undergone considerable change. Though the majority of the cases

---

[3] *McLaren* v. *Aikman* 1939 S.C. 222 per Lord Wark at 230.
[4] J. M. Bell's *Treatise on the Law of Arbitration in Scotland* (2nd edn. 1877) has achieved almost institutional status.
[5] Later supplemented and amended by the Arbitration Act 1975.
[6] *APS* 1427 c. 6.
[7] Discussed in paragraphs 12.21–12.24 below.

were decided during or since the nineteenth century, by which time law reporting had become quite sophisticated, some of them are earlier and the reports of them are difficult to interpret. A purist might regard many of the nineteenth and twentieth century precedents as of doubtful application, since these often arose out of proceedings in statutory regimes rather than ordinary arbitration. The structural basis of the law is therefore not very satisfactory, and discourages reference to arbitration in Scotland in international commercial cases, though it is familiar enough to Scots lawyers and arbiters, and fortunately the courts have been willing to treat statutory regimes and ordinary arbitration as subject to the same procedural principles except in so far as legislation expressly provided otherwise.[8]

12.5.   **Contract — implied terms**. There are two main factual grounds upon which a term may be held to be implied in a submission. One is, that otherwise the arbiter would be unable to explicate the jurisdiction,[9] or in other words to perform all the duties of the office sufficiently thoroughly to enable a valid award to be issued. For example, if the matter in dispute is connected with the condition of property in the possession of one of the submitters, the arbiter must have power to require personal access to it for this purpose. The implication of all powers necessary to explicate the jurisdiction is the equivalent for arbitration of 'business efficacy' in mercantile affairs generally.[10] The other is, that it is required by a custom which is either known to the parties or so notorious that they must be taken to have contracted on that basis.[11] For example, the practice of certain mercantile arbiters in taking evidence was held acceptable because —

> 'the mode of proceeding which the arbiters adopted [was] according to the custom of the place.'[12]

The arbiter's procedural powers, duties and discretion

12.6.   **Powers**. The procedural powers granted to an arbiter by the general law are wide, and include all those which are necessary

---

[8] See e.g. *Mitchell-Gill* v. *Buchan* 1921 S.C. 390 per L. P. Clyde at 395; *Johnson* v. *Gill* 1978 S.C. 74 per Lord Kissen at 83.
[9] Erskine, *Inst.* I.2.8.
[10] *McWhirter* v. *Longmuir* 1948 S.C. 577 per Lord Jamieson at 589.
[11] Walker, *Contracts*, 22.7.
[12] *Hope* v. *Crookston Brothers* (1890) 17 R. 868 per L. J. C. MacDonald at 875.

in the particular case to enable proceedings to be effectively conducted.[13] It is therefore strictly unnecessary, though it remains common practice,[14] to grant power expressly in a submission to 'receive the claims and answers of parties and take all manner of probation' he or she may 'think necessary by writ, witnesses or oath of party.' But though an arbiter's powers are wide, they are limited by the duties of the office and the court's conception of the nature of the arbiter's functions. The law has for example never accepted the existence of an implied power in the arbiter to prorogate (extend the duration of) the jurisdiction[15] or to ordain that security be found for the payment of expenses or of sums which might be found due under a final award.

12.7. **Duties.** The procedural duties of an arbiter — which may be numerous depending on the terms and nature of the submission — can be arranged under three heads corresponding to the fundamental duties of the office:-

(a) fairness as between the submitters;
(b) observance of the terms of the submission; and
(c) reasonable dispatch.

So long as an arbiter complies with these general duties he or she is 'master of all incidental procedure'[16] and is at liberty to exercise discretion.

12.8. The obligation of *fairness* is fundamental to the nature of arbitration as adjudication.[17] The parties cannot contract out of it without depriving the proceedings of their judicial character[18] and the decision of its enforceability as an award.[19] However informal proceedings may be, they must be fair.[20]

12.9. The meaning of fairness or 'natural justice' in the context of arbitration proceedings cannot be adequately summarised in a

[13] Erskine, *Inst.* I.2.8.
[14] Irons, *Arb.* 143.
[15] Bell J. M., *Arb.* paragraph 325.
[16] Guild, *Arb.* 56; *Glasgow Corporation* v. *Paterson & Sons Ltd.* (1901) 3 F. (H.L.) 34 per Lord Robertson at 40.
[17] *Sharpe* v. *Bickersdyke* (1815) III Dow. 102.
[18] *Holmes Oil Co. Ltd.* v. *Pumpherston Oil Co. Ltd.* (1891) 18 R. (H.L.) 52.
[19] *Maule* v. *Maule* (1816) IV Dow. 363.
[20] *Black* v. *John Williams & Co. (Wishaw) Ltd.* 1923 S.C. 510 per L. P. Clyde at 514.

concise definition. Pithy phrases may be helpful up to a point, but must be treated with caution because they give a misleading impression of simplicity. One of these phrases is the expression 'hear both sides' — sometimes expressed in the Latin tag *'audi alteram partem'*. The notion that both the parties to a dispute should be given a hearing is an important one, but fairness involves more than this, and the meaning of 'hearing' differs according to the circumstances. For example, both parties must normally be given an opportunity to present evidence and to address the arbiter in argument, but sometimes, as when persons of skill are appointed to determine a dispute over the value of an object, neither proof nor hearing is required;[21] and though in very formal arbitrations, in which the fairly complex general pattern of an ordinary action in the Sheriff Court is followed, fairness generally requires that the parties be permitted to be heard through legal representatives unless they have expressly agreed otherwise, in simpler proceedings legal representation may be regarded as unnecessary.[22]

12.10. Another way of expressing the obligation of fairness is to say that the parties must be treated equally. Thus if an intimation of some step in proceedings such as a visit by the arbiter to inspect property is given to one party it must be given to both[23]; advice or assistance in carrying out any arbitral functions should not be accepted from one party without the agreement of the other[24]; one party must not be excluded from the presence of the arbiter if the other is allowed to remain[25]; and an opportunity to present evidence or argument given to one must be given to both.[26] Equality of treatment is an essential element in fairness, but it must not be interpreted too literally. It might for example be most unfair to allocate to each party an equal amount of time for the presentation of evidence.

12.11. It is often said that 'justice should not only be done but should manifestly and undoubtedly be seen to be done'.[27] This

---

[21] *Logan* v. *Leadbetter* (1887) 15 R. 115.
[22] *Glasgow Corporation* v. *Paterson & Sons Ltd.* (1901) 3 F. (H.L.) 34.
[23] Guild, *Arb.* 60–1.
[24] *Johnson* v. *Lamb* 1981 S.L.T. 300 at 306. *Campbell* v. *McHolm* (1863) 2 M. 271 seems now of doubtful authority and should be confined to its own facts if followed at all.
[25] *Barrs* v. *British Wool Marketing Board* 1957 S.C. 72.
[26] *Sharpe* v. *Bickersdyke* (1815) III Dow. 102.

dictum emphasises the importance of conducting proceedings in a manner which will maintain confidence in their impartiality. If for example an arbiter were to accept hospitality from one party during an arbitration, this would inevitably give rise to a suspicion that the opportunity would be used to discuss the case outwith the presence of the opponent, even if the arbiter had not been affected in the least and no improper communications had taken place. Though it may not always be unlawful, it is always undesirable.[28] Though meetings outside the context of the arbitration may be hard to prevent, especially where the arbiter and the submitters are in the same trade, contact between the arbiter and one party should if possible be avoided.[29]

12.12.   Though fairness is hard to define, its importance cannot be overemphasised. The point has never been better expressed than by an English judge in the following passage[30] —

'It may be that there are some who would decry the importance which the courts attach to the observance of the rules of natural justice. "When something is obvious", they may say, "why force everybody to go through the tiresome waste of time involved in framing charges and giving an opportunity to be heard? The result is obvious from the start." Those who take this view do not, I think, do themselves justice. As everybody who has anything to do with the law well knows, the path of the law is strewn with examples of open and shut cases which, somehow, were not; of unanswerable charges which, in the event, were completely answered; of inexplicable conduct which was fully explained; of fixed and unalterable determinations that, by discussion, suffered a change. Nor are those with any knowledge of human nature who pause to think for a moment likely to underestimate the feelings of resentment of those who find that a decision against them has been made without their being offered any opportunity to influence the course of events.'

---

[27] *R. v. Sussex Justices, ex parte McCarthy* [1924] 1 K.B. 256 per Lord Hewart, C. J. at 259. See also *Barrs* v. *British Wool Marketing Board* 1957 S.C. 72.

[28] *Tranent Coal Co.* v. *Polson and Robertson* (1877) 15 S.L.R. 184.

[29] Mustill, *Comm. Arb.* 220. The circumstances of *Halliday* v. *Duke of Hamilton's Trustees* (1903) 5 F. 800 are unusual: on this point the decision should be confined strictly to its own facts.

[30] In *John* v. *Rees and Others* [1969] 2 All E.R. 274 per Megarry V.C. at 309.

If these words were more generally acted upon there would be fewer unjust awards and (slightly) fewer aggrieved submitters.

12.13. The second basic duty of the arbiter is to *observe the terms of the submission.* The most important element in this duty is the requirement to do everything necessary in conducting proceedings to ensure that an award can be issued which deals fully with all the issues presented for decision[31] without going beyond them.[32] It would be possible to subsume all the duties of the arbiter under the heading of compliance with the terms of the submission, this being an implied term of the appointment contract, but some duties are laid down mandatorily by law and it would be unwise to suggest that they are subject to alteration by the parties.

12.14. The duty to observe the limits of the jurisdiction is itself not without procedural implications. For example, at any time during an arbitration the arbiter may have to determine whether a particular claim or counterclaim may be entertained. Though the mere fact that the arbiter has allowed a claim which is outwith the scope of the submission to be lodged does not justify an action to interdict the proceedings,[33] and though it is readily assumed that an arbiter will keep within the jurisdiction,[34] a step may be taken early in an arbitration which 'must render the award, when pronounced, bad' and incline the court to intervene.[35]

12.15. The third basic duty of the arbiter is reasonable *dispatch* in the execution of the functions of the office.[36] The obligation has long been part of the law,[37] but its precise meaning is still not entirely clear. It probably does not mean that proceedings must be pushed ahead by the arbiter even though neither party is urging action.[38] If therefore there is no response by either party to a letter sent to both of them by the arbiter on appointment, inviting them

---

[31] *Halkerton* v. *Wishart* 30 June 1625 Mor. 645.
[32] *Carruthers* v. *Hall* (1830) 9 S. 66.
[33] *Moore* v. *McCosh* (1903) 5 F. 946 per Lord Trayner at 949.
[34] *Bennets* v. *Bennet* (1903) 5 F. 376 per L. P. Kinross at 381.
[35] *Birkmyre Brothers* v. *Moore and Weinberg* (1907) 14 S.L.T. 702.
[36] Bell J. M., *Arb.*, paragraph 377.
[37] It is acknowledged in Balfour, *Practicks*, 413.
[38] So, at least, it has been observed in England: *Bremer Vulkan Schiffbau und Maschinenfabrik* v. *South India Shipping Corporation* [1981] 1 Ll. Rep. 253 per Lord Diplock at 261.

to lodge statements of claim or to suggest a date for a preliminary meeting, the arbiter is under no obligation to press the matter.

12.16. It is not certain whether an arbiter has an obligation to maintain the *privacy* of proceedings generally as distinct from the confidentiality of particular items of evidence. There has been no legislation or caselaw on the matter in Scotland, and it is questionable whether such an obligation could properly be regarded as being, on the basis of custom, an implied term in the arbiter's contract. Doubts are increased by the fact that writers of textbooks on comparable legal systems in which arbitration law is more highly developed than in Scotland either do not mention any obligation to maintain privacy[39] or state merely that it —

'is not a legal requirement [but] has been sanctioned by long-standing practice.'[40]

12.17. **Discretion.** Subject to compliance with the three basic obligations abovementioned — and many particular duties may be imposed under the general heading of compliance with the submission — an arbiter has a wide discretion to determine how proceedings should be conducted. *'Prima facie* it is for the arbiter to decide questions of procedure'.[41] Or as Lord President Clyde once put it,[42]

'On the one hand, an arbiter carries on his shoulders all the obligations of justice which rest upon a regularly constituted court of law. On the other hand, he is dispensed — in his own discretion — from the observance of those well-tried forms of procedure which, in the case of an ordinary court, provide the instruments by which the judicial function is performed.'

A party cannot during the course of an arbitration insist that a formal procedure be followed,[43] but it is permissible to stipulate for this in the contract of submission or, in relation to the arbiter, in an implementing deed following upon an ancillary arbitration agreement.

---

[39] The following have been consulted: Holmbäck, *Arb. Swe.*; Robert, *Arb.*; Robert and Carbonneau, *Arb.*; Mustill, *Comm. Arb.*; Russell, *Arb.* 1982.

[40] Domke, *Comm. Arb.*, 24.05.

[41] *Glasgow Corporation* v. *Paterson & Sons Ltd.* (1901) 3 F. (H.L.) 34 at 40.

[42] In *Black* v. *John Williams & Co. (Wishaw) Ltd.* 1923 S.C. 510 at 514.

[43] *Ibid.*

12.18. Unless the submission provides for institutional arbitration, in which case the procedure is likely to be laid down in some detail, the parties may not know what is to be done until the arbiter tells them. If therefore the arbiter does not give clear and precise directions, injustices may easily occur. For example, it is obvious that each party should have proper notice of the case that has to be met.[44] Under the rules of the ordinary courts service on the defender is the responsibility of the pursuer; in some tribunals, such as the industrial tribunal, service of the originating application is the responsibility of the secretary of the tribunal. In each case it is clear who must act. In arbitration there is no established order, and it is therefore important that the arbiter gives clear instructions, unless a special system is imposed by the submission itself or rules incorporated therein.

12.19. It should not be thought that the possession of wide procedural discretion necessarily makes an arbiter's task easier. To follow a detailed set of rules may often be irksome and inconvenient, but if they are followed any procedural decisions made are likely to be safe from legal attack. Wide discretion means that great care must be taken to see that nothing is done or omitted which could reasonably be said to be unfair, and it requires both a sharp appreciation of the implications of procedural situations and a capacity for quick and decisive action to avoid falling into error.

Procedural duties of the submitters

12.20. Attention has been focussed in the foregoing paragraphs upon the powers, duties and discretion of the arbiter and little has been said of the submitters. This is not intended to suggest that the latter have no powers or duties of any importance. That they have, should become apparent from the discussion which follows on the rules contained in the twentyfifth Article of Regulation.

Grounds of challenge relating to procedure

12.21. The formal grounds upon which procedural faults may be attacked are —

[44] *Walker* v. *AUEW* 1969 S.L.T. 150.

(i) bribery, falsehood and corruption in terms of Article 25 of the Articles of Regulations 1695; and
(ii) misconduct, that is, a material breach of the express or implied terms of the submission.[45]

Article 25 of the Articles of Regulation refers to corruption, bribery or falsehood 'to be alleged against the judges-arbitrators', and doubts have been expressed whether such conduct on the part of the submitters can be the basis of an action based on the 1695 legislation,[46] but it must constitute a material breach of the terms of the submission by the parties thereto, and would justify the opponent in rescinding it and obtaining reduction of a decree arbitral based thereon.[47]

12.22. **Bribery** has not been the subject of much litigation, no doubt because it is extremely difficult to prove if those who commit it take elementary care to conceal their nefarious activities. There have been only two reported cases in which it has been expressly alleged,[48] though there have also been some in which acts which might have been regarded as bribery have been dealt with as 'corruption'.[49] It is therefore difficult to find any authoritative definition of the meaning of the term in this context, but arguably it includes the demanding and the acceptance of 'any payment, favour or consideration from or on behalf of either of the parties . . . with a view to influencing [the arbiter's] judgment in their favour',[50] or indeed as a reward for doing or forbearing to do anything in respect of the arbitration otherwise than in payment for fees and expenses properly earned. In an old case, an award was reduced on the ground of bribery because the arbiter had demanded a fee as a condition of its release.[51] This might suggest that in Scotland it is not considered proper to intimate to parties that the award may be uplifted on payment of the arbiter's fees and expenses, but when the case was decided arbitration was regarded as gratuitous, and it is very doubtful if this view would now be taken.

---

[45] *Adams* v. *Great North of Scotland Railway* (1890) 18 R. (H.L.) 1 per Lord Watson at 79.
[46] *Logan* v. *Lang* 15 Nov. 1798, Mor. Appx. I., No. 6, 9.
[47] *Ibid*.
[48] *Blair* v. *Gib* Jan. 12 1738, Mor. 664; *Girdwood* v. *Hercules Insurance Co.* (1833) 11 S. 351.
[49] E.g. *Mitchel* v. *Fullerton & Weir* Jan. 14 1715, Mor. 663.
[50] Irons, *Arb.*, 391.
[51] *Blair* v. *Gib* Jan. 12 1738 Mor. 664.

12.23. **Falsehood**. The meaning of this term in the context of the Articles of Regulation is equally obscure and for similar reasons. It has been suggested that 'falsehood' is confined to forgery of the submission or decree arbitral,[52] but in other cases in which falsehood has been alleged[53] the court does not seem to have regarded as irrelevant an averment that one of the submitters had concealed relevant writings or that the award contained lies. It seems that 'falsehood' must include the intentional and dishonest uttering of a forged deed,[54] and may include the concealment of relevant and admissible documentary evidence.

12.24. **Corruption**. There were quite a number of decisions reported during the nineteenth century concerning the meaning of this term in the context of the Articles of Regulation, though only two[55] since 1900. As a result of *dicta* in *Adams* v. *Great North of Scotland Railway Co.*[56] it is now reasonably clear what 'corruption' does not mean — it does not cover conduct which is not dishonest but merely careless or erroneous. The concept of 'constructive' or 'legal' corruption developed earlier by some judges[57] was there emphatically disapproved, except in so far as it was used to indicate that corruption might be inferred from the terms of the award.[58] A more positive definition is harder to come by, and here it may be helpful to have regard to the probable deprivation of the twentyfifth Article of Regulation from the concept of *dolus malus* in the civil law.[59] *Dolus* meant any kind of

'guile, chicanery or trick used to circumvent, defraud or dupe another person',[60]

---

[52] *Hardie* v. *Hardie* 18 Dec. 1724, Mor. 664 (marginal note). This is consistent with *Mell* v. *Graham* 2 Jan. 1700, IV Bro. Supp. 471.

[53] *Hetherington* v. *Carlyle* 21 June 1771 F.C.; *Hart, Petitioner* 1795, Session Papers 202:6 (Signet Library); *Blain* v. *Crawford* (Unreported, but referred to in *Hetherington*).

[54] *Ogilvie* v. *Ogilvie* 2/28 Nov. 1728, Mor. 5198 and Appx. II (Elchies), Improbation.

[55] *Robson* v. *Menzies* 1913 S.C. (J.) 90; *Cook* v. *Angus* (1943) 59 Sh. Ct. Rep. 167.

[56] (1890) 18 R. (H.L.) 1.

[57] E.g. by Lord Cockburn in *Mowbray* v. *Dickson* (1848) 10 D. 1102 at 1125 and by Lord President Inglis in *Alexander* v. *Bridge of Allan Water Co.* (1869) 7 M. 492.

[58] Per Lord Watson at 8–9.

[59] See paragraph 2.33 above.

[60] Thomas, *Text*. 228.

and in arbitration the *exceptio doli* was available in Roman law where an arbiter had been —

'led by corrupt material gain or partiality for one party to pronounce his decision as he did.'[61]

Dolus was presumed if less than a third of what was just had been decreed.[62] There has never been any suggestion in Scotland that infringement of Article 25 was presumed on such a basis, but it seems reasonable in the light of this derivation that 'corruption' includes any behaviour other than bribery and falsehood which in the opinion of a reasonable person arises from —

'some perversion of the moral feeling either by interest or passion or partiality'[63]

and could influence the outcome of the arbitration.

12.25. **Misconduct**. This concept is used in the regulation of ordinary arbitration proceedings in Scotland only in judicial decisions and juristic writing. It does not occur in legislation. Unfortunately its meaning is uncertain. Misconduct has been said[64] to involve breach of —

'the express conditions contained in the contract of submission, or any one of those important conditions which the law implies in every submission.'

The meaning of 'condition' in Scots law is not clear due to the influence of the English meaning of this term,[65] but it is probable that Lord Watson was using the word in the sense of a material or fundamental term, breach of which would justify interdict against the continuation of the arbitration or reduction of any final award. Thus, any breach of any express or implied term of the submission which of its nature could distort the outcome of the proceedings by giving the submitters something different from what they contracted for would constitute misconduct. There seems no good reason to apply the term only to behaviour of the arbiter, though that party's control of the proceedings is such that there are few

---

[61] Julien, *Ev. hist.* 225.
[62] *Ibid.* 228–9.
[63] *Cameron* v. *Menzies* (1868) 6 M. 279 per Lord Neaves at 280.
[64] By Lord Watson in *Adams* v. *Great North of Scotland Railway* (1890) 18 R. (H.L.) 1 at 8.
[65] Walker, *Contracts*, 19.3.

acts or omissions of the submitters falling short of those struck at by article 25 of the 1695 Articles of Regulation which could have a significant effect on the award.

12.26. The question remains, what implied conditions are there, breach of which would constitute misconduct on the part of an arbiter? It is probable that there are two — failure to ensure fairness and failure to observe the limits of, and yet to exhaust fully, the matters referred by the parties for arbitral decision — in brief, conduct contrary to 'natural justice' or involving jurisdictional error.

12.27. With regard to the former, it seems clear that an honest mistake can constitute misconduct. In one case[66] the arbiter honestly believed, as a result of an error on the part of his clerk, that a letter had been received from each of the submitters to the effect that they had nothing further to add to their pleadings and had been sufficiently heard. In fact one of them had not even sent such a letter, and had not concluded his case. The award was nevertheless reduced.

12.28. The latter is more controversial. It is possible to derive from Lord Watson's speech in *Adams* the conclusion that 'misconduct' does not extend beyond acts contrary to natural justice. This appears to have been the opinion of Lord Maxwell in *Johnson* v. *Lamb*.[67] The adoption of this view would however leave a conceptual gap in the law. Jurisdictional error on the part of an arbiter can certainly lead to reduction of the award[68]; just as certainly, an error of this kind does not, as such, come within the twentyfifth article of the Articles of Regulation. Therefore, if jurisdictional error is not misconduct, it will be necessary to invent another name for it. Since neither acts contrary to natural justice nor jurisdictional error necessarily involve any moral fault, and since both may result in the reduction of any award thereafter pronounced, it would seem appropriate in the interests of a rational and coherent structure of principle to regard both as types of misconduct.

[66] *Sharpe* v. *Bickersdyke* (1815) III Dow. 102.
[67] 1981 S.L.T. 300 at 305.
[68] *Halkerton* v. *Wishart* 30 June 1625, Mor. 645; *Carruthers* v. *Hall* (1830) 9 S. 66.

12.29. The conception of misconduct expounded above as being the law of Scotland is close to, but not identical with, the same conception expounded by Mustill[69] as the law of England. This branch of English law has a statutory basis in section 23 of the Arbitration Act 1950, and has been shaped by courts which have enjoyed under that Act and its predecessors a wider discretion in deciding whether to set aside an award than that possessed by their Scottish counterparts. It would seem that in England an act or omission may constitute misconduct without necessarily being such as to induce a court to set any subsequent award aside, and it is regarded as misconduct to 'behave in a way regarded by the courts as contrary to public policy'.[70] On the other hand, since the English courts are generally more willing than those of Scotland to accept a term as being implied in the submission, cases are likely to occur in which on the same facts an English court would hold that the arbitrator had not exceeded the jurisdiction, and had thus not committed any misconduct, while a Scots court would come to the opposite conclusion. It is therefore dangerous to regard English authorities on arbitral misconduct as being persuasive in Scotland.

Remedies

12.30. The remedies for bribery, falsehood, corruption and misconduct are interdict against the continuance of the arbitration or reliance upon a subsequent award, suspension of any diligence used to enforce an award, reduction of the award, and an order to the arbiter to implement his or her duties under the submission. Interdict and the order to implement are considered in this chapter; reduction and suspension are considered in chapter fourteen which deals with the award. It has been suggested[71] that the Court of Session has power to remove an arbiter —

'either in virtue of its *nobile officium* or its inherent power to redress a wrong'.

but if it exists it appears never to have been exercised. This may be because however convenient it may be to eject an unsatisfactory arbiter without thereby terminating the proceedings, unless there

---

[69] *Comm. Arb.* 494–6.
[70] Mustill, *Comm. Arb.* 494.
[71] Irons, *Arb.* 126.

is also power to appoint a replacement — and there is certainly no such power — it is unlikely to be more useful than interdict.

12.31. Interdict. This is —

'a remedy by decree of court, either against a wrong in course of being done, or against an apprehended violation of a party's rights, only to be awarded on evidence of the wrong, or on reasonable grounds of apprehension that such violation is intended.'[72]

Interdict may be granted at the instance of one of the submitters if it is clear that the arbiter does not have the jurisdiction he or she has been called upon to exercise,[73] or has become disqualified from acting,[74] or has taken some step which would inevitably prove fatal to the award if the proceedings were allowed to continue to that point.[75] Interdict will be an appropriate remedy where there are circumstances which suggest that the demand for arbitration is no more than a delaying tactic. This may be so where, for example, there is no real question to determine,[76] or the relationship between the submitters[77] or the nature of the claim[78] is such that there is clearly no right to call for arbitration on the matter. Even a submitter who nominated the arbiter who is discovered to be disqualified may bring the action,[79] since he or she runs the risk of expense and delay if the proceedings are prolonged only to be rendered abortive by the reduction of the award. A judicial assignee of a submitter, having been excluded from participation in the proceedings, may seek interdict against their continuance.[80]

12.32. The grant of interdict is however in the discretion of the court, and there is great reluctance to interfere with an ongoing

---

[72] *Hay's Trustees* v. *Young* (1877) 4 R. 398 per Lord Ormidale at 401.

[73] *Glasgow and South Western Railway Co.* v. *Caledonian Railway Co.* (1871) 44 Sc. Jur. 29 per Lord Neaves at 31; *McCoard* v. *Glasgow Corporation* 1934 S.N. 112.

[74] *McKenzie* v. *Clark* (1828) 7 S. 215.

[75] *Birkmyre Brothers* v. *Moore & Weinberg* (1906) 14 S.L.T. 702.

[76] *Parochial Board of Greenock* v. *Coghill* (1875) 5 R. 732; *Albyn Housing Ltd.* v. *Taylor Woodrow Homes Ltd.* 1985 S.L.T. 309.

[77] *Cormack* v. *McIldowie's Trustees* 1974 S.L.T. 178.

[78] *Glasgow and South West Railway Co.* v. *Boyd & Forrest* 1918 S.C. (H.L.) 14 (*res judicata*).

[79] *Magistrates of Edinburgh* v. *Lownie* (1903) 5 F. 711.

[80] *Rutherford* v. *Licences & General Insurance Co. Ltd.* 1934 S.L.T. 31.

arbitration.[81] It is not lightly assumed that arbiters will exceed the limits of their jurisdiction.[82] A submitter who is adversely affected by some act or omission of an arbiter ought to draw the matter to his or her attention and if possible allow an opportunity for the matter to be put right before seeking the assistance of the court,[83] and if a disqualified person has been appointed to act under an ancillary submission, but no disputes have yet arisen for determination, application for interdict will be regarded as premature.[84] Where there is doubt it may be convenient to apply[85] to have a case stated for the opinion of the court on a question of law instead of seeking an interdict.

12.33. A submitter who during the proceedings becomes aware of some ground of objection which he or she could make to their continuance must state that objection timeously, and not allow the opponent to incur trouble and expense in the belief either that no objection exists or that such objection as there is has been waived. Failure to object at the proper time will mean that an attempt later to have the award reduced will be met by a plea of acquiescence and will fail. Nevertheless a submitter who during proceedings states an objection to their continuance is not compelled to elect between standing on the objection and declining to appear further or waiving the objection.[86] Objection during the proceedings is all that is required to avoid the plea of acquiescence being successfully urged at a later date — there is no need to raise an action of interdict.

12.34. **Order to implement**. The enforcement of the positive obligations of an arbiter, notably the obligation of reasonable dispatch, has been thought[87] to give rise to some difficulty. The expressions of doubt may have been caused by the failure of the submitter in some old cases[88] to obtain redress by 'letters of

---

[81] *Farrell* v. *Arnott* (1857) 19 D. 1000 per Lord Mackenzie at 1001; *Christison's Trustee* v. *Callendar-Brodie* (1906) 8 F. 928.

[82] *Dumbarton Water Commissioners* v. *Lord Blantyre* (1884) 12 R. 115 per Lord Shand at 120; *Bennets* v. *Bennet* (1903) 5 F. 376.

[83] *Wemyss* v. *Ardrossan Harbour Co.* (1893) 20 R. 500 per Lord McLaren at 505.

[84] *Caledonian Railway Co.* v. *Magistrates of Glasgow* (1897) 25 R. 74.

[85] Under s. 3 of the Administration of Justice (Scotland) Act 1972.

[86] *Johnson* v. *Lamb* 1981 S.L.T. 300.

[87] *Marshall* v. *Edinburgh and Glasgow Railway Co.* (1853) 15 D. 603 per L. P. McNeill at 605.

[88] E.g. *Cheisly* v. *Calderwood* 13 Jan. 1699, Mor. 632.

horning',[89] an old and now obsolete means of enforcement which led to the forfeiture to the Crown of the moveables of the offender as an assumed rebel.[90] The failure to obtain redress there arose from the absence of any signed consent on the part of the arbiter to any document including an express promise to hear and determine the cause within a stated time, a penalty clause, and a clause of registration for execution. It is questionable whether the absence of an express consent to hear and determine within a stated time would nowadays lead to the unenforceability of the obligation, for an aggrieved submitter has been known to raise a petition[91] in the Court of Session — not the sheriff court[92] — to ordain a dilatory arbiter to meet and hear parties and thereafter proceed as might be just. Refusal to comply with such an order would presumably, as in the case of failure to obey an interdict, constitute contempt of court[93] and would be punishable as such by the imposition of a fine or even imprisonment.

Procedure

12.35. The procedure by which an interdict or order for implement may be sought against an arbiter is an application for judicial review[94] under Rule 260B of the Rules of Court.[95] That rule provides that —

'an application to the supervisory jurisdiction of the court which immediately before the coming into operation of this rule would have been made by way of summons or petition, shall be made by way of an application for judicial review in accordance with the provisions of this rule.'

[89] These were available to enforce submissions: Mackenzie, Sir George, *Institutions of the Law of Scotland*, Edinburgh, 1684, IV.3.
[90] Erskine, *Principles of the Law of Scotland*, Edinburgh, 1754 (18th edn. 1890), II.5.24–6; IV.3.8.
[91] *Watson* v. *Robertson* (1893) 22 R. 362; *Marshall* v. *Edinburgh & Glasgow Railway Co.* (1853) 15 D. 603.
[92] *Forbes* v. *Underwood* (1886) 13 R. 465.
[93] As defined in *H.M. Advocate* v. *Airs* 1975 S.L.T. 177.
[94] This procedure was used in *O'Neill* v. *Scottish J.N.C.* 1987 S.C.L.R. 275, though it should be noted that there the petitioner was seeking reduction of a decree arbitral.
[95] Established in its modern form by Act of Sederunt (Rules of Court Amendment No. 2) (Judicial Review) 1985 (S.I. 1985 No. 500 (S. 48)). On this procedure generally see St. Clair J. and Davidson N. F., *Judicial Review in Scotland*, Edinburgh, 1986.

The application is by means of a petition. Rule 260B has been said to provide no remedy of relief which did not previously exist in some form,[96] and there would seem therefore to be no alteration to the principle that an arbiter as a private judge is subject to the supervisory jurisdiction of the Court of Session in the same way as an inferior public judge.[97] Though the procedure for the reduction of an award was formerly an ordinary action for reduction as if the award were a private deed, this was not wholly inconsistent with its being in a sense an application to the supervisory jurisdiction of the court. The new rule does appear to cover cases in which the proceedings were formerly instituted by summons as well as those initiated by petition, but it is 'not available where other means of review are provided and those means have either not been made use of or have been used without success'.[98]

Enforcement of procedural orders against submitters

12.36. The procedural orders of an arbiter may be enforced against a submitter at least to the extent of any penalty specified in the submission.[99] Where the submission contains both a penalty clause and a clause of registration for execution the penalty may be enforced immediately by the opponent. If there is no such clause of registration, it may be that application could be made to the court as in cases where it is the arbiter who is at fault, but this does not appear to have been attempted in any reported case. This is probably because it is unnecessary. Though an arbiter probably cannot grant decree by default,[100] he or she may proceed *ex parte* — in the absence of the recalcitrant submitter — to take such evidence as may be available, and normally this will be sufficient grounds upon which to base a decree. The absent party, who is obviously unable to discharge any burden of proof, may then be held as confessed.[101]

---

[96] *O'Neill* v. *Scottish J.N.C. (supra).*
[97] *Forbes* v. *Underwood* (1886) 13 R. 465 per L. P. Inglis at 470.
[98] *O'Neill* v. *Scottish J.N.C. (supra).*
[99] Stair, *Inst.* IV.39.14.
[100] *United Collieries Ltd.* v. *Gavin* (1899) 2 F. 60 per L. P. Balfour at 65.
[101] *Mitchell* v. *Cable* (1848) 10 D. 1297 per Lord Fullerton at 1308.

CHAPTER THIRTEEN

THE CONDUCT OF ARBITRATION PROCEEDINGS: 2 PRACTICE

Introduction

13.1. This chapter is divided into two sections: the first deals with general points of practice, including some which are likely to arise early in proceedings and the second with the course of an arbitration. Chapter fourteen deals with two special topics — evidence and the stated case. All that can usefully be done in discussing practice is to indicate how the principles set out in the preceding chapter may be applied, and to provide some general guidance. There is no set pattern which all arbitrations must follow — what is acceptable in an agricultural arbitration[1] or a technical reference in a mercantile dispute[2] may be quite inappropriate and even unlawful in a case which in its nature requires to be handled with some formality.[3]

General points of practice

13.2. **Co-operation between arbiters.** If more than one arbiter has been appointed, they must all — apart from the oversman — act together from the outset in performing the judicial and administrative or ministerial functions of their office.[4] Nothing of any importance, not even the appointment at the outset of a clerk, should be undertaken until all the arbiters have been appointed. An award made without the participation of one of the appointed arbiters, is a nullity,[5] and the same may probably be said of any other judicial act. Disagreements between two arbiters may

[1] As in *Davidson* v. *Logan* 1908 S.C. 350.
[2] As in *Barr* v. *Wilson's Trustee* (1852) 15 D. 21 (ship's accounts).
[3] As in *McLaren* v. *Aikman* 1939 S.C. 222.
[4] Irons, *Arb.* 168.
[5] Bell, J. M., *Arb.* paragraph 783.

be resolved by devolution upon the oversman. Where there are three or more arbiters it seems that they may act by a majority unless the submission otherwise provides,[6] though if no express power to do so is given the dissenters must at least execute the decree arbitral to indicate by this means not only their disagreement but also their participation in the decision.[7]

13.3. **Appointment of oversman.** Where there is an even number of arbiters they have an implied power to appoint an oversman unless the submission provides otherwise.[8] It is generally preferable to exercise this power at the outset so that the appointment is not affected by any disagreement that may later arise on a substantive issue in the arbitration. It may also be convenient for the oversman to sit in on proceedings where appropriate, though he or she should not participate in any decisions taken by the arbiters.[9] It is perfectly competent to appoint an oversman before a difference has arisen between the arbiters unless to do so would be contrary to the submission.[10] The appointment of an oversman must be distinguished from the devolution of the arbitration upon that person. The latter, discussed below,[11] is permissible only[12] where there has arisen —

'such a difference of opinion between arbiters — either on the merits of the questions involved or on the proper procedure to be followed — as brings the proceedings to a deadlock.'[13]

13.4. In nominating an oversman the arbiters must take as much care as should have been taken by the submitters over their own nomination.[14] The nomination and appointment of an oversman by the arbiters is sometimes referred to as a 'judicial act'.[15] This

[6] Erskine. *Inst.* IV.3.34.
[7] *Ibid.*; *McCallum v. Robertson* (1825) 4 S. 66, affd. 2 W. & S. 344; *Love v. Love* (1825) 4 S. 53.
[8] Arbitration (Scotland) Act 1894 s. 4.
[9] *Frederick v. Maitland and Cunningham* (1865) 3 M. 1069 at 1072.
[10] *Crawford v. Paterson* (1858) 20 D. 488 per L.P. McNeill at 492; *Sellar v. Highland Railway Co.* 1918 S.C. 838 per Lord Johnston at 853, affd. 1919 S.C. (H.L.) 19.
[11] Paragraphs 13.51.–13.53.
[12] *Gibson v. Fotheringham* 1914 S.C. 987 per Lord Salvesen at 994.
[13] *Ibid.* per Lord Guthrie at 996.
[14] *Sellar v. Highland Railway Co.* 1919 S.C. (H.L.) 19 per Lord Finlay at 25.
[15] E.g. by Guild, *Arb.* 51.

description is acceptable in so far as it emphasises the need for care, and in particular the avoidance of any procedure whose outcome depends upon the operation of chance. The latter is unlawful unless it is accepted by all the nominators that all the persons upon whom the lot may fall are equally suitable.[16] In the event of the arbiters failing to agree on a nomination, any of the submitters may apply to the court to make an appointment,[17] and may do so even if the arbiters have not yet differed on the merits of the dispute.[18]

13.5. The nomination and appointment of the oversman should be effected in writing,[19] and if the submission itself has been formally executed the offer of appointment and the oversman's acceptance should be equally formal,[20] though in mercantile arbitrations informal letters passing between the arbiters and their nominee have been held sufficient[21] and probably telex is now acceptable.

13.6. **Appointment of clerk.** Arbiters in Scotland normally appoint a clerk at a very early stage in proceedings. The clerk is usually a solicitor with experience of arbitration practice, and his or her duties include the safe custody of written pleadings and other documents, and the provision of advice to the arbiter on procedure and on the drafting of interlocutors and decrees arbitral. If the arbiter does not have access to office facilities, the clerk provides them, and acts as the main channel of communication between the arbiter and the submitters, and also as administrative assistant dealing, for example, with such matters as the hire of rooms if this is necessary. The arbiter's clerk fulfils at proofs and hearings and other meetings the functions of a clerk to a tribunal, ensuring that witnesses enter promptly in the expected order, and that works of reference, written pleadings, documentary evidence and other productions are available. When not otherwise occupied he or she also keeps a note of the evidence given by witnesses,

---

[16] *Smith* v. *Liverpool and London and Globe Insurance Co.* (1887) 14 R. 931 per L.P. Inglis at 937.

[17] Arbitration (Scotland) Act 1894 s. 4.

[18] *Glasgow Parish Council* v. *United Collieries Ltd.* (1907) 15 S.L.T. 232.

[19] The authorities are old and generally do not distinguish between nomination, appointment and devolution: *Middleton* v. *Chalmers* (1721) Rob. 391; *Colquhoun* v. *Corbet* (1784) 2 Paton 626.

[20] Irons, *Arb.* 174.

[21] *Mackenzie* v. *Hill* (1868) 40 Sc. Jur. 499.

except in the rare cases in which a shorthand writer is employed. The employment of a clerk does not guarantee that no procedural errors will occur[22] but it probably reduces their incidence. It also reduces the temptation upon an arbiter to accept professional assistance from a person who is solicitor to one of the submitters, a practice which appears to be acceptable in England[23] but is possibly misconduct in Scotland.[24]

13.7. Where the proceedings are likely to be of any legal complexity or to involve lengthy written pleadings or a substantial volume of documentary evidence the appointment of a clerk is desirable, and indeed the procedure laid down in the Rules of Court for making application for a stated case for the opinion of the court on a question of law appears to assume[25] that a clerk will have been appointed. There are however several types of case in which the employment of a clerk is unusual. Where the sums at stake are very small the expense of a clerk is not justified, and in technical references, where it is apparent from the start that there will be no written pleadings and that only the arbiter's personal examination of some lands or buildings or accounts or other objects is required, there is little for a clerk to do. The terms of the submission may forbid the appointment of a clerk, but this is probably rare. Apart from such stipulation the arbiter has a discretion whether to appoint a clerk[26] and whom to choose to fill the office. No person should be appointed who has any family or business connection with either of the submitters or any interest in the outcome of the proceedings since justice might then not be seen to be done. There is however probably no objection to the appointment of a partner of the arbiter.[27]

13.8. **Appointment of assessors.** It has long been accepted[28] that an arbiter may not delegate any of the judicial functions of the

---

[22] As appears from *Sharpe* v. *Bickersdyke* (1815) III Dow 102.

[23] *Bunten and Lancaster (Produce) Ltd.* v. *Kiril Mischoff Ltd.* [1964] 1 Ll. Rep. 386.

[24] This could be inferred from dicta in *Johnson* v. *Lamb* 1981 S.L.T. 300 at 306.

[25] Especially in Rule 277.

[26] *Fletcher* v. *Robertson* (1918) S.L.T. 68 at 69, revd. on other grounds 1919 S.L.T. 260.

[27] *Laughland* v. *Galloway* 1968 S.L.T. 272 (J.P. Fiscal and J.P. Clerk).

[28] *Stark* v. *Thumb* 20 Mar. 1630, Mor. 6834. The rule may be derived from canon law, on which see Hostiensis, *Comm.*, X.1.43.–13. Fol. 209, r°, 210°.

office to another person[29] without the express consent of all the submitters.[30] It is however permissible to appoint an assessor to give advice on a matter on which the arbiter has no knowledge.[31]

13.9. **Determination of procedural law.** Just as an arbiter cannot finally determine the scope of the jurisdiction,[32] so he or she cannot finally determine what is the 'curial law', that is, the law governing the procedure to be followed and the admissibility and weight of evidence presented in the arbitration. This does not however mean that no decision at all can be made on this matter, and in cases with an international element such a decision may indeed be necessary.

13.10. The curial law of the arbitration, which comes into effect when the arbiter has been properly appointed and is in a position to determine the procedure to be adopted,[33] is distinguishable both from the law governing the obligations of the submitters in the dispute which is the subject of the arbitration and from the law governing the contract of submission itself. This follows from the fact that arbitration has a jurisdictional as well as a contractual element. From the point of view of the legal system which enforces arbitral awards, an arbiter exercises an inferior jurisdiction.[34] Therefore, while the submitters are in Scots law permitted a wide discretion in framing or adopting from institutional sources rules to govern arbitration proceedings and while the arbiter is permitted an equally wide discretion, subject to any rules the submitters may have prescribed, in determining how proceedings are to be conducted,[35] both the submitters' rules and the arbiter's discretion are governed by the curial law of the arbitration.

---

[29] *Skerret* v. *Oliver* (1896) 23 R. 468 at 482; *Paton* v. *Abernethy Co-operative Society Ltd.* (1923) 39 Sh. Ct. Rep. 283.

[30] As in *Crudens Ltd. Petitioners* 1971 S.C. 64.

[31] Bell J. M., *Arb.* paragraph 470; *Caledonian Railway Co.* v. *Lockhart* (1860) III Macq. 808 per L. C. Campbell at 812–13.

[32] *Caledonian Railway Co.* v. *Greenock & Wemyss Bay Railway Co.* (1872) 10 M. 892 per Lord Kinlock at 898, affd. (1874) 1 R. (H.L.) 8.

[33] So, at least, it has been held in England: *International Tank and Pipe S.A.K.* v. *Kuwait Aviation Fuelling Co. K.S.C.* [1975] Q.B. 224 per Lord Denning at 233.

[34] *Forbes* v. *Underwood* (1886) 13 R. 465 per L.P. Inglis at 467.

[35] *Holmes Oil Co.* v. *Pumpherston Oil Co.* (1890) 17 R. 624 per Lord Rutherfurd Clark at 656, expressly approved in the House of Lords by Lord Robertson in *Glasgow Corporation* v. *Paterson & Sons Ltd.* (1901) 3 F. (H.L.) 34 at 40.

Though arbitral awards which are valid and enforceable in one country are regularly enforced in another as a result of international agreement, it would be surprising if the law of Scotland permitted arbitration proceedings taking place in this country to be governed by a law other than the law of Scotland simply because the submitters had so contracted.

13.11. The rules upon which the curial law of an arbitration has to be determined have not yet been decided by a Scottish court, but they have been considered by the House of Lords in a case concerning an arbitration taking place in Scotland. That decision[36] is obviously of great weight even though it occurred in the context of an appeal from an English court. The case arose out of a contract between an English and a Scottish company in the form of the 1963 English edition of the Royal Institute of British Architects' standard form. The contract was negotiated in England and executed in Scotland, and concerned construction work to be performed in Scotland. A dispute arose and the Scottish company applied to the President of the RIBA for the appointment of an arbiter. The application was made on a standard RIBA form which contained a reference to the English Arbitration Act 1950. The President appointed a Scottish architect as arbiter, and he appointed a Glasgow solicitor as clerk and conducted the proceedings in Scotland in accordance with Scottish practice. The English company did not object to this manner of proceeding, but later requested the arbiter to state his award in the form of a special case for the opinion of the English High Court. The arbiter refused on the ground that under Scots law he had no duty or even power to comply with that request. The English company applied to the High Court in England to order him to do so. The matter ultimately came before the House of Lords, where the main question was whether the procedure of the arbitration was governed by Scots or English law.

13.12. A majority of the judges were of opinion that the proper law of the main contract was English law, and they were unanimous that the arbitration proceedings were governed by Scots law. In so doing they recognised unequivocally that the curial law of arbitration proceedings and the law governing the

---

[36] In *James Miller and Partners* v. *Whitworth Street Estates (Manchester) Ltd.* [1970] A.C. 583.

issues in dispute may be different. The grounds upon which they thought that the curial law had to be determined are however less clear. While there was general agreement that in the absence of any agreement between the submitters to the contrary the curial law must be the law of the place of the arbitration, some judges[37] appear to have accepted without question that it was open to the submitters to choose what that law should be, while others[38] seem to have doubted whether the curial law could ever be other than the law of the place at which the proceedings took place. It is submitted that the latter view is more consistent with the view hitherto taken by the courts in Scotland that arbitration in Scotland is an inferior jurisdiction supervised in the manner of its exercise by the Scottish courts and governed in the last resort by rules and principles forming part of the law of Scotland. However wide may be the discretion allowed by Scots law to submitters in choosing the place in which and in prescribing the rules by which an arbitration is to be held and to arbiters in determining subject to any such provisions where and how proceedings are to be conducted, the curial law of proceedings conducted in Scotland is almost certainly the law of Scotland irrespective of any provision by the submitters to the contrary. As a similar attitude is likely to be taken by courts elsewhere in relation to proceedings conducted within the area of their jurisdiction, and as it would be confusing for a single arbitration to be conducted according to different laws, it is unwise for an arbiter to conduct different parts of an arbitration in different countries. If evidence required in a Scottish arbitration has to be obtained abroad, it should be taken on commission.

13.13. **Determination of procedure**. Subject to the general duties referred to in the previous chapter, which include compliance with the terms of the submission so far as these are lawful, an arbiter has under the law of Scotland a wide discretion to determine how proceedings are to be conducted.[39] At the more formal end of the spectrum there is the adversarial type of procedure patterned on the ordinary action in the Sheriff Court. For the benefit of lay arbiters this is described below.[40] At the

---

[37] Such as Lord Guest at 608.
[38] E.g. Lord Wilberforce at 616 and Lord Hodson at 606.
[39] *Holmes Oil Co.* (*supra* note 35).
[40] Paragraphs 13.23, 13.27.–13.30.

informal end, there is personal examination of an object by the arbiter. In between there is a range of procedures which combine in various ways adversarial and investigatory and structured and informal methods of doing justice. The arbiter's approach to procedure must be affected by the nature and complexity of the matters in issue, the agreed views of the submitters, and his or her own knowledge and expertise.

13.14. The issues in an arbitration are broadly classifiable into questions of law,[41] fact, quality and value, and combinations of any two or more of these. Sometimes it is suggested that questions of quality or value are of their very nature suitable for simple personal investigation by the arbiter, but they may be associated with questions of fact which require evidence to be taken from witnesses. For example, in a dispute over the quality of certain roughcasting work, a plasterer was appointed arbiter. He inspected the work, discovering that coke breeze had been used for part of it instead of granite chips. The contractor then alleged that he had been authorised by the client to use coke breeze. The terms of the submission were such that the arbiter, who had probably expected to be required merely to carry out a physical examination of the building, properly considered that he had to enquire into the truth of this allegation, and he therefore took evidence informally from the submitters and certain of their employees, who were examined outwith the presence of their employers in order to prevent intimidation. The award, which was subsequently challenged on the grounds of procedural misconduct but upheld,[42] ultimately turned not simply on the mixed question of fact and quality relating to the roughcasting work itself, but on the actings of the parties and the legal implications thereof. It is therefore wise to give consideration to the manner of proceeding not only at the outset of an arbitration but also later if the circumstances make this appropriate.

13.15. **Communications with submitters.** Communications between the arbiter and the submitters should be open, definite, clear, and secure, and decisions once intimated should be consistently acted upon. Openness, definiteness, clarity and

[41] The nature of a question of law is discussed below, paragraphs 14.2–14.26.
[42] *Black* v. *John Williams & Co. (Wishaw) Ltd.* 1923 S.C. 510, 1924 S.C. (H.L.) 22.

consistency are required of an arbiter by the obligation to act fairly; security is to some extent a requirement of fairness and a protection against future allegations of unfairness. An arbiter should in general make every reasonable effort to defer to the convenience of the submitters, and to do so in a manner which treats them equally.

13.16. Openness is an important means of protecting the integrity of an arbitration. Both the submitters — all of them if there are more than two — must be made aware of everything of importance that is communicated by the arbiter to one of them. The courts are not so pedantic as to disapprove of trivial incidental contacts in private such as a visit to deposit documents,[43] but justice must be seen to be done.[44] Private conversations between the arbiter or the clerk and a submitter by telephone or face to face should be minimised and confined to such matters as inviting and making suggestions as to convenient dates for meetings. Both the submitters should receive copies of all written communications, including telexes, dealing with matters which it would be improper to communicate in private conversation.

13.17. An arbiter should communicate his or her intentions and instructions to the submitters in clear, precise and definite terms. There may sometimes be a reluctance to issue peremptory orders in what is assumed to be a relatively amicable proceeding, but it is unwise to be so relaxed that parties are left in any uncertainty as to what is expected of them or what the arbiter intends to do. For example, it is inappropriate for an arbiter to intimate to the submitters that he or she 'hopes' to have certain documents by a specified date, for this does not put them on notice that if the documents have not been produced by then the arbiter will decide without them. To issue in such terms what is intended to be an order has been held in England to amount to misconduct,[45] and it seems likely that a Scottish court would come to a similar conclusion provided that the aggrieved party did whatever was possible to provide the arbiter with an opportunity to retrieve the error.

---

[43] *Barr* v. *Wilson's Trustee* (1852) 15 D. 21 per Lord Robertson at 24.
[44] *Barrs* v. *British Wool Marketing Board* 1957 S.C. 72.
[45] The '*Myron*' (*Owners*) v. *Tradax Export S.A.* [1969] 1 Ll. Rep. 411.

13.18. Since injustice may arise from failure or delay in communication, arbiters should ensure, normally through their clerks, that intimation is effected by the most secure means. For protection against false or erroneous allegations of non-receipt, interlocutors — formal orders of a procedural nature — and important documents should normally be sent by recorded delivery post, and the arbiter should retain copies of all correspondence with the submitters and postal receipts along with the bundle of documents — called in Scotland the 'process' — containing the claims and answers, documentary productions, and copies of motions and interlocutors.

13.19. An arbiter should seek to be consistent and thereby to fulfil the expectations that he or she has created in the minds of the submitters. For example, if after a proof the arbiter has intimated to the submitters a willingness to receive from them any final written statements that they may wish to make, a reasonable time must be allowed to enable them to do this.[46] Similarly, if an intention to hold a meeting or to inspect a site has been expressed, it should be adhered to unless explicitly and timeously revoked. In an English case,[47] an arbiter had written to the parties' solicitors indicating that before the hearing he would personally view the property which was the focus of the dispute. In the event, he did not do so, and one of the parties, who was unaware of this and who at the hearing had called no expert evidence and had conducted his case on the basis that the arbiter would by then have viewed the property, successfully brought an action to have the award set aside. It seems likely that a Scottish court would come to a similar conclusion if the arbiter had failed to rectify the error on being given an opportunity so to do.

13.20. So far as possible an arbiter should consult the convenience of the parties when arranging the dates of meeting and should always give reasonable notice. What constitutes reasonable notice in a particular case will depend on the nature of the meeting, the complexity of the case and the distance the parties and their witnesses have to travel. The absence of reasonable notice will usually constitute a breach of natural justice and therefore misconduct.[48] There is nevertheless a limit to the patience an

---

[46] *Walker* v. *AUEW* 1969 S.L.T. 150 at 153.
[47] *Micklewright* v. *Mullock* (1974) 232 E.G. 337.
[48] *Walker* v. *AUEW* 1969 S.L.T. 150 at 151.

arbiter should show to parties who seek without reasonable justification to delay the progress of the arbitration. It is not corruption or misconduct to refuse a request that a hearing be indefinitely postponed or adjourned until certain evidence alleged to be vital and in existence becomes available,[49] or until the party concerned has had time to consult counsel on a matter which is not of any great legal complexity or on which advice could have been obtained earlier, even if not from the chosen advocate.[50] In general it is for the party seeking delay to satisfy the arbiter fully that the request is reasonable and does not involve unfairness to the opponent.

13.21. Representation. Subject to the terms of the submission, an arbiter has a discretion whether or not to allow parties to be represented, and if so whether by solicitors or counsel.[51] That discretion must however be exercised 'according to the subject matter ... in hand, and the resulting considerations of convenience and justice.'[52] Where a very formal mode of procedure with full written pleadings has been adopted, the denial of professional assistance would be unfair since such procedures can be effectively operated only by people who are trained to use them. Also, if it is considered appropriate to exclude the submitters personally, which may be done in the interests of eliciting truthful evidence from a witness who is subject to the power of one of them — for example because of being in that person's employment[53] — they should be allowed representation by professional persons who are aware that they have duties not only to their clients but to the administration of justice. In relatively simple proceedings it may often be appropriate to refuse to allow professional representation, especially where there is a great disparity of means between the parties, financial assistance under the statutory legal aid scheme not being available in arbitration proceedings. Having once approved professional representation, an arbiter should not withdraw that approval without good cause and due notice, for to

---

[49] *Livingstone* v. *Black & Knox* 16 Jan. 1809 F.C.

[50] *Spearman* v. *Pitloh* (1828) 6 S. 645.

[51] *Kirkaldy* v. *Dalgairns* June 16 1809 F.C.

[52] *Glasgow Corporation* v. *Paterson & Son Ltd* (1901) 3 F. (H.L.) 34 per Lord Robertson at 40.

[53] *Black* v. *John Williams and Co. (Wishaw) Ltd.* 1923 S.C. 510 per L.P. Clyde at 515.

do so is misconduct.[54] It is equally incumbent upon a submitter to give reasonable notice to the arbiter and to the opponent of an intention to be represented professionally in any proceedings in the arbitration. If failure to do so is likely to prejudice the opponent, it will justify the arbiter in refusing to hear the representatives.

The course of an arbitration

13.22. **Preliminary proceedings.** Where the procedure to be followed is not laid down expressly and in detail in rules incorporated into the submission, or impliedly by custom of trade, a meeting may be convened by the arbiter to obtain the views of parties on procedural matters. It appears, however, that in Scotland the holding of a preliminary meeting is less common than in England.[55] Though the general character of the procedure and its initial stages such as the time limits for lodging claims and answers should be determined by the arbiter at the outset, it is usually inappropriate to establish a rigid timetable for the whole arbitration at this point unless the arbiter's own availability is restricted, for problems are quite likely to arise which could make strict adherence to it difficult and even productive of injustice.

13.23. **Lodging of claims and answers.** Except in technical references in which only the arbiter's personal investigation of material objects is required,[56] the submitters will usually require to lodge claims and answers with the arbiter's clerk. Unless a timetable for doing these things is laid down in rules incorporated into the submission, the arbiter must determine it. In proceedings of the more formal type, the arbiter's orders are issued to both or all of the submitters in the form of interlocutors,[57] and the claims and answers of the parties are presented as if they were initial writs and defences, all in a manner similar to the practice of the sheriff courts. Copies of the claims and defences are intimated by the parties to their opponents, the principal being lodged with the arbiter's clerk. It is not legally necessary to be so formal, however.

---

[54] *Walker* v. *AUEW* 1969 S.L.T. 150 at 153.
[55] Hawker and Ors., *ICE Arb.*, 106.
[56] *Dundas* v. *Hogg & Allan* 1937 S.L.T. (Sh. Ct.) 2.
[57] Useful styles may be found in Halliday, *Conveyancing*, Vol I., paragraphs 14–40 to 14–49 and 14–51 to 14–54.

All that is essential is that in good time before the hearing each of the submitters is made aware of the facts which the opponent intends to prove and the legal basis of any claim that is being made,[58] and that the arbiter receives notice of these matters in sufficient time to grasp the nature of the case before having to listen to evidence and argument upon it.

13.24. **Absence of defender.** If claims have been lodged with the arbiter but the defender has failed to lodge defences within the time specified, the arbiter may proceed to determine the case and issue an award in the absence of the defender,[59] provided always that proper intimation has been made to him or her of all stages of the proceedings, and that sufficient evidence has been taken to satisfy the arbiter that the facts are as claimed by the pursuer.[60]

13.25. **Late claims or counterclaims.** It is usually wise for the arbiter to entertain late claims or counterclaims, under reservation of the liability of the party concerned for any consequent expenses. In one case[61] in which the arbiter refused to receive late counterclaims lodged by the defender after the arbiter had issued proposed findings, he was held[62] to have committed a 'denial of justice' and his award based on the existing claims and defences was reduced. Where arbitration proceedings have been initiated under an ancillary arbitration clause, and a party lodges late claims which are within the scope of that clause but not related to the issues originally presented to the arbiter, their admissibility will depend on the terms of any institutional rules governing the arbitration and on whether the arbiter has agreed to act in any matter arising under the ancillary clause or only under the implementing deed. It has been held in England that an arbiter appointed to act generally under the ancillary clause must entertain such claims,[63] and this seems persuasive.

13.26. **Interlocking claims.** Where the same arbiter has been appointed under separate arbitration agreements and is presented

---

[58] *Walker* v. *AUEW* 1969 S.L.T. 150 at 151; *Brown* v. *Herriot* 22 Jul. 1675 II Bro. Supp. 187; *A* v. *B* 7 Jan. 1617 Mor. 662.
[59] *Mitchell* v. *Cable* (1848) 10 D. 1297 per Lord Fullerton at 1308.
[60] *United Collieries Ltd.* v. *Gavin* (1899) 2 F. 60.
[61] *Drummond* v. *Martin* (1906) 14 S.L.T. 365.
[62] By Lord Ardwall at 366–7.
[63] *Telfair Shipping Corporation* v. *Intersea Carriers S.A.* (*The 'Caroline P'*) [1983] 2 Ll. Rep. 351.

with interlocking claims involving several parties, it may be convenient to deal with them together in a single arbitration. This may not be legally possible, however. It has been held in England[64] that this depends on whether all the parties to all the agreements have agreed to this course of action, and the decision seems persuasive.

13.27. Clarification of claims and defences. Where a formal procedure has been adopted, the clarification of the parties' averments of fact and pleas in law is achieved by a process of 'adjustment' leading to a 'closed record' containing the final pleadings of both sides. Though in arbitration such pleadings do not set rigid limits to the evidence and arguments which the parties may present,[65] they can — if well drafted on both sides — assist the arbiter in discovering very precisely where the submitters are at odds and in preventing surprise. In less highly structured arbitrations there is greater risk of injustice from surprise unless care is taken to clarify before the hearing any serious uncertainties or inadequacies in the pleadings. Unless prohibited by the submission, an arbiter may seek to minimise such risks and to facilitate a thorough grasp of the issues by requiring, on his or her own initiative or on the application of a party, such further particulars to be provided of specified matters in the claims or defences as may be necessary for these purposes.

13.28. Where a formal procedure has been adopted, the timetable for adjustment of pleadings is strictly controlled by the arbiter in consultation with the submitters. When claims and answers have been lodged, the arbiter allows a specified time for the parties to alter their pleadings so that each averment and plea in law made by one is dealt with by the other. New claims and counterclaims, and new averments of fact, may be freely added at this stage — provided always that the boundaries of the submission are not overstepped. The 'record'[66] is then closed, and the claims and answers are then combined in a single document of numbered paragraphs in which the averments of one side are placed opposite

[64] In *Oxford Shipping Co. Ltd.* v. *Nippon Yusen Kaisha* (*The 'Eastern Saga'*) [1984] 2 Ll. Rep. 373.
[65] *Miller and Partners Ltd.* v. *Edinburgh Corporation* 1978 S.C. 1 per L.J.C. Wheatley at 11.
[66] Pronounced here with an emphasis on the second syllable.

the admissions and denials of the other, for easy reference. The closed record establishes the limits of the facts which the parties will later be permitted to prove and the legal pleas which they will be permitted to present. Until shortly before the date fixed for a proof it may be opened up and amended on the application of either party, but a successful application for amendment usually carries with it a liability for consequential expenses

13.29. **Debate**. In formal procedure, a legal debate is often held shortly after the closing of the record, to deal with preliminary pleas which, if upheld, would restrict the extent of the proof or even eliminate the necessity for it altogether. It may happen, however, that it is difficult to judge the merits of pleas to the relevancy and competency until at least some evidence has been heard, and in such cases a 'proof before answer' may first be held.

13.30. A debate is likely to be required at some stage where the defender has entered a plea either to the competency or the relevancy of the pursuer's case. A plea that the pursuer's claims are incompetent may for example be made where the defender alleges that the arbiter cannot grant them because they lie outside the jurisdiction defined by the submission, or because they have already been determined in other judicial proceedings that have taken place between the parties ('*res judicata*') or that they have no legal foundation at all. The defender may allege that the pursuer's claims are irrelevant because the averments are an insufficient legal basis for the remedy sought. The plea that an opponent's case is irrelevant because lacking in specification[67] serves a similar purpose in Scottish pleading to a request for 'further and better particulars' in English practice.[68] If a party faced with such a plea fails to make more detailed averments of fact and does not succeed in arguing that the plea of irrelevancy is unjustified because the existing averments are adequate, any claim based on irrelevant pleadings may be dismissed,[69] though it is said[70] that arbiters are often too reluctant to dismiss claims on this ground. Even if no debate is required, it is common practice to hold a meeting to enable the proceedings to concentrate on the matters really in

[67] On which see Dobie, *Sh. Ct. Pr.*, 167.
[68] On which see Russell, *Arb.* 1982, 255–6.
[69] Dobie, (*supra* note 67).
[70] Source: Mr A. M. Hamilton, CBE, Solicitor, Glasgow.

dispute[71] and to obtain the submitters' agreement to exclude from proof matters on which they are not at issue.

13.31. Interim protection orders. These include orders for the preservation or custody of property which is the subject of dispute or which has evidentiary value therein, or for obtaining security for the payment of expenses or other sums which may be found due under an award. Arbiters are not granted any such powers by legislation, and it is unlikely — the point appears not to have been raised in any reported case — that they have any implied powers under the common law. The courts in Scotland have since the middle of the nineteenth century evinced a restrictive attitude to the implied powers of arbiters, and have generally not been willing to extend them further than the minimum required to enable an arbiter to perform the functions of the office. Since the purpose of a power to issue interim protection orders is to make the award effective rather than to assist the arbiter in conducting the proceedings, an arbiter in Scotland probably has no implied power under the submission to make any kind of interim protection order. If therefore the submitters wish the arbiter to have such powers, they must grant them expressly.[72] If this has not been done, the only means of protection is by raising an action in the courts. In that context arrestment of moveable goods and inhibition against disposal of heritable property may be sought 'on the dependence' of the action. An order may also be sought under Rule 95A of the Rules of Court for the preservation of any documents or other property on which any question may relevantly arise in the cause. This has the additional advantage that its scope is not confined to property belonging to one of the litigants. In admiralty causes the Court of Session has power in an action *ad rem* under Rules of Court 136, 137 and 140 to order the arrestment of a ship or its cargo. The arrestment of a ship relates to the action, and is probably not available as security for compliance with an arbitral award, but only for decree conform thereto in the court action.[73] A defender might however be willing to gain release of the vessel by finding other security in the shape of a bond

[71] Guild, *Arb.* 56.
[72] This may be done by incorporating institutional arbitration rules, such as the ICE Arbitration Procedure for Scotland, rule 6 of which gives an arbiter power to order certain protective measures. See Hawker and Ors., *ICE Arb.*, 115–6.
[73] So, at least, it has been held in England: *The 'Golden Trader'* [1974] 1 Ll. Rep. 378 at 384.

covering the award also. Though this stratagem has been judicially disapproved by an English court,[74] the decision has been subjected to strong attack,[75] and is in any event based on technicalities of English law. When the appropriate orders have been obtained the action may then be sisted pending the outcome of the arbitration.

13.32. **Productions.** A party who is in possession of a document or material object upon which he or she founds any part of the case, should lodge it in process. If this is not done the arbiter may order it, either *ex proprio motu* or on the application of the other party. If the submission contains a clause of registration for execution such an order may be enforced at the instance of one of the submitters by registration of the submission along with the order in the books of the court; otherwise application must be made to the court for assistance.

13.33. If documents or other material objects required as evidence in the arbitration are in the hands of a person who is not a party to the arbitration, and a mere request proves insufficient to induce its production to the arbiter, a submitter may send to the arbiter a list of the items sought — in Scottish legal practice called a 'specification' — along with a request that an interlocutor be issued certifying that they are required in the arbitration. The list and request must be intimated to the opponent, who may lodge an objection to the production of some or all of the items on the ground that they are irrelevant or are protected from production by their confidentiality. If necessary, the arbiter may hear parties concerning the specification. Once an order has been made for the recovery of all or some of the documents contained in the specification, application may if necessary be made to the court for assistance in enforcing it. On the application of one of the submitters the court will grant warrant to cite the persons stated to be in possession of the items mentioned in the arbiter's order — the 'havers' in Scots legal terminology — to produce them to a commissioner.[76] The Court of Session has granted such warrant even where the haver was in England.[77]

---

[74] In *The 'Cap Bon'* [1967] 1 Ll. Rep. 543.
[75] In Mustill, *Comm. Arb.* 299.
[76] *Crichton* v. *North British Railway Co.* (1888) 15 R. 784; *Crudens Ltd., Petitioners* 1971 S.C. 64.
[77] *Blaikie Brothers* v. *Aberdeen Railway Co.* (1851) 13 D. 1307.

13.34. **Inspection of property.** Unless the submission otherwise provides, an arbiter has an implied power to require a submitter to allow inspection of any property in his or her possession such as buildings, land, animals, vehicles, and equipment which is the subject of dispute in the arbitration. Whether the submitters may attend during the inspection is for the arbiter to decide, but if one of them is invited or is merely likely to be there at the time the other should be invited also. Though the courts have on occasion taken a relaxed view of chance encounters on site[78] they have not always done so,[79] and it is dangerous to assume that the relaxed view will prevail. A further reason for issuing an invitation to both is that the parties are both able to see what the arbiter does, and to point out features of the property which they regard as important.[80] A party who has had such an opportunity cannot thereafter be heard to complain if the arbiter has omitted to observe something. The courts are reluctant to interfere with an award on the ground that it is based on inadequate inspection,[81] though reduction has been granted where the arbiter's failure was such that his duties under the submission had not been fulfilled.[82] An arbiter is entitled to prefer the evidence of his or her own eyes to oral evidence later led on behalf of a submitter.[83]

13.35. An arbiter has no power to inspect or to have inspected any property in the hands of third parties. There is no exact Scottish equivalent of subsection 12(6)(g) of the Arbitration Act 1950 under which the High Court in England may authorise an arbiter to inspect such property, but since an arbitral award is likely to give rise to proceedings in court if only for decree conform thereto it is arguable that an application might be made by a submitter under Rule of Court 95A for inspection of such property by an arbiter. A haver who refused to permit inspection in spite of a court order for any reason not coming within the terms of subsection 1(4) of the Administration of Justice (Scotland) Act 1972 would be in contempt of court.

[78] *Campbell* v. *McHolm* (1863) 2 M. 271.
[79] *Heggie & Co.* v. *Stark and Selkrig* (1825) 3 S. 488; *McNair's Trustee* v. *Roxburgh & Faulds* (1855) 17 D. 445.
[80] Bell, J. M., *Arb.* paragraph 279.
[81] *Johnson* v. *Lamb* 1981 S.L.T. 300 at 306; *Sim* v. *McConnell & Stevenson* (1936) 52 Sh. Ct. Rep. 324.
[82] *McNair's Trustee* (*supra* note 79) per L.P. McNeill at 449.
[83] *McNabb* v. *A. & J. Anderson* 1955 S.L.T. 73.

13.36.   **Citation of witnesses.** Since an arbiter has no power over any persons other than the submitters, the assistance of the court is required for the citation of witnesses resident in Scotland. A submitter who is doubtful of the willingness of a proposed witness to appear before the arbiter may ask the arbiter to certify that there is good reason to require that person's attendance to give evidence, and on the basis of the arbiter's certificate an application may be made to the court for warrant for citation.[84] Failure to appear before the arbiter will then constitute contempt of court.

13.37.   The attendance of witnesses resident outwith Scotland cannot be compelled, and if the evidence of such a person is required in an arbitration it is necessary to have it taken on commission. This must be done even if the witness is resident in England,[85] there being no Scots equivalent of subsection 12(4) of the English Arbitration Act 1950. A submitter seeking to have the evidence of such a witness taken must first apply to the arbiter for a note respectfully recommending the Lords of Council and Session to sanction and confirm the appointment of a particular person as commissioner and to require and enforce the attendance of the witness before that person. The Court may then be petitioned to interpone their authority to the arbiter's note and to grant warrant for letters of diligence. If the witness is still unwilling to testify, application must then be made to the appropriate court in the country in which the witness resides.[86] An arbiter has an implied power to approve an application to take evidence on commission even where the witness resides within Scotland,[87] but the exercise of this power is probably now rare.

13.38.   In very exceptional circumstances the court will grant warrant to take evidence on commission in connection with a dispute which has not yet been submitted to an arbiter. This has been done in a dispute which was within the scope of an ancillary arbitration clause and the person for whose evidence the commission was requested was about to depart to reside permanently abroad.[88] The evidence taken by a commissioner in

---

[84] *Harvey* v. *Gibson* (1826) 4 S. 809.
[85] *Highland Railway Co.* v. *Mitchell* (1868) 6 M. 898.
[86] *John Nimmo & Son Ltd., Petitioners* (1905) 8 F. 173.
[87] *Berry* v. *Watson* (1827) 6 S. 256, (1831) 9 S. 337; Bell J. M., *Arb.*, paragraph 287.
[88] *Galloway Water Power Co.* v. *Carmichael* 1937 S.L.T. 188.

such circumstances lies 'in retentis' — that is, it is retained in the records of the court — until such time as it is required in arbitration proceedings.

13.39. **Proof.** In arbitration proceedings a proof is any occasion arranged primarily for the purpose of enabling the arbiter to receive oral evidence in connection with the matters submitted for his or her determination, whether the proceedings are formally structured on the model of an ordinary action in court, or not. Its object is to ensure that the arbiter receives —

'all the evidence of fact which can enable him to arrive at a proper and just conclusion.'[89]

It matters not whether the evidence is led by the submitters or investigated by the arbiter.

13.40. The fact that a submission contains no express grant of power to hold a proof does not mean that the arbiter possesses no such power. In general an arbiter has an implied power to take evidence whenever this is required to explicate the jurisdiction.[90] In a technical reference to a person of skill the circumstances may be such that proof is incompetent,[91] but even here power is implied where it is necessary to enable the arbiter to bring the proceedings to a successful conclusion by an award which exhausts the submission.[92] On the other hand, the fact that a submission expressly gives power to hold a proof does not itself imply that it imposes a duty to do so,[93] or that the arbiter must listen to all the evidence that a submitter wishes to present.[94] As has been said,[95]

'it is not a necessary allowance to the course of "eternal justice" to hear interminably.'

13.41. The exercise of discretion in deciding what evidence to receive calls for delicate judgment. On the one hand an arbiter

---

[89] *Holmes Oil Co. Ltd.* v. *Pumpherston Oil Co. Ltd.* (1891) 18 R. (H.L.) 52 per Lord Watson at 55.
[90] Erskine, *Inst.* I.2.8.
[91] *Logan* v. *Leadbetter* (1887) 15 R. 115 per L.P. Inglis at 116.
[92] *Cochrane* v. *Guthrie* (1859) 21 D. 369.
[93] *MacDonald* v. *MacDonald* (1843) 6 D. 186 per Lord Fullerton at 189; *Graham* v. *Mill* (1904) 6 F. 886 per Lord Trayner at 892.
[94] *Ledingham* v. *Elphinstone* (1859) 22 D. 245.
[95] *Brakenrig* v. *Menzies* (1841) 4 D. 274 per Lord Moncreiff at 286.

must minimise the risk of denying to a submitter the opportunity to present evidence which is neither incompetent nor irrelevant nor superfluous, and must not proceed to judgment before the case is ripe for decision.[96] On the other hand nothing must be done by entertaining irrelevant evidence to create an inference that the jurisdiction will be exceeded. Though the courts have not lightly drawn that inference,[97] they have sometimes done so, and have then granted interdict to halt the arbitration.[98] The leading of irrelevant or superfluous evidence is moreover a 'waste of time'[99] and of money, and its exclusion 'cannot infringe the principles of natural justice'.[100] It is not unknown for an unscrupulous litigant to seek to wear down the resistance of the opponent by dragging out the proceedings, and an arbiter should be alert to this possibility and should seek to defeat such attempts to pervert justice.

13.42.   A proof may be heard in whatever manner the arbiter may decide, subject to the terms of the submission. It may be formal or informal, adversarial or investigatory. If there is a need for a debate on the parties pleas in law, the proof is normally arranged to take place after that event, but the order may be reversed, in which case the proof is said to be 'before answer'.

13.43.   It is common practice for the arbiter to ask each party to provide before the proof a list of witnesses in the order in which it is intended to call them, for the assistance of the clerk at the hearing. Some institutional rules provide for disclosure or exchange of the 'precognitions',[101] as statements made by witnesses as recorded by parties' law agents are called in Scots practice.

13.44.   It is not customary in formal adversarial proceedings in Scotland for opening statements to be made by the parties or their representatives, but where there are no formal pleadings an arbiter may find it helpful to ask each side for a verbal summary of the case before evidence is presented. Usually the pursuer presents

---

[96] *Mitchell* v. *Cable* (1848) 10 D. 1297 per Lord Mackenzie at 1307.
[97] *Bennets* v. *Bennet* (1903) 5 F. 376 per L.P. Kinross at 381.
[98] *Glasgow and South West Railway Co.* v. *Caledonian Railway Co.* (1871) 44 Scot. Jur. 29; *Birkmyre Brothers* v. *Moore & Weinberg* (1907) 14 S.L.T. 702 per Lord Mackenzie.
[99] Walkers, *Evidence* 5.
[100] *Brown & Son* v. *Associated Fireclay Companies Ltd.* 1937 S.C. (H.L.) 42.
[101] See e.g. Rule 16.3 of the ICE Arbitration Procedure for Scotland.

evidence first, but where it is the facts alleged by the defender that are in question it may be appropriate for the defender to lead.[102] Where averments are made by the defender, and that party leads evidence relating thereto, the pursuer is entitled then to lead further evidence in reply.[103] The defender is entitled to lead no further evidence unless he or she can show that the nature of the pursuer's further proof is such that justice requires this to be allowed. The arbiter may exclude a submitter if he or she considers there is a possibility that a witness may otherwise be unwilling to give truthful evidence, but this should not be done unless a professional representative is allowed to remain.[104]

13.45. An arbiter may administer an oath or affirmation to witnesses, but is not obliged to do so unless this is required by the submission.[105] The forms used in civil proceedings in Scotland are the same as those laid down by Act of Adjournal[106] for criminal cases, and are set out in Appendix II hereof. Witnesses other than the submitters themselves who have not yet given evidence are not normally permitted to be present in the room where the proof is being taken,[107] but this is merely a rule of practice. They should not be prevented from giving evidence if due to inadvertence or the unavoidable absence of suitable accommodation for them this rule has not been observed.

13.46. In adversarial procedure the parties should each be permitted to present the evidence of their own witnesses and test by questioning any substantial allegation by any witness adduced by the opponent. They should not however be allowed either to suggest to their own witnesses, by means of 'leading questions' or otherwise, what they should say on any controversial matter, or to bully or harass opposing witnesses. The arbiter should personally keep a note of the evidence given, though the notes taken by the clerk, when that person is not otherwise engaged, may be used as a check. Some institutional rules which follow a generally adversarial pattern nevertheless enable an order to be made for

---

[102] Walkers, *Evidence*, 65–6.
[103] In formal terms, a 'conjunct probation': on which see *Magistrates of Edinburgh* v. *Warrender* (1862) 1 M. 13.
[104] *Black* v. *John Williams & Co. (Wishaw) Ltd.* 1923 S.C. 510 affd. 1924 S.C. (H.L.) 22.
[105] *Hope* v. *Crookston Brothers* (1890) 17 R. 868 per L.J.C. MacDonald at 874–5.
[106] Form of Oaths, S.I. 1976 No. 172.
[107] Dobie, *Sh. Ct. Pr.*, 214.

expert witnesses to be examined first by the arbiter and thereafter by the submitters or their representatives and then only at the arbiter's discretion.[108]

13.47. An arbiter is entitled to make use of his or her own personal knowledge of matters which fall into one or other of the following categories: —

(a) *matters within 'judicial knowledge'*, that is, 'matters which can be immediately ascertained from sources of indisputable accuracy or which are so notorious as to be indisputable'[109]; and

(b) *matters within local knowledge or the scope of the trade or profession* which the arbiter carries on and on account of which he or she has been appointed.[110]

Otherwise, though the rules of evidence which apply in the ordinary courts do not apply in arbitration in Scotland,[111] ordinary fairness to the parties normally demands that the arbiter does not rely upon private sources of information without at least inviting the parties to comment and lead evidence on the point if they wish,[112], though it has been considered that an expert arbiter may without reference to the submitters make use of his or her own knowledge of changes in circumstances occurring between the final proof or hearing and the promulgation of the award.[113] It has been held by a judge in the Outer House that the report of an expert appointed by the arbiter may be received without providing copies of it to the submitters or allowing them to make any representations concerning it,[114] but this does not seem a desirable course of action.

13.48. Any conduct which clearly indicates that the arbitral mind was made up before the evidence and argument was fully heard[115]

---

[108] See ICE Arbitration Procedure for Scotland, Rule 13(1)(c).

[109] Walkers, *Evidence*, 47.

[110] *Black* v. *John Williams & Co. (Wishaw) Ltd.* 1924 S.C. (H.L.) 22 per Lord Shand at 28; *Keane* v. *Mount Vernon Colliery Co.* 1932 S.C. 492 affd. 1933 S.C. (H.L.) 1; *Miller & Partners* v. *Edinburgh Corporation* 1978 S.C. 1 per L.J.C. Wheatley at 8–10.

[111] *Walker* v. *AUEW* 1969 S.L.T. 150 at 151.

[112] *Dyer* v. *Wilson & Clyde Coal Co. Ltd.* 1915 S.C. 199.

[113] *Miller and Partners Ltd.* v. *Edinburgh Corporation* 1978 S.C. 1 per L.J.C. Wheatley at 11.

[114] *Masinimport* v. *Scottish Mechanical Light Industries Ltd.* 1976 S.C. 102 at 108.

[115] *Pekholtz* v. *Russell* (1899) 7 S.L.T. 135; *McLauchlan and Brown* v. *Morrison*

or which reveals serious prejudice against a submitter or a witness
— such as 'Italians are all liars ... but ... Norwegians generally are
a truthful people'[116] should be avoided, though the expression of
what amounts merely to a preliminary view of the case appears to
be acceptable.[117]

13.49. A witness may express reluctance to give evidence on a
matter because of fear of making a defamatory statement. In
Scotland witnesses in judicial proceedings enjoy absolute privilege
in relation to statements made when giving evidence,[118] and for this
purpose an arbitration counts as a judicial proceeding.[119] The same
applies to the arbiter and to professional representatives of the
submitters.[120] The submitters, however, enjoy only a qualified
privilege, though this covers statements made in written pleadings
as well as those uttered during a hearing. Hence, if malice and facts
and circumstances from which malice can be inferred are alleged
and can be proved, a submitter is not immune from liability.[121]
Arbiters are probably in the same position in this matter as
submitters.[122]

13.50. **Hearing.** This is not a technical term, and in connection
with arbitration it can mean any occasion arranged primarily for
the purpose of enabling the submitters to present to the arbiter
argument on questions of law or fact relating to the matters in
issue.[123] Such occasions include debates on the parties' pleas in law,
but the term is normally used to refer to occasions when final
arguments are presented after the proof. Hearings may thus be
distinguished from ordinary meetings arranged to enable the

(1900) 8 S.L.T. 279; *Aviemore Station Hotel Co. Ltd. v. James Scott & Son* (1904)
12 S.L.T. 494.
[116] An arbitrator's aside considered in *Re an Arbitration between the Owners of
the steamship 'Catalina' and Others and the Owners of the motor vessel 'Norma'*
(1938) 61 Ll. L. Rep. 360.
[117] *Halliday* v. *Duke of Hamilton's Trustee* (1903) 5 F. 800 per L.J.C.
MacDonald at 808. A similar view has been taken in England: see *Hagop
Ardahalian* v. *Unifest International SA* (*The 'Elissar'*) [1984] 1 Ll. Rep. 206.
[188] *Macintosh* v. *Weir* (1875) 2 R. 877.
[119] *Neill* v. *Henderson* (1901) 3 F. 387; *Slack* v. *Barr* 1918 1 S.L.T. 133.
[120] *Slack (supra).*
[121] *Hay* v. *Cameron* (1898) 6 S.L.T. 48; *Neill (supra* note 119).
[122] *Auchincloss* v. *Black*, 1793, Hume's *Decisions*, 595; *McMillan* v. *Free Church
(No. 2)* (1862) 24 D. 1282.
[123] Bell J. M., *Arb.* paragraph 293.

arbiter informally to obtain the views of the submitters on uncontroversial procedural questions. The usefulness of a hearing has been well described by J. M. Bell.[124]

'The frank collision of earnest discussion between antagonists has the effect of letting in light upon many bearings of both sides of a cause, which might escape the calm scrutiny even of an acute and intelligent person, who, like the arbiter, stands free of the promptings of self-interest on either side, and is thoroughly indifferent between the parties and their claims.'

In any case in which evidence has been led or which is of any legal complexity — that is, except in such cases as technical references[125] and 'documents only' arbitrations — the submitters should, and indeed are entitled to, be heard[126] unless they have mutually agreed otherwise. Natural justice requires that if an opportunity to make representations is given to one party, it must be given to all, and all are entitled to be present if they wish to hear their opponents' arguments.[127] Usually there is at least one hearing — immediately following the proof, when parties address the arbiter on the implications of the evidence led and elaborate the legal grounds of their claims and defences. Hearings may be arranged at other stages also, to debate preliminary pleas or to enable the submitters to make representations on the arbiter's proposed findings.

13.51. **Devolution on oversman.** Though an oversman may be appointed at any stage in an arbitration unless the submission provides otherwise, the issues may only be devolved upon him or her when the arbiters have reached deadlock,[128] though disagreement on a procedural or administrative matter is thought to be sufficient.[129] If an act of appointment is intended also to have effect as a devolution it should say so expressly, for devolution is not inferred without very good reason.[130] In law an act of devolution probably does not have to be in probative writing[131] and

---

[124] *Ibid.*
[125] *Latta* v. *MacRae* (1852) 14 D. 641; *Nivison* v. *Howat* (1883) 11 R. 182; *Dundas* v. *Hogg & Allan* 1937 S.L.T. (Sh. Ct.) 2.
[126] *Glennie* v. *MacPhail* (1825) 3 S. 574.
[127] *Earl of Dunmore* v. *McInturner* (1835) 13 S. 356 per L.J.C. Boyle at 360; *Henderson* v. *McGown* 1915 2 S.L.T. 316.
[128] *Gibson* v. *Fotheringham* 1914 S.C. 987.
[129] Guild, *Arb.*, 52.
[130] *Telfer & Co.* v. *Bell* (1823) 2 S. 167; *Brysson* v. *Mitchell* (1823) 2 S. 382.
[131] *Dick* v. *Inglis* (1907) 15 S.L.T. 615; *French* v. *Durham* (1911) 27 Sh. Ct. Rep. 77.

perhaps not even in writing at all,[132] though obviously writing is desirable on practical grounds. The view that formality is required is probably the result of confusion between devolution and appointment.

13.52.   Matters of substance on which the arbiters can agree and which are able to be separated from those on which there is deadlock, may be made the subject of part awards[133] unless the submission provides otherwise. This prevents uncertainty over the identification of issues not devolved. Moreover, it is extremely confusing   to   have   two   arbitral   tribunals   dealing contemporaneously with the same submission,[134] even though arbiters may competently continue to deal with any issues remaining after some have been devolved on the oversman. Where the arbiters have no power under the submission to issue part awards they must devolve the whole matter in dispute upon the oversman. This must be done even where there is power to issue interim awards, because these, unlike part awards, are not final on the matters included therein. It may nevertheless be convenient in many cases to issue interim awards on agreed matters before devolution, so that the attention of the oversman and of the submitters can be focussed on the remaining issues. An oversman should always be careful to avoid dealing with any matters which have been decided in part awards, and to deal with those included in interim awards, for otherwise there is a risk of overstepping or failing to exhaust the issues which have been devolved, and all the awards may be subject to challenge.[135]

13.53.   Once any issue has been devolved upon the oversman the arbiters have completed the judicial duties of their office in relation to it: in other words, they are '*functi* (*functae*) *officio*' in relation to it. From that point, the oversman alone decides how proceedings should be conducted on that matter and what the final award on it should contain. Subject to express stipulation in the submission to the contrary, the oversman has the same powers as the arbiters.[136] If the oversman then dies or becomes incapacitated, the situation is

---

[132] *Middleton* v. *Chalmers & Others* (1721) Rob. 391; *Sinclair* v. *Fraser* (1884) 11 R. 1139.
[133] See paragraph 15.11. below.
[134] *Lang* v. *Brown* (1855) II Macq. 93 per L. C. Cranworth at 96.
[135] *Runciman* v. *Craigie* (1831) 9 S. 629.
[136] *Glover* v. *Glover* (1805) IV Dow 655.

the same as if a single arbiter had been thus struck down: the issues do not revert to the original arbiters, who have no power (unless the submission otherwise provides) to make a new appointment,[137] and equally the court has no power to intervene to prevent the proceedings from being abortive.

13.54.   **Tenders.** A tender is 'a judicial offer to pay a part of the sum asked by [the] adversary'.[138] It must be 'explicit and free from qualifications and conditions'.[139] In an arbitration a defender may make an offer to settle the dispute in one of three ways. An offer may be made to the pursuer 'without prejudice', or as a sealed tender, or as an open tender. In the first case it is not a tender and has no effect on the proceedings: neither party may refer to it and it is not lodged in process. An open tender is normally made by a minute lodged in process but may be made on record in the pleadings. There is no obligation on the parties not to refer to it and the arbiter obviously acquires knowledge of it before deciding upon the award on the merits of the case. A sealed tender, which is perhaps less common in Scots than in English practice, is lodged in process and intimated openly to the pursuer but its contents are not disclosed to the arbiter until after he or she has come to a final decision upon the merits of the award. Since the tenderer may reasonably feel that if the arbiter becomes aware even that a tender has been made the award may be affected, the tender may be held by the clerk on behalf of both parties and its existence not disclosed to the arbiter until after the merits of the award have been determined. Alternatively, the procedure suggested by Mr. Justice Donaldson in an English case[140] may be adopted. The arbiter may towards the close of proceedings invite the defender to lodge in process a sealed envelope which may contain either a tender or a statement to the effect that no tender has been made.

13.55.   A tender offering a sum which, when interest is taken into account, is equal to or in excess of the sum awarded by the arbiter on the substance of the dispute — it must include the expenses of the arbitration — has the effect, other things being equal, that the pursuer should be held liable for any expenses incurred in the

---

[137] Irons, *Arb.*, 180.
[138] Maxwell, *Ct. of Sess. Pr.*, 245.
[139] *Bisset* v. *Anderson* (1847) 10 D. 233 per Lord Cockburn at 234.
[140] *Tramountana Armadora SA* v. *Atlantic Shipping Co. SA* [1978] 2 All E.R. 870 at 876.

arbitration after the tender was intimated, since failure to accept the tender has caused a waste of time and money. A reasonable time should be allowed for acceptance of a tender, and what is reasonable for this purpose depends on the circumstances of the case.[141] In a case[142] in which there were two defenders, the first defender made an offer subject to the concurrence of the second defender to admit liability to make reparation jointly and severally with the second defender, on condition that the defenders were liable *inter se* to contribute to the damages and expenses of the pursuer in the proportion three quarters by the first defender and one quarter by the second defender. The second defender refused to concur, and the jury found for the pursuer, the defenders having contributed in the proportion two-thirds by the first and one-third by the second defender. The court ordered that all the pursuer's expenses should be paid in the proportions found by the jury up to the date of the offer, but that the subsequent expenses both of the pursuer and the first defender should be paid by the second defender.

13.56. Proposed findings. It is a common practice among arbiters in Scotland to frame and issue to parties at a late stage in proceedings a note of the findings in fact and law that they propose to make.[143] Proposed findings may take the form of a draft of an award and a note of the arbiter's reasons. The adoption of this practice helps to minimise the risk of injustice and of errors such as the inadvertent transposition of the names of the parties in calculating part of the amounts due.[144] Since there is obviously no point in issuing proposed findings if no opportunity is to be allowed for the submitters to comment thereon, they should not be issued if the time specified under the submission for issuing the award is about to expire. Where proposed findings are issued, intimation should simultaneously be made of the date by which any written representations relating thereto must be lodged. An arbiter who issues a final award without waiting a reasonable time for parties to lodge written representations against proposed

---

[141] *Smeaton* v. *Dundee Corporation* 1941 S.C. 600.

[142] *Williamson* v. *McPherson* 1951 S.C. 438.

[143] *Miller and Partners Ltd.* v. *Edinburgh Corporation* 1978 S.C. 1 per L.J.C. Wheatley at 8.

[144] As occurred in an English arbitration which was the subject of *Mutual Shipping Corporation of New York* v. *Bayshore Shipping Co. of Monrovia* [1985] 1 All E.R. 521.

findings is likely to be held to have committed misconduct.[145] Where proposed findings are not going to be issued, some possible causes of misunderstanding[146] may be removed if at the end of what is expected to be the final proof or hearing the arbiter asks the parties to confirm that their cases are closed and that they have nothing further to add on any matter. Their replies should be recorded in writing at the time.

13.57. **Questions of law for the court.** Section 3 of the Administration of Justice (Scotland) Act 1972 has introduced a procedure by which either of the submitters may ask the arbiter to state a case for the opinion of the court in Scotland on a question of law arising in the arbitration. That procedure is discussed in detail in the next chapter,[147] but at this stage attention is drawn to the fact that the right to make such a request may be excluded, but only if the submitters have so provided in the 'agreement to refer to arbitration'. If the arbitration is based upon an arbitration clause, a purported agreement to exclude it which is not contained in the arbitration clause is ineffective.[148] Where the right has not been validly excluded, it can be exercised at any stage in proceedings up to, but not at or beyond, the point when the arbiter issues the final award on the issue on which the court's opinion is sought. It is probable that an arbiter who deliberately hastened the promulgation of the award in order to deny a party the opportunity of obtaining a stated case would be guilty of misconduct.[149]

13.58. Under Article 177 of the Treaty of Rome establishing the EEC, a 'court or tribunal of a Member State' of the European Community may obtain a preliminary ruling from the Court of Justice of the European Communities on a question of European Community law. A question may arise, whether an arbiter in Scotland under an ordinary submission is a 'court or tribunal of a Member State' for this purpose. This question has to be considered in the light of a decision of the European Court relating

---

[145] *McLaren* v. *Aikman* 1939 S.C. 222 per Lord Wark at 230.

[146] Such as have occurred in England: *Sokratis Rokopoulos* v. *Esperia SpA* (*The 'Aros'*) [1978] 1 Ll. Rep. 456.

[147] Paragraphs 14.11.–14.34.

[148] *Clydebank District Council* v. *Clink* 1977 S.C. 147.

[149] So, at least, it was considered in England when a similar procedure existed there: *Food Corporation of India* v. *Carras (Hellas) Ltd.* [1980] 2 Ll. Rep. 577.

to arbitration in Germany.[150] In his reference to the Court the German arbiter had observed that under German law —

'a mistaken application of the law [by the arbiter] in so far as it does not involve an offence against public morality or public policy [Paragraph 1041(1)(2) of the *Zivilprozessordnung*] cannot be rectified in proceedings for enforcement or to have the award set aside. Consequently, if arbitration tribunals are denied jurisdiction to refer matters to the Court of Justice for a preliminary ruling the uniform application of Community law will be jeopardised in a field of vital importance for the European Communities, namely commercial law.'

The Court nevertheless held that the German arbiter was not authorised to make a reference to it because —

'the link between the arbitration procedure in this instance and the organisation of legal remedies through the courts in the Member State in question is not sufficiently close for the arbitrator to be considered a 'court or tribunal of a Member State' within the meaning of Article 177.'

The considerations which induced the European Court to arrive at this opinion were that the submission to arbitration was entirely voluntary, and that the German public authorities were neither involved in the decision to opt for arbitration nor called upon to intervene automatically in the arbitration proceedings.

13.59. There is little doubt but that compulsory arbitration regimes in Scotland come within the scope of Article 177.[151] The main question is, whether ordinary arbitration in Scotland is sufficiently similar to arbitration in Germany to bring it clearly within the scope of the European Court's ruling in the German case. It is probable that it is. The mere fact that the Scottish courts regard ordinary arbitration as a form of subordinate jurisdiction[152] is probably not of itself sufficient to have the effect that an ordinary arbiter in Scotland is a 'court or tribunal of a member state'. German law appears to allow the courts in that country to exercise over arbitration only slightly greater control than that which is exercised over ordinary arbitration by the courts in Scotland. The

---

[150] *Nordsee Deutsche Hochseefischerei GmbH* v. *Reederei Hochseefischerei AG and Co. KG and Another* (Case 102/81) [1982] E.C.R. 1095.
[151] *Vaassen-Göbbels* v. *Beambtenfonds voor het Mijnbedrijf* [1966] E.C.R. 261.
[152] *Forbes* v. *Underwood* (1886) 13 R. 465 per L.P. Inglis at 467.

main difference would appear to be that in Scotland under the system of registration of a decree arbitral for execution its enforcement can be automatic, subject to the possibility of reduction of the decree on grounds no wider than those on which an award may be reviewed in Germany. It is arguable that where the submission includes consent to registration for execution the intervention of official enforcement machinery is sufficiently automatic to satisfy the European Court's criteria for the designation of proceedings as a 'court or tribunal', and that here a Scots arbiter may make a direct reference. It is however probable that where there is no such consent this is not competent. If in such a case reference to the European Court is desired, an application must first be made to a Scottish court for an opinion on a question of law.

CHAPTER FOURTEEN

THE CONDUCT OF ARBITRATION PROCEEDINGS: 3 EVIDENCE AND THE STATED CASE

Arbitration and the rules of evidence

14.1. Whether the rules of evidence are binding in arbitration. The rules of evidence applicable in a court of law are not binding as such upon an arbiter in Scotland, because it has long been accepted that an award cannot be reduced merely on the ground that the arbiter received and founded on evidence which would have been excluded in a court, or that he has rejected evidence which a court would have entertained.[1] There is however some doubt concerning the basis of this principle. Three possible grounds for this assertion have been advanced.

14.2. One is that the courts will not interfere with an arbiter merely because he or she has gone wrong in law.[2] This is no longer plausible, given the strict view that is now taken of an arbiter's obligation to adhere to the law.[3]

14.3. A second is that the parties may be taken to have impliedly given the arbiter a discretion to disregard the strict rules of evidence.[4] This appears to be the approach of English law.[5] The difficulty with this is that, if — as is suggested[6] — the rules of evidence are strictly part of the general law, it is difficult in a Scottish context at least to reconcile such discretion with the arbiter's obligation to adhere to the law.

14.4. A third view is that the rules of evidence are, like the rules of procedure, binding only on the ordinary courts, and that an

[1] Bell J. M., *Arb.* paragraphs 258–259.
[2] *Spearman v. Pitloh* (1828) 6 S. 645 per Lord Glenlee at 646.
[3] *Mitchell-Gill v. Buchan* 1921 S.C. 390 per L.P. Clyde at 395.
[4] *Alston v. Chappell* (1839) 2 D. 248.
[5] Mustill, *Comm. Arb.* 310–11.
[6] *Ibid.*

arbiter is therefore free to admit or refuse to entertain evidence as fairness and the effective exhaustion of the submission dictate. There is, after all, nothing in the rules of evidence themselves that expressly requires their application outside the courts.

14.5.   Against the third view it could be argued that it appears to have been thought necessary to provide expressly that (for example) industrial tribunals are not bound by the ordinary rules of evidence.[7] This could however be regarded as simply a wise precaution against the legalism which inevitably tends to intrude where lawyers are employed to chair proceedings or to represent parties. Moreover, the view that the rules of evidence normally apply only to the ordinary courts is consistent with the language of the regulation governing industrial tribunals at least, and has some support from the most recent[8] and the most ancient[9] of the Scottish judicial decisions in which the subject is considered.

14.6.   Though the rules of evidence applicable in a court do not apply in arbitration in Scotland, this does not mean that in arbitration evidence cannot be inadmissible in law at all. An instrument which falls into a category which is required by law to be impressed with a revenue stamp, and which does not bear such a stamp, cannot be admitted. Subsection 14(4) of the Stamp Act 1891 provides that —

> 'an instrument executed in any part of the United Kingdom, or relating, wheresoever executed, to any property situate, or to any matter or thing done or to be done, in any part of the United Kingdom, shall not ... be given in evidence, or be available for any purpose whatever, unless it is duly stamped in accordance with the law in force at the time when it was first executed.'

14.7.   **The guiding principle in the admission of evidence.** While in a Scots arbitration evidence cannot be inadmissible in law merely on the ground that it would be excluded by the rules of evidence, an arbiter must in fairness admit any evidence which is clearly not superfluous and which is relevant to the issues raised, unless the parties have agreed to restrict the kinds of evidence

---

[7] Industrial Tribunals (Rules of Procedure) (Scotland) Regulations 1985, S.I. 1985 No. 17, Schedule 1, paragraph 8(1).
[8] *Walker* v. *AUEW* 1969 S.L.T. 150 at 151.
[9] *Garven* v. *Trotter* 13 Jan. 1681, II Bro. Supp. 266.

which may be entertained.[10] The principle governing the admission of evidence was stated thus by Lord Watson[11] —

'The principles of natural justice require that before proceeding to decide [a disputed question of fact] the arbiter shall receive from the parties all the evidence of fact which can enable him to arrive at a proper and just conclusion.'

This broad view of the arbiter's responsibilities concerning the admission and assessment of evidence seems consistent with the tendency which has been observeable since the seventeenth century towards greater freedom of proof.[12] It is, indeed, the strictness of the ordinary law of evidence that now requires justification.[13] Some justification for it does exist, now that belief in a universal cognitive capacity has been shaken by some contemporary writing on psychology,[14] but given that an arbiter is selected by or with the consent of the submitters, and is usually chosen because of his or her special expertise, there is little reason to hedge the process of fact-finding in arbitration with strict technical rules on the admissibility of evidence.

14.8. **Relevance.** Relevant evidence has been described as evidence which is 'logically connected with [the] matters in dispute between the parties'.[15] It may be direct or indirect. An example of direct evidence is the testimony of someone who asserts that he or she saw what happened[16] on an occasion concerning which the parties are at issue. Indirect evidence is

'evidence of any fact which renders probable or improbable the existence of the fact in issue'[17]

or which gives rise to inferences relating to the truthfulness or reliability of a witness. Whether a particular item of evidence is or is not relevant is for the arbiter to decide.[18]

---

[10] As for example in 'documents only' arbitrations.
[11] *Holmes Oil Co.* v. *Pumpherston Oil Co.* (1891) 18 R. (H.L.) 52 at 55.
[12] *Young* v. *Pearson* Jul. 2 1678, II Bro. Supp. 230 (Stair); Walker D. M., 'Evidence', in *Scot. Leg. Hist.*, 305 ff.; Cohen L. J., 'Freedom of Proof' in Twining W. (ed.), *Facts in Law*, Wiesbaden, 1983, 1 at 8–12.
[13] Cohen, (*supra*) 5.
[14] *Ibid.*, 16–19.
[15] Walkers, *Evidence*, 5.
[16] *Ibid.*
[17] *Ibid.*, 6.
[18] *Brown & Sons Ltd.* v. *Associated Fireclay Companies Ltd.* 1937 S.C. (H.L.) 42 per Lord Thankerton at 45.

14.9.   **The 'best evidence' rule.** One effect of the fact that arbitration in Scotland is not subject to the courts' rules of evidence is that the role of what is known as the 'best evidence rule' is changed. In the context of the rules of evidence the best evidence rule —

'excludes indirect evidence where direct evidence is, or ought to be, available.'[19]

In particular it excludes what is known as 'secondary hearsay', that is, evidence of what another person has said, offered as indirect evidence of the facts asserted in that person's statement.[20] Only where the person being quoted is at the time of the proof dead or permanently insane or a prisoner of war, so that his or her personal testimony is unavailable, can secondary hearsay be admitted in a court of law.[21] For similar reasons, the 'best evidence rule' excludes oral testimony concerning the terms of documents or the features of objects[22] which it would be practicable to produce or, if large, to visit. In arbitration, however, the 'best evidence rule' becomes, unless the submission requires adherence to the strict rules of evidence, a criterion not of the admissibility but of the weight of the evidence. Secondary hearsay is of less value than direct evidence, but in some cases it may be all that is available, or at least all that can be obtained without incurring expense which is out of all proportion to the value of the matters in issue. Injustice is then more likely to arise from its exclusion than its admission.

14.10.   **Burden of proof.** In arbitration this concept is stripped of its more technical refinements and becomes simply an aid in the assessment of the evidence and in structuring the order of proceedings in a proof. In the context of arbitration it means that initially the party who asserts something must prove it,[23] unless the fact in issue is 'peculiarly within the knowledge' of the opponent.[24] The burden of proof is shifted by the presentation of convincing if not conclusive evidence.

[19] Walkers, *Evidence*, 394.
[20] 'Primary hearsay', that is, evidence of what someone has said when the fact of his or her having said it is itself in issue, is acceptable even under the rules of evidence: Walkers, *Evidence*, 394.
[21] *Ibid.*
[22] *Ibid.*, note 5.
[23] *Ibid.*, 67.
[24] *Ibid.*, 68.

The 'stated case'

14.11. General nature and purpose. The stated case is a means by which a ruling may be obtained from a court on a matter which has arisen in proceedings before an inferior tribunal. The essential element is that the court is presented with a question — such as 'is the arbiter entitled to order the landlord to carry out certain specified repairs to the property leased by the tenant?',[25] together with a statement of the relevant facts and legal provisions out of which the question has arisen. Normally only a question of law may be entertained, but this is not an essential feature of the institution.[26] Again, it usually operates only as a means of obtaining guidance on difficult or controversial questions arising in the course of proceedings, but in some systems it is used as a means of reviewing decisions.[27]

14.12. Origins. The stated case was introduced into ordinary arbitration in Scotland by section 3 of the Administration of Justice (Scotland) Act 1972,[28] which came into force on April 2nd 1973.[29] It was not then a novel procedure in the law in Scotland, however, having been previously introduced into a number of statutory arbitration regimes[30] since the enactment of section 84 of the Excise Act 1827.[31] A form of the procedure is known to have existed in 1207.[32]

14.13. The 1972 provisions. *Legislative purpose.* The ostensible reasons for the introduction of section 3 of the 1972 Act were stated by Baroness Tweedsmuir during debate in the House of Lords. She said[33] —

'While accepting that the relative speed and finality of arbitration proceedings should not be lightly discarded, it is the Government's view that where an arbiter has made a patent

---

[25] As in *Chalmers Property Investment Co.* v. *Bowman* 1953 S.L.T. (Sh. Ct.) 38.
[26] Walker D. M., *The Scottish Legal System* 4th edn., Edinburgh, 1974, 494.
[27] Dobie, *Sh. Ct. Pr.*, 540–1.
[28] For the text, see Appendix I hereto.
[29] Administration of Justice (Scotland) Act 1972 (Commencement) Order 1973 (S.I. 1973 No. 339 (C. 11)).
[30] Such as those under the Agricultural Holdings (Scotland) Acts.
[31] 7 & 8 Geo. IV, Ch. 53, considered in *Steele* v. *McIntosh Brothers* (1879) 7 R. 192.
[32] *Cambuskenneth Abbey* v. *Dunfermline Abbey*, Cooper, *Sel. Scot. Cas.* 13.
[33] Hansard, *Parl. Deb. (H.L.)*, 9 Mar. 1972, Vol. 329, Col. 221.

error in law, it should be possible to correct that error on appeal; but in order to preserve as far as possible the present advantages of this method of settling disputes, the provision is expressly confined to questions of law. On questions of fact the arbiter's award is, and would remain, final. Certain Scottish statutory arbitration codes ... make provision for such appeals. The clause therefore brings Scots law into line with these statutory codes.'

If the Government's intention truly was to enable arbitral errors in law to be corrected on appeal, the provisions which were actually introduced (and which, apart from the addition of a 'contracting out' clause, were not significantly altered during the Parliamentary process) were not an appropriate means of achieving it, since the form of words chosen had already been judicially held to mean that the question could not be stated once the decision had been made.[34] Subsection 3(1) of the 1972 Act therefore could not provide, as Baroness Tweedsmuir suggested, for an appeal, and the court has since held that indeed it does not do so.[35] There is indeed a case for making the award of an arbiter in Scotland more open to challenge or review than it is,[36] but this measure does not have that effect. It may be interpreted as a minimal response to conflicting pressures[37] by a Government not seriously interested in the reform of Scots arbitration law.

14.14. *Effect.* Subsection 3(1) of the 1972 Act states that in certain specified circumstances an arbiter or oversman may or must state a case for the opinion of the Court of Session on any question of law arising in the arbitration. This provision poses a number of questions relating to —

(a) the circumstances in which an arbiter or oversman —
   (i) is at liberty, or
   (ii) has an obligation
   to state a case;
(b) the types of question that can be stated;

---

[34] *Johnston's Trustees* v. *Special Committee of the Corporation of Glasgow* 1912 S.C. 300 per L.P. Dunedin at 303; *Smith* v. *Scottish Legal Life Assurance Society* 1912 S.C. 611.

[35] *Fairlie Yacht Slip Ltd.* v. *Lumsden* 1977 S.L.T. (Notes) 41.

[36] As Mr. Robert Howie, Advocate, has argued in an illuminating but as yet unpublished research paper.

[37] Arising out of the decision in *James Miller and Partners Ltd.* v. *Whitworth Street Estates (Manchester) Ltd.* [1970] 1 All E.R. 796.

(c) the manner in which a case should be stated; and
(d) the effect of the opinion of the court.

14.15. As to the *circumstances* in which a case may or must be stated, three conditions must be satisfied before an arbiter or oversman is at liberty or may be required to state a case for the opinion of the court.

14.16. *First*, the submitters must not have inserted an 'express provision to the contrary in an agreement to refer to arbitration'. The meaning of 'agreement to refer' has already been considered.[38] Here let it be said merely that this includes any contract of submission whether contained in an ancillary arbitration clause or an *ad hoc* deed of submission. It matters not for this purpose whether the contract is contained in a formal deed or in informal letters. The submitters may by express provision thus exclude resort to the stated case procedure, but they may *only* do so in the 'agreement to refer'; no subsequent agreement, however clear or emphatic, will be effective,[39] except possibly where it formally amends the original agreement. If an ancillary submission has been entered into without excluding the stated case, the submitters would have to abandon it unequivocally and enter into a new 'agreement to refer' if they wished to achieve this effect.[40] It is not certain whether or not the parties may in the agreement to refer exclude the stated case in particular kinds of dispute only. Partial exclusion has been permitted in some cases arising out of certain statutory regimes,[41] and there seems no reason to hold that the rule should be otherwise under the 1972 provision.

14.17. It is not certain what the force and effect of the indefinite article in the phrase 'an agreement to refer to arbitration' is. Arbitration proceedings sometimes come to cover matters not originally submitted either as a result of additional contracts or other actings made effective by homologation or *rei interventus*. Does an agreement to exclude the stated case in an ancillary clause or even *ad hoc* submission apply in relation to issues incorporated later into the arbitration without any further act of exclusion? The

[38] Paragraphs 3.12–3.16 above.
[39] *Clydebank District Council* v. *Clink* 1977 S.C. 147.
[40] *Ibid.*, per Lord Emslie at 154.
[41] *Broxburn Oil Co. Ltd.* v. *Earl of Buchan* (1926) 42 Sh. Ct. Rep. 30.

indefinite article could found an argument that it does, and this would have the practical result that the same rule applied to all the issues in the proceedings.

14.18.   *Second*, one of the submitters must apply to the arbiter asking for a stated case. The arbiter may not state a case on his or her own initiative. The procedure for making an application is laid down in Rules of Court 277–8.[42] A minute must be lodged with the clerk to the arbitration, setting forth the questions on which the opinion of the court is desired. The clerk (presumably the arbiter acts in this capacity if no clerk has been appointed) then intimates the application to the other party, who is entitled within seven days of the *receipt* of the intimation to lodge a minute setting forth additional questions. There appears to be no statutory requirement that parties should be heard on whether a case should be stated, but since the opponent is asked to show cause why the arbiter should not state a case if the court is ultimately asked to compel the arbiter to act, it would seem appropriate for the arbiter to receive written representations and even hear parties orally on the matter.

14.19.   *Third*, the application must be made before the final award is issued.[43] What constitutes the promulgation or issuing of an award is considered in the next chapter. At this point it may be said briefly that an award has been issued if it has either been sent or handed to a party as a completed deed and not merely as a draft, or if it has been placed in the hands of the clerk to hold it for the submitters. Whether the clerk holds an award for the arbiter or for the submitters is a question of fact which has to be determined in the light of the circumstances of each particular case.[44] Probably the promulgation of a partial award (as distinct from an interim award) prevents an application being made thereafter for a stated case on the matters dealt with in that award, because the arbiter, having discharged his or her whole duties therein, could not give effect to the court's opinion, as normally he or she would be obliged to do.[45] A decision in an old case under section 84 of the

[42] *John L. Haley Ltd.* v. *Dumfries and Galloway Regional Council* 1985 S.L.T. 109.
[43] *Fairlie Yacht Slip Ltd.* v. *Lumsden* 1977 S.L.T. (Notes) 41.
[44] *Johnson* v. *Gill* 1978 S.C. 74 per Lord Kissen at 84.
[45] *Johnston's Trustees* v. *Special Committee of the Corporation of Glasgow* 1912 S.C. 300 per L.P. Dunedin at 303.

Excise Act 1827[46] that a decision might be pronounced subject to the opinion of the court on the case stated, can be distinguished on the ground that the wording of that Act was different and the body concerned was an inferior court not an arbiter. The fact that expenses in the arbitration still have to be taxed (that is, formally assessed and approved by the Auditor of Court) does not mean that every stage of the arbitration has not been completed.[47] It is probably misconduct for an arbiter to hasten the promulgation of an award to forestall an application for a stated case.[48]

14.20.   An arbiter may be *obliged* to state a case if the court on the application of one of the submitters so orders. An arbiter who decides to refuse an application for a stated case must immediately intimate this decision to the submitters, and must grant a certificate of refusal, accompanied by a note of, or a sufficient reference to, either the averments or admissions of the parties or to findings in fact if any have been made.[49] The certificate must specify the date of and the reason for refusal, but the court may be willing to interpret an uninformative certificate as being based on the acceptance of submissions made by one of the parties.[50] Within *fourteen days* of the date of refusal of the application, the submitter concerned may apply by written note to the Inner House of the Court of Session for an order requiring the opponent to show cause why a case should not be stated.[51] (This time limit is strictly enforced[52] for, though the court has a discretion to dispense a party from the strict observance of the Rules of Court,[53] that power is exercised only in exceptional circumstances and in such a manner as will not frustrate the objects of the rule concerned.[54]) The note, which must state shortly the nature of the case, the facts, and the question which the applicant desires to raise, must be accompanied

---

[46] *Steele* v. *McIntosh Brothers* (1879) 7 R. 192 per L.P. Inglis at 196.
[47] *Fairlie Yacht Slip (supra).*
[48] So, at least, it was held in England when a similar procedure obtained there: *Food Corporation of India* v. *Carras (Hellas) Ltd.* [1980] 2 Ll. Rep. 577.
[49] Rule of Court 277(d).
[50] *Gunac Ltd.* v. *Inverclyde District Council* 1983 S.L.T. 130 at 132.
[51] Rule of Court 278.
[52] *John L. Haley Ltd.* v. *Dumfries and Galloway Regional Council* 1985 S.L.T. 109.
[53] Act of Sederunt (Rules of Court, Consolidation and Amendment) 1965 (S.I. 1965 No. 321).
[54] *Grieve* v. *Batchelor and Buckling* 1961 S.C. 12 per L.P. Clyde at 15; Maxwell, *Ct. of Sess. Pr.,* 62–3.

by the arbiter's certificate of refusal. An arbiter who refused or delayed to issue a certificate, would probably commit misconduct, but the problem would probably be resolved in practice by an exercise of the rarely used dispensing power of the court.

14.21. Two provisions place a restriction on the *types of question* that may be posed in a stated case. Subsection 3(1) of the 1972 Act states that only a 'question of law arising in the arbitration' may be the subject of a stated case, and the Rules of Court permit an arbiter to refuse an application on several grounds. Furthermore, it has been suggested that it may not be competent to state a case on a matter which has not been argued at all before the arbiter.[55]

14.22. There are two approaches to the problem of determining whether an issue is a question of law. One is, to search through the reports — with the assistance perhaps of a list of cases such as that most helpfully provided by Mustill[56] — for a precedent as close as may be to that which is presented. The difficulty here is that, if no direct case in point is found, the precedents will not provide much assistance because of their lack of any consistent approach to the problem. Another approach, which is adopted here, is to seek to discover the rational basis of the distinction between questions of fact and questions of law. If the following discussion is insufficient reference may be made to the sources on which it is based.[57]

14.23. The questions which may be presented to an arbiter may be classified broadly under three headings:

(a) truth-questions;
(b) probability-questions; and
(c) description-questions, or questions of meaning, interpretation or clarification.

Truth-questions and probability-questions are questions of fact. The difficulty arises with description-questions, because some of these may legitimately be treated as questions of fact, and some of them as questions of law.

[55] *Williamson* v. *Hay* 1952 S.L.T. (Sh. Ct.) 93.
[56] *Comm. Arb.* Appendix 5.
[57] Principally Wilson W. A., 'A Note on Fact and Law' (1963) 26 *M.L.R.* 609; Jackson J. D. and Ockelton M., 'Questions of Fact and Questions of Law' in Twining W. (ed.) *Facts in Law*, Wiesbaden, 1983. On the lighter side, see Herbert A. P., *Uncommon Law*, London, 1969, 18–23, which shows how the question 'is a golfer a gentleman?' could become a question of law.

14.24. The difference between these three types of question may be illustrated by means of the following example. Suppose that a question is raised before an arbiter relating to the cause of delay in completion of certain contract works, and suppose that under the contract a legitimate cause of delay is 'exceptionally adverse weather conditions'.[58] One of the parties leads the evidence of an expert who states that the mean temperature during the month of January as recorded at a local weather station was − 5°C, and that the average mean daylight temperature for January there for the last 20 years was 1°C. Any question about whether the expert is telling the truth or is a reliable witness, or whether the mean temperature in January in the relevant year was really − 5°C is a '*truth-question*'. There then arises a question whether, assuming the expert may be believed, the temperature at the construction site was also − 5°C. If the only evidence about the temperature is that of the expert concerning the conditions at the local weather station, the arbiter has to make an inference therefrom on the basis of, say, further evidence about matters such as the relative heights of the weather station and the construction site above sea-level. This is a '*probability-question*'. Assuming this question to have been decided in the affirmative, the arbiter then has to determine whether a mean temperature of 6°C below the average for the month constituted, amounted to, or counted as, 'exceptionally adverse weather conditions' in terms of the contract. This is a '*description-question*' concerning the meaning of this phrase in the context of the contract. Because of its legal context, it might be regarded as a question of law, However, the phrase 'exceptionally severe weather conditions' is not a legal term of art; it has no special meaning in law distinct from its meaning in ordinary life, and in ordinary life words and phrases do not have definite and clear meanings in isolation from their contexts. The question would therefore probably be regarded as a question of fact, like the preceding truth-questions and probability questions. If, however, the phrase has appeared previously in legislation applicable to the industry concerned, or had been the subject of a judicial decision which had given it a definite legal meaning in a specified context or in general, the question arising in the example given above would become a question of law.

14.25. A question of law may arise concerning whether the arbiter has acted properly in the conduct of proceedings or in

[58] As in clause 25.4.2. of the RIBA Scottish form of building contract.

arriving at certain findings of fact, in spite of the absence of detailed rules of procedure and evidence, because the arbiter remains governed by broad legal requirements of fairness and of care.

14.26. Finally in this context, it may be noted that if the arbiter were asked whether the meaning of 'exceptionally severe weather conditions' in the contract was or was not a 'question of law' in terms of subsection 3(1) of the 1972 Act, that would be a 'description-question' which was clearly a question of law, because the phrase 'question of law' has itself acquired a legal meaning even if that meaning is extremely obscure.

14.27. The other restrictions on the liberty to state a case are contained in Rule of Court 277(d). This rule provides that an arbiter may refuse to state a case for the opinion of the court on any one of three grounds: —

(i) 'that the proposed question does not arise'; or
(ii) 'that a decision upon it is unnecessary for the purpose of the appeal' [*sic*]; or
(iii) that the proposed question 'is frivolous'.

These rules, which apply equally to all forms of application for a stated case, are similar to but not identical with the rules which applied in England when the institution of the 'special case' existed there.[59] The differences are sufficient to make the application of English precedents hazardous. The Court of Session has considered that the mere fact that one of its own decisions was directly in point did not mean that the question was 'frivolous', where the pursuer wished the matter to be heard by a court of seven judges.[60]

14.28. The *manner of stating a case* is prescribed in some detail in Rules of Court 277–80. Where the arbiter decides to state a case, and the party who first applied for it decides to proceed with it, the timetable is as follows —

(a) Intimation by arbiter of decision to state a case — Within 28 days of application.

---

[59] As stated, e.g. in *Halfdan Greig and Co. A./S.* v. *Sterling Coal and Navigation Corporation and Another* [1973] 2 All E.R. 1073.
[60] *Pumpherston Oil Co. Ltd.* v. *Caveney* (1903) 5 F. 663.

(b)	Submission of draft case by arbiter to parties	Within 14 days of intimation of decision to state case.
(c)	Return of draft by parties	Within 21 days of receipt of draft.
(d)	Final settlement by arbiter of terms of case	No specific time limit.
(e)	Delivery of case as authenticated by clerk to party who first requested it.	No specific time limit.
(f)	Intimation by applicant party to opponent and lodging of principal case with Deputy Principal Clerk of Court.	Within 7 days of delivery of case.
(g)	Lodging by applicant party of copy of case in General Department of Court of Session with usual process in terms of Rules 20 and 25(b), and delivery of 10 copies to opponent with intimation of lodging in the General Department.	Within 14 days of receipt by Deputy Principal Clerk of principal copy.

The total time for stating case from first application to the beginning of its consideration by the court, assuming that at each stage the maximum time is taken and assuming that the arbiter takes no more than 21 days to settle final terms of the case and deliver it to the applicant party, will be four calendar months. This assumes also that either the application was presented after the facts have been ascertained by the arbiter, or that the arbiter has not decided, in terms of Rule 277(c), to postpone further consideration of the case until the necessary facts have been ascertained.

14.29. The lodging of the stated case and process in the General Department of the Court of Session must be accompanied by the enrolling of a motion for an order for a hearing. The motion must be intimated to the opponent. At any time before the final disposal of the case the court may allow it to be amended with consent of the parties, and may remit it back to the arbiter for restatement or further amendment. This has been done in a number of cases arising out of statutory arbitration proceedings.[61] If any enquiry

[61] *Lendrum* v. *Ayr Steam Shipping Co.* 1914 S.C. (H.L.) 91 per Lord Dunedin at

into matters of fact is competent and required for the disposal of the case, and it is not possible or not convenient to remit the case back to the arbiter for further findings of fact, the court may remit to a Lord Ordinary or to a reporter or to one of their own number to take evidence.

14.30. The form which the stated case should take is laid down in general terms of Court 279 and Form 43 in the Appendix thereto. Within that framework it is a matter for the arbiter, subject always to the power of the court to remit it back for clarification or elaboration. Though obviously the submitters must have a strong — if unanimous a very strong — influence at the drafting stage, it is the arbiter who finally determines how the case is stated.[62] If either party is dissatisfied he or she must apply to the court to have the case remitted back.[63]

14.31. A stated case should refer to the statute under which it is presented, and then go on to indicate—

'in articulate numbered paragraphs the facts and circumstances out of which the case arises, as the same may be agreed or formed.'[64]

The facts are most unlikely to be the arbiter's final findings, because these are not normally established until the final award is issued. It is, moreover, competent for an arbiter appointed for his or her special skill and knowledge to take account of altered circumstances since the date of the last proof or hearing.[65] The proposed findings in a stated case are sufficient for the purpose where they —

'represent the definite conclusion [of the arbiter] on matters of fact which, subject always to the possible effect of representations made by the parties, will form the basis of [the] decree arbitral.'[66]

102; *Campbell* v. *Rivet, Bolt and Nut Co. Ltd.* 1925 S.L.T. 177; *McNaught* v. *Garrallan Coal Co.* 1926 S.C. 351.

[62] *McNaught* (*supra* note 61) per L.P. Clyde at 355.
[63] *Forsyth-Grant* v. *Salmon* 1961 S.L.T. (Notes) 38 per L.J.C. Thomson at 39.
[64] Rule of Court 279(a).
[65] *Miller & Partners Ltd.* v. *Edinburgh Corporation* 1978 S.C. 1 per L.J.C. Wheatley at 11.
[66] *Mackenzie* v. *MacGillivray* 1921 S.C. per L.P. Clyde at 729–30.

When a question has arisen concerning whether there is evidence to support a proposed finding of fact,

'the salient features of the evidence should be stated, not at length, but in brief summary, in the body of the case itself.'[67]

The case should finally set out the question which the court has to answer.

14.32.   So far as ordinary arbitration is concerned, there appears to be no provision in the Rules of Court in terms of which an arbiter could be ordered to transmit to the court any notes of evidence or other documents relating to a stated case. Such an order has been made in the context of a statutory arbitration in which the arbiter was a sheriff,[68] but this step seems to have been taken on the basis of the power in what is now Rule of Court 104 to require transmission of the process of an inferior court. The order was made reluctantly even in that context, and similar orders have been refused in other cases.[69]

14.33.   Where a party who has applied for a stated case decides not to proceed with it, he or she must return the principal case to the clerk to the arbitration who must thereupon deliver it to the opponent who may then proceed as the original applicant might have done. Failure either to proceed with the case by lodging the principal copy with the Deputy Principal Clerk of Session or to intimate a decision not to proceed by returning it to the arbiter's clerk will entitle the opponent to apply to the arbiter to have the proceedings disposed of.[70] A party who has failed to lodge a copy of the case in the General Department of the Court of Session along with the usual process, and has not been reponed against that failure — that is, relieved by the court from the consequences that would otherwise follow from it — upon a motion to that effect within seven days of the expiry of the time limit, will be regarded as having abandoned the application.[71] The Deputy Principal Clerk of Session will then endorse a certificate of abandonment on the case and retransmit it to the arbiter who may then, on the application of either party, dispose of the proceedings.[72]

[67] *Differ* v. *Cadzow Coal Co. Ltd.* 1941 S.C. 162.
[68] *Brydon* v. *Railway Executive* 1957 S.C. 283.
[69] E.g. *Scott* v. *Mitchell* 1930 S.C. 105.
[70] Rule of Court 277(h)(ii).
[71] Rule of Court 277(k)(i).
[72] Rule of Court 277(k)(iii).

14.34. The *effect of the court's opinion* in a stated case is that the arbiter is bound to give effect to it.[73] In dealing with a stated case the court may deal with the expenses of the proceedings before it,[74] but the expenses of the preparation of the case will be regarded as expenses in the arbitration[75] for which the arbiter allocates responsibility.

[73] *Johnston's Trustees* v. *Special Committee of the Corporation of Glasgow* 1912 S.C. 300 per L.P. Dunedin at 303; *Mitchell-Gill* v. *Buchan* 1921 S.C. 390 per L.P. Clyde at 395.
[74] *McQuater* v. *Ferguson* 1911 S.C. 640.
[75] *Thomson* v. *Earl of Galloway* 1919 S.C. 611.

CHAPTER FIFTEEN

THE DECREE ARBITRAL OR AWARD — 1

Introduction

15.1. In this chapter the decree arbitral or award — the terms are interchangeable[1] — is discussed under the following heads —

(a) definitions;
(b) the main types of award;
(c) features of common styles of award;
(d) characteristics of a valid award;
(e) the legal effect of an award.

The following chapter deals with the challenge and interpretation of an award and the enforcement of foreign awards in Scotland.

Definitions

15.2. A decree arbitral or award is a decision[2] reached by a qualified[3] and properly appointed[4] arbiter or arbiters or oversman, without misconduct, corruption, bribery or falsehood,[5] upon questions[6] properly submitted[7] on the basis of a valid and subsisting contract of submission,[8] and issued[9] to the submitters in such form[10] and at such time[11] or place[12] as the law or the contract requires. If only one award is made in a submission of existing

[1] *Mackenzie* v. *Girvan* (1843) II Bell 43 per Lord Brougham at 49.
[2] Paragraphs 1.1–1.13 and 8.31 above.
[3] Paragraphs 4.32–4.56 above.
[4] Paragraphs 11.28–11.40 and 13.3–13.5 above.
[5] Paragraphs 12.21–12.29 above.
[6] Paragraphs 6.2–6.8 and 11.6 above.
[7] Paragraphs 6.9–6.15 above.
[8] See above paragraphs 4.3–4.31 (capacity and power of submitters); 5.3–5.21 (constitution and proof); and chapter 7 (circumstances of formation).
[9] Paragraph 15.61 below.
[10] Paragraphs 15.26–15.30 below.
[11] The submission may impose limits, but Scots law does not.
[12] Scots law does not specify a place of issue or deposit.

disputes, it must exhaust all the questions at issue; if there are more awards than one, all the part awards must together exhaust those questions.[13] An award issued by an oversman must be based on a proper devolution of the matters determined by the decree[14].

15.3. The decree arbitral or award should be the accurate[15] embodiment of the arbiter's own[16] clear[17], precise,[18] internally consistent,[19] self-contained and unconditional[20] judgment (not mere hope or opinion[21]) upon the question or questions submitted by the submitters for determination. Once the submitters have agreed on the whole or part of the matter in issue, then that matter cannot form the subject of a decree arbitral.[22]

Types of award

15.4. In Scots law three categories of arbitral awards are usually distinguished — final awards, partial awards, and interim awards. Since the term 'final award' is used in two senses, the term 'terminating award' is here introduced to carry the less important of its two meanings.

15.5. **Final award**. This term is primarily used to mean an award by which the arbiter makes her or his irrevocable decision on the issue or issues dealt with therein. In this sense an award which conclusively determines only part of the subject matter of the arbitration is a final award, but the term is also used more loosely to mean a terminating award. Once a final award has been issued on any matter, the judicial powers of the arbiter in relation to it are spent, and his or her duties are discharged. In other words, he or she is *'functus (functa) officio'*.[23]

---

[13] Paragraph 15.46 below.
[14] Paragraphs 13.51–13.53 above.
[15] Paragraph 15.31 below.
[16] Paragraph 13.8 above.
[17] Paragraph 15.33 below.
[18] Paragraph 15.34 below.
[19] Paragraph 15.37 below.
[20] Paragraph 15.38 below.
[21] Paragraph 15.40 below.
[22] *Maule* v. *Maule* (1816) IV Dow 363.
[23] Bell J. M., *Arb.* paragraph 449.

15.6. Terminating award. It may be convenient to use this term to refer to an award which deals fully and conclusively with all the matters submitted, or all the matters which have not already been conclusively determined in part awards, and which therefore completes the judicial proceedings in an arbitration. It may be the only award in an arbitration, or the last in a series. All 'terminating awards' must therefore be 'final awards', but a 'final award' is not necessarily a 'terminating award'.

15.7. A terminating award must deal with any matters previously determined in a provisional manner by means of interim awards. If there have been any interim awards it is desirable though not formally necessary to make reference to them in the terminating award, indicating whether and to what extent they are confirmed or altered, and whether any sums found due in the terminating award are in addition to, or merely comprise, sums thus provisionally awarded.

15.8. A terminating award should narrate the promulgation of any part awards that have been made in the arbitration, and do so in such a way that their character as such is clear and that the issues dealt with therein are not inadvertently dealt with again in the terminating award.

15.9. To reduce the risk of reduction of a terminating award on the ground of failure to exhaust the submission, it is appropriate, but again not formally necessary, to narrate that the arbiter has considered all items of claim by both parties and the answers thereto, and to specify which claims or counterclaims have finally been upheld in whole or in part. The form of a terminating award should include words which indicate that it is a full as well as a final award, that it determines all the issues, or all the remaining issues, which have been submitted. If this is done, a court is likely to find that it follows by necessary implication that no sums were found due except those mentioned.[24]

15.10. Interim and part awards. An interim award in Scots law is an award which determines the issues mentioned therein only provisionally, not conclusively and irrevocably. It may (but need not) deal with the whole of the issues submitted. An interim

---

[24] *Donald* v. *Shiell's Executrix* 1937 S.C. 52 per L.J.C. Aitchison at 62.

decree is inherently subject to recall or alteration by a subsequent award.[25] An old decision, in which the court held that, if two decrees were made by the same arbiters on the same matter between the same two parties, 'the last makis derogatioun to the first'[26] is probably best understood as involving an interim and a final terminating decree. It has been held that an interim decree which dealt with the whole issue in a submission, but which had not been followed by any subsequent decree could stand as if it were a final decree,[27] but this seems anomalous and of very doubtful authority. An interim decree which, albeit provisionally, exceeds the matters submitted, is liable to reduction but the court has shown some unwillingness to reduce an interim decree on this ground where the alleged irregularity is readily capable of rectification by the arbiter.[28]

15.11.   A part award, by contrast, is one which deals conclusively and irrevocably with part only of the matters submitted,[29] and is a 'final award' in the sense defined in paragraph 15.5 above. Since the submission must be exhausted, if one part award has been issued it must normally be accompanied by another, and all the part awards must, taken together, exhaust the submission.

15.12.   There are two kinds of circumstance in which difficulties may arise in practice in applying the rule that a submission must be exhausted. One is where there has been an *ad hoc* general submission of 'all disputes'. Though this expression has in this context to be interpreted as including only those disputes which were being actively pursued when the contract was executed,[30] so that the scope of the submission is ascertainable in principle, in practice it may be difficult for an arbiter to be sure that what he or she intends as the terminating award is not in fact merely a part award. The problem may, as J. M. Bell suggested,[31] be obviated by insisting at the outset on formal proceedings with a closed record containing a distinct statement that all claims competent under the

---

[25] *Edinburgh & Glasgow Railway Co.* v. *Hill* (1840) 2 D. 486.
[26] *Maxwell* v. *Walkinshaw* 19 Dec 1561, Mor. 643.
[27] *Taylor* v. *Neilson & Fulton* (1822) 1 S. 278.
[28] *Edinburgh and Glasgow Railway Co.* v. *Hill* (1840) 2 D. 486 per Lord Mackenzie.
[29] Bell J. M., *Arb.*, paragraphs 501–2.
[30] Paragraph 10.15 above.
[31] *Arb.* paragraph 108.

submission have been stated therein. Another is to issue proposed findings in terms which make it clear that the arbiter assumes that there are no further questions to be decided under the submission. In the latter case, if neither of the parties takes the opportunities presented of making any representation to the contrary, both will be personally barred from arguing subsequently that the award did not exhaust the submission.

15.13. The other difficulty arises in ancillary submissions of future disputes. In relation to such a submission any award is actually or potentially only a part award and does not act as a terminating award. It would, however, clearly be ridiculous for an award which had dealt with all the issues presented to the arbiter to be held invalid on the ground that it had not exhausted the submission. In this context the rule must require only that any award which expressly or impliedly purports to deal with all matters within the scope of the submission which have been presented to the arbiter must actually have done so. The scope of such matters is easier to ascertain if the ancillary contract has been followed by an implementing deed of submission.

15.14. The phrase 'interim award' is sometimes used loosely, even by judges, to refer to or include part awards.[32] Care must therefore be used when interpreting judicial decisions in this field. This inexactitude may be due in some degree to the fact that interim awards (in the strict sense) generally do not deal with the whole subject matter of the arbitration, and also to the fact that Scots usage differs from but is subject to strong influence by English law. It would appear that in England what in Scots law is called an 'interim award' is not competent at all, and that the term 'interim award' is reserved for deeds which in Scotland are called 'part awards'.[33]

15.15. It is desirable that an interim or part award should contain in its own text (*'in gremio* of the deed') an indication of its nature.[34] If this is not done, and a deed intended as a part award comes to be interpreted by the court as being *ad interim* only, there is some risk that the terminating award in the submission will be reduced on the ground that it has failed to exhaust the submission; conversely,

---

[32] See e.g. *Lyle* v. *Falconer* (1842) 5 D. 236.
[33] Mustill, *Comm. Arb.* 331–2.

if a deed intended as an interim award comes to be regarded as a part award, the power to reconsider the issues therein dealt with will be excluded.

15.16. There is no legal presumption, as there appears to be in some other countries,[35] that an arbiter may make a part award. An arbiter cannot issue an interim or a part award unless power has been expressly or impliedly granted for that purpose.[36] Where no express provision has been made, the power of the arbiter to issue part or interim awards depends on the readiness of the courts to interpret submissions as containing an implied grant. The authorities suggest that in general the courts are willing to imply a power to issue such awards whenever the language of the submission gives any reasonable warrant for such a conclusion. Though the precedents on this matter are derived from the early part of the nineteenth century they have escaped disapproval during the 'strict constructionist' era associated with Lord President Inglis during the latter part of the nineteenth century.

15.17. A number of examples of this liberal approach may be cited. It has been suggested, though not decided, that a general submission of 'all claims' imports an implied power to pronounce part decrees at least where the matters in dispute are 'articulate and separable'.[37] An ancillary submission of 'any dispute or difference' arising during the currency or after the expiry of the main contract has been held necessarily to imply a power to pronounce a part award.[38] Consent to the registration of part decrees implies a grant of power to issue such a decree.[39] It is probable therefore that in disputes arising under submissions which are ancillary to contracts for construction works in which it is quite likely that a succession of claims and counterclaims will occur, all affecting the total sums ultimately due under the contract, an arbiter will be held to have power to issue both part and interim awards.

[34] Bell J. M., *Arb.* paragraph 506.
[35] E.g. Sweden (Arbitration Act 1929 s. 19) and England (Arbitration Act 1950 s. 14).
[36] Parker, *Arb.*, 162, 164.
[37] *Lyle* v. *Falconer* (1842) 5 D. 236; the reference is to 'interim' decrees, but the sense indicates that part decrees are meant.
[38] *Montgomerie* v. *Carrick & Napier (No. 2)* (1849) 12 D. 274; here again the term 'interim' decree was used, but the sense indicates that part decrees were meant.
[39] *Lyle* v. *Falconer* (1842) 5 D. 236.

15.18. Where power to issue part awards exists, it may not always be appropriate to use it. Mustill and Boyd advise[40] that while it may sometimes be possible to —

'achieve a saving of time and expense by breaking down a dispute ... into separate issues and making a [part][41] award on one issue before embarking on an investigation of the next, ... in practice this tends to increase rather than reduce the duration and cost of the reference'.

In any event, if there is any prospect of dividing up the matters in a complex dispute so that they may be dealt with by a series of part awards, the decision to do so should be taken at an early stage in the proceedings.

15.19. It is possible, but not judicially decided or even considered, that a Scots arbiter permitted by the submission to issue interim awards might use this power to take provisional measures to safeguard property or to effect the securing of the sum in dispute. It appears that in Sweden interim awards are used for two distinct purposes.[42] One is as a —

'provisional award (*interimistisk dom*) whereby, for instance, the claimant is awarded a sum at an early stage of the proceedings on account of the damages he may eventually be found entitled to recover'.

The other is as a means of effecting a 'security measure (*säkerhetsåtgärd*) such as a preservation order'. Circumstances could arise in Scotland in which an arbiter, faced with the possibility that his or her final award might be made wholly ineffective if interim security measures were not taken, might find it appropriate to use for this purpose an ordinary power to make interim awards.

Features of common styles

15.20. **Sources.** Proven styles of decree arbitral may be found in a number of sources.[43] Those contained in English publications

---

[40] *Comm. Arb.* 331–2.
[41] Naturally they adopt the English usage and call these 'interim' awards.
[42] Holmbäck, *Arb. Swe. 1984*, 128.
[43] E.g. Halliday, *Conveyancing*, Vol. I, paragraphs 14.55 to 14.62; Keith J., and

should be treated with caution even if (perhaps especially if) they purport to give Scottish forms.[44] Use of a proven style is not required in law, but they have been developed by notarial tradition over many years — indeed centuries[45] — and usually provide a sound foundation upon which to build.

15.21. **Structure.** A formal decree arbitral normally contains three main parts — a narrative clause, an adjudicative clause, and a testing clause.[46]

15.22. The purpose of the *narrative clause* is to identify the arbiter (or arbiters or oversman), the submitters, the contract on which the arbitration is based, and the matters in issue, and to recite the events in the proceedings which affect the content of the award. These may include for example the date of the appointment of the arbiter, any devolution upon an oversman, the fact (if it is a fact) that the arbiter has received parties' claims and answers, viewed property, allowed and held a proof, heard parties, issued proposed findings, and noted parties' representations thereon. The narrative clause also notes any special powers granted to the arbiter, any acts of prorogation of the submission, and any interim or part awards previously issued. Traditionally it has concluded

---

Brown J. (eds.) *Encyclopaedia of Scottish Legal Styles*, Edinburgh, 1935, Vol. I, 280–90; Irons, *Arb.*, 449–56; Weir, *Arb.*, Appendix II, 158–66.

[44] E.g. the style given in (1979) 45 *Arbitration*, 126–9. Its heading 'In the matter of the Arbitration Act 1894', a meaningless transposition of the English style 'In the matter of the Arbitration Act 1950', betrays its foreign origin.

[45] Compare the styles in the publications mentioned in note 43 above with, for example, (1) the decree arbitral between the Abbey of Cambuskenneth and William of Fentoune and another, 13 Feb. 1349, in Fraser W. (ed), *Registrum Monasterii S. Marie de Cambuskenneth*, Grampian Club, Edinburgh, 1872, 259–61; and (2) the decree arbitral between Andrew Bishop of Moray and Hugh Ross of Kilravock, 13 Aug. 1492, in *Registratum Episcopatus Moraviensis*, Bannatyne Club, Edinburgh, 1937, 243–6. A distinguished English arbitrator has shrewdly commented that the modern formal Scots award retains 'a touch of clericalism with traces of liturgical embellishment': Barclay C., 'The Arbitration Award', (1979) 45 *Arbitration* 120. Probably the practice of having a solicitor as arbiter's clerk is derived from mediaeval usage, and that notarial tradition is responsible for continuing similarities in the form of award, and for the modelling of formal arbitration upon court procedure. N.B., in the context of the similarity between modern formal arbitration and sheriff court procedure, the comment of *Regiam Majestatem* (II.1.1) in the early 14th century that arbitration proceedings are 'framed on the model of the judicial process'.

[46] Bell J. M., *Arb.*, paragraph 455.

with an affirmation that the arbiters, having considered all the claims and answers of parties, are now 'well and ripely advised' and have 'God and a good conscience before their eyes', but these flourishes are now usually omitted.

15.23. The *adjudicative clause* contains the arbiter's judgment on matters submitted, and should indicate whether the judgment is final or only *ad interim*, and whether it is a part or a terminating award. If it is a terminating award and one or more interim awards have already been issued, it should refer to them and affirm them either completely or with such modifications as are thought appropriate. Reasons are not normally given in the decree itself, but are sometimes attached in an ancillary note, which usually expressly contains a statement to the effect that it is not part of the decree. Where the submission authorises registration for preservation and execution, a clause of registration is inserted at the end of the adjudicative clause.

15.24. The *testing clause* narrates the names and designations of any witnesses — formal execution requires two — and the date and place (or dates and places, if there are several arbiters who sign separately) of the execution of the deed.

Characteristics of a valid award

15.25. The characteristics of a valid award are discussed below under two main heads — compliance with formal requirements, and compliance with substantive requirements. Certainty and the absence of errors of expression are here regarded as substantive requirements. An invalid award may be a nullity, or be liable to reduction[47] following upon an action in the Court of Session, or may be unenforceable. A party may however become personally barred by homologation, *rei interventus*, or adoption from obtaining reduction, unless the grounds of invalidity are not such as may be waived.[48] A party may be held to have homologated the decree if he or she has received or done any thing in terms thereof,

[47] For grounds of reduction, see paragraph 16.2 below.
[48] *Elgin Lunacy Board* v. *Bremner and Elder* (1874) 1 R. 1155 per Lord Neaves at 1168, affd. (1875) 2 R. (H.L.) 136; *Hepburn* v. *Hepburn* Dec. 1 1736 Mor. 5658.

'albeit the samin be never so litill'.[49] Probably registering a decree for preservation constitutes homologation.[50]

15.26.   **Formal requirements**. The rules governing the formal validity of decrees arbitral in Scotland are derived mainly from judicial decisions which are old, laconically reported, and sometimes conflicting. For this reason it is difficult to expound the law on this matter with certainty, and prudential advice is often all that can be offered.

15.27.   Most modern systems of law require that an arbitration award must be in writing and model laws drawn up by international bodies are usually framed on this assumption.[51] In Scots law there is a residual category of awards which do not require to be in writing — those which follow upon verbal submissions entered into 'between country people (*inter rusticos*), for matters of small importance',[52] but it is obsolete and may be ignored. It is not competent to prove an award by the oath of an arbiter.[53] For practical purposes, therefore, it can be stated that a decree arbitral must be in writing and signed by the arbiter. In a submission to a plurality of arbiters, all must participate in the whole proceedings[54] and then sign the award[55] unless power has been given to decide by a majority. In that event a dissenter cannot hold up proceedings by withdrawing or refusing to sign the award,[56] and the signatures of the majority are sufficient.

15.28.   Given that an award must be in writing, must the writing be formally executed? It has been held that it must either be so executed before two witnesses or be holograph (in the handwriting) or adopted as holograph of the arbiter, unless it falls into one of two categories of exception.[57]

---

[49] *Montgomery* v. *Semple* Feb. 23 1566, Mor. 5619.
[50] *Laird of Ruthven* v. *Laird of Banff* 31 Jul. 1560, Mor. 5619.
[51] See e.g. Article 31(1) of the Model Law adopted on June 21 1985 by the United Nations Commission on International Trade Law (UNCITRAL).
[52] *A* v. *B* 19 Dec. 1746, Mor. 8475.
[53] *Ferrie* v. *Mitchell, Ewing and Others* (1824) 3 S. 113.
[54] Bell J. M., *Arb.*, paragraph 786. The same view is judicially taken in England; *European Grain and Shipping Ltd.* v. *Johnston* [1983] 2 W.L.R. 24.
[55] *Sutherland* v. *Torrie* 5 June 1605 Mor. 14719; *Freeland* v. *Freeland* 28 Feb. 1666 Mor. 646. *Paton* v. *Leith* 7 July 1708 Mor. 16988.
[56] *McCallum* v. *Robertson* (1825) II W. & S. 344; *Love* v. *Love* (1825) 4 S. 53.
[57] *McLaren* v. *Aikman* 1939 S.C. 222 per L.J.C. Aitchison at 227; *Earl of Hopetoun* v. *Scots Mines Co.* (1856) 18 D. 739 per Lord Deas at 753.

(1) An award which follows upon a submission which is not, and does not require to be, holograph or tested, merely has to be signed by the arbiter.[58] There are four main examples of awards in this category:

(a) those dealing with disputes arising out of mercantile transactions' (*'in re mercatoria'*)[59];
(b) those arising out of relations between tenants of agricultural holdings and their landlords[60];
(c) those arising between incoming and outgoing agricultural tenants[61]; and
(d) those which are opinions of counsel on a matter submitted by way of joint memorial.[62]

In an exceptional case which probably would not now be followed, the submitters each accepted bills to each other and consigned them into the hands of the arbiter, the creditor in each case having indorsed the bill blank. The arbiter gave judgment by filling up one of the bills with the sum which the arbiter thought due, and delivering both into the hands of the successful party. No signed award was given at all. The court sustained the bill which the arbiter had filled up.[63]

(2) An award in a Scots arbitration which is executed outside Scotland is valid if it is executed according to the law of the place where the award is executed.[64] In practice an award which is executed outside Scotland is likely to follow upon proceedings outside Scotland, and is for that reason most unlikely to be an arbitration whose proceedings are governed by Scots law.[65] The requirements for awards in foreign arbitrations are discussed below.[66]

15.29. An award which has not been executed according to appropriate formalities, but which is still a writing clearly

[58] *Dykes* v. *Roy* (1869) 7 M. 357 per Lord Neaves at 360.
[59] *McLaren* (*supra* note 57); *Dykes* (*supra* note 58); *Steel* v. *Swan* (1869) 6 S.L.R. 387.
[60] *Nivison* v. *Howat* (1883) 11 R. 182.
[61] *Cameron* v. *McKay* (1938) 54 Sh. Ct. Rep. 276.
[62] *Fraser* v. *Lord Lovat* (1850) VII Bell 171; *Earl of Hopetoun* v. *Scots Mines Co.* (1856) 18 D. 739 per Lord Deas at 753.
[63] *Kerr* v. *Clark* 19 Feb. 1751 Mor. Appx. II (Elchies), Bill of Exchange, 50.
[64] *Earl of Hopetoun* (*supra*).
[65] *James Miller and Partners Ltd.* v. *Whitworth Street Estates (Manchester) Ltd.* [1970] 1 All E.R. 796; and see paragraph 13.9–13.12 above.
[66] Paragraphs 16.26–16.52 below.

emanating from the arbiter, may be validated by homologation,[67] *rei interventus*[68] or adoption[69]; otherwise it is a nullity.

15.30. For the avoidance of doubt, it may be pointed out that certain features commonly required by modern legal systems elsewhere are *not* required by Scots law.

(a) Reasoned or 'motivated' awards are now required by many legal systems except where the submitters have agreed otherwise,[70] and in some where the law does not require reasons they are normally given.[71] English law now gives the court power in certain circumstances to order an arbiter to give reasons.[72] Scots law nevertheless does not in ordinary arbitration require a decree arbitral to include reasons,[73] though it is a common practice, as apparently in England[74] for arbiters to issue a separate note of reasons, expressly stating that it does not form part of the award, and though reasoned awards have been required in some statutory régimes.[75] Submitters may of course expressly stipulate for a reasoned award, and this should be done if there is any possibility that the award may have to be enforced in a country which for reasons of public policy requires motivation as a condition of enforcement.

(b) Some legal systems require specification of the arbiters' names, the matters in dispute, and the date and place of the award, or of at least some of these matters.[76] Though all these are normally included in an award which follows the formal Scottish style, none

---

[67] *Robertson* v. *Boyd and Winans* (1885) 12 R. 419; *Dykes* (*supra* note 58).

[68] *Otto* v. *Weir* (1871) 9 M. 660 per L.J.C. Moncreiff at 661.

[69] *Dykes* (*supra* note 58).

[70] See e.g. the French Code of Civil Procedure, Articles 1471, 1480. Mediaeval French law was similar to Scots: Jeanclos Y. *L'arbitrage en Bourgogne et en Champagne du XII au XV siecle*, Dijon, 1977, 244. The UNCITRAL Model Law, Article 31(2) appears to assume that most countries already require reasoned awards, and that others will be ready to do so.

[71] E.g. in Sweden: Holmbäck, *Arb. Swe. 1984*, 134.

[72] Arbitration Act 1979 s. 1(5)(6).

[73] *Williamson* v. *Fraser* 12 Dec. 1739 Mor. 665; *Rogerson* v. *Rogerson* (1885) 12 R. 583.

[74] Mustill, *Comm Arb.* 541–3; *Intermare Transport GmbH* v. *International Copra Export Corporation* (*The 'Ross Isle' and 'Ariel'*) [1982] 2 Ll. Rep. 589 per Staughton J. at 593.

[75] See those mentioned in *Alexander* v. *Bridge of Allan Water Co.* (1869) 7 M. 492; *Paynter* v. *Rutherford* 1940 S.L.T. (Sh. Ct.) 18; *Dunlop* v. *Mundell and Others* 1943 S.L.T. 296.

[76] See e.g. the French Code of Civil Procedure, Articles 1471, 1472 and 1480.

of them — not even the arbiters' names[77] — are legally required. (c) At one time decrees arbitral had to be stamped, but this requirement was abolished by the Finance Act 1949.[78]

15.31.   **Substantive requirements:** (*a*) *Absence of error in expression.* A clerical error may be committed in framing or transcribing the award. Unless the submitters agree, the arbiter has no power to alter a final and promulgated award, but application may be made to the court to permit rectification.[79]

15.32.   An arbiter may make a mistake in reasoning which results in the promulgation of an erroneous award. If the error is a mere error in calculation the court will allow it to be rectified,[80] but otherwise the award will be sustained as issued, on the ground that the errors of an arbiter in point of principle on the matter in issue in the submission cannot be corrected.[81] Section 8 of the Law Reform (Miscellaneous Provisions) (Scotland) Act 1985, which provides for the rectification of certain defectively expressed documents, does not apply to an arbitral award, because an award is intended neither 'to express or to give effect to an agreement' nor to 'create, transfer, vary or renounce a right'. The distinction between an error in calculation and an error in point of principle has been the subject of helpful discussion in an English case.[82] A dispute had arisen between the owners and the charterers of a ship regarding the amount of fuel used. The owners contended that it was 7.176 tons per day, whereas the charterers contended it was 4.5 tons per day. The arbitrator accepted the charterers' figure, but by mistake transposed the names of the parties in one of the documents in which he worked out his reasoning. As a result, the award was almost the opposite of what it should have been. The court remitted the award back to the arbitrator to correct the error in terms of section 22 of the Arbitration Act 1950. Sir John Donaldson said[83] —

---

[77] *Kerr* v. *Clark* 19 Feb. 1751, Mor. Appx. II (Elchies), Bills of Exchange, 50.
[78] S. 35, Schedule 8, paragraph 6.
[79] See paragraph 16.6 below.
[80] *Hetherington* v. *Carlyle* 21 June 1771 F.C.
[81] *Morrison* v. *Robertson* (1825) 1 W. & S. 143; *Nasmyth* v. *Magistrates of Glasgow* 18 Nov. 1777, V Bro. Supp. 427.
[82] *Mutual Shipping Corporation of New York* v. *Bayshore Shipping Co. of Monrovia* (*The 'Montan'*) [1985] 1 All E.R. 520.
[83] At 526.

'... It is the distinction between having second thoughts or intentions and correcting an award or judgment to give true effect to first intentions which creates the problem. Neither an arbitrator nor a judge can make any claim to infallibility. If he assesses the evidence wrongly or misconstrues or misappreciates the law, the resulting award or judgment will be erroneous, but it cannot be corrected.'

Sir John then considered whether there had been 'a mistaken appreciation of the evidence or of the law' or 'an accidental slip or omission'. He decided that the arbitrator had —

'accepted the evidence of the charterers' expert and he does not have any second thoughts about having done so. Having accepted that evidence he sought to give effect to his acceptance in his award. That he did not succeed was due solely to the accidental attribution of the evidence to the wrong party in his reason which he used as a tool in constructing his award. This seems to me a classic case of error in an award arising from ... accidental slip in the recording of material contained in the reasons.'

The error would not have come to light had not the arbitrator issued a note of his reasons along with the award. The possibility of this kind of error is good reason for adopting, in Scotland, the practice of issuing proposed findings.

15.33. **Substantive requirements:** (*b*) *Certainty.* An award, says J. M. Bell,[84]

'should be clear and perspicuous in its language, and free of ambiguity; so that the parties may learn with certainty, by perusing it, what are their respective rights and obligations, as settled by the arbiters.'

Though it is impossible to categorise or enumerate all the ways in which an award may be unclear or indefinite, decided cases illustrate some of them.

15.34. Lack of sufficient clarity or precision may arise either from a failure to take sufficient care in expressing a decision in appropriate terms, or from a failure to grasp either the precise

[84] *Arb.* paragraph 476.

nature of the dispute or what is necessary to determine it. Two examples must here suffice. (1) A submission in England directed an arbitrator to determine the price at which certain property should be purchased by A or B. The arbitrator simply directed that A or B should pay a price which he specified. The court in England held the award void for uncertainty, because it did not indicate which of the submitters should make the payment.[85] (2) D alleged that W, when clearing a gott[86] between their respective lands, had brought down its sides in several places, damaging D's property. The question submitted to arbitration was, whether W was liable to make reparation, and if so to what extent. The arbiters ordered W to repair those places which he had damaged, but without indicating just where those places were. The court were unable to enforce the decree in the form in which it was issued.[87]

15.35.   An award may be obscure because in framing it the arbiter made an assumption of fact or law which turns out to be wrong or at least highly questionable. Though in the only Scottish case[88] in which this situation arose the court rather surprisingly found that there was in fact no obscurity, it seems clear that reduction may be obtained if as a result of such an erroneous assumption the meaning of the award is uncertain as distinct from erroneous. Two proprietors, L and G, submitted to arbitration their differences over the line of the march between their respective lands. In his award, the arbiter made reference to part of the line as running up a burn to its 'source'. In so doing he clearly assumed that the burn had a definable source. L sought to have the award reduced on the ground of uncertainty, and offered to prove that the burn had more than one source. The Lord President said[89] that it would be dangerous to allow a decree arbitral to be disturbed 'on the evidence of Highland witnesses' whom he apparently regarded as inherently unreliable as a class, and therefore refused to entertain the notion that the position of the source of a Highland burn could be a matter of doubt.

[85] *Lawrence* v. *Hodgson* (1826) 1 Y. & J. 16.
[86] *Anglicé* a 'ditch': Robinson M., *The Concise Scots Dictionary*, Aberdeen, 1985, 241.
[87] *Williamson* v. *Dinwiddie* 18 June 1777, V Bro. Supp. 428.
[88] *Lumsden* v. *Gordon* (1842) 4 D. 1353.
[89] At 1354.

15.36. Where the submission relates to several claims, a terminating award should make it clear that they have all been considered and determined. Where claims are all of the same kind (*'eiusdem generis'*) or are all due under a single contract for work done and materials supplied, it is permissible to award a single lump sum after narrating that all claims have been considered.[90] Where the claims are different in character, and liability depends on different circumstances, the separate claims should be separately identified in the award.[91] If this is not done, and a question arises whether a particular claim has been dealt with, the absence of competent and available means of interpreting the award may lead to its reduction.[92] Where there are reciprocal claims, and the arbiter makes a single finding disposing of them all *'hinc inde'*, this will be taken to mean that the arbiter —

'wishes to make it plain that he is disposing of the whole matter on both sides'.[93]

It is preferable, however, to say this (and everything else in the award) in plain English instead of in a language which is not now generally understood, and the interpretation of which is thus particularly likely to give rise to litigation.

15.37. A final award must be internally consistent,[94] and consistent with any other final awards in the same proceedings. If it is not, it may be reduced, as occurred in a case in which the arbiter determined upon modes of taxing heirs and singular successors in a feu holding in terms so inconsistent as to be inextricable.[95] An interim award, which is inherently liable to be recalled and the decision which it embodies modified, may be inconsistent with a later interim or final award which supersedes it.

15.38. The meaning and effect of an award should not normally be conditional upon the taking of some further decision or the occurrence of some other act or event,[96] unless this is clearly

---

[90] *Miller & Son* v. *Oliver & Boyd* (1903) 6 F. 77, per Lord Trayner at 88; *Glasgow Corporation* v. *Paterson & Son Ltd.* (1901) 3 F. (H.L.) 34 per Lord Robertson at 39–40.

[91] *Miller & Son* (*supra* note 90).

[92] As in *Donald* v. *Shiell's Executrix* 1937 S.C. 52.

[93] *Farrans Ltd.* v. *Roxburgh County Council* 1969 S.L.T. 35 at 36.

[94] Bell J. M., *Arb.* paragraph 482.

[95] *Gray* v. *Ferguson* (Unreported) discussed in Parker, *Arb.*, 176–7.

[96] Bell J. M., *Arb.*, paragraph 485.

envisaged in or permitted by the submission. In particular, it should not use terms or expressions whose meaning is in dispute between the parties and is not resolved by the award itself. The only reported decision of the Scottish courts on this matter appears to reveal a willingness to allow the enforcement of awards which are uncertain for this reason,[97] but the sheer practicalities of enforcement must — at least in the case of final awards — make this decision of doubtful authority. In England and Sweden a different and, it is submitted, more reasonable view has been taken. In a dispute between the buyers and sellers of certain goods, an arbitrator in England awarded that —

'buyers shall pay sellers the said sum of US\$224,000 — ... less such sums as the buyers shall have paid the pre-sellers in settlement of the sellers' liability to those pre-sellers over and above the said market price of US\$137.00 per metric ton in respect of the quantities shipped.'

An English court found that the award was unenforceable by reason of uncertainty.[98] In a Swedish case, W contracted to supply and install a marine engine ordered on behalf of a company that was in process of formation. It was agreed that if delivery should be delayed, W was to pay each of the shareholders interest at 20 per cent per annum on the amount paid by the shareholder in respect of his holding on the date fixed for delivery. Delivery was in fact delayed, and in the subsequent dispute the arbiters ordered W to pay three shareholders, K, A, and L 20 per cent interest from the date fixed for delivery on the capital they had respectively paid up on that date. The Swedish Supreme Court, by a majority, found the award unenforceable by reason of its obscurity.[99]

15.39. It is however clear that in Scotland an effectively conditional award may be acceptable if it inevitably depends wholly or partly on the determination of a question which the arbiter has no jurisdiction to decide. Where it is clearly necessary or required by the submission that an award must be issued before the extraneous question has been disposed of, the arbiter has no option but to issue an award in an alternative form. In practice this

[97] *Duffus* v. *Petrie* (1833) 12 S. 205.
[98] *River Plate Products Netherland BV* v. *Etablissment Coargrain* [1982] 1 Ll. Rep. 628.
[99] *Kristensen* v. *Wennberg* 1901 Nytt Juridiskt Arkiv 590; considered in Holmbäck, *Arb.Swe.* 152–3 and *1984*, 147.

problem appears to arise mainly in the context of statutory arbitration régimes, but it can occur in ordinary arbitration also. In one case a tenant of an agricultural holding made a claim for compensation against the Board of Agriculture (as the Department of Agriculture and Fisheries for Scotland was then called). The Board had taken possession at Martinmas 1914 of lands which included the tenant's holding, and the tenant claimed that the previous owner had extended the lease to Martinmas 1915. An arbiter was appointed to determine whether any compensation was due to the tenant, but he had no jurisdiction to deal with the question whether the tenancy had in fact been extended. He therefore issued an award in the alternative, reaching one conclusion on the basis that the lease had terminated at Martinmas 1914, and a different conclusion on the basis that it had been extended to Martinmas 1915. The House of Lords considered, but did not formally have to decide, that the award was valid.[100]

15.40.   An expression of mere hope or opinion cannot be a valid award.[101] Since arbitration is supposed to be a relatively amicable proceeding, it may sometimes be thought inappropriate to issue a judgment in firm language, but it is no service to the submitters to be tentative. Where a submission has been constituted by a joint memorial to counsel, a subsequent award should not (as an ordinary opinion might) merely express a view as to the right of parties, but should firmly determine what they are.

15.41.   It is of course, impossible to frame an award in such exact and unequivocal terms that it cannot under any circumstances give rise to dispute, if only because 'in some particular sense every word is ambiguous'.[102] An arbiter can do no more than give judgment in terms sufficiently clear to determine to the satisfaction of a court the issue actually presented. An illustration of the problem of anticipating every possible source of ambiguity is provided by a case in which three landowners, C, H, and D were in dispute over rights of property and servitude in a loch and its surrounding shores. The matter was submitted in 1807 to arbitration, and the

[100] *Glendinning* v. *Board of Agriculture* 1918 S.C. (H.L.) 56; see also *Scott Plummer* v. *Board of Agriculture* 1916 S.C. (H.L.) 94.

[101] Irons, *Arb.* 188.

[102] Ziembinski Z. (Trans. Ter-Oganian L.), *Practical Logic* (for lawyers), Warsaw, 1976, 166. (N.B. in particular Chapter XI on 'Causes of misunderstanding').

arbiter found that the right of property in the loch belonged to C, subject to servitude rights in H and D of fishing in and shooting over the loch, pasturing cattle at low water, and cutting reeds and rushes. Some twenty five years later C brought an action to interdict D and his tenant from making drains to reduce the level of the loch, and from cutting grass on the extended area of dry land. D defended on the ground (among others) that the right of cutting reeds and rushes included the right of cutting grass. The sheriff considered the decree arbitral ambiguous, and ordered a proof as to the condition of the reeds and rushes and the practice of cutting them. On appeal, the Court of Session held that the right to cut reeds established by the decree arbitral (the validity of which was not doubted) did not include the right to cut grass used for fodder.[103] An award will not be reduced for failing to deal clearly with issues not effectively raised in the proceedings.

15.42. It is not yet certain whether in Scots law an award of interest at a rate based on a specified standard which may fluctuate is enforceable. An award in such terms is no more uncertain than some which have in the past been upheld, but since in an ordinary action a court will not grant decree for payment of interest calculated in such a manner,[104] it should be avoided.

15.43. An award which states the arbiter's decision in such a way that mere arithmetical calculation is sufficient to bring out its meaning is apparently valid. In one case,[105] two railway companies had entered into an agreement for working certain lines. Disputes arose over the allocation of receipts from traffic, and these were submitted to arbitration. The arbiter decided that receipts from traffic were to be divided between the companies in accordance with mileage and the rules of the clearing house. The House of Lords upheld the award. In another case, an oversman found the successful party entitled to 'two thirds expenses'. In an action of reduction at the instance of the unsuccessful party the award was upheld.[106]

15.44. **Substantive requirements:** (*c*) *Possibility of compliance.* The Scottish courts do not appear to have been called

[103] *Cuninghame* v. *Dunlop and Others* (1836) 15 S. 295.
[104] *Royal Bank of Scotland* v. *Geddes* 1983 S.L.T. (Sh. Ct.) 32.
[105] *Highland Railway Co.* v. *Great North of Scotland Railway Co.* (1896) 23 R. (H.L.) 80.
[106] *Paterson* v. *Sanderson* (1829) 7 S. 616.

upon in any reported case to consider the validity of a decree arbitral which purported to ordain a submitter to do something which was altogether impossible or illegal, but there can be no serious doubt but that such a deed would be invalid.[107] Nevertheless the mere fact that what the arbiter ordained was beyond the financial or physical means of a particular party would be legally enforceable.

15.45. **Arbitral propriety**. The arbiter must not have been disqualified[108] or have acted falsely[109] or corruptly[110] or with misconduct.[111] The parties may expressly or impliedly waive their objections to most types of disqualification[112] including, it would seem, all types of improper behaviour during the proceedings.[113]

15.46. **Compliance with a subsisting submission**. It has long been established that a valid award must be 'precisely commensurate with the submission'[114]; it must both exhaust the matters submitted[115] and refrain from going beyond them (*'ultra fines compromissi'*).[116] The submission — which of course must be valid and subsisting when the award is made — has to be respected not only in relation to the scope of the matters in dispute, but also the extent of the arbiter's duty to exercise powers which he or she has been granted. As a submission may contain implied as well as express terms, the former being peculiarly subject to judicial policy in their definition,[117] the implications of the rule unfortunately cannot be discovered simply by the exercise of intelligent commonsense. Moreover, many of the reported cases were decided over a century ago, and though the contemporary Scottish bench is notoriously reluctant avowedly to depart from

---

[107] Irons, *Arb.* 205.
[108] Grounds of disqualification are discussed above, paragraphs 4.32–4.56.
[109] On this, see paragraph 12.23 above.
[110] On this, see paragraph 12.24 above.
[111] On this see paragraphs 12.25–12.29 above.
[112] See paragraphs 4.37–4.40 and 4.48–4.56 above.
[113] See paragraphs 4.34 and 12.32 below.
[114] Bell J. M., *Arb.* paragraph 474.
[115] *Lovat* v. *Fraser of Phopachy* 22 June 1738 Mor. 625; Bell J. M., *Arb.*, paragraph 394; Balfour, *Practicks*, 413; D.4.8.19.1.
[116] *Carruthers* v. *Hall* (1830) 9 S. 66; Bell J. M., *Arb.*, paragraph 475; Balfour, *Practicks*, 413; *Cambuskenneth Abbey* v. *Dunfermline Abbey* (1207) Cooper, *Sel. Scot. Cas.* 13–14.
[117] See discussion in paragraphs 10.5–10.11 above.

precedents laid down during the 'Inglis era', it may be that not all of those precedents carry the weight they once did.

15.47. The interpretation of terms defining the matters in dispute raises some problems which can be discussed in general terms. Where claims are similar in character and the amount of each claim and liability to pay are related to similar facts, an arbiter has no duty to specify what is awarded under each head of claim unless the submission clearly so requires.[118] If in such circumstances an arbiter awards a lump sum, this does not constitute a failure to exhaust the submission. Again, the absence of any express reference to the view the arbiter has taken on a disputed averment does not as such constitute such a failure,[119] though the final and terminating award must not leave the decision on any important part of the case to stand on mere inference.[120] It is therefore only if the parties expressly ask for a decision on a point not merely as being incidental to a claim, but as being itself one of the primary matters submitted, that the arbiter must deal with it specifically and expressly in the award.

15.48. General problems of the exhaustion of the submission are also raised in connection with implied terms defining the arbiter's powers and her or his duty to exercise them, as for example in connection with the award of interest and expenses. An arbiter has an implied power to award interest on sums found due,[121] and to award expenses,[122] but no implied duty to do so. Failure to award interest or to deal with expenses does not constitute failure to exhaust the submission, unless a specific claim for interest or expenses has been made,[123] or the question submitted is one of accounting between the parties, in which case it is implied that interest must be determined.[124] It appears that here Scots law differs from English law, under which the award of a sum of money

---

[118] *Glasgow Corporation* v. *Paterson & Son Ltd.* (1901) 3 F. (H.L.) 34; *Donald* v. *Shiell's Executrix* 1937 S.C. 52 per L.J.C. Aitchison at 62.

[119] *Farrans Ltd.* v. *Roxburgh County Council* (*No. 2*) 1970 S.L.T. 334 at 335.

[120] *Mitchell* v. *Brand and Dean* (1865) 1 S.L.R. 68 per Lord Barcaple at 69; *Mackenzie* v. *Inverness and Aberdeen Junction Railway Co.* (1866) 38 Sc. Jur. 429 per Lord Deas at 432.

[121] Irons, *Arb.*, 219.

[122] *Pollick* v. *Heatley* 1910 S.C. 469 L.P. Dunedin at 480.

[123] *Ibid.*

[124] Irons, *Arb.*, 219.

without reference to any interest that may be legally due constitutes misconduct.[125]

15.49. It is often difficult for an arbiter to determine precisely what would constitute acting beyond the scope of the jurisdiction ('*ultra fines compromissi*'), and reported cases cannot provide a guide to the solution of every conceivable problem. All that can be done is to comment on some common situations.

15.50. An arbiter must judge according to the law and base his or her findings of fact upon the evidence presented or discovered in the proceedings.[126] If an award provides clear evidence that the decision which it contains has been made in ignorance or disregard of the law it is liable to reduction,[127] as being beyond or otherwise contrary to implied terms of the submission.[128] If however there has merely been an erroneous application of the law to the facts found, this is irremediable.[129]

15.51. In the course of reaching a decision on an disputed issue an arbiter almost inevitably has to determine incidentally a number of subordinate questions of fact or law. That such questions were not themselves separately submitted does not mean that by incidentally deciding them the arbiter exceeded the jurisdiction.[130] Equally, the fact that these questions have thus been incidentally decided does not mean that they have become judged issues ('*res judicata*') between the parties.

15.52. Damages may only be awarded if power has been expressly given to this effect.[131] The power to award interest is

---

[125] Mustill, *Comm. Arb.*, 345, citing *Panchaud Frères SA* v. *Pagnan & Fratelli* [1974] 1 Ll. Rep. 394.

[126] *Mitchell-Gill* v. *Buchan* 1921 S.C. 390 per L.P. Clyde at 395.

[127] *Clyne's Trustees* v. *Edinburgh Oil Gas Light Co.* (1835) II Sh. & McL. 243 per Lord Brougham at 271.

[128] *Adams* v. *Great North of Scotland Railway Co.* (1890) 18 R. (H.L.) 1 per Lord Watson at 8.

[129] *Mitchell-Gill* v. *Buchan* 1921 S.C. 390 per L.P. Clyde at 395; *Brown & Son Ltd.* v. *Associated Fireclay Companies Ltd.* 1936 S.C. 690 per Lord Fleming at 705, affd. on other grounds 1937 S.C. (H.L.) 42.

[130] *Farrans Ltd.* v. *Roxburgh County Council (No. 2)* 1970 S.L.T. 334.

[131] *Aberdeen Railway Co.* v. *Blaikie Brothers* (1852) 15 D. 20; *North British Railway Co.* v. *Newburgh & North Fife Railway Co.* 1911 S.C. 710 at 718.

however regarded as inherent.[132] The parties may specify the rate of interest payable and the point from which it runs, but otherwise these matters are laid down by law. If an award contains a decision on interest which on its face complies neither with the submission nor with general legal rules, as for example by finding interest due on damages for breach of contract from a date other than the date on which the claim was made in the arbitration[133] or at a rate different from that fixed in relation to court decrees,[134] then unless there has been a mere erroneous application of correct law to the facts, the award is liable to reduction. It is permissible for an award to be made in a foreign currency if that is required by the express or implied terms of the submission.[135]

15.53. Questions sometimes arise over whether counterclaims may be entertained. In principle, a counterclaim must be as clearly within the scope of the submission as the original claim. Where the submission is a general one of all existing disputes between the parties, a counterclaim will be admissible if it existed and was disputed when the submission was entered into. It has long been established, however, that the mere fact that two parties have agreed to submit certain disputes between them to arbitration under a special submission does not mean that other matters — even matters very closely connected with the specified issues — are within the jurisdiction of the arbiter[136]; a counterclaim must be clearly specified in a special submission before it can be entertained.

15.54. The amount finally awarded in a decree arbitral may not be in excess of the amount claimed, even if a claim for a greater amount would have been justified in law.[137]

---

[132] Irons, *Arb.*, 219. On interest generally, see Walker D.M., *Civil Remedies*, Edinburgh, 1974, Ch. 23.

[133] *Dean Warwick* v. *Borthwick* 1983 S.L.T. 533.

[134] By statutory instrument under the Administration of Justice (Scotland) Act 1933. It is incorporated in Rule 66 of the Rules of Court.

[135] *Commerzbank Aktiengesellschaft* v. *Lange* 1977 S.L.T. 219; Craig Sir T., *Jus Feudale*, 1603/1655, Stair Soc. edn., Edinburgh, 1934, I.16.22–3. A similar view to that of Craig has now been taken by the House of Lords in an English appeal: *Miliangos* v. *George Frank (Textiles) Ltd.* [1975] 3 All E.R. 801.

[136] *McEwan* v. *Middleton* (1866) 5 M. 159; *Cambuskenneth Abbey* v. *Dunfermline Abbey* (1207) in Cooper, *Sel. Scot. Cas.* 13–14.

[137] *Napier* v. *Wood* (1844) 7 D. 166.

15.55. An award may include an order for specific performance if this —

'may without straining the language of the submission, fairly and reasonably be held to be within its terms'[138]

always provided that what is ordered is lawful, within the power of the submitters to transact, and necessary to ensure implementation of legal obligations. An arbiter may for example order a submitter to execute a deed,[139] or perform specified works,[140] and may interdict a submitter from entering on specified property[141] and give a decree dissolving a partnership.[142] An award does not by itself transfer property from one person to another,[143] but it may order such a transfer to be carried out. Nowadays a decree ordering that a party must —

'remove his residence ... out of the parochionis of Stramiglo and Kilgour in all tyme tocum'

would not be as favourably regarded by the courts as formerly it was.[144] Once a final award has been issued in any matter, the arbiter has no power to supervise compliance with any order made therein for specific performance.[145] Therefore, where an order to execute a deed is intended, the deed should at least be framed to the arbiter's satisfaction before the final decree is given. Enforcement of its execution may then be safely left to the court.

15.56. Power to award expenses is implied in any submission.[146] Normally no express provision is made specifying the rules in terms of which expenses must be allocated, but if this has been done, the rules must be adhered to, even if difficult to apply. In one case,[147] the submission required that expenses should be awarded against 'the losing party'. The dispute concerned a count and reckoning relating to a business with a turnover of £45,000 (at

---

[138] Irons, *Arb.*, 221.
[139] *Tait* v. *Wilson* (1831) 9 S. 680; Bankton, *Inst.*, I.23.23.
[140] *Connal* v. *Coldstream* (1829) 7 S. 726.
[141] *Gray* v. *Brown* (1833) 11 S. 353.
[142] *Duthie* v. *Milne* 1946 S.L.T. (Sh. Ct.) 14.
[143] *Erskine* v. *Cochrane* 30 Jul. 1714, Mor. 649.
[144] *Lundy and Others* v. *Ramsay* 4 Nov. 1495, *ADC*, 418.
[145] Erskine, *Inst.*, IV.3.3.2; though *contra* Bankton, *Inst.*, I.23.23.
[146] *Pollick* v. *Heatley* 1910 S.C. 469.
[147] *Gye & Co.* v. *Hallam* (1835) I. S. & McL. 347.

1829 prices). The arbiter brought out a figure of £4:3:11 due to the pursuer, but found the pursuer liable to pay the expenses of £693:16:8 because he considered that, since the sum awarded was very small both in absolute terms and by comparison with what had been claimed, the pursuer was the losing party. The House of Lords upheld this decision, but with a comment to the effect that the circumstances were very unusual.

15.57.   If in awarding expenses an arbiter has exercised his or her discretion in a judicious manner, the court will not interfere even if it would have come to a different decision.[148] Nevertheless an arbiter, like a judge,

> 'must have materials upon which, if he does not follow the usual course of awarding expenses to the successful party, he can take any other line of action'.[149]

The Scottish courts have not considered what 'materials' an arbiter is entitled to rely upon. In England it has been suggested[150] that —

> 'an arbitrator must confine his attention strictly to facts connected with or leading up to the litigation which have been proved before him or which he has himself observed during the progress of the case, and must not take into account conduct unconnected with the cause of action or (of course) prejudice of race or religion, or sympathy with the unsuccessful party.'

Among the circumstances which in England[151] are regarded as justifying departure, wholly or partially, from the normal rule that expenses follow success are —

(a) failure by the otherwise successful party on an issue on which a large amount of time had been spent;

(b) refusal by the successful party of a tender of a sum equal to or greater than the sum ultimately awarded;

(c) extravagance in the employment of professional representatives or witnesses; and

(d) any unreasonable or obstructive behaviour which has increased the expense of proceedings to the unsuccessful party.

---

[148] *McArdle v. J. and R. Howie Ltd.* 1927 S.C. 779.

[149] *Feeney v. Fife Coal Co. Ltd.* 1918 S.C. 197 per Lord Salvesen at 201.

[150] Mustill, *Comm. Arb.* 347.

[151] Mustill, *Comm. Arb.* 349; N.B. also Stephenson D. A., 'Awarding Costs in Arbitration', (1983) 48 *Arbitration* 244–5.

These opinions are highly persuasive. It is submitted however that if legislation has provided in an analogous case that no expenses should be awarded at all except against a party who has acted frivolously, vexatiously or otherwise unreasonably, then provided that the legislation is not applied inflexibly as if it had been binding,[152] it may form the basis for an additional reason for departing from the normal rule. Thus for example if an arbiter has to determine a dispute between an employer and a worker — for example over contractual pension rights — which would have been heard by an industrial tribunal if it had arisen in the context of compensation for unfair dismissal, then provided there has been no unreasonable behaviour on either side the normal rule relating to expenses in industrial tribunal proceedings may properly be followed.

15.58.   An award of expenses must be made in or prior to the promulgation of the terminating award in the arbitration, because thereafter the arbiter has no further power to bind the submitters.[153] If no exact amount is specified, the award cannot be enforced by summary diligence,[154] but it is perfectly legitimate to refrain from specifying an amount if a direction is given that expenses are to be taxed (assessed) by a particular person, usually — but not necessarily — the Auditor of Court. If one party is not liable for the expenses of the whole proceedings, the arbiter must give clear directions as to the proportions of the whole amount or the parts of proceedings for the expenses of which each party is liable; but if this is done taxation can be regarded as a matter of mere calculation or (as Guild[155] suggests) as a purely 'ministerial' or administrative act.

15.59.   Expenses are normally allowed on a 'party and party' scale in relation to the whole proceedings from (in *ad hoc* arbitrations) the framing of the submission or (in ancillary submissions) the initial notice to refer or implementing deed of submission, through the conduct of the case up to the terminating award[156] and the

---

[152] *Breslin* v. *Barr & Thornton Ltd.* 1923 S.C. 90.
[153] *Jack* v. *King* (1932) 48 Sh. Ct. Rep. 242 at 244. *Obiter dicta* of Lord Curriehill to the contrary in *Paul* v. *Henderson* (1867) 5 M. 613 at 626 seem contrary to principle.
[154] *Paterson* v. *Sanderson* (1829) 7 S. 616.
[155] *Arb.* 78.
[156] Irons, *Arb.*, 228.

taxing process itself. The expense of recording an interim decree has been allowed as part of the expenses of the proceedings,[157] but it has been doubted whether the recording of the terminating decree is in the same category, since this is an act which occurs after the arbiter's judicial powers are at an end.[158] Yet either registration for execution or proceedings to obtain decree conform is necessary to put a decree arbitral on an equal footing with a decree of a court, and the mere fact that registration occurs after the terminating award is not significant because, if it were, an arbiter could not include in such an award an order for specific performance of any kind. It is therefore arguable that registration — for which consent must in any event have been given in the submission — constitutes a legitimate expense in the arbitration and may be included for the purposes of taxation.

15.60. In styles of submission it is still quite common,[159] though not universal,[160] practice to include a provision for a penalty to be paid over and above performance in the event of failure promptly to implement an arbiter's decree. Consent to payment of a penalty was once essential to the enforcement of a decree arbitral in civil,[161] though not in canon,[162] law, and was exacted as an alternative to performance. The civil law rule applied in Scots law until the latter part of the sixteenth century,[163] but appears to have fallen into desuetude in the seventeenth.[164] The insertion of a clause of registration for execution had by then come to be a more effective means of enforcing implementation, and though penalty clauses continued to be used also,[165] they were in the modern form already mentioned. In modern law a penalty cannot be truly a penalty — that is, a punishment.[166] The amount of a penalty therefore cannot amount to more than a reasonable prior assessment of the loss sustained through failure to implement the award, and given that it

---

[157] *Anderson v. Kinloch* (1836) 14 S. 447.
[158] *Ibid.*
[159] E.g. Weir, *Arb.* Appx. II, 156, 158.
[160] E.g. Halliday, *Conveyancing*, Vol. I, paragraphs 14–35 to 14–39.
[161] *Regiam Maj.* II.8.2.
[162] Where an oath was sufficient: Julien, *Ev. hist.*, 207.
[163] Balfour, *Practicks*, 412.
[164] Stair, *Inst.*, I.17.20. Similar developments were occurring elsewhere in Europe at the time: for France see Targowla M., *L'arbitrage dans l'ancien droit français*, Paris, 1953.
[165] Dallas, *Stiles*, 814; Carruthers, *Stiles*, 273.
[166] *Robertson v. Driver's Trustees* (1881) 8 R. 555 per Lord Young at 562.

is intended to be over and above performance it cannot be more than such sum as would cover the creditor's expenses.[167] An arbiter may not decern for payment of a penalty unless there is warrant in the submission.[168] J. M. Bell suggested[169] that penalty clauses might be framed so as to empower the arbiter to impose a penalty for delay in implementing procedural orders, but this does not seem to have been taken up.

Promulgation

15.61. A decree arbitral is not valid and effective as such unless and until it has been issued or promulgated[170] — these terms are used synonymously — in compliance with any rules required by law and the submission. An award which has not been issued is a mere draft or proposed award.

15.62. The law of Scotland imposes no general requirements for the promulgation of awards,[171] nor does it connect promulgation with registration or deposit with any official body or otherwise insist upon such registration, though it does enable awards which follow upon a submission containing an appropriate consent to be registered in the books of a court for preservation and execution. The Commission of the European Communities may require the communication to itself of an award relating to a provision in an agreement which would, apart from special exemption, offend against the provisions of Article 85(1) of the Treaty of Rome.[172] Such a requirement does not, however, appear to make such communication a condition of the validity of an award.

15.63. Promulgation of a duly executed decree arbitral may be effected by an arbiter in any one of a number of ways —

(a) by delivering the principal decree or a certified copy thereof to either of the parties[173];
(b) by registering the principal decree in terms of the submission

---

[167] Bell J. M., *Arb.* paragraph 435.
[168] *Groset* v. *Cunningham* 24 Jan. 1739, Mor. 626; Erskine, *Inst.* IV.3.32.
[169] *Arb.*, paragraph 436.
[170] *Gray & Woodrop* v. *McNair* (1831) V W. & S. 305 at 312–13.
[171] *Dickson* v. *Shirreff* (1830) 9 S. 100.
[172] As e.g. in *Papeteries Bolloré/Braunstein Agreement* [1972] C.M.L.R. D.94.
[173] *Gray & Woodrop* (*supra* note 170).

in the books of a court for preservation or preservation and execution[174];

(c) by delivering the principal decree to the clerk in the arbitration, in a manner which indicates that the clerk is to hold it on behalf of the submitters[175];

(d) by giving clear authority for any of the foregoing acts to be done.[176]

It is the third of these methods of delivery which causes most difficulty,[177] because the intention of the arbiter must in this case be made particularly clear. The clerk is normally the servant of the arbiter, and holds documents on behalf of the arbiter, not on behalf of the parties.[178] This presumption, if it can be called such, is nevertheless relatively easily displaced, at least if there is any risk that the award might become time-barred, because the courts are generally unwilling to hold an award invalid for purely technical reasons.[179] To avoid misunderstandings it is desirable that an award should generally not be executed until it is to be issued, that where there are more arbiters than one their signatures should follow one another very closely in time, and that once an award has been fully executed it should be speedily issued in a manner which leaves no doubt what is intended.

Effect of awards

15.64. The effect of a valid award upon the arbiter depends in some respects upon whether or not it is a final award. Once a final award — and this category includes part awards — has been issued, the judicial powers and duties of the arbiter in relation to the matters included in that award are at an end. She or he is in these matters '*functa (functus) officio*' and cannot bind the submitters by any further orders in that connection.[180] No case on those matters may be stated for the opinion of the court,[181] and no correction of

---

[174] *Ibid.*

[175] *McQuaker* v. *Phoenix Assurance Co.* (1859) 21 D. 794; *Johnson* v. *Gill* 1978 S.C. 74.

[176] *Gray & Woodrop* (*supra* note 170).

[177] As in *Macrae* v. *Edinburgh Street Tramways Co.* (1885) 13 R. 265.

[178] *Robertson* v. *Ramsay* 20 Nov. 1782, Hailes' *Decisions* 912, per Lord Hailes.

[179] *McQuaker* (*supra* note 175).

[180] Bankton, *Inst.*, I.23.22; Bell J.M., *Arb.*, paragraph 449.

[181] *Fairlie Yacht Slip Ltd.* v. *Lumsden* 1977 S.L.T. (Notes) 41.

inadvertent slips in the award may be made except with the consent of all the parties to the submission.[182] If however the award is provisional in nature — in other words, if it is an interim award — the arbiter's legal powers are unaffected. Where the obligations which are in dispute in the arbitration are in their nature continuing and subject to alteration in the light of changing circumstances, an award relating thereto is inherently subject to prospective alteration,[183] and thus has some of the characteristics of an interim award, though it is final in its retrospective effect.

15.65. Even after the promulgation of a final award, certain administrative or ministerial duties may remain. Productions may have to be returned to the submitters, accounts are likely to have to be paid for the services of the clerk and in some cases also the hire of rooms. For these matters the arbiter is responsible to the submitters, though many of the duties are carried out by the clerk.

15.66. The effect of a valid award upon the submitters depends to some extent upon whether or not they have agreed — as is usual in formal arbitrations — that the submission and any decree arbitral following thereon may be registered in the books of a court (normally the Books of Council and Session) for preservation and execution. The agreement for registration need not be contained in the original contract of submission: it may be contained in an implementing deed of submission or a minute of agreement.[184] The agreement itself (or an extract thereof, if it has itself already been registered) must be produced when the decree is presented for registration.[185] Where only certified copies of the decree have been provided to the submitters, registration of the principal decree is usually effected by the clerk to the arbitration in whose hands it has been retained. There is no obligation on either party to register a decree. In a case in which the principal decree had been delivered to the successful party, the court, in a judgment which contains the only explicit and authoritative recognition of the value of privacy in arbitration, refused an application by the unsuccessful party to order registration.[186] Normally, however, the successful party will

[182] Bell J. M., *Arb.*, paragraph 489.
[183] *Summers* v. *William Baird and Co. Ltd.* 1926 S.C. (H.L.) 24.
[184] *Baillie* v. *Pollock* (1829) 7 S. 619.
[185] *Muirhead* v. *Stevenson* (1848) 10 D. 748.
[186] *Dickson* v. *Shirreff* (1830) 9 S. 100.

register a decree and obtain an official extract of it, because such an extract is warrant for enforcement by summary diligence, including the arrestment in the hands of third parties of sums due to the unsuccessful party, pointing (*anglicé* 'attachment') and sale of moveable goods, and inhibition and adjudication of heritable property.

15.67. If the submitters have not given their express consent to registration for execution, the arbiter may still order or permit registration, but for preservation only.[187] In order to put the decree into effect, the successful party must then bring an ordinary action in court for decree conform to the award.

15.68. The authorities are not fully in agreement concerning the precise basis of this type of action. J. M. Bell said[188] that the basis of the action was that —

'taken along with the submission, the award has precisely the force of a written contract'.

This is very similar to the position in England as described by Mustill and Boyd.[189] There, apparently,

'a valid award confers on the successful claimant a new right of action, in substitution for the right on which his claim was founded. Every submission to arbitration contains an implied promise by each party to abide by the award of the arbitrator . . . It is on this promise that the claimant proceeds, when he takes action to enforce the award.'

A rather different view of Scots law is taken by Irons and Melville,[190] who assert that —

'a valid award in a voluntary arbitration is a final judgment between the parties regarding all matters referred by the submission. It is final and binding both as to the facts and the law, and that so effectively as to bar the parties from an appeal to any other tribunal forming as it does a good plea of *res judicata*, to the same extent and effect as a decree pronounced in a court of law.'

[187] Parker, *Arb.*, 187.
[188] *Arb.*, paragraph 742.
[189] *Comm. Arb.* 27.
[190] *Arb.*, 346.

15.69. Bell may have been influenced by two considerations. First, he must have been aware of the practice, then not long discontinued, by which the submitters left blank and signed a space on the back of the submission which the arbiter was expected to fill up with the award. This practice seems to have arisen between the beginning of the sixteenth and the end of the seventeenth centuries, for it appears first in styles of the latter part of that period.[191] It was during the seventeenth century that the offices of arbiter and arbitrator became confused in Scots law, the latter having always had a tendency to shade into that of the 'amicable compositor' whose primary function was to bring disputing parties to agreement. As a result, the contractual element in ordinary arbitration was given a stronger emphasis, which is revealed in a number of eighteenth century cases, such as *Logan* v. *Lang*,[192] in which it was argued by the successful pursuers that —

'the submission and decree founded on it, form a contract, which like every other may be set aside for any reason necessarily implying an inconsistency with the consent of parties at entering into it'.

The second consideration which Bell may have had in mind was the report of the decision in *Lang* v. *Brown and Others*,[193] in which Lord Chancellor Cranworth remarked[194] that —

'every award has its force, not by virtue of the award itself, but by virtue of the previous contract of the parties giving it effect.'

That case was however concerned mainly with 'the construction to be put upon the contracts of parties',[195] and the dictum may be interpreted as meaning no more than that an arbiter does not have jurisdiction over the submitters except in so far as they have agreed to accept it.

15.70. During the latter part of the nineteenth century the Court of Session came, under the leadership of Lord President Inglis

---

[191] See e.g. Dallas, *Stiles*, 813–14; the practice was recognised by Mackenzie, *Inst.*, IV.3. Compare the decree of 13th August 1492 in the arbitration between the Bishop of Moray and Hugh Ross of Kilravock, in *Registratum Episcopatus Moraviensis*, (Bannatyne Club), Edinburgh, 1937, 243.

[192] 15 Nov. 1798 Mor. Appx. I, No. 6, 9.

[193] (1855) II Macq. 93.

[194] At 94.

[195] *Ibid.*

which reached its climax after the last edition of Bell's book appeared, to take a less contractualist and more jurisdictional view of arbitration.[196] Irons and Melville, writing just after the turn of the century, reflect this change of emphasis, though their authority — *Fraser* v. *Lord Lovat*[197] — predates the influence of Inglis. In this case the House of Lords upheld a judgment of the Court of Session that a certain action which had been brought was incompetent as the issue was '*res judicata*' having already been determined by an arbiter. The case seems sound authority for Irons and Melville's view, for it is difficult to see how an act which has the force of a judgment can be regarded as having the force merely of a contract.

15.71. The position adopted by Irons and Melville on this matter is in accordance both with the nature of the procedure by which enforcement of a decree arbitral is sought and with the historical acceptance by the Scottish courts that a valid submission to arbitration ousts their jurisdiction on the merits of the case.[198] Where there has been no consent to registration for execution, a decree arbitral is enforced through an action for decree conform thereto. In granting such a decree, a Scottish court performs a function similar in appearance to that of a French court in granting an '*ordonnance d'exequatur*',[199] which gives compulsory force to an award which already possesses '*force de la chose jugée*'.[200] It is said that[201] —

'the decision which is the outcome of the proceedings is clothed with all the qualities of a jurisdictional act and thus deserves the assistance of authority for its execution. The *exequatur* is thus merely an administrative control permitting execution ... [though] it opens the way to judicial control at the instance of the parties.'

It would appear that a French court, in issuing the *exequatur*, does not consider that it is simply enforcing a contract. It is submitted

---

[196] See e.g. *Forbes* v. *Underwood* (1886) 13 R. 465.

[197] (1850) VII Bell 171. See also *Johne of Spottiswood* v. *Andro Mowbra* 5 Nov. 1479, *ADC* 40; Erskine, *Inst.*, IV.3.29; *Caledonian Railway Co.* v. *Turcan* (1898) 25 R. (H.L.) 7 per Lord Watson at 16; *Farrans* v. *Roxburgh County Council* 1969 S.L.T. 35.

[198] *Sanderson* v. *Armour & Co.* 1922 S.C. (H.L.) 117 per Lord Dunedin at 126.

[199] On which see Robert, *Arb.*, 282.

[200] Robert & Carbonneau, *Arb.*, paragraph 4.02.

[201] Robert, *Arb.*, 259.

that a Scottish court in issuing decree conform is in a similar position, and the Irons and Melville's understanding on the effect of a decree arbitral is correct. Though it is enforceable against the submitters *because* there has been a contract, it is not enforced *as* a contract but as a judgment.

15.72. The State Immunity Act 1978 has limited the extent to which states may claim immunity from the jurisdiction of the Scottish courts in proceedings relating to arbitration. Section 9 of the Act provides that —

'Where a State has agreed in writing to submit a dispute which has arisen, or may arise, to arbitration, the State is not immune as respects proceedings in the courts of the United Kingdom which relate to the arbitration'

unless the agreement provides otherwise. The section does not however apply to agreements which only involve states as parties, and section 13 provides that the property of a state shall not be subject to any process for the enforcement of an arbitration award unless the state consents or the property is being used or intended for use for commercial purposes.

15.73. A valid decree arbitral may have an effect on persons other than the original submitters. A person who claims through one of the submitters, or who has formally been sisted as a party[202] or who has become sisted by reason of his or her actings[203] is bound by a subsequent award. Likewise a cautioner (*anglicé* 'guarantor') is bound by an award against the principal debtor, even if neither called nor sisted as a party in the arbitration.[204] The assignee of a contract to which an ancillary submission is appended is bound by an award given in an arbitration under that submission,[205] and an award in a submission completed before the death of a submitter is enforceable against his or her heirs[206] — nowadays effectively the executor,[207] though particular debts may fail to be paid out of particular parts of the estate.

---

[202] *Henry* v. *Hepburn and Burns* (1835) 13 S. 361.

[203] *Brown* v. *Gardner* 10 Jan. 1739, Mor. 5659.

[204] *Anderson* v. *Wood* (1821) 1 S. 31.

[205] *Whately* v. *Ardrossan Harbour Co.* (1893) 1 S.L.T. 382.

[206] *Laird of Lochinvar* v. *Earl of Cassilis* 1583, Mor. 624, Spottiswood, *Practicks*, 14 (citing Bartolus); *Robertson* v. *Cheyne* (1847) 9 D. 599 per Lord Mackenzie at 603.

[207] Succession (Scotland) Act 1964 s. 14.

15.74. The effect of an invalid decree arbitral depends upon whether it was void from the outset (*ab initio*) or merely voidable. A void decree has no effect at all upon the issues which it purports to determine, and it technically does not require to be formally reduced by a court,[208] though where there is any question whether an award is void or voidable an action of reduction,[209] with an alternative conclusion for declarator that the decree is void, is appropriate. What effect it has upon the arbitration proceedings is a separate question. It has been considered, in a case in which an award was held void on the ground that it had not been properly executed, that an arbiter retains power to issue a new award unless the submission has expired in the meantime.[210]

15.75. A voidable decree is effective as a valid decree until successfully challenged.[211] What the consequences of reduction of such a decree are upon the powers of the arbiter is not clear. A tentative opinion has been judicially expressed to the effect that once a decree has been reduced the jurisdiction of the arbiter does not revive.[212] This view has the merit of common sense, at least in an *ad hoc* submission where the reason for reduction related to the misconduct, corruption, bribery or falsehood of the arbiter, and the problem would be entirely academic in most cases in which the reason for reduction was the disqualification of the arbiter. It could be justified theoretically on the ground that the arbiter had broken a material term of his or her contract with the submitters, though that could equally happen where the decree was void.

15.76. Where the arbitration is based on an ancillary submission of future disputes to an unnamed arbiter the matter is more complex. The question may arise whether either the arbiter whose decree has been reduced, or a new arbiter, has jurisdiction to deal with the dispute which was the subject of the abortive proceedings or with other disputes. It has been judicially suggested in a case of alleged failure to exhaust the reference[213] that —

---

[208] Walker D. M., *The Law of Civil Remedies in Scotland*, Edinburgh, 1974, 145.
[209] As in *Clark* v. *Clark's Trustees* 1948 S.L.T. (Notes) 58.
[210] *Bannatyne* v. *Gibson & Clark* (1862) 1 M. 90; the position appears to be the same in Sweden: Holmbäck, *Arb. Swe. 1984*, 138.
[211] *Sellar* v. *Highland Railway Co.* 1919 S.C. (H.L.) 19 per Lord Buckmaster at 23.
[212] *Miller & Son* v. *Oliver & Boyd* (1906) 8 F. 390 per Lord McLaren at 403.
[213] In *Farrans Ltd.* v. *Roxburgh County Council* 1969 S.L.T. 35 at 37.

'there is no warrant in practice or authority which would allow a party to an arbitration to permit the defective decree to stand and to raise an action for payment with the intention . . . that the arbiter should take up the reference again'

and decide the matters inadvertently or erroneously omitted. Though the matter is by no means free from doubt, it is therefore probable that, apart from stipulation to the contrary in the submission, the parties are not bound by an arbitration agreement in relation to any dispute in which a voidable decree has been issued and subsequently reduced, so that neither the old arbiter nor any new one can, without further agreement on the part of the submitters, deal with matters which have not been determined under the submission by a valid award. It would seem however that the parties remain bound in relation to disputes not covered by the reduced award. As substantial inconvenience may often result from an abortive arbitration, a submission or implementing deed should normally provide that —

'in the event that no valid final decree arbitral shall follow hereupon, all probation to be taken by . . . [name] . . . as arbiter shall be held and received as legal probation, of as much weight and quality, in any subsequent arbitration proceedings or process at law between us.'[214]

---

[214] Slightly adapted from Irons, *Arb.*, 415.

CHAPTER SIXTEEN

THE DECREE ARBITRAL OR AWARD — 2

Challenge and interpretation of awards

16.1. There are five means by which the validity of an award may be challenged, its effect avoided, or its terms corrected. These are —

(a) an action of reduction of a voidable award;
(b) an action of declarator of nullity of a void award;
(c) a petition for the correction of a clerical error in a valid award;
(d) a petition for suspension of a charge on a void or voidable award;
(e) a plea in defence to an action based on an award, that it should for the purposes of the action be set aside by way of special exception (*'ope exceptionis'*).

The first three means of recourse mentioned above are competent only in the Court of Session; the fourth is competent in the court in whose books the decree arbitral or decree conform thereto has been registered, and the fifth in the court in which the action concerned has been raised. In practice a petition for the correction of a clerical error appears to be rare: normally application is made in the context of an action for reduction. The law makes no provision for appeal to the court against a decree arbitral: the Arbitration Act 1979 of the Parliament of the United Kingdom, section 1 of which established a right of appeal in England and Wales, does not apply to Scotland.[1]

16.2. **Reduction.** A decree arbitral which is voidable may be reduced. The four grounds on which reduction may be sought are —

(a) the disqualification of the arbiter[2];

[1] S. 8(4).
[2] *Smith* v. *Liverpool and London and Globe Insurance Co.* (1887) 14 R. 931.

(b) jurisdictional or procedural misconduct of the arbiter[3];

(c) corruption, bribery or falsehood in terms of article 25 of the Articles of Regulation 1695; and

(d) reduction or lawful rescission of the submission upon which the decree is based.[4]

A decree arbitral cannot be reduced on the ground that new evidence not available at the time of the arbitration has come to light.[5]

16.3. The procedure for reduction is now by way of a petition for judicial review in terms of the Act of Sederunt (Rules of Court Amendment No. 2) (Judicial Review) 1985.[6] This form of review is available only where no other means of review exists,[7] but since there exists no appeal against decrees arbitral petition for judicial review is normally competent. It has been suggested[8] by Lord Jauncey in the Outer House that where a petitioner could have sought a stated case under section 3 of the Administration of Justice (Scotland) Act 1972 a petition for judicial review of the arbiter's award is incompetent. This is surely incorrect except in the case of an interim award, because an application for a stated case must be made before the final award has been issued.[9] A failure during the arbitration proceedings to seek a stated case for the opinion of the court cannot therefore properly be regarded as an alternative to a petition for reduction of a final award.

16.4. Though reduction is technically not necessary where the decree concerned is void, in practice it is often sought, with an alternative conclusion for declarator of nullity. An award may be reduced if it does not possess the characteristics of a valid award mentioned above.[10] Verbal submissions do not come within the scope of article 25 of the 1695 Articles of Regulation, and awards

---

[3] *Holmes Oil Co. Ltd.* v. *Pumpherston Oil Co. Ltd.* (1891) 18 R. (H.L.) 52 per Lord Watson at 55.

[4] E.g. rescission of the submission on the grounds of fraud of one of the submitters in presenting the case: *Logan* v. *Lang* 15 Nov. 1798, Mor. Appx. I, No. 6, 9.

[5] *Sharp* v. *Bury* (1813) I Dow 223.

[6] S.I. 1985 No. 500 (S. 48).

[7] *Brown* v. *Hamilton District Council* 1983 S.L.T. 397 per Lord Fraser at 414.

[8] *O'Neill* v. *Scottish J.N.C.* 1987 S.C.L.R. 275 at 278.

[9] *Fairlie Yacht Slip Ltd.* v. *Lumsden* 1977 S.L.T. (Notes) 41.

[10] Paragraphs 15.25 to 15.59 above: see also the brief summary in paragraphs 15.2–15.3.

following upon them may therefore still be reduced for 'enorm lesion', but as they are almost never both valid and provable and are unknown in practice they can be ignored.

16.5. A decree arbitral may be reduced wholly or in part.[11] Reduction in part is however only granted where two conditions are satisfied. These are —

(i) that the good and bad parts of the decree can be separated[12]; and
(ii) that the remaining parts of the decree (in the case of part awards, when taken together with any other subsisting part awards) still exhaust the submission.[13]

The implication of the second of these conditions is that, except where the decree which is under attack is a part award, partial reduction is only possible if the ground of reduction is that the decree has gone beyond the matters submitted (*'ultra fines compromissi'*). It is arguable that the second condition is based on mere *obiter dicta*, but it seems probable that they would be followed.

16.6. **Declarator of nullity**. A decree arbitral is void if it deals with a matter which is beyond the power of the submitters to transact or is contrary to public policy; or if it has not been properly executed[14]; or if the submission on which it purports to be based is itself void. Since it is analogous to a decree of a court in that it can form the basis for a plea of *res judicata*,[15] and as a court decree requires to be reduced if it cannot be reviewed on appeal,[16] it might be argued that it is incompetent to seek a declarator of nullity of a void award. However, the reason why a court decree requires reduction is that until reduced it stands in the records of the court. A decree arbitral only stands in the record of a court if it

[11] *Laird of Inchaffray* v. *Oliphant* 4 Mar. 1607, Mor. 5063; *Groset* v. *Cunningham* 24 Jan. 1739, Mor. 626; *Ferrier* v. *Alison* (1843) 5 D. 456 affd. (1845) IV Bell 161; *Cox Brothers* v. *Binning & Son* (1867) 6 M. 161.
[12] *Reid* v. *Walker* (1826) 5 S. 140; *North British Railway Co.* v. *Barr & Co.* (1855) 18 D. 102; *Miller & Son* v. *Oliver & Boyd* (1903) 6 F. 77. In these cases the bad and the good parts were on the particular facts held inseparable.
[13] *Miller & Son* v. *Oliver & Boyd* (1906) 8 F. 390 per Lord McLaren at 403–4; *Farrans Ltd.* v. *Roxburgh County Council* 1969 S.L.T. 35 at 37.
[14] *Bannatyne* v. *Gibson & Clark* (1862) 1 M. 90.
[15] *Fraser* v. *Lord Lovat* (1850) VII Bell 171.
[16] Walker D. M., *The Law of Civil Remedies in Scotland*, Edinburgh, 1974, 171.

has been registered therein in terms of consent given in the submission, or if decree conform thereto has been granted. Except in those two cases, therefore, an action for declarator of nullity of a void decree is competent, but an action of reduction is the normal means of challenge.

16.7. **Correction of clerical errors.** Where a clerical error either is discovered in an award in the course of an action for decree conform, or forms the basis of an action for the suspension of a charge based upon it, there is sufficient equitable power in the court to rectify it. It may also be competent to petition the Court of Session under its general equitable power or *'nobile officium'* to alter a clerical error in an extract registered award, since such a power has been exercised for the purpose of correcting a slip in an extract registered court decree,[17] but there has been no reported case of this having been done. There is no Scottish equivalent of section 17 of the English Arbitration Act 1950.

16.8. **Petition for suspension.** A petition for suspension — usually combined with interdict — is competent as a means of preventing diligence proceeding upon (*anglicé* enforcement of) a decree arbitral which is void or voidable. The court may require that any sum awarded in the decree be consigned in court or that caution (security) be found for payment of an equivalent amount before the petition may be proceeded with.

16.9. **Setting aside by exception (*'ope exceptionis'*).** Where a decree arbitral is being founded on in an action either in a sheriff court or in the Court of Session, the defender may seek to have it set aside by way of exception (*'ope exceptionis'*) without having to raise an action of reduction in the Court of Session. There is however some conflict of authority concerning the circumstances in which this is competent.

16.10. According to one strand of authority, exception as a defence to an action based on an award is not competent where it is based on —

'forgery, fraud, corruption, or any other objection which is extrinsic, not appearing from the terms of the decree itself,'[18]

[17] *Benhar Coal Co. Ltd., Liquidators of, Petitioners* (1891) 19 R. 108.
[18] *Whitehead* v. *Finlay* 16 Nov. 1833 F.C., (1833) 11 S. 170. See also *Thomson* v. *Munro* (1882) 19 S.L.R. 739; *Waugh* v. *Baxter & Sons* 1922 S.L.T. (Sh. Ct.) 61.

and may be stated only where the objection 'is to be proved from the terms of the decree itself.'

16.11. On the other hand, there are quite a number of cases in which decrees were set aside in sheriff court actions where the objection involved the leading of extrinsic evidence.[19] This was done on the basis of Rule 50 in Schedule 1 of the Sheriff Courts (Scotland) Act 1907 or its predecessor. That Rule provided — and still provides[20] — that

> 'when a deed or writing is founded on by any party in a cause, all objections thereto may be stated and maintained by way of exception, without the necessity of bringing a reduction thereof.'

The sheriffs who accepted the competency of a request to set an award aside by exception took the view that a decree arbitral was not the same thing as a judgment of a court, but a deed or writing. They also appear to have been influenced by considerations of convenience and the avoidance of expense.[21] It has already been argued that a decree arbitral is analogous to a decree of a court,[22] and though the context is different it would be somewhat inconsistent not to argue here that the sheriffs were wrong in holding that a decree arbitral was not analogous to a court judgment, though it has to be accepted that there was undeniable authority for their view that court decrees are not — for this purpose at least — deeds or writings.[23] Guild considered that there is a distinction between formal and informal decrees arbitral, and that setting aside by exception under Rule 50 is only competent in the case of informal decrees. It is respectfully submitted that Guild's view on this matter[24] has no secure foundation, as in the case cited as authority[25] an action of reduction was brought by the defender in the action for payment based on the award.

---

[19] *Sundt & Co.* v. *Watson* (1915) 31 Sh. Ct. Rep. 156; *Kilmaurs Dairy Association* v. *Brisbane and Beatties Dairies* 1927 S.L.T. (Sh. Ct.) 65; *Blythe Building Co. Ltd.* v. *Mason's Executrix* (1937) 53 Sh. Ct. Rep. 180. N.B. also *Nivison* v. *Howat* (1883) 11 R. 182 per Lord Lee at 189.

[20] S.I. 1976 No. 744.

[21] *Sundt & Co.* (*supra* note 19) at 158; *Kilmaurs Dairy Association* (*supra* note 19) at 67.

[22] Paragraphs 15.67–15.70 above.

[23] *Leggat Brothers* v. *Gray* 1912 S.C. 230.

[24] *Arb.* 85.

[25] *Nivison* v. *Howat* (1883) 11 R. 182.

Nevertheless it must be admitted that practical convenience is entirely on the side of the shrieval approach, and on a doubtful question such as this it should tip the balance.

16.12. **Interpretation of awards.** Restrictions have been placed by the courts on the types of evidence which may competently be admitted for the purposes of determining whether a decree arbitral is valid or not. In the analysis of these restrictions it is possible to distinguish the following main situations, to which different sets of rules apply:
(i) those in which the validity of the decree is challenged on grounds relating to —

(a) the behaviour of the arbiter or of either of the submitters during the arbitration proceedings (the *'res gestae'*);
(b) the capacity or power of the arbiter to conduct, or of either of the parties to submit to, arbitration proceedings in general or in the particular case; and
(c) the circumstances surrounding the contracts of submission or of appointment of the arbiter; and

(ii) those in which the validity of the decree is challenged on grounds relating to —

(a) its own form or content;
(b) the content of the judgment which it is supposed to embody; and
(c) the form or content of the contract of submission on which the decree is based.

16.13. The first of the two main categories mentioned in the previous paragraph gives rise to little difficulty. Here the special rules on the admission of evidence for the purposes of interpreting deeds do not apply. In cases which can be grouped under this heading it is competent to examine the arbiter personally concerning events which took place during the proceedings,[26] and to have regard to the notes of the arbiter made at the time,[27] and any other relevant evidence which is generally admissible.

16.14. The second of the two main categories has given rise to serious problems, which are centred upon the fact that a decree

---

[26] *Grant* v. *Grant* 9 Dec. 1679, II Bro. Supp. 253; *Black* v. *John Williams & Co. (Wishaw) Ltd.* 1923 S.C. 410, affd. 1924 S.C. (H.L.) 22.
[27] *Wauchope* v. *Edinburgh & Dalkeith Railway Co.* (1846) 8 D. 816.

arbitral is a written document.[28] Under the general rules of the law of evidence relating to the explanation of written documents —

'when the language of the writing is clear and applies without doubt to the facts of the case, extrinsic evidence is neither necessary nor admissible for its interpretation.'[29]

At first sight, such a rule seems plain and easy to apply, but clarity in a decree arbitral is itself unfortunately an ambiguous concept. It may be very plain what the arbiter has decided — for example that A & Co. shall pay B & Co. the sum of £100,000 — but it may still be far from obvious whether in so ordaining the arbiter has considered, say, item 14 of the disputed heads of claim, in which B & Co. sought payment of £543:63p, or has had regard to the fact that A & Co. is alleged to be owed some £986:05p under another contract not covered by the submission. Taken by itself, the decree is clear, and extrinsic evidence to explain it is unnecessary and should be inadmissible; taken in conjunction with the submission, it is utterly obscure and cries out for explanation by means of any extrinsic evidence that may be available.

16.15.   The obscurity of a decree arbitral may be mitigated, and its compliance with the terms of the submission made assessable, simply by adducing the evidence of the submission itself. The submission is now regarded as extrinsic to the award, though it was once suggested that the two documents formed part of one contract,[30] perhaps because for a time in the seventeenth and eighteenth centuries it was the practice to insert the award on the back of the paper containing the submission, the submitters having subscribed it in blank.[31] The documents are however so closely connected that it would be carrying technical rules to absurd lengths to prevent the decree being read in the light of the submission.

16.16.   Not all problems of interpretation can be overcome by the simple expedient of adducing the evidence of the submission. The details of claims are often not stated in the submission, and

---

[28] A verbal award is most unlikely to be valid, and none appear to have been the subject of litigation for over a century.

[29] Walker, *Evidence*, 282.

[30] Though this view has been put forward, e.g. by the successful pursuer in *Logan* v. *Lang* 15 Nov. 1798 Mor. Appx. I, No. 6, 9.

[31] Dallas, *Stiles*, 813; Carruthers, *Stiles*, 271.

counterclaims rarely so. It is moreover possible for the scope of a submission to be widened by the pleadings and other actings of the parties.[32] It is therefore appropriate that evidence of such actings and pleadings is admitted,[33] though it is required not directly to explain the award but to explain the submission on which it is based. It appears that the personal testimony of the arbiter — who in this context is simply a witness — and the notes taken by the arbiter at the time, are both admissible on these and indeed other matters concerning the arbitration proceedings,[34] or *'res gestae'* as they are sometimes called.

16.17.　After all relevant and admissible evidence concerning the scope of the submission and the details of the parties' claims and pleadings have been adduced, the answer to the question whether the award exhausts and observes the limits of the matters submitted may still be uncertain. Such uncertainty is relatively common where what is awarded is a single lump sum covering several heads of claim. In such a case, it might be thought that the award was obscure, however clear its order might be for the payment of a specified sum by one party to the other, and that it was therefore legitimate to adduce extrinsic evidence for its clarification. That has not however been the view generally adopted by the courts.

16.18.　The approach of the courts has been to assert a presumption of congruence with the submission except where it is alleged that the arbiter has exceeded the bounds of the submission and thus encroached on their own jurisdiction. The presumption appears from a dictum of Lord Stevenson in *Donald* v. *Shiell's Executrix*.[35] His Lordship remarked that —

'it being the duty of an arbiter to pronounce a final and exhaustive award, the presumption is that he intended that his award should be, and that it is in fact, such an award. The Court

[32] *North British Railway Co.* v. *Barr & Co.* (1855) 18 D. 102 per Lord Deas at 107; Bell J. M., *Arb.*, paragraph 100.
[33] *Wauchope* v. *Edinburgh & District Railway Co.* (1846) 8 D. 816 per L. J. C. Hope at 820.
[34] *Young* v. *Pearson* 2 July 1678, II Bro. Supp. 230; *Colquhoun* v. *Corbet* 26 July 1784, III Paton 1; *Clippens Oil Co. Ltd.* v. *Edinburgh and District Water Trustees* (1901) 3 F. 1113 per Lord Kinnear at 1128, affd. (1902) 4 F. (H.L.) 40; *Black* v. *John Williams & Co. (Wishaw) Ltd.* 1923 S.C. 410, affd. 1924 S.C. (H.L.) 22.
[35] 1937 S.C. 52 at 57.

is therefore disposed to construe an award as embracing and disposing of all matters submitted if it can reasonably admit of such a construction.'

The restricted scope of the presumption appears from the fact that Lord Stevenson seems expressly to confine it to the exhaustion of the submission, and from the jealousy of the courts to prevent arbiters from assuming a wider jurisdiction that the submitters have clearly agreed upon. As Lord President Inglis put it in *Calder* v. *Mackay*,[36]

'an arbiter cannot be allowed to oust the jurisdiction of the courts, nor can the parties be considered as intending to do so, except to the extent which they have expressly specified.'

The operation of these contrary presumptions means that expressions in an award which would be regarded as ambiguous in the context of an averment of usurped jurisdiction are likely to be considered sufficiently clear in the context of an averment of failure to exhaust the submission.

16.19. It would be virtually impossible in any but the clearest case to succeed in showing that an award had failed to exhaust the submission, were it not for the fact that in certain circumstances the courts imply into the submission what amounts to a formal requirement that the award must specify the amount (if any) awarded under each head of claim. This requirement is assumed to have been inserted where the arbiter —

'is asked to decide upon a variety of claims different in character, and where the amount of each and the liability for which depend on different circumstances.'[37]

It is probable that this means that a detailed award is required if either the claims are different in character or the amount and liability depend on different circumstances or the claims have a different legal foundation. It is of course open to the parties to make alternative provisions in the contract or implementing deed of submission concerning detailed findings in the award.

16.20. If the arbiter has failed to comply with express or implied formal requirements, and has awarded, say, a single lump sum

---

[36] (1860) 22 D. 741 at 744.
[37] *Miller & Son* v. *Oliver & Boyd* (1903) 6 F. 77 per Lord Trayner at 88–9.

where specification of the amount awarded under each of several heads of claim is required, the decree may be reduced even if in fact the arbiter did take into account all the claims and did not go beyond the matters submitted. Giving the unanimous judgment of the court in *Miller & Son*,[38] Lord Trayner said that such a decree,

> 'must be set aside, because it is consistent with (that is, does not exclude) the view that the arbiter has not exhausted the reference.'

Where a decree is attacked on this formal ground, no extrinsic evidence is required, which is just as well from the point of any party seeking reduction, for no such evidence is admissible. A decree —

> 'must be read and construed as issued, and its validity determined, as at the date of its issue without any explanation or addition which does not appear on the face of the decree itself.'[39]

16.21. Where an award is ambiguous or obscure taken on its own, extrinsic evidence becomes admissible to explain its meaning, though it appears that the presumptions above-mentioned — of validity in the case of failure to exhaust the submission,[40] and of invalidity in the case of exceeding the jurisdiction[41] — still apply in assessing the effect of that evidence upon the award. The question then arises whether any kinds of extrinsic evidence are here inadmissible. Since it is the interpretation of the language of the award, not that of the scope of the submission, that is in issue, the focus must be upon evidence which might indicate what was in the arbiter's mind when framing the decree — the personal testimony of the arbiter, any statement of reasons issued by the arbiter along with the award, and notes made by the arbiter when preparing the award.

16.22. The personal testimony of the arbiter may be admitted in so far as it relates to events during the proceedings (the *'res gestae'*) but evidence of what the arbiter or anyone else did or said during that period is unlikely to be helpful in determining the meaning of expressions used in the award. In most cases the important

---

[38] *Ibid.* at 89.
[39] *Ibid.*
[40] *Johnson* v. *Lamb* 1891 S.L.T. 300.
[41] *Calder* v. *Mackay* (1860) 22 D. 741.

question is, whether the personal testimony of the arbiter is admissible for this purpose. There are some old judicial *dicta* which cast doubt on the admissibility of this evidence in this context,[42] and more recently Lord Kinnear said,[43] after accepting that the evidence of an arbiter on the *res gestae* was competent, that nevertheless —

> 'no question can be put to him for the purpose of proving how the award was arrived at, or what items it included, or what was the meaning which he intended to be given to it. The decree arbitral must speak for itself.'

Against that view can be placed the slightly different opinion of the same judge in another case,[44] where he appears to have accepted the competence of examining an arbiter in relation to matters of jurisdiction, but not as to his reasoning. In other cases it has been held competent to ask an arbiter how he construed the submission,[45] and other questions to the same effect.[46]

16.23. It is submitted that the view that an arbiter's

> 'evidence is competent on any matter which would entitle the court to interfere with his award'[47]

is sound. The contrary view, to the effect that 'the decree arbitral must speak for itself' would exclude not merely the testimony of the arbiter but all other evidence. This would be consistent, but it would mean that a decree arbitral would be treated even more strictly than other deeds, and it is hard to see why this should be so. It is one thing to say that no extrinsic evidence should be admitted unless the deed is ambiguous; it is quite another to say that no such evidence should be admitted however ambiguous it is. In giving evidence to a court about the meaning of a decree that he or she has issued, an arbiter is not acting as arbiter, but simply as a witness.

[42] *Woddrop* v. *Finlay* 4 Feb. 1794 Mor. 628.
[43] *Clippens Oil Co. Ltd.* v. *Edinburgh & District Water Trustees* (1901) 3 F. 1113 at 1128, affd. (1902) 4 F. (H.L.) 40.
[44] *Lanarkshire and Dumbartonshire Railway Co.* v. *Main* (1895) 22 R. 912 at 918.
[45] *Black* v. *John Williams & Co. (Wishaw) Ltd.* 1923 S.C. 510 at 512, affd. 1924 S.C. (H.L.) 22; *Fleming* v. *Fleming* 5 Apr. 1555 Mor. 624.
[46] *Glasgow City and District Railway Co.* v. *MacGeorge, Cowan and Galloway* (1886) 13 R. 609.
[47] Walkers, *Evidence*, 388. See also MacPhail, I. D., *Research paper on the Law of Evidence in Scotland*, Scottish Law Commission, Edinburgh, 1979, paragraph 3.15.

The proceedings are not analogous to a stated case, where reference is made to the arbiter as such. The fact that she or he has discharged the judicial duties of the office (is *'functa (functus) officio'*) is therefore no obstacle.

16.24. The rule quoted in the previous paragraph does not of course mean that the arbiter may be examined on his or her reasoning on the substantive merits of the decision. It is clear that here the arbiter's testimony is incompetent,[48] but this is due not to any special rule relating to that testimony, but to the fact that the court cannot itself review the award on grounds of error of fact or of law not appearing on the face of the award.

16.25. In so far as the personal testimony of the arbiter is admissible, the notes of the arbiter must also be admissible except to the extent that they are excluded by the 'best evidence' rule.[49] The notes made by an arbiter when formulating the award have been admitted to show that the submission had been exhausted.[50] It has further been observed[51] that —

'in considering the effect of a decree arbitral a Court of Law is bound to take into account and to read along with that decree the findings of the arbiter upon which it proceeds as explanatory of the views to which by his formal judgment he intended to give effect.'

It is submitted that this comment should not be taken to mean that the notes of an arbiter may be looked at even if the decree is unambiguous in itself; it is only if it is obscure that such extrinsic evidence is admissible.

16.26. The rules that apply to the notes of an arbiter also apply to other forms of extrinsic evidence, including any statement of reasons which the arbiter may have issued along with, but not as part of, an award. It is sometimes argued that these are wholly excluded from the view of the court by the contract of the parties. Though the point appears not yet to have been raised in Scotland,

---

[48] *Campbell* v. *Campbell* (1843) 5 D. 530.
[49] On which see paragraph 14.9 above.
[50] *Alston & Orr* v. *Allan* 1910 S.C. 304 per Lord Ardwall at 311. See also *Farrans Ltd.* v. *Roxburgh County Council (No. 2)* 1970 S.L.T. 334 at 336; *Johnson* v. *Lamb* 1981 S.L.T. 300.
[51] *Holmes Oil Co.* v. *Pumpherston Oil Co.* (1891) 18 R. (H.L.) 52.

it has been considered in England,[52] where awards are said often to be accompanied by a document giving reasons, but headed by a note to the following effect —

'These reasons do not form part of the award. They are issued after its publication and are given on the understanding that no use shall be made of them in any proceedings arising on or in connection with the award'.

Documents of this kind are apparently so commonplace in maritime arbitrations that in England the courts have readily accepted that it is implied by custom that an arbiter may if he or she wishes issue reasons headed by such a note.[53]

16.27. It has been held in England that any agreement between the parties to the effect that a document of this kind could not be presented in evidence to a court was void as amounting to the ousting of the jurisdiction of the court.[54] It is submitted that in Scotland, where the rule in *Czarnikow* v. *Roth, Schmidt and Co.*[55] on which that decision was based does not apply, the parties could competently agree that such reasons could not be presented. If the parties may competently oust the jurisdiction of the courts by submitting a matter to arbitration,[56] they may surely agree, as between themselves, not to present certain evidence to a civil court. However, a Scottish court might require very compelling evidence that such an agreement existed, just as it requires such evidence of the existence and scope of arbitration agreements.[57] It is one thing to separate reasons from an award to ensure that the rules relating to extrinsic evidence exclude reference to the reasons unless the award is ambiguous; it is another thing to exclude all reference to the reasons. In so far as the document simply provides evidence of the arbiter's reasoning on the matters submitted, the court will not have regard to it, because the arbiter's judgment on the merits is not reviewable unless it is clear on the face of the award that either the law or the evidence have not merely been

---

[52] In *Mutual Shipping Corporation of New York* v. *Bayshore Shipping Co. of Monrovia* (*The 'Montan'*) [1985] 1 All E.R. 520; *Intermare Transport GmbH* v. *International Copra Export Corporation* (*The 'Ross Isle' and 'Ariel'*) [1982] 2 Ll. Rep. 589.

[53] *Intermare Transport* (*supra* note 52).

[54] *Mutual Shipping* (*supra* note 52).

[55] [1923] 2 K.B. 478.

[56] *Sanderson* v. *Armour & Co.* 1922 S.C. (H.L.) 117.

[57] *Calder* v. *Mackay* (1860) 22 D. 741.

misapplied or misapprehended but disregarded.[58] It is only in so far as it assists in explaining a decree which is obscure or in correcting clerical errors that it can be relevant. Whether on these matters it is admissible is still an open question in Scotland.

Enforcement of external arbitral awards

16.28. Under this heading will be considered the means by which, and the conditions under which, the courts in Scotland will enforce an award which has been issued outside Scotland and which has not been transformed into the judgment of a foreign court. The matter is now regulated to a substantial extent by legislation, giving effect in some cases to international conventions, but the common law retains at least a marginal relevance, and is worthy of some consideration.

16.29.   **Common law**. Apart from statute, the enforcement of an award issued outside Scotland (here referred to generally as an 'external award') is sought in Scotland by means of an action for decree conform thereto. As to the conditions which must be satisfied, it has been suggested by a leading juristic authority[59] that there are seven. These are —

(1) that the submission upon which it is based is valid according to its own proper law, even if it would not have been valid under the law of Scotland[60];

(2) that the arbiter had jurisdiction under the submission and under the proper law of the submission to make the award;

(3) that the award was formally valid under the law of the country in which it was issued[61];

(4) that the award was final and is not the subject of any proceedings contesting its validity in the country in which it was issued;

(5) that to grant decree conform to the award would not be contrary to 'deeply rooted and important considerations of public policy'[62];

(6) that the issue decided by the award had not previously been

---

[58] *Mitchell-Gill* v. *Buchan* 1921 S.C. 390 per L.P. Clyde at 395.
[59] Professor A. E. Anton, 'Arbitration: International Aspects', 1986 S.L.T. (News) 53 at 54–5.
[60] *Hamlyn & Co.* v. *Talisker Distillery Co.* (1894) 21 R. (H.L.) 21.
[61] *Earl of Hopetoun* v. *Scots Mines Co.* (1856) 18 D. 739.

decided in Scotland in litigation or arbitration proceedings between the same parties; and

(7) that the award was not vitiated by fraud or based on proceedings contrary to natural justice.[63]

16.30. It is arguable that condition (7) could be subsumed within the terms of condition (5), and clear Scottish authority for conditions two, four and six is lacking, but with one minor qualification all these propositions are consistent with the general rules of Scots arbitration or general private international law and it is difficult to envisage their being disapproved by any Scottish court. The qualification relates to conditions (1) and (3). There is some dispute among juristic authorities in Scotland whether external submissions and awards affecting rights to heritable property in Scotland require to be executed according to the formalities of Scots law. Bell asserts that any award which 'purports directly to affect Scottish heritage' must be so executed.[64] Irons and Melville[65] argue that such formalities are only required of external awards which purport to convey heritable property in Scotland, and cite the authority of Bell himself[66] for the view that they are not required of awards which affect heritage by obliging a party to execute a deed. It is submitted that the view of Irons and Melville is here to be preferred. The effect is a qualification of conditions (1) and (3).

16.31. **Legislation.** So far as statutory provisions are concerned, a distinction must be drawn between external awards issued outside the United Kingdom and those issued in a part of the United Kingdom other than Scotland. The principal statutes applicable to awards made outside the United Kingdom are Part II of the Arbitration Act 1950 and the Arbitration Act 1975, which are intended respectively to give effect to the Geneva Convention on the Execution of Foreign Arbitral Awards 1927[67] and the New York Convention on the Recognition of Foreign Arbitral Awards 1958.[68] The latter is intended eventually to supersede the former.

[62] *Hamlyn & Co.* v. *Talisker Distillery Co.* (1894) 21 R. (H.L.) 21 at 27.
[63] *Hope* v. *Crookston Brothers* (1890) 17 R. 868 at 875.
[64] *Arb.* para. 842.
[65] *Arb.* 417.
[66] *Arb.* para. 842.
[67] 92 *League of Nations Treaty Series* 301; also reproduced in Schedule 2 to the Arbitration Act 1950.
[68] 330 *United Nations Treaty Series* 3.

The Arbitration (International Investment Disputes) Act 1966 is of rather limited concern and is not considered in any detail here. Only brief mention is made of the Administration of Justice Act 1920 Part IV and the Foreign Judgments (Reciprocal Enforcement) Act 1933, which apply to certain awards which have been confirmed by the judgments of foreign courts. The main provisions of the Civil Jurisdiction and Judgement Act 1982 were brought into force with effect from 1st January 1987.[69] As yet no legislation has been proposed to incorporate the UNCITRAL[70] Model Law[71] into the law of any part of the United Kingdom to regulate either international or domestic arbitration, but committees have been established in both Scotland and England to consider this matter.[72] As some of the provisions of the model law relating to the supervisory powers of the courts have not attracted favourable opinions from influential English judges expert in commercial law,[73] and as it is unlikely that different provisions of the Model Law would be adopted for different parts of the United Kingdom, the chances are that it will be adopted, if at all, only in part.

16.32. *Civil Jurisdiction and Judgments Act 1982.* This Act was passed to give effect within the United Kingdom to the Convention on Jurisdiction and the Enforcement of Judgments in Civil Matters signed at Brussels in 1968. So far as Scotland is concerned, however, it lays down new rules of jurisdiction for the Scottish courts which apply, for the most part, whether the Convention is applicable or not. The Convention does not apply to arbitration awards, but it has been remarked[74] that the effect of this exclusion is not wholly clear.

---

[69] Civil Jurisdiction and Judgments Act 1982 (Commencement No. 3) Order 1986, S.I. 1986 No. 2044 (C. 78). The promulgation of this Order completed the process of bringing this Act into effect.

[70] United Nations Commission on International Trade Law.

[71] Adopted 21 June 1985. The final English text may be found in Lew J.D.M. (ed) *Contemporary Problems in International Arbitration*, London, 1986, 176–187.

[72] The Lord Advocate has established a committee to advise on whether, and if so to what extent, it should be implemented in Scotland: 1986 S.L.T. (News) 306.

[73] See e.g. Kerr, Sir Michael, 'Arbitration and the Courts: the UNCITRAL Model Law', (1985) 34 *International and Comparative Law Quarterly* 1–19.

[74] Anton A. E., 'Arbitration: International Aspects', 1986 S.L.T. (News) 53 at 56.

16.33. The main effect of the 1982 Act on the enforcement of arbitration awards outside the jurisdiction in which they have been made is upon such enforcement within the various parts of the United Kingdom. Section 18(2)(*e*) provides that

'an arbitration award which has become enforceable in the part of the United Kingdom in which it was given in the same manner as a judgment given by a court of law in that part'

may be enforced as a judgment by registration if it is certified by a court that it contains money provisions. If it does not, application must be made to the court of the part of the United Kingdom where it is being enforced, and enforcement will be granted unless 'compliance with the non-money provisions ... would involve a breach of the law of that part of the United Kingdom'.[75]

16.34. *Arbitration Act 1975.* The operation of this Act is based on the definition which subsection 7(*c*) contains of a '*Convention award*' as —

'an award made in pursuance of an arbitration agreement in the territory of a state, other than the United Kingdom, which is a party to the Convention.'

The Act does not indicate in what precise circumstances an award may be said to have been 'made' for this purpose, but probably the word should be interpreted in accordance with the law governing the validity of the award. Since the Convention is concerned with states, not legal systems, it does not apply to awards made in another part of the United Kingdom.

16.35. An '*arbitration agreement*' is defined in the same section to mean —

'an agreement in writing (including an agreement contained in an exchange of letters or telegrams) to submit to arbitration present or future differences capable of settlement by arbitration.'

It has been held in Italy[76] that a clause in a contract of sale submitting disputes to arbitration under the auspices of a certain trade association and referring to its model contract is a written

---

[75] Schedule 7 paragraph 5(5).
[76] *Société Italo-Belge pour le Commerce et l'Industrie* v. *IGOR SpA* [1982] Eur. Law Dig. 323.

agreement under the Convention and there seems no reason to doubt that subsection 7(c) of the 1975 Act would be interpreted to as to have a similar effect.

16.36. It is doubtful whether 'arbitration' includes for this purpose forms of arbitration — such as the Italian 'informal' arbitration — which have as their outcome awards which are unenforceable as such in the country by whose law they are governed, because otherwise they would have an effect abroad as 'Convention awards' which they would not have at home. A German court has held an Italian informal arbitration award unenforceable on this ground.[77] It is however often argued that some forms of international commercial arbitration are in effect 'delocalised', so that an award which is unenforceable in the country in which it was made is nevertheless not prevented from being enforceable elsewhere. One of the most powerful advocates of the delocalisation of international commercial arbitration appears now to accept that it is now 'most unlikely that an award annulled in its country of origin will be given life elsewhere'.[78]

16.37. It is not certain on what basis the courts in this country will hold that differences are 'capable of settlement by arbitration'. Different legal systems have different rules on this matter. It is submitted that in the statutory context in which it occurs, the phrase will be taken to mean 'capable of settlement by arbitration under the law governing the arbitration agreement'. There is sufficient safeguard in the 'public policy' provision of the Act[79] to prevent Convention awards on issues which for deep-rooted and important reasons are not capable of being determined by arbitration in Scotland from being enforced in this country.

16.38. Whether an award is governed by the law of a state other than the United Kingdom which is party to the Convention is immaterial. What matters is whether it was made within the territory of a state which, at the time the award is presented to the court for enforcement,[80] is a party to the Convention. The fact that

---

[77] Bundesgerichthof III 2R 42/60, 8 Oct. 1981, [1982] Eur. Law Dig. 414.

[78] Paulsson J., 'The extent of independence of international arbitration from the law of the *situs*', in Lew J.D.M. (ed), *Contemporary Problems in International Arbitration*, London, 1986, 141 at 148.

[79] S. 5(3).

[80] *Minister of Public Works of the Government of Kuwait* v. *Sir Frederick Snow and Partners and Others* [1983] 1 W.L.R. 818 per Kerr L.J. at 826.

a state is party to the Convention may be, and in many cases has been, conclusively established by Order in Council.[81] However, the fact that a state is not mentioned in the current Order as being a party to the Convention does not mean that a court in the United Kingdom cannot entertain an averment that it is a party.

16.39. Section 4 of the Act provides that a party seeking to enforce a 'Convention award' must produce —

'(a) the duly authenticated original award or a duly certified copy of it; and
(b) the original arbitration agreement or a duly certified copy of it; and
(c) where the award or agreement is in a foreign language, a translation of it certified by an official or sworn translator or by a diplomatic or consular agent.'

Though it is not expressly provided that an award, as distinct from an arbitration agreement, must be in writing, section 4(a) has the effect of requiring this in practice.

16.40. Section 5 of the 1975 Act provides that —

'Enforcement of a Convention award shall not be refused except in the cases mentioned in this section'.

Those do not include the case of an award which has been confirmed by a judgment of a foreign court to which Part I of the Foreign Judgments (Reciprocal Enforcement) Act 1933 applies. Section 6 of the latter Act provides that —

'no proceedings for the recovery of a sum payable under a foreign judgment to which this Part of the Act applies, other than proceedings by way of registration of the judgment, shall be entertained by any court in the United Kingdom.'

This section is, it is submitted, inconsistent with section 5 of the 1975 Act. On ordinary principles of statutory interpretation the later Act should prevail, but there is disagreement among eminent jurists in England on this point,[82] and the matter has not yet come before the courts in any reported case.

[81] In 1986 the current Order in Council was the Arbitration (Foreign Awards) Order 1984, S.I. 1984 No. 1168.
[82] Compare Dicey & Morris, *The Conflict of Laws*, 10th edn., London, 1980, Vol. 2, 1155, note 17, and Mustill, *Comm. Arb.*, 373.

16.41. The remaining subsections of section 5 of the 1975 Act specify the circumstances in which enforcement of a Convention award may be refused. Subsection (2) provides for five situations. These are —

(a) *Incapacity of a party to the arbitration agreement.* Since the arbiter is not normally a party to that agreement, the incapacity of the arbiter appears not to be covered. The rules of modern legal systems relating to the capacity to undertake arbitration are generally similar, but there are some peculiarities. Italian law for example is said to require that in arbitration proceedings taking place in that country (which is a party to the Convention) the arbiters must be Italian citizens.[83] Proceedings for the enforcement of an award made in Italy by an arbiter who was not an Italian citizen might have to be sisted in terms of subsection 5(5) of the 1975 Act pending the outcome of proceedings in Italy for its reduction.

(b) *Invalidity of the arbitration agreement* under 'the law to which the parties subjected it or, failing any indication thereon, under the law of the country where the award was made'.

(c) *Certain procedural irregularities.* Among the irregularities which the 1975 Act specifies as justifying refusal of enforcement are absence of 'proper notice of the appointment of the arbitrator or of the arbitration proceedings' and generally anything which makes a party 'unable to present his case'. This provision goes in some respects beyond ordinary Scots concepts of procedural unfairness, and is in other respects more restrictive. However, in so far as any unfairness is not covered by this subsection and is regarded in Scotland as being very serious, it would be covered by the 'public policy' provision of subsection (3).

(d) *The award deals with matters not submitted.* The subsection enables, but does not require, a court to refuse enforcement. It is therefore conceivable that an award might be upheld in spite of its having gone beyond the terms of the submission. This is consistent with subsection 5(4), which provides that an award which has gone beyond the matters submitted may be enforced 'to the extent that it contains decisions on matters submitted to arbitration which can be separated from those on matters not so submitted.' There is no provision in the 1975 Act under which an award which does not exhaust the submission may be refused enforcement on that ground.

[83] Bernini G., in Sanders P. (ed), *Yearbook on Commercial Arbitration*, Deventer, 1981, Vol. 6, 24 at 36.

(e) *The composition of the 'arbitral authority' of the procedure followed was 'incorrect'*, that is, it was not in accordance with the agreement of the parties or, failing such agreement, with the law of the country where the arbitration took place. This provision does not appear to let in the objection that the composition of the authority or the procedure, while in accordance with the agreement, was contrary to mandatory provisions of the law of the country where the arbitration took place.

(f) *The award has not yet become binding, or has been set aside or suspended*, by a competent authority of the country in which or under the law of which it was made. Subsection (5) enables the court, in its discretion, to sist proceedings where an application has been made to set aside or suspend the award. The court may also, in such circumstances, require the party seeking adjournment to give security, presumably for payment of any amount which the debtor is obliged to pay in terms of the award.

16.42.   Subsection (3) of the section entitles a court to refuse enforcement on the ground that the matter 'is not capable of settlement by arbitration' or that enforcement would be 'contrary to public policy'. Though the Act does not so specify, Article V(2)(*a*) of the Convention makes it clear that in enforcement proceedings in the Scottish courts it would be the principles of Scots law relating to what matters are arbitrable that would apply. Equally, the Convention makes it clear in Article V(2)(*b*) that in such proceedings it would be by Scots public policy that the appropriateness of enforcement would be judged.

16.43.   The effect of a Convention award which complies with the conditions laid down in the Act is that it is enforceable by action or, where the arbitration agreement contains consent to registration in the Books of Council and Session for execution, and the award has been so registered by summary diligence.[84] If a question were raised whether an award so registered does in fact comply with the Act, an action of suspension and interdict would have to be brought to prevent diligence proceeding.

16.44.   The 1975 Act is intended ultimately to replace Part II of the Arbitration Act 1950, which gives effect to the Geneva Convention of 1927. Consistently with this intention, it is provided in section 2 that —

[84] S. 3.

'where a Convention award would, but for this section, also be a foreign award within the meaning of Part II of the Arbitration Act 1950, that Part shall not apply to it.'

However, the provisions of the 1975 Act are without prejudice to any right to enforce or rely on an award otherwise than under the 1975 Act or Part II of the 1950 Act.[85] Rights of action and defences based on the common law are thus preserved.

16.45. *Arbitration Act 1950, Part II.* This Act defines certain kinds of award as 'foreign awards', and provides for the manner in which such awards are proved and for the conditions subject to which they are enforceable by the courts of the United Kingdom.

16.46. A *'foreign award'* is defined for the purposes of the 1950 Act partly in terms of the nature of the agreement upon which it is based and partly in terms of the place in which it was made.[86] The agreement on which it is based must be one to which the protocol set out in the first schedule to the Act applies, and must be between persons who are 'subject to the jurisdiction' of different states, each of which must have been declared by Order in Council to be a party to the Geneva Convention. The phrase 'subject to the jurisdiction' of different states has been interpreted by a court in England to mean that the parties must reside or carry on business in two different contracting states.[87] Since England and Scotland are not — and have not for over two and a half centuries been — different states, an award based on an arbitration agreement entered into between parties resident in England and Scotland cannot, wherever it may have been made, be a 'foreign award' under the 1950 Act. The submission must not be governed by the law of Scotland,[88] and the award itself must have been made in a territory declared by Order in Council to be one to which the Geneva Convention applies.

16.47. A party seeking enforcement of a 'foreign award' is required by section 38(1) of the Act to produce —
(a) 'the original award or a copy thereof duly authenticated in the manner required by the law of the country in which it was made';

[85] S. 6.
[86] S. 35(1).
[87] *Brazendale and Co. Ltd.* v. *Saint Frères SA* [1970] 2 Ll. Rep. 34.
[88] Ss. 40(*b*) and 41(2).

(b) 'evidence that the award has become final';
(c) evidence that the award is a foreign award; and
(d) evidence that the three conditions of enforceability specified in subsections 32(1)(*a*)–(*c*) are satisfied.

In addition, under section 38(2) where any document required to be produced under subsection (1) is in a foreign language, a certified translation must also be produced. There is no requirement that either the award or the arbitration agreement be in writing, but the evidentiary requirements of subsection 38(1) effectively require the award to be written. If the law governing the arbitration agreement requires it to be in writing, evidence that that condition was satisfied must be produced.

16.48.   *The conditions for the enforcement of foreign awards* are set out in section 37 of the Act, as applied to Scotland in terms of section 41(2). They are —
(a) the arbitration agreement upon which the award was based must be valid 'under the law by which it was governed';
(b) the arbitration tribunal must have been constituted in accordance with the agreement. This rule would seem to exclude arbiters appointed by the court where the appointment under the agreement had failed;
(c) the award must have been made in conformity with the law governing the arbitration procedure. This rule would seem to exclude cases where the law governing the arbitration procedure was different from the law governing the award, and the award was valid only in terms of its own law. Usually, of course, the law governing the procedure also in practice governs the award;
(d) the award had become 'final' in the country in which it was made. The word 'final' has caused difficulty, in spite of the definition of 'final award' in section 39. The word does not have the same meaning in this context as it has in the context of domestic Scots law. Under the 1950 Act an award may not be deemed to be final if proceedings to contest its validity are pending in the country where it was made, but the absence of such proceedings does not necessarily mean that it is final,[89] for it may be final even if under the law of the country where it was made it requires a court order for its enforcement[90];

[89] Dicey & Morris (*supra*) at 1145.
[90] *Union Nationale des Co-operatives Agricoles de Céréales* v. *Robert Catterall & Co.* [1959] 1 Ll. Rep. 111.

(e) the award deals with matters which may lawfully be referred to arbitration under Scots law;

(f) enforcement must not be contrary to the public policy of the law of Scotland. The reference to the law of Scotland seems not to imply that the substantive law of Scotland governing, for example, the arbitration procedure[91] or the content of the award must be complied with. Only a mandatory legal rule which relates to enforcement appears to be meant[92];

(g) the award has not been annulled in the country where it was made;

(h) the party against whom enforcement is sought was given notice of the arbitration proceedings in sufficient time to present his case, or being under some legal incapacity was properly represented;

(i) the award does not fail to exhaust or go beyond the matters submitted. The court may however postpone enforcement or enforce an award subject to the giving of security by the person seeking to enforce it.

16.49.   If a 'foreign award' complies with the provisions of Part II of the 1950 Act, it may be enforced by action for decree conform or, if the submission contains an agreement to registration in the Books of Council and Session for execution and is so registered, by summary diligence.[93] It may also be relied on in defence or otherwise used in any legal proceedings in Scotland.[94] Where a question of the compliance of an award with the conditions laid down in the Act arises in the case of a registered award, it is necessary to bring an action of suspension and interdict to prevent diligence from proceeding.

16.50.   *Other statutory provisions.* Awards which have become enforceable in the same manner as a decree of a court in the country where they were made may in certain circumstances be enforceable in Scotland upon registration in terms of the Administration of Justice Act 1920 or the Foreign Judgments (Reciprocal Enforcement) Act 1933. Under the 1920 Act the definition of a 'judgment' is wide enough to include an arbitral award. Section 35(1) and paragraph 4 of Schedule 10 to the Civil Jurisdiction and Judgments Act 1982 extend the scope of the 1933 Act so that it also

---

[91] *Masinimport* v. *Scottish Mechanical Light Industries Ltd.* 1976 S.C. 102.
[92] Dicey & Morris, (*supra* note 82).
[93] S. 41(3).
[94] S. 36(2).

applies to arbitral awards which have become enforceable as court judgments. Registration of a foreign decree under the Acts of 1920 and 1933 is sought by petition in terms of rule 248 or 249 of the Rules of the Court of Session, and where Part I of the 1933 Act applies, no other method of enforcement is permissible.[95]

16.51. The Arbitration (International Investment Disputes) Act 1966 was passed to facilitate the enforcement of awards rendered under the auspices of the International Centre for Settlement of Investment Disputes (ICSID) established by international convention. The procedure for registration of awards rendered under the convention is laid down in Rule 249A of the Rules of the Court of Session. ICSID arbitration is likely to concern the Scottish courts only rarely, when a foreign state seeks to enforce an award against a person or corporation resident in Scotland. A fuller discussion of ICSID arbitration may be found in specialist sources.[96]

[95] 1933 Act s. 6.
[96] E.g. Delaume R., 'ICSID Arbitration' in Lew J.D.M. (ed), *Contemporary Problems in International Arbitration*, London, 1986, 23–39.

PART D

QUASI-ARBITRAL AND EQUITABLE PROCEDURES

CHAPTER SEVENTEEN

INTRODUCTION

17.1. Numerous types of procedures exist which in one way or another bear some resemblance to ordinary arbitration. Some have already been alluded to in passing in Chapter One.[1] A few are governed by the common law, but most are regulated to a greater or lesser extent by statute. It is not possible in a general work of this kind to mention, let alone describe in full, all the procedures that exist. Three only are considered here in any detail — judicial reference, agricultural arbitration under the Agricultural Holdings (Scotland) Act 1949, and industrial arbitration, least being said about the last, because it has no peculiarly Scottish legal features of any importance, and is discussed in standard works on labour law.[2] Arbitration on compulsory taking of property, which was extensively discussed by Irons and Melville,[3] will not be dealt with here. Though the principal Act under which compensation in such circumstances was determined by arbitration — the Lands Clauses (Scotland) Act 1845 — is still in force and occasionally the subject of legal proceedings,[4] the functions which used to be performed by arbiters under that Act are now generally undertaken by the Lands Tribunal for Scotland established under the Land Compensation Act 1963.

17.2. Where a procedure called 'arbitration' is established by legislation, the freedom of parties to a dispute to which the legislation applies is usually restricted to some extent. The law may for example lay down how and from among what group of persons the 'arbiter' is to be selected, how many 'arbiters' there are to be, how the proceedings are to be conducted, and in what form and within what period the 'award' must be issued. Usually the law

[1] Paragraphs 1.4–1.6 and 1.18–1.29 above.
[2] See e.g. Smith I. T. and Wood J. C., *Industrial Law*, 3rd edn, London, 1986, 26–39; Dickens L. and Others, *Dismissed: A Study of Unfair Dismissal and the Industrial Tribunal System*, Oxford, 1985, Chapter 9, 'An Arbitral Alternative'; Wedderburn and Davies, *Empl. Griev. Proc.*, Chapter 9.
[3] *Arb.* 243–345.
[4] See e.g. *Rogano* v. *British Railways Board* 1979 S.C. 297.

requires that disputes of a specified type are dealt with under the prescribed procedure and expressly or impliedly prohibits an arbiter from entertaining any claims outside the specified categories, so that interdict may be granted if an attempt is made to exercise a jurisdiction which is not within the statute,[5] and an 'award' dealing with matters outside the scope of the statutory scheme may be reduced.[6] Occasionally a party aggrieved by an 'arbiter's' decision is given the right to have it reviewed on the merits by a court. There is, for example, a right of appeal in certain circumstances against the award of an arbiter acting under the Agricultural Holdings (Scotland) Act 1949.[7]

17.3. But though an institution thus established may have some of the features of a statutory tribunal — an arbiter appointed by the Secretary of State or the Land Court under the 1949 Act comes within the purview of the Scottish Committee of the Council on Tribunals[8] — to call it 'arbitration' is not necessarily inappropriate. The institution may have grown out of a form of ordinary arbitration, or the law may leave some important matters such as the nomination of the arbiter to be established in the first instance at least by the agreement of the parties. The 'arbiter' may be given as much freedom to determine how proceedings are to be determined as is common in ordinary arbitration. The fact that the procedure is designated 'arbitration' is an indication that where a point is not regulated by the statute establishing the procedure, the matter has to be determined in accordance with the law governing ordinary arbitration. From this point onwards, therefore, the distinction between such a procedure and ordinary arbitration will not be emphasised by placing references to the former in inverted commas.

[5] *Dumbarton Water Commissioners* v. *Lord Blantyre* (1884) 12 R. 115 per Lord President Inglis at 119 (though in this case interdict was not granted).
[6] E.g. *Glasgow City and District Railway* v. *MacGeorge, Cowan and Galloway* (1886) 13 R. 609.
[7] See paragraph 19.53 below.
[8] Tribunals and Inquiries Act 1971, Schedule 1 Part II.

CHAPTER EIGHTEEN

JUDICIAL REFERENCE

Definition

18.1.   A judicial reference is a procedure by which issues which are being litigated in an ordinary court are referred by agreement of the litigants and the approval of the court to the decision of a person other than the public judge who is hearing the case. It has been authoritatively defined as —

'the submission by the parties to a cause, with the approval of the Court, of the whole subject matter of the cause, or any part or parts thereof, to a referee'.[1]

It is an act of the court, and does not take the cause out of the court,[2] though with certain exceptions which will be noted below,[3]

'an award in a judicial reference is as sacredly fixed and conclusive as the most formal decree arbitral'.[4]

Litigants may agree by joint minute lodged in the court process that the matters in issue between them, or some part thereof, shall be determined by a specified person. They then jointly crave the court to interpone its authority to the minute and to remit the matters to the referee. This may be done at any stage in the court proceedings before the matters to be referred have been heard by the court itself.[5] When the referee has given a decision, it is reported formally to the court and either of the litigants may — indeed must if the decision is to receive legal effect[6] — then move the court to grant decree conform to it.[7]

[1] MacLaren, *Ct. of Sess. Pract.*, 511.
[2] *Clyne's Trustees* v. *Edinburgh Oil Gas Light Co.* (1835) II Sh. & MacL. 243 per Lord Brougham at 268.
[3] Paragraph 18.8.
[4] *Mackenzie* v. *Girvan* (1840) 3 D. 318 per Lord Moncreiff at 327, affd. (1843) II Bell 43 per Lord Brougham at 49.
[5] Bell, *Arb.* paragraph 509.
[6] *Mackenzie* v. *Girvan* (1843) II Bell 43 per Lord Brougham at 49.
[7] Bell, *Arb.* paragraphs 533–4.

Distinction from ordinary arbitration

18.2. Judicial reference is similar in most respects to ordinary arbitration, but it is dependent on the curial proceedings out of which it arises, and the judicial referee is an officer of the court[8] even though appointed with the consent and on the nomination of the litigants. The similarities to ordinary arbitration lie in the application to judicial reference of the basic rules which apply to ordinary arbitration,[9] including the twenty fifth Article of Regulation 1695.[10]

18.3. **Similarities.** Just as in ordinary arbitration a submission binds only the parties thereto, so in judicial reference where there are several parties involved in a lawsuit the decision of the judicial referee is binding only on those who concurred in the reference.[11] The effect of a reference is to remove such aspects of the case as have been specified, which may include the whole cause, from the court to the referee.[12] A judicial referee, like an arbiter, must exhaust, but must not exceed, the matters submitted,[13] must proceed in a fair manner,[14] and must not be disqualified by interest.[15] A clerk may be appointed in a judicial reference, and he or she is entitled to a fee in the normal way.[16] The referee has the same procedural freedom as an ordinary arbiter, so that even if the court has prior to the reference issued an interlocutor allowing a proof, the referee is not as a result bound to take it.[17] At one time the judicial referee differed from an ordinary arbiter in that, as an officer of the court, the former was entitled to a fee[18] while the latter was not,[19] but ordinary arbiters are also now entitled to remuneration.[20]

[8] *Drummond* v. *Leslie* (1835) 13 S. 684 per L. J. C. Boyle.
[9] *Brakenrig* v. *Menzies* (1841) 4 D. 274 per Lord Meadowbank at 280; *Watmore* v. *Burns* (1841) 4 D. 150; *Campbell* v. *Campbell* (1843) 5 D. 530 per L. J. C. Hope at 537.
[10] *Brakenrig* v. *Menzies* (1841) 4 D. 274 per Lord Moncreiff at 284.
[11] *Macintosh* v. *Robertson* (1834) 12 S. 321; *Stewart* v. *Hickman and Marriott* (1843) 6 D. 151 (cautioner).
[12] *Reid & Co* v. *Firth and Stott* (1886) 23 S.L.R. 845.
[13] *Shiels* v. *Shiels' Trustees* (1874) 1 R. 502.
[14] Ibid.
[15] See paragraphs 4.48–4.55 above.
[16] *Jackson* v. *Galloway* (1867) 5 S.L.R. 130.
[17] *Colquhoun* v. *Haig* (1825) 3 S. 424.
[18] *Drummond* v. *Leslie* (1835) 13 S. 684; *Beattie* (1873) 11 M. 954.
[19] *Stewart* v. *Ross* (1822) 1 S. 335.
[20] *Macintyre Brothers* v. *Smith* 1913 S.C. 129.

18.4. It has been said that it would be competent to object to a motion craving the court to interpone its authority to a judicial referee's report

'on any ground which would be competent and sufficient for setting aside an extrajudicial decree arbitral'.[21]

If a report is successfully objected to on such a ground it is probable that the judicial reference is at an end,[22] unless the grounds of the objection come within the limited power of the court to remit the matter back to the referee for reconsideration.[23]

18.5. **Differences.** The differences between judicial reference and ordinary arbitration arise from the connection of the former with an action in court. This is apparent in the rules governing the *scope of a reference* and its relation to the referee's report. It is not possible to submit to a person in his or her capacity as judicial referee any matters which are not at issue in the cause before the court,[24] though the mere fact that something is in issue before the court does not give the judicial referee jurisdiction to decide questions, such as matters of status, which ordinary arbiters cannot entertain.[25] Only the court has the power to amend the record, which defines the scope of the reference, but the judicial referee may permit the amendment of pleadings formulated within the reference itself. This, at least, appears to be the best reconciliation of the slightly different expressions of opinion by Lord McLaren and Lord Kinnear in *Brown's Trustee* v. *Horne*.[26] There is, of course, no reason why additional matters may not be submitted to the same individual acting as an ordinary arbiter, but the decision upon them would require to be contained in a decree arbitral separate from the report to the court made in the judicial reference. Where the matters submitted to a referee consisted of 'this cause and all matters in difference between the parties', it was

[21] *Mackenzie* v. *Girvan* (1840) 3 D. 318 per Lord Moncreiff at 327; *Hook* v. *Lodge Colinton and Currie* (1931) 47 Sh. Ct. Rep. 144 at 145.
[22] Guild, *Arb.* 112. Though this seems reasonable, the supporting authorities are not strong.
[23] Below, paragraph 18.8.
[24] *Mackenzie* v. *Girvan* (1840) 3 D. 318 per Lord Moncreiff at 327, affd. (1843) II Bell 43.
[25] See paragraphs 6.9 and 6.11–6.12 above.
[26] 1907 S.C. 1027.

held that this must be taken to mean 'all questions in dispute between the parties in the cause referred'.[27]

18.6. Because an agreement to enter into a judicial reference is simply 'a step of procedure in the depending action'[28] it is not binding in itself. A party may *resile* from a joint minute until the court has expressly or impliedly interponed its authority thereto,[29] though the court has no authority to put an end to the contract contained therein.[30] Normally the court interpones its authority expressly in an interlocutor, but it has been known for this step to be omitted. In such a case the parties have been held bound if they have agreed to the reference in open court and permitted the reference to go on without making any objection.[31] A formal acceptance of office by the referee is not required, but is obviously desirable.[32]

18.7. The rules governing the duration of a judicial reference differ from those governing that of ordinary arbitration proceedings. Essentially, the duration of the former is related to the litigation proceedings out of which it arises. If the litigation is terminated, so is the reference,[33] and as long as the litigation continues in existence, the report of the referee will not be time-barred,[34] though where the cause has 'fallen asleep' during the reference it must be 'wakened' before the report of the referee can be received.[35] Though the court may itself without any warrant in the joint minute of reference set a time limit within which the referee must present the report, if in such circumstances it permits a report to be received late and grants decree conform thereto, a litigant may not suspend the decree on the ground that the report was time-barred.[36] Since a cause in court does not terminate on the

---

[27] *Clyne's Trustees* v. *Edinburgh Oil Gas Light Co.* (1835) II Sh. and MacL. 243 per Lord Brougham at 268.

[28] Bell, *Arb.* paragraph 512.

[29] *Reid (Rae's Trustee)* v. *Henderson* (1841) 3 D. 1102.

[30] *Walker & Co.* v. *Stewart* (1855) II Macq. 424, per Lord Cranworth at 429.

[31] *Fairley* v. *McGown* (1836) 14 S. 470.

[32] Bell, *Arb.* paragraph 526.

[33] *Gillon* v. *Simpson* (1859) 21 D. 243, per L. J. C. Inglis at 249.

[34] Bell, *Arb.* paragraph 551.

[35] Bell, *Arb.* para. 553; *Stewart* v. *Hickman* (1843) 6 D. 151.

[36] *Robertson and Stevenson* v. *Stewart* 15 Jan. 1818, Parker, *Arb.* Synopsis, xxxiii.

death of a party, neither does a reference arising out of it.[37] The death of the referee, however, appears to leave either party free to resume the action in court,[38] except possibly where the parties had not themselves nominated a referee, but had agreed to refer to such person as might be nominated by the court. It is however normal for the litigants to agree on a nomination for approval by the court.

18.8. The report of a judicial referee is similar to a decree arbitral, and need not, for example, contain reasons,[39] but the former is subject to additional judicial powers. These powers are not as clearly defined as they might be, but it appears at least that if a referee's report is ambiguous,[40] or cannot in practice be complied with,[41] or if there is some defect in it arising from the manner in which proceedings were conducted — for example a failure to hear parties sufficiently[42] — the court may make a remit back if a request to do so is made before decree conform to the report has been granted. A report may not, however, be amended by the court: it is either accepted, and decree given conform to its terms, or it is sent back to the referee for reconsideration.[43] If the referee is or has become disqualified, failure to approve the report implies the failure of the reference. It is not necessary to raise a formal action of reduction of a referee's report.[44] The court will not remit back, and will on the contrary if requested grant decree conform, if the objection to the report is merely that the referee has in the judgment committed either an error of law which does not appear on the face of the report or an error of fact.[45] Once a report has been approved by the court, it is not competent to bring forward any objection to it.[46]

---

[37] *Watmore and Taylor* v. *Burns* (1839) 1 D. 743 per Lord Mackenzie; *Robertson* v. *Cheyne* (1847) 9 D. 599.

[38] Bell, *Arb.* paragraph 555.

[39] *Rogerson* v. *Rogerson* (1885) 12 R. 583.

[40] *Anderson and others* v. *Pott and another* (1832) 10 S. 534.

[41] *Lord Advocate* v. *Heddle* (1856) 18 D. 1211.

[42] *Baxter* v. *Macarthur* (1836) 14 S. 549; *Hilton* v. *Walkers* (1867) 5 M. 969 per Lord Curriehill at 971; *Lord Advocate* v. *Heddle* (1856) 18 D. 1211; *Lyle* v. *Neilson* (1844) 6 D. 1163.

[43] MacLaren, *Ct. of Sess. Pract.*, 515.

[44] *Mackenzie* v. *Girvan* (1840) 3 D. 318 per Lord Moncreiff at 327.

[45] *Mackenzie* v. *Girvan* (1840) 3 D. 318 per Lord Moncreiff at 329; *Brakenrig* v. *Menzies* (1841) 4 D. 274 per Lord Moncreiff at 284; *Campbell* v. *Campbell* (1843) 5 D. 530 Per L. J. C. Hope at 539.

[46] *Hunter* v. *Cochrane's Trustees* (1831) 9 S. 477.

Distinction from judicial remit

18.9.   A judicial reference must be distinguished from a judicial remit. A court may remit to a person possessing appropriate professional knowledge or skill to report on a matter of fact or carry out one of the administrative functions of the court such as the 'taxing' (assessment) of expenses. This is usually done with the consent of the parties to the cause, but the court may act in this matter on its own initiative. In practice a judicial remit appears to be more common in causes initiated by petition than by action.[47] The reporter is not in any sense a judge, but where the remit has been made with the consent of the parties or has been acquiesced in and has been made without reservation of further proof, no other proof is allowed.[48]

Contemporary importance

18.10.   Almost all the reported litigation concerning judicial reference took place between 1825 and 1867. Though the procedure is of some antiquity and was and is competent in lower[49] as well as superior civil courts, there appears to have been only one clear reported case on issues concerning judicial reference prior to 1825,[50] only seven of the forty three cases were decided after 1867, and only one since 1916 and that in the sheriff court.[51] Since judicial reference is said now to be rare,[52] those who find the above account of it lacking in sufficient detail may find a fuller discussion in chapter XIV of J. A. Maclaren's work on Court of Session Practice, written in 1916.

[47] Maxwell, *Ct. of Sess. Pract.*, 259.
[48] *Pearce* v. *Irons* (1869) 7 M. 571; *Rowat* v. *Whitehead* (1826) 5 S. 19; Maxwell, *Ct. of Sess. Pract.*, 314–5.
[49] Sheriff courts — see e.g. *Low* v. *Banks* (1836) 14 S. 869 — and the former burgh courts — see e.g. Shearer, A., *Extracts from the Dunfermline Burgh Records*, Dunfermline, 1951, 197.
[50] *McMath* v. *Poure* 10 Jan. 1624, Mor. 14719.
[51] *Hook* v. *Lodge Colinton and Currie* (1931) 47 Sh. Ct. Rep. 144.
[52] Maxwell, *Ct. of Sess. Pract.*, 259.

CHAPTER NINETEEN

AGRICULTURAL ARBITRATION

Introduction

19.1. Relations between landlords and tenants of agricultural holdings have always been a fruitful source of disputes. Long before the emergence of statutory arbitration régimes with the Agricultural Holdings Act (Scotland) 1883 these were often determined by ordinary arbiters, generally small farmers and minor landowners. Normally, each party chose one arbiter with an oversman to break any deadlock that might arise. The courts did not expect agricultural arbiters to be very sophisticated, particularly in matters of procedure, and allowed them considerable licence.[1] Given the chronic financial insecurity of the small tenant farmer, the awards of such arbiters could nevertheless sometimes have grave consequences: one caused ruin to the father of the poet Robert Burns,[2] and his fate was probably not unusual.

19.2. The 1883 Act required certain kinds of dispute between such parties to be decided in accordance with a special statutory scheme. This was succeeded by a number of Acts with the similar purpose of creating a more regular and satisfactory system. These were increasingly precise in their provisions, regulating not only the number and manner of appointment of arbiters, but also enabling a party to require an arbiter to state a case for the opinion of a sheriff on a question of law. Gaps were however filled by reference to rules of ordinary arbitration derived from the common law, and the tradition that agricultural arbiters were allowed considerable latitude was retained.[3] The rules governing agricultural arbitration are now to be found mainly in the Agricultural Holdings (Scotland) Act 1949.

---

[1] See e.g. *McGregor* v. *Stevenson* (1847) 9 D. 1056; *Nivison* v. *Howat* (1883) 11 R. 182.
[2] Letter of Gilbert Burns to Mrs. Dunlop, quoted in Crawford T., *Burns: A study of the poems and songs*, Edinburgh, 1978, 8.
[3] See e.g. *Cameron* v. *Nicol* 1930 S.C. 1.

19.3. Though the scope of the issues which are required to be dealt with in terms of that Act is very wide, there are some matters expressly excluded. The remedy of removing for non-payment of rent may only be granted by a sheriff,[4] and certain types of application are within the exclusive jurisdiction of the Land Court.[5] By virtue of section 75(4), section 74 of the 1949 Act does not apply to certain valuations, notably items of obligatory waygoing valuation and bound sheep stocks, which are governed by a special régime under the Sheep Stocks Valuation (Scotland) Act 1937 and the Hill Farming Act 1946, the latter having been amended by section 32 of the Law Reform (Miscellaneous Provisions) (Scotland) Act 1985. Separate provision is made under the Allotments (Scotland) Act 1922 for disputes between the landlord and tenant of an 'allotment garden', but other allotments cultivated by the occupier not for the production of vegetable crops for himself and his family but for business purposes may be a holding to which the 1949 Act applies. Disputes between landlord and tenant of an agricultural holding concerning the landlord's amount of any compensation due for complete or partial cessation of milk production are referred to arbitration under the 1949 Act as modified by the regulations concerned.[6] Except where a matter is statutorily required to be decided by a court or by some other arbitration régime, types of issue excluded from the scope of the 1949 Act may if the parties so agree be decided by ordinary arbiters.

The 1949 Act régime

19.4. The arbitration régime provided for by the Agricultural Holdings (Scotland) Act 1949 has been discussed at some length in some fairly recent works on agricultural law, and those who find the present writer's treatment of this subject insufficient are referred to them.[7] There have, however, been some developments

---

[4] S. 19.
[5] See in particular ss. 26 and 52 of the 1949 Act.
[6] Milk (Community Outgoers' Scheme) (Scotland) Regulations 1986 (S.I. 1986 No. 1613 (S. 122); Milk (Partial Cessation of Production) (Scotland) Scheme 1986 (S.I. 1986 No. 1614 (S. 123)).
[7] Gill B., *Agr. Hold.*, chapters 25, 34 and 35. See also Campbell K. M., 'Arbitration' in *Aspects of Agricultural Law*, Law Society of Scotland, Edinburgh, 1981, pp. 20–33; Campbell K. M., 'Arbitration under the 1949 Act'

since they were published, and these are noted here. By way of introduction it may be remarked that though the 1949 Act regulates the procedures to which it applies in quite a detailed way, where it is silent the gap is filled by the ordinary common law rules.[8]

19.5. **Jurisdiction.** In compulsory statutory arbitration régimes such as that existing under the 1949 Act, the scope of the arbiter's jurisdiction is laid down by the statute. On a matter which is within the statutory provisions — here contained in sections 68 and 74 — the jurisdiction of the ordinary courts is excluded for the purposes of determining the merits of the dispute. A landlord and tenant may not agree upon a different system of arbitration — say by two arbiters and an oversman under an ordinary submission — but those whose disputes are not governed by the Act, such as incoming and outgoing tenants, may do so, because

'no statutory provision which interferes with freedom of contract is to be stretched beyond the precise language used.'[9]

19.6. The effect of the statute is that the jurisdiction of the ordinary courts is ousted in like manner as if there had been a submission to an ordinary arbiter, with one important exception. This is that the parties cannot by agreement expressly or impliedly prorogate the jurisdiction of the ordinary courts,[10] though a landlord and tenant may agree that, instead of the single arbiter to whom a dispute is normally referred in terms of section 75 of the Act, the matters in issue between them may be determined by the Land Court.[11] Statutory provisions which are in imperative terms, as these are, and which are introduced for reasons of general public policy rather than for the benefit of a class of individuals, cannot be waived even impliedly by failing to plead them,[12] though they are

in *Post Qualifying Legal Education: Agricultural Law*, Law Society of Scotland, Edinburgh, 1982, pp. 30–61.

[8] *Mitchell-Gill* v. *Buchan* 1921 S.C. 390 per L. P. Clyde at 395.

[9] *Roger* v. *Hutcheson* 1921 S.C. 787 per Lord Salvesen at 805; affd. 1922 S.C. (H.L.) 140. See also *Westwood* v. *Barnett* 1925 S.C. 624 per L. J. C. Alness at 628.

[10] *Brodie* v. *Ker*, *McCallum* v. *Macnair* 1952 S.C. 216; *Houison-Craufurd's Trustees* v. *Davies* 1951 S.C. 1 per L. J. C. Thomson at 8.

[11] 1949 Act s. 78.

[12] *Craig and Another*, *Apps.* 1981 S.L.T. (Land Ct.) 12; *Taylor* v. *Brick* 1982 S.L.T. 25. For an example of judicial acceptance of a waiver of an imperative statutory provision made solely for the benefit of a class of private individuals see *Suggett* v. *Shaw* 1985 S.L.C.R. 80 at 88.

strictly construed.[13] If a question which should under the Act be
referred to arbitration arises in the course of an action in court,
such as for example an action of removing, the action must be
sisted pending arbitration.[14] The court does, of course, retain the
power to decide whether a matter does or does not require to be
determined by arbitration under the Act.[15] An arbiter can deal with
a question relating to his or her own jurisdiction if it is raised
during the proceedings, but any decision then arrived at may be
reviewed by the ordinary courts in an action of interdict[16] or by
means of the stated case procedure to be found in paragraph 19 of
the Sixth Schedule to the Act or in the course of an appeal to the
Land Court under section 75(1A) of the 1949 Act[17] against an
arbiter's award.

19.7. The jurisdiction of an arbiter under the 1949 Act is laid
down mainly in section 74, which provides that —

'Save as otherwise expressly provided in this Act, any question
or difference of any kind whatsoever between the landlord and
the tenant of an agricultural holding arising out of the tenancy or
in connection with the holding (not being a question or
difference as to liability for rent) shall, whether such question or
difference arises during the currency or on the termination of
the tenancy, be determined by arbitration'.

Such questions may include matters of valuation,[18] except that
items of obligatory waygoing valuation are excluded by s. 75(4). By
virtue of section 75(1), the reference in the non-excluded cases is to
a single arbiter — two arbiters are normal in such waygoing
valuations — and the procedure and award are governed by the
Sixth Schedule to the Act. The provisions of the Arbitration
(Scotland) Act 1894 do not apply in this context.

---

[13] *Westwood* v. *Barnett* 1925 S.C. 624 per L. J .C. Alness at 628.
[14] *Brodie* v. *Ker* 1952 S.C. 216 (conventional irritancy); *Houison-Craufurd's Trustees* v. *Davies* 1951 S.C. 1 (resumption); *McCallum* v. *Macnair* 1952 S.C. 216 (notice to quit).
[15] *Cormack* v. *McIldowie's Trustees* 1974 S.L.T. 178.
[16] *Christison's Trustee* v. *Callendar-Brodie* (1906) 8F 928 per L. P. Dunedin at 931; *Trustees of Donaldson's Hospital* v. *Esslemont* 1925 S.C. 199 per L.P. Clyde at 205.
[17] Inserted by the Agricultural Holdings (Amendment) (Scotland) Act 1983 s. 5(1).
[18] *Stewart* v. *Williamson* 1910 S.C. (H.L.) 47 per Lord Loreburn L.C. at 48.

19.8. A number of other provisions[19] require certain further types of question to be submitted to this form of arbitration. The overlap between these provisions and those of section 74 is such that it has been suggested by an authoritative writer that the former 'may be thought unnecessary'.[20] The drafting might certainly have been improved, integrating more closely into the scheme of the Act the matters here dealt with in sections derived from previous legislation. There are however some instances in which it seems at least not wholly clear that the circumstances are covered by s. 74.[21] Also, in arbitrations under certain sections particular limitation provisions apply[22]; other sections lay special duties upon[23] or grant special powers to[24] an arbiter, and an award has in some cases a particular effect.[25] Moreover Parliament has recently laid it down that slightly different rules relating to the stated case procedure shall apply in arbitrations based on section 7(1) of the Act. It is therefore important to be clear under which section of the Act arbitration is being sought.

19.9. Some words and phrases in section 74 merit particular attention. The reference to a *'question or difference'* indicates that before arbitration under the section can be competently demanded there must be a real point at issue between the parties which is capable of decision.[26] In a case in which the landlord had brought an action for declarator that the tenant had incurred an irritancy of his lease because he had been sequestrated, and in which the tenant had in his pleadings admitted the sequestration, the preliminary plea that the matter should be referred to arbitration under a provision similar to section 74 of the 1949 Act was rejected because there could be no dispute for the arbiter to determine.[27]

---

[19] Ss. 2(2), 4(1), 5(5), 6(1)(2), 7(1), 8(4), 9(1), 12(3), 15(2), 22, 34, 61 and 66(4).

[20] Gill, *Agr. Hold.*, paragraph 330.

[21] In particular, the questions whether or not a lease is simply a grazing lease (s. 2); what terms should be included in a lease where no written lease exists or it is defective (s. 4); and what compensation may be claimed by a tenant from a landlord for damage by game (s. 15).

[22] Ss. 6(1), 7(3), 15(1)(*b*), 27(2), 68(2)(4).

[23] Ss. 4(2) and (3), 7(2), 34, 43, 53, 61.

[24] Ss. 6(3), 9(2).

[25] S. 6(4).

[26] *Brodie* v. *Ker, McCallum* v. *MacNair* (*supra* note 10). See also *Brown* v. *Simpson* 1910 1 S.L.T. 183 at 184.

[27] *Department of Agriculture for Scotland* v. *Fitzsimmons* 1940 S.L.T. (Sh. Ct.) 37.

19.10. The question between the parties must arise in their respective *capacities as landlord and tenant* of an agricultural holding.[28] In a case in which the persons in dispute happened to be landlord and tenant, but the question between them arose in connection with their occupation of adjoining lands, arbitration under the 1949 Act was held not to be competent.[29] Disputes between incoming and outgoing tenants are not determinable by arbitration under the 1949 Act,[30] though of course ordinary arbitration is competent if the parties so agree.

19.11. The terms 'landlord' and 'tenant' are defined in section 93(1) of the Act and 'agricultural holding' in section 1. 'Landlord' includes 'any person for the time being entitled to receive the rents and profits or to take possession of any agricultural holding', and 'tenant' means 'the holder of land under a lease and includes the executor, administrator, assignee, heir-at-law, legatee, disponee, next-of-kin, guardian, curator bonis, or trustee in bankruptcy of a tenant'.[31] Thus, where an estate was sold with entry at Martinmas, and on that date the tenant, by arrangement with the person who was selling it, gave up the holding, the 'landlord' who might be liable to pay compensation to the tenant was the selling owner not the purchaser of the estate.[32] It was considered that the phrase 'for the time being' referred to the point of time, whatever it might be, which was 'relevant' in the context of the particular dispute, such as the date of the termination of the tenancy. The parties must therefore be or have been in the relationship of landlord and tenant of an agricultural holding at the time when there occurred the events which have given rise to the issue between them, though of course, subject to provisions which effectively limit the time within which certain kinds of claims can be made,[33] an arbiter may be appointed and claims presented in the arbitration after the tenant has left the holding. A question may be within the jurisdiction of an arbiter under the Act if it arises between landlord and tenant 'on the termination of the tenancy', but this does not mean that any question between them in connection with the

---

[28] *Exven* v. *Lumsden* 1982 S.L.T. (Sh. Ct.) 105.
[29] *Cameron* v. *Haldane* (1945) 61 Sh. Ct. Rep. 12.
[30] *Roger* v. *Hutcheson* 1922 S.C. (H.L.) 140 per Lord Dunedin at 143.
[31] 1949 Act s. 93(1).
[32] *Waddell* v. *Howat* 1925 S.C. 484.
[33] Ss. 6(1), 7(3), 15(1), 27(2), 68(2)(4), Sixth Schedule paragraph 5.

holding arising out of events occurring after the end of the tenancy must be submitted to arbitration. It has been said[34] that —

> 'these words are clearly intended to be read along with the rest of the section and relate to questions such as the compensation on its termination'.

19.12.   The parties must be landlord and tenant respectively of an *agricultural holding*. A lease of ground which in its terms is clearly a lease for grazing does not create an agricultural holding,[35] and a farm from which the tenant has been ordered by a court to remove because the landlord intends to occupy it himself has been held no longer to be a holding.[36]

19.13.   Section 74 makes provision for the *types of question* which are within the jurisdiction of arbiters under the 1949 Act. With certain specified exceptions, any question 'of any kind whatsoever ... arising out of the tenancy or in connection with the holding' must be referred to arbitration. This is a very wide category, but if it can be established that the issues between the parties lie outside it, an arbiter may be interdicted from acting.[37] It has been considered that a claim for damages based on allegations of delict is not arbitrable under the 1949 Act because —

> 'the law of reparation sits very uneasily with the whole code of the Agricultural Holdings Acts' and 'resort to the ordinary courts cannot ... be ousted unless parties have unequivocally agreed to resolve their differences by arbitration or they are unequivocally statutorily required to do so.'[38]

In that case there was a dispute between a landlord and tenant over whether a certain red stable was within the holding let to the tenant. This was however merely ancillary to the main issue which was whether the landlord was liable to make reparation to the tenants for the death of or injury to some cattle caused, it was alleged, by their having been poisoned by red paint in that stable. The Land Court, to which the tenants' request to appoint an

---

[34] *Craig and Another, Applicants* 1981 S.L.T. (Land Ct.) 12.
[35] *Love* v. *Montgomerie and Logan* 1982 S.L.T. (Sh. Ct.) 60, not following *MacLean* v. *Galloway* 1979 S.L.T. (Sh. Ct.) 32.
[36] *Hendry* v. *Walker* 1926 S.N. 157.
[37] *Love* v. *Montgomerie and Logan* 1982 S.L.T. (Sh. Ct.) 60.
[38] *McDiarmid* v. *Secretary of State for Scotland* 1970 S.L.T. (Land Ct.) 17 at 19; *Cameron* v. *Haldane* (1945) 61 Sh. Ct. Rep. 12.

arbiter had been addressed because the landlord was the Secretary of State,[39] were prepared to appoint an arbiter for the limited purpose of determining whether the red stable formed part of the subjects let, but the parties agreed in terms of section 78 that the whole matter should be dealt with by the Land Court itself. The Court considered, however, that there was no statutory warrant in terms of which either it or an arbiter could entertain the claim for damages, which was based alternatively on delictual and contractual grounds.

19.14. *Certain types of issue are excluded* from arbitration under the 1949 Act. In addition to the matters reserved to the Land Court by that Act and section 11(7) of the Agriculture (Miscellaneous Provisions) Act 1968, questions of liability for rent are expressly excluded by section 74 from arbitration under the Act. In *Brodie* v. *Ker*[40] the court considered whether a question as to liability for rent was raised —

'when a tenant claims to retain rent admittedly due either in security for performance of the landlord's obligations, or as a compulsitor upon the landlord to fulfil some obligation under the lease alleged to have been left unimplemented by him'.

It held that in such circumstances that question was not raised, because questions of liability for rent required to be —

'confined to cases in which the liability to pay the rent sued for is disputed upon grounds which, if sustained, in law extinguish "liability"'.

In another case, where the parties had agreed that a number of questions should be determined by the Land Court, the landlord's solicitor argued, notwithstanding the joint nature of the application, that two of the issues raised by the tenant were incompetent. The tenant, who admitted that some rent was payable, had claimed that it should be reduced because the land had been flooded, and desired the Land Court to fix the rent. The objection to the competency was repelled. A dispute as to the amount of rent payable was not a question of 'liability for rent'.[41]

---

[39] S. 77.
[40] 1952 S.C. 216.
[41] *Boyd* v. *MacDonald* 1958 S.L.C.R. 10.

19.15.   Section 75(4) provides that section 74 does not apply to —

'valuations of sheep stocks, dung, fallow, straw, crops, fences and other specific things the property of an outgoing tenant, agreed under a lease to be taken over from him at the termination of a tenancy by a landlord or the incoming tenant, or to any questions which it may be necessary to determine in order to ascertain the sum to be paid in pursuance of such agreement, and that whether such valuations and questions are referred to arbitration under the lease or not.'

The valuation of bound sheep stocks in such cases is governed by other legislation and is discussed briefly below.[42]

19.16.   **Demand for arbitration.** In arbitrations under the 1949 Act, either party may in most types of case demand arbitration, though naturally the demand must be in clear terms.[43] There are however some types of case in which only the landlord,[44] or only the tenant, may demand arbitration, and that within a specified period. A landlord's demand under section 6(1) for arbitration of compensation for his or her tenant's failure to discharge liability for maintenance etc. of fixed equipment must be made within the 'prescribed period', i.e. one month from the date on which the transfer took effect.[45] Similarly, a tenant's demand under section 27(2) for arbitration of questions arising in certain circumstances out of a notice to quit must be made within one month of the service of that notice.[46] The consequence of a demand for arbitration in this last case is that the tenant's counter notice — which would otherwise render the notice to quit inoperative unless confirmed by the Land Court — is of no effect.[47]

19.17.   Though the language of the sections does not seem to identify demand for arbitration with agreement to appoint an arbiter or application to the Secretary of State as described in the next paragraph, it would seem wise in default of such agreement to

---

[42] Paragraphs 19.53–19.58.

[43] *Jack* v. *King* (1932) 48 Sh. Ct. Rep. 242.

[44] Who may be an uninfeft proprietor: *Black and Sons* v. *Paterson* 1968 S.L.T. (Sh. Ct.) 64.

[45] Agricultural Holdings (Scotland) Regulations 1950 (S.I. 1950 No. 1553) reg. 5.

[46] *Ibid.* reg. 7(1).

[47] Agriculture (Miscellaneous Provisions) Act 1976 s. 14(2).

make an application to the Secretary of State within the time specified by the statute (and indicated here in the preceding paragraph) for demanding arbitration.

19.18. Delay in demanding arbitration on a claim may on general legal principles bar a claim where the delay is such that it has led the other party reasonably to believe that the claim has been abandoned and would cause prejudice were the claim to be entertained.[48] In some circumstances it may have the result that the claim cannot be made the subject of a counterclaim in an action by the other party, and that the court refuses to sist the action pending arbitration.[49] Also, certain types of claim become unenforceable after the expiration of periods prescribed by statute.[50] If the period for making a particular type of claim has admittedly elapsed, a reference to arbitration under the Act will become incompetent, because there will in effect be no dispute which an arbiter could properly entertain.

19.19. Special rules apply where either landlord or tenant demands arbitration of a claim arising on or out of the termination of the tenancy of the holding or part thereof. A claim must be made within two months from the termination of the tenancy.[51] Within one month from the expiration of the period allowed under section 68(3) for the settlement of the claim — four months with the possibility of up to two two-month extensions on application to the Secretary of State — or such longer time as the Secretary of State may in special circumstances allow, either an arbiter must have been appointed by agreement between the parties or an application must have been made to the Secretary of State (or Land Court, if appropriate) for an appointment.[52] There is no obligation on the Secretary of State to reveal the special circumstances which weighed with him in allowing an extension of time.[53]

---

[48] Walker D. M., *The Law of Civil Remedies in Scotland*, Edinburgh, 1974, 1259; *Taylor* v. *Earl of Moray*, (1892) 19 R. 399 per Lord Kinnear at 402; *Evans* v. *Cameron* 6 March 1981 (Unreported) Elgin Sheriff Court.

[49] *Shewan* v. *Johnston* (1933) 49 Sh. Ct. Rep. 285 at 287; but see *Galbraith* v. *Ardnacross Farming Co.* 1953 S.L.T. (Notes) 29.

[50] For such periods, see e.g. ss. 15(1), 68(2).

[51] s. 68(2).

[52] 1949 Act s. 68(4).

[53] *Crawford's Trustees* v. *Smith* 1952 S.L.T. (Notes) 5.

19.20. **Appointment of arbiter**. This is regulated by section 75 of the Act and paragraph 1 of the Sixth Schedule. Arbitration must be by a single arbiter[54]; reference to two arbiters with an oversman, which was once common in agricultural disputes, is no longer competent in cases governed by the 1949 Act.

19.21. The parties may make an appointment by *agreement*. This requires —

'a document in writing under the hands of the landlord and tenant (or it may be their agents) appointing a named arbiter to determine a specified dispute'.[55]

Presumably the appointment must be successful — in other words the parties must earlier have approached the person nominated and obtained his or her consent.

19.22. In the *absence of agreement* — and agreement need not have been attempted[56] — either party may apply in writing to the Secretary of State (or the Land Court where the Secretary of State is a party)[57] for the appointment of an arbiter. This should be done in one of the forms specified in Schedule 2 to the Agricultural Holdings (Specification of Forms) (Scotland) Order 1983.[58] Though the use of the form seems from the permissive language of regulation 3 of the Order not to be mandatory, it is desirable, because it directs attention to the need to provide certain information, in particular the nature of the issue between the parties. It has been wisely remarked[59] that —

'in the application form the question or difference should be formulated with care because the wording used by the applicant will be repeated by the Secretary of State in the instrument of appointment'

of the arbiter.

19.23. Where the appointment is made by the Secretary of State or the Land Court the arbiter is selected from a panel of persons

[54] S. 75.
[55] *Chalmers Property Investment Co.* v. *MacColl* 1951 S.C. 24 per L. P. Cooper at 29.
[56] *Ibid.* at 30.
[57] 1949 Act s. 77.
[58] S.I. 1983 No. 1073 (S. 100).
[59] Gill, *Agr. Hold.*, paragraph 338.

appointed in terms of section 76 of the 1949 Act. Before the letter containing an appointment is issued by the Secretary of State, the agreement of the selected person is first obtained informally,[60] so that in effect the arbiter offers his or her services and the appointment completes the transaction. It has been held unnecessary for the selected person formally to intimate acceptance.[61] It is the practice for a copy of the letter of appointment to be sent to each of the parties at the same time as the original is sent to the arbiter.[62]

19.24.   The selection has been held to be an administrative act[63] but it is subject to the supervisory jurisdiction of the Court of Session at least for the purposes of ensuring that the Secretary of State acts within his or her statutory powers.[64] The extent of that jurisdiction is not wholly clear. For example, though it may be that the Secretary of State, like the court which was itself in a similar position under previous legislation, should not take account of matters external to the particular dispute concerned when deciding whether to make an appointment,[65] it does not follow that a court could give a remedy if such matters were considered. However, if a person who was not on the statutory panel were to be appointed, an application for judicial review under Rule 260B of the Rules of Court[66] would be likely to succeed. It might also succeed if the choice had fallen on a person who, for reasons of his interest in the case or relationship to one of the parties, would certainly be disqualified on ordinary common law grounds,[67] for this would surely be struck down as unreasonable.[68]

19.25.   In certain circumstances a *new arbiter* may be appointed as if the first appointment had never been made. This may be done if

---

[60] Gill, *Agr. Hold.*, paragraph 340.
[61] *Sheriff* v. *Christie* (1953) 69 Sh. Ct. Rep. 88 at 92.
[62] *Suggett* v. *Shaw* 1985 S.L.C.R. 80 at 87.
[63] *Ramsay* v. *McLaren and Others* 1936 S.L.T. 35 per Lord Mackay at 36.
[64] *Moss' Empires* v. *Assessor for Glasgow* 1917 S.C. (H.L.) 1 per Lord Shaw at 11. For a recent discussion of the scope of judicial review see St. Clair J. and Davidson N. F., *Judicial Review in Scotland*, Edinburgh, 1986, chapter 3.
[65] *Easson* v. *Morison* (1890) 6 Sh. Ct. Rep. 46.
[66] Inserted by Act of Sederunt (Rules of Court Amendment No. 2) (Judicial Review) 1985, S.I. 1985 No. 500 (S. 48).
[67] See paragraphs 4.49–4.55 above.
[68] *Brown* v. *Hamilton District Council* 1983 S.L.T. 397 at 414, accepting the dictum of Lord Greene M. R. in *Associated Provincial Picture Houses Ltd.* v.

the original arbiter has died, or is 'incapable of acting', or has failed to act within seven days after receiving notice in writing from either party requiring action.[69] It has been held that the phrase 'incapable of acting' may include incapacity due to removal for misconduct or valid revocation of the appointment, for its meaning —

'is not . . . limited to incapacity to act by reason of some physical or mental disability, but means incapacity to act however that incapacity may arise.'[70]

The fact that the date of the new arbiter's appointment occurs after the expiry of any mandatory period within which an original appointment must be made does not invalidate the new appointment if the first appointment was timeous.[71]

19.26. An arbiter's appointment may be *revoked* by the parties only by notice in writing under the hands of both of them.[72] The wording of the Sixth Schedule to the Act does not suggest that an appointment by either the Secretary of State or the Land Court is immune from revocation by agreement of the parties.[73]

19.27. **Appointment of clerk.** An arbiter may appoint a clerk in the arbitration, but unless the appointment is made after the submission of the claim and answers to the arbiter and with either the consent of the parties or the sanction of the sheriff, the clerk's remuneration and expenses cannot be charged against any of the parties.[74] The object of this rule is no doubt to keep expense to a minimum; its effect is presumably that failure to comply means that the arbiter has to pay the clerk out of his or her own pocket, as the clerk's contract is with the arbiter, not the parties.[75] A sheriff will not reject an arbiter's request to sanction the appointment of a clerk if the arbiter specifies the legal questions which he or she thinks arise in the arbitration, and if the sheriff thinks these are —

Wednesbury Corporation [1948] 1 K.B. 223 as stating a principle which was also part of the law of Scotland.

[69] Sixth Schedule, paragraphs 2 and 4.
[70] *Dundee Corporation* v. *Guthrie* 1969 S.L.T. 93 per L. J. C. Grant at 98.
[71] *Ibid.*; *Graham* v. *Gardner* 1966 S.L.T. (Land Ct.) 12.
[72] Sixth Schedule paragraphs 3 and 4.
[73] This is also the opinion of Gill, *Agr. Hold.*, paragraph 343 and J. Muir Watt, *Agricultural Holdings* 12th edn. 1967, 525.
[74] Sixth Schedule, paragraph 18.
[75] See paragraph 3.28 above.

'such that it would be reasonable that a lay arbiter should have the assistance of a lawyer for their decision.'[76]

19.28. Statement and particulars of case. Paragraph 5 of the Sixth Schedule requires that —

'each of the parties to the arbitration shall within twenty-eight days[77] from the appointment of the arbiter deliver to him a statement of that party's case with all necessary particulars ...'

The Schedule does not require a copy to be sent to the opposing party, but it is contrary to fair pleading not to do so. The arbiter should enquire whether this has been done, and ensure that each party receives proper notice of the opposing case.

19.29. No provision is made in the Act for extension of time, even by leave of the arbiter, and it has been held[78] that the paragraph has to be read as imposing an 'absolute obligation' on the parties to lodge their claims within the specified period. However, it has since been considered on the basis of the principle of waiver[79] that —

'while ... an arbiter cannot by order strictly extend the peremptory time limit of 28 days, he can nevertheless within his discretion give effect to an agreement between parties that he should entertain a late statement of claim'.[80]

The period of 28 days runs from the date of the arbiter's appointment, not from the date of any subsequent letter to the parties informing them of the appointment or requesting them to lodge statements of their cases.[81]

19.30. It is thought that the statement of the case and the particulars are not necessarily two separate documents,[82] but it seems clear that the statement must,

[76] *Henderson* v. *Dunnet and Haldane* 1935 S.L.T. (Sh. Ct.) 41.
[77] Twenty one days in milk quota compensation cases under S.I. 1986 No. 1613 reg. 15, and in S.I. 1986 No. 1614.
[78] *Jameson* v. *Clark* (1951) 67 Sh. Ct. Rep. 17 at 19–20. This case was decided prior to the amendment of the Sixth Schedule by the Agriculture (Miscellaneous Provisions) Act 1963, when the period was 14 days.
[79] Citing with approval Maxwell Sir P. B., *The interpretation of statutes*, 12th edn., London, 1969, 328.
[80] *Suggett* v. *Shaw* 1985 S.L.C.R. 80 at 88.
[81] *Ibid.* at 89.
[82] Gill, *Agr. Hold.*, paragraph 346.

'while probably not implying a condescendence and pleas in law, . . . mean a document with short averments or statements of fact setting out the nature of the claim and whether, for example, it is founded on obligations contained in the lease or on statutory provisions'.[83]

It has been indicated that where a party wishes to raise a question of competency, fair pleading demands that this should be done formally by the stating of a plea in law.[84] As to the particulars, it has been declared[85] that these must —

'afford to the recipient fair notice of the basis of the demand which is being made against him . . .'

19.31. Except with the consent of the arbiter, the statement and particulars of the case may only be adjusted or otherwise amended or added to within the initial 28-day period.[86] It has been wisely suggested[87] that —

'an arbiter ought normally to allow to each party, as soon as the statements of claim are lodged, a period within which to answer the other's averments in order that the issues of fact may be properly focussed.'

In England it has been held that extensive amendments may be allowed,[88] and there is no reason to believe that a Scottish court would come to a different conclusion.

19.32. **The hearing**. The Sixth Schedule to the 1949 Act does not regulate in detail the procedure at and immediately prior to the hearing. Where it lays down no specific rules, the rules and principles which govern ordinary arbitrations apply.[89] Broadly speaking, these allow the arbiter a wide discretion in matters of procedure, subject to the duty to act fairly as between the parties.[90] The Schedule does however contain some specific rules.

---

[83] *Robertson's Trustees* v. *Cunningham* 1951 S.L.T. (Sh. Ct.) 89 at 92.

[84] *Boyd* v. *MacDonald* 1958 S.L.C.R. 10 at 12.

[85] In *Simpson* v. *Henderson* 1944 S.C. 365 per L. J. C. Cooper at 370.

[86] Sixth Schedule paragraph 5(a).

[87] Gill, *Agr. Hold.*, paragraph 347. N.B. dicta in *Robertson's Trustees* v. *Cunningham* 1951 S.L.T. (Sh. Ct.) 89 at 92.

[88] *E.D. and A.D. Cooke Bourne (Farms)* v. *Mellows* [1983] Q.B. 104.

[89] For a detailed discussion, see Chapters Twelve and Thirteen above.

[90] *Holmes Oil Co.* v. *Pumpherston Oil Co.* (1890) 17 R. 624, affd. 18 R. (H.L.) 52; *Dundas* v. *Hogg and Allan* (1937) S.L.T. (Sh. Ct.) 2 at 4.

19.33. It clearly confines the parties at the hearing to 'the matters alleged in the statement and particulars'.[91] Since it is facts, not pleas in law, which can in normal parlance be said to be 'alleged', the statute may not debar a party from presenting at the hearing legal arguments for which a basis had not previously been laid, but it would normally be contrary to fair pleading to do so[92] and the arbiter should therefore exercise his procedural discretion — which is very wide[93] — to prevent surprise. It has been considered by a sheriff that matters not contained in the statement or particulars, as duly amended, are not rendered admissible by their having been referred to in evidence by the opposing party.[94]

19.34. A more investigatory procedure than that of the ordinary courts is apparently envisaged, for paragraph 6 of the Schedule requires the parties and all persons claiming through them, to

'submit to be examined by the arbiter on oath or affirmation in relation to the matters in dispute'

unless they can state a legal objection,[95] though the arbiter has no duty to administer an oath or affirmation.[96] It also obliges them to —

'produce before the arbiter all samples, books, deeds, papers, accounts, writings and documents within their possession or power respectively which may be required or called for, and do all other things which during the proceedings the arbiter may require.'

The requirements of the arbiter may include entry on property for the purposes of inspection. At least, given that it is recognised that an arbiter may, and sometimes — as for example where the dispute relates to the value of certain things — must, make an inspection,[97] it would be inconsistent to permit his or her exclusion.

19.35. An expert arbiter is generally entitled to base his or her

[91] Paragraph 5(b).
[92] *Adam* v. *Smythe* 1948 S.C. 445 per Lord Keith at 455–6.
[93] *Dundas* v. *Hogg and Allan* (*supra* note 90); *Christison's Trustee* v. *Callendar-Brodie* (1906) 8 F. 928 per L.P. Dunedin at 931.
[94] *Stewart* v. *Brims* 1969 S.L.T. (Sh. Ct.) 2.
[95] See on the oath generally, Walkers, *Evidence*, paragraph 337.
[96] *MacLean* v. *Chalmers Property Investment Co. Ltd.* 1951 S.L.T. (Sh. Ct.) 71.
[97] *Graham* v. *Mill* (1904) 6 F. 886.

conclusions on personal inspection[98] without recourse to proof,[99] since the rules of evidence applied in ordinary court proceedings do not apply in arbitration,[100] and arbiters normally have a very wide discretion in matters of procedure.[101] There are however circumstances in which even an expert arbiter must be careful to apprise the parties of information which is within his or her own knowledge and which is intended to be used in coming to a decision. This is particularly true in cases concerned with the determination of rent under section 7 of the 1949 Act. In one such case it was judicially remarked[102] that while an arbiter —

> 'may indeed have to exercise investigatory powers to obtain proper evidence or in the event of a dearth of evidence to introduce his own comparative evidence ... [he] must act judicially in accordance with the rules of natural justice which entails [*sic*] that he must divulge to parties for their comment at or before the hearing any specific facts or specific comparables on which he expects to base his rental determination. This also applies to improvements, which not infrequently come to light at inspection having been overlooked in formal evidence. Both sides must be present for comment.'

An arbiter does not, however, require in such cases to 'go out to look for' evidence relating to the factors listed in section 7(1A), but merely to 'consider' evidence that apparently exists.[103] Moreover, it is not open to a party to bring an award under review merely on the basis of an allegation that the arbiter's inspection was insufficient,[104] for it is apparently presumed that the arbiter, having been selected for his or her expertise, will have exercised it properly. It has been suggested[105] that, since the Land Court has applied in its own proceedings the normal requirements of legal proof where the facts are not especially open to the special expertise of members of the Court,[106] arbiters should do likewise. It is no doubt in many instances wise to follow such a principle, but it

---

[98] *McNabb* v. *A. and J. Anderson* 1955 S.L.T. 73 at 77.

[99] *Fletcher* v. *Robertson* 1918 1 S.L.T. 68.

[100] *Earl of Seafield* v. *Stewart* 1985 S.L.C.R. 64 at 73.

[101] Discussed in Chapters Twelve and Thirteen above.

[102] *Earl of Seafield* v. *Stewart* (*supra* note 100) at 72.

[103] *Aberdeen Endowments Trust* v. *Will* 1985 S.L.C.R. 38 at 56.

[104] *Johnson* v. *Lamb* 1981 S.L.T. 300; *Secretary of State for Scotland* v. *Young*, 1960 S.L.C.R. 31; *Sim* v. *McConnell and Stevenson* (1936) 52 Sh. Ct. Rep. 324.

[105] Gill, *Agr. Hold.*, paragraph 375.

[106] *Smith* v. *Marquis of Aberdeen's Trustees* 1916 S.C. 905.

is submitted that in view of the wide discretion of arbiters generally this is not required by law.

19.36. The Secretary of State has power under section 75(2) to make rules by statutory instrument to make such provision as he thinks desirable for expediting proceedings in arbitrations under the 1949 Act, but the power has not yet[107] been exercised.

19.37. **The stated case.** There are now only two situations in which there is no power at all in an arbiter to state a case or in parties to require a case to be stated — an ordinary arbitration in which the parties have expressly provided, in the agreement to refer to arbitration, that a case may not be stated,[108] and in milk quota compensation cases.[109] However, since the coming into force of the Agricultural Holdings (Amendment) (Scotland) Act 1983 the stated case in statutory régimes has been governed by slightly different provisions, according to whether the arbiter was appointed by agreement of the parties on the one hand or by the Secretary of State or the Land Court on the other. Party-appointed arbiters are governed by paragraph 19 of the Sixth Schedule which provides that —

'The arbiter may at any stage of the proceedings, and shall, if so directed by the sheriff (which direction may be given on the application of either party), state a case for the opinion of the sheriff on any question of law arising in the course of the arbitration.'

It has been judicially remarked[110] that the object of a similar section in a previous Act was —

'to give the parties to the arbitration, and the arbiter himself, the advantage of the services of a legal assessor, whenever that seems to be desirable.'

19.38. In arbitrations under section 7(1) of the Act concerning variation of rent, where the arbiter has been appointed by the Secretary of State or the Land Court, a new paragraph 20A

---

[107] 1 May 1987.
[108] The decision in *Johnson-Ferguson* v. *Board of Agriculture* 1921 S.C. 103 is superseded.
[109] Under S.I. 1986 No. 1613 reg. 15(3)(*d*) and S.I. 1986 No. 1614.
[110] *Cathcart* v. *Board of Agriculture for Scotland* 1916 S.C. 166, per L.P. Strathclyde at 167.

applies, having been inserted into the 1949 Act of section 5(2)(*f*) of the 1983 Act. The new paragraph provides that in such cases paragraphs 19 and 20 of the Sixth Schedule shall not apply, but instead —

> 'the arbiter may at any stage in the proceedings state a case (whether at the request of either party or on his own initiative) on any question of law arising in the course of the arbitration for the opinion of the Land Court, whose decision shall be final.'

19.39.   The terms of paragraph 19 and 20A are similar, but not identical, to each other and to the terms of section 3(1) of the Administration of Justice (Scotland) Act 1972, which by virtue of subsection (2) of that section does not apply to arbitrations under the 1949 Act. The most important difference between paragraphs 19 and 20A of the Sixth Schedule to the 1949 Act (as amended) on the one hand and section 3(1) of the 1972 Act on the other is that the 1949 Act provisions, unlike those of the 1972 Act, enable the arbiter to state a case on his or her own motion. In one respect, however, paragraph 19 and Section 3(1) — which both enable a party to seek the assistance of the court[111] to require an arbiter to state a case — are more similar to each other than either is to the new paragraph 20A, which makes no such provision. Arbiters officially appointed in cases of variation of rent under section 7(1) of the 1949 Act, cannot now be compelled, though they may be requested by either party, to state a case. An application may be made to the sheriff — either the sheriff or the sheriff principal[112] — for a direction only in relation to party-appointed arbiters, and it should be noted that a motion for such a direction made in the course of a hearing on a case already stated does not constitute an 'application'.[113]

19.40.   There is no mechanism by which the parties can dictate the content of the case which is stated.[114] All that can be said is that there are two ways of influencing it, namely either —

[111] Under paragraph 19 the sheriff.

[112] When the 1949 Act was framed, the Interpretation Act 1889 s. 28, being uncontradicted, had the effect of including both sheriff and sheriff substitute. S. 4 of the Sheriff Courts (Scotland) Act 1971 and Schedule 1 of the Interpretation Act 1978 have the same result. In any event, s. 91 of the 1949 Act itself suggests that (to use the modern terms) either sheriff principal or sheriff may exercise these powers.

[113] *Wilson-Clarke* v. *Graham* 1963 S.L.T. (Sh. Ct.) 2 at 4.

[114] *Forsyth-Grant* v. *Salmon* 1961 S.L.T. (Notes) 38.

'by persuasion [of the arbiter] at adjustment, ... [or] by persuading the sheriff that there are proper grounds for putting some pressure on the arbiter to amplify or explicate the original case.'[115]

Only the first of these applies where officially-appointed arbiters are concerned. In other cases the sheriff may remit a case back to the arbiter to have certain findings explained, but

'it is not, in general, the function of the Court in a stated case to entertain the kind of representations which may be made to an arbiter against his own proposed findings.'[116]

19.41. The opinion of the sheriff or of the Land Court is binding on the arbiter.[117] In cases not involving officially-appointed arbiters either party may within three months[118] appeal against the opinion of the sheriff by applying to the Court of Session in accordance with Rules of Court 267–273. There is here no appeal from the decision of the Court of Session.[119] There is no appeal from the opinion of the Land Court under paragraph 20A.

19.42. Once the award itself has been promulgated—and the question of what amounts to the promulgation of an award has been discussed above[120] — it is no longer competent for the arbiter to state a case, or for a party to request this to be done,[121] though an attempt by the arbiter to avoid doing so by hastening to promulgate the award might in some circumstances be regarded as misconduct. It has long been the practice for arbiters to issue proposed findings,[122] and it is perfectly competent for a stated case to be requested and made after this has been done.[123] From the point of view of one or other of the parties proposed findings at this stage may be helpful for they may facilitate a decision whether to request a stated case.

[115] Ibid. per L.J.C. Thomson at 39.
[116] *Chalmers Property Investment Co.* v. *Bowman* 1953 S.L.T. (Sh. Ct.) 38.
[117] *Mitchell-Gill* v. *Buchan* 1921 S.C. 390 per L.P. Clyde at 395.
[118] Act of Sederunt (Rules of Court, Consolidation and Amendment) 1965 (S.I. 1965 No. 321) as amended by S.I. 1974 No. 845; Sheriff Courts (Scotland) Act 1907, First Schedule, paragraph 86.
[119] Sixth Schedule, paragraph 20.
[120] Paragraphs 15.61–15.63.
[121] *Johnson* v. *Gill* 1978 S.C. 74.
[122] *Baxter* v. *Macarthur* (1836) 14 S. 549.
[123] *Mackenzie* v. *MacGillivray* 1921 S.C. 722.

19.43. **The award.** Awards under the 1949 Act have always been regulated more closely by the law than awards in ordinary arbitration, but since the coming into force of the Agricultural Holdings (Amendment) (Scotland) Act 1983 the requirements in variation of rent cases under section 7(1) of the 1949 Act have become more stringent. It has been judicially remarked[124] that —

> 'Agricultural arbiters ... now have higher standards imposed upon them by statute and statutory regulation. These changes appear designed to tighten up and clarify decisions in statutory arbitrations where the awards are now to be made publicly available.'

19.44. The law regulates the following aspects of an arbitral award made under the 1949 Act —

(a) the time within which it must be made and signed (paragraph 8);

(b) the form of the award (paragraph 10 and regulations made thereunder[125]); and

(c) the content of the award (paragraphs 9, 9A, and 11–13).

It also permits an arbiter to make an interim award for the payment of a sum on account of that to be finally awarded,[126] and to correct clerical mistakes or errors arising from any accidental slips or omissions,[127] and provides that, subject to the right to appeal introduced by section 5(1) of the 1983 Act,[128] an award is final and binding on the parties and any persons claiming right under them.[129]

19.45. Certain statutory *time limits* must be observed. The arbiter must 'make and sign' the award within three[130] months of the appointment or such longer period as may be agreed to in writing by the parties or be fixed by the Secretary of State.[131]

---

[124] *Earl of Seafield* v. *Stewart* 1985 S.L.C.R. 64 at 71.

[125] On which see below paragraph 19.46.

[126] Paragraph 9.

[127] Paragraph 15.

[128] By inserting a new subsection 1A into section 75 of the 1949 Act.

[129] Paragraph 14.

[130] Amended period prescribed by section 5(2)(a) of the 1983 Act. In milk quota compensation cases the period is thirty five days: S.I. 1986 No. 1613 reg. 15(3)(b) and S.I. 1986 No. 1614.

[131] Sixth Schedule, paragraph 8.

Whether this means that it must not only be drafted and signed but also promulgated is unclear, since the reported cases on promulgation arise out of different statutory language. The form by which an arbiter may apply to the Secretary of State for extension of time is laid down in Schedule 2 to the Agricultural Holdings (Specification of Forms) (Scotland) Order 1983.[132] Extension may be sought and granted before or after the original time limit has expired.[133] Since there is no legal restriction on the grant of an extension, and since an award issued outwith the time limit — original or extended — is invalid, and since it has been held to be misconduct for an arbiter to issue his or her award outwith that time limit,[134] an arbiter must request an extension if there is any risk that the award will not be completed in time, rather than issue an award out of time and hope that nobody will notice the defect.

19.46. The *form* of an award under the 1949 Act is regulated by the 1983 Order mentioned above. If the appropriate form is used, it is sufficient in law,[135] though it should of course be signed. In a case in which a typewritten award was delivered to the parties unsigned, proof was allowed whether the award was genuine.[136] The validity of the award had not been challenged by the defender in his pleas, no action of reduction had been raised, and no attempt had been made to set the award aside *ope exceptionis*. The case must therefore be treated with reserve.

19.47. Where the arbiter has been appointed by the Secretary of State or the Land Court, he or she must if either party so requires, state the reasons for the decision.[137] Similarly, if the appointment so made is, in terms of section 7 of the 1949 Act, for the purpose of determining the rent payable in respect of the holding as from the next ensuing day on which the tenancy could have been terminated by notice to quit, the arbiter is obliged in terms of paragraph 9A of the Sixth Schedule (as amended) to state in writing the findings of fact and the reasons for the decision, and to make such statement available not only to the parties but also to the Secretary of State.

---

[132] S.I. 1983 No. 1073 (S. 100).
[133] *Dundas* v. *Hogg and Allan* 1937 S.L.T. (Sh. Ct.) 2.
[134] *Halliday* v. *Semple* 1960 S.L.T. (Sh. Ct.) 11.
[135] Sixth Schedule, paragraph 23.
[136] *Cameron* v. *McKay* (1938) 54 Sh. Ct. Rep. 276.
[137] Tribunals and Inquiries Act 1971 s. 12 and Schedule I Part II.

These rules do not apply in 'private' arbitrations where the parties have agreed on the appointment.[138]

19.48.   Paragraphs 11 to 13 of the Sixth Schedule to the 1949 Act contain a number of mandatory provisions relating to the *content* of awards. The arbiter is required —

(a) to state separately in his or her award the amounts awarded in respect of the several claims referred;
(b) to specify, on the application of either party, the amount awarded in respect of any particular improvement or any particular matter which was the subject of the award; and
(c) to fix a day not later than one month after delivery of the award for the payment of any money awarded as compensation, expenses or otherwise.[139]

Where the Act provides for compensation under an agreement to be substituted for compensation under the Act, the arbiter must award accordingly. In addition, the rules of ordinary arbitration require that the award shall exhaust and must not exceed the matters submitted. Paragraphs 16 and 17 allow the arbiter discretion in directing by whom 'the expenses of and incidental to the arbitration and award' are to be paid, but require that the reasonableness of the parties' respective claims and behaviour in conducting the case must be taken into account. The expenses incurred in preparing and submitting a stated case are for the arbiter to deal with,[140] but those incurred in sheriff court proceedings and in any appeal against the sheriff's decision are for the court.[141]

19.49.   Section 13 of the Agriculture (Miscellaneous Provisions) Act 1976 gives an arbiter a power to issue certain directions in cases where the dispute relates to the fact that the landlord has under section 25(2)(*e*) of the 1949 Act served on the tenant a demand in writing to remedy a breach of a term in the lease by doing remedial work. Section 13 gives the arbiter power to alter or specify the period during which the work must be done, in accordance with

[138] *Aberdeen Endowments Trust* v. *Will* 1985 S.L.C.R. 38 at 41.
[139] In milk quota compensation cases, a day may be fixed for payment of money awarded only in respect of expenses: S.I. 1986 No. 1613 reg. 15(3)(*c*); S.I. 1986 No. 1614.
[140] *Thomson* v. *Earl of Galloway* 1919 S.C. 611.
[141] *McQuater* v. *Fergusson* 1911 S.C. 640.

what in the circumstances he or she feels is reasonable, or to delete items which are unnecessary or unjustified, or substitute a different method or material for that demanded, where the latter would involve undue difficulty or expense. Apart from such substitution, there is no power to amend the demand.

19.50. The detailed requirements of the Act concerning the factors which arbiters have to take into account when deciding the different types of case which may arise are not considered here, as this work is concerned with arbitration, not agricultural law. Suffice it to say that normally an award will be sufficient if all the headings to part IV of the style of schedule set out in Schedule 1 of the 1983 Order have been completed by listing the relevant facts found to have been proved, and that the style need not be slavishly followed, but may be modified or supplemented as circumstances require.[142]

19.51. **Remedies.** A dissatisfied party has a remedy either against the arbiter personally or against the award. So far as the arbiter personally is concerned, application may be made to the sheriff to remove him or her for misconduct.[143] The nature of misconduct has been discussed earlier[144] so far as ordinary arbitration is concerned. Probably 'misconduct' under the 1949 Act includes behaviour which would constitute corruption, bribery or falsehood under item twenty-five of the Articles of Regulation 1695. In general, however, the same rules apply in the context of arbitration under the 1949 Act as in ordinary arbitration. In addition, a failure on the part of the arbiter to comply with a peremptory requirement,[145] but not a discretionary provision,[146] of the Act will constitute misconduct.

19.52. Paragraph 22 of the Sixth Schedule to the 1949 Act gives power to the sheriff to set an award aside[147] where the arbiter who issued it has misconducted himself, or the award has been improperly procured. It is incompetent, in the course of

---

[142] *Earl of Seafield* v. *Stewart* 1985 S.L.C.R. 64 at 71.
[143] Sixth Schedule, paragraph 21.
[144] In paragraphs 12.25–12.29 above.
[145] *Halliday* v. *Semple* 1960 S.L.T. (Sh. Ct.) 11.
[146] *MacLean* v. *Chalmers Property Investment Co. Ltd.* 1951 S.L.T. (Sh. Ct.) 71.
[147] Except in milk quota compensation cases under S.I. 1986 No. 1613 reg. 15(3)(*d*) and S.I. 1986 No. 1614.

proceedings to set aside an award, for the arbiter to lodge a minute offering to make good the error complained of.[148] In addition to the statutory remedies, an award may be reduced under the ordinary common law powers of the Court of Session.[149]

19.53. Since the coming into force of the 1983 Act, which inserted a new subsection (1A) into section 75 of the 1949 Act, there has been provision for appeal against the award of an arbiter in certain cases of variation of rent brought under section 7(1) of the 1949 Act. The right of appeal only applies where the arbiter was appointed by the Secretary of State or the Land Court, and may be exercised by application to the Land Court within two months of the date of issue of the award complained of. The appeal may however raise not only questions of law but also questions of fact, and in an appropriate case the Land Court may decide to hear the whole case *de novo*.[150]

Bound sheep stock valuations

19.54. Detailed discussion of bound sheep stock valuation procedures may be found in specialist literature on agricultural law.[151] The subject is worth mentioning here so that attention may be drawn to legislation enacted since the main works on agricultural law were written.

19.55. Valuations of sheep stocks, though subject to quite detailed legislative regulation concerning the matters to be taken into account by arbiters and as to the particulars required to be shown in awards, are closer to ordinary arbitration than those governed by the 1949 Act, and the Arbitration (Scotland) Act 1894 is not excluded. The stated case provisions of the Administration of Justice (Scotland) Act 1972 do not, however, apply to valuations of bound sheep stocks.[152] Sheep stock valuations to which neither

---

[148] *Duke of Argyll* v. *MacArthur and Campbell* 1943 Sh. Ct. Rep. 91.

[149] *Dunlop* v. *Mundell and others* 1943 S.L.T. 286; *Brodie-James* v. *Brown* 1917 1 S.L.T. 49.

[150] As in *Earl of Seafield* v. *Stewart* (*supra* note 142) and *Aberdeen Endowments Trust* v. *Will* (*supra* note 138).

[151] See e.g. Gill *Agr. Hold.*, Chapter 25.

[152] In the opinion of the present writer they are excluded by subsection 3(2) of the 1972 Act. For a contrary view see Gill, *Agr. Hold.*, paragraph 335.

the 1949 Act nor the 1937 Act apply may be ordinary arbitrations governed by the rules expounded in Parts B and C of this book.

19.56. Section 1 of the 1937 Act does not itself require arbitration, but it does provide that where under a lease the tenant must leave the stock of sheep on the holding to be taken over by the landlord or incoming tenant at an arbiter's valuation, the arbiter must show the basis of the valuation of the stock and state separately in the award any amounts included for special factors such as acclimatisation. This provision is amplified by section 28 of and the Second Schedule to the Hill Farming Act 1946, which lay down a method of valuation. This schedule was by 1985 considered to be outdated, and provision was made in section 32 of the Law Reform (Miscellaneous Provisions) (Scotland) Act 1985 for regulations to be made varying it for the purposes of valuations made in respect of leases entered into after the making of the variation. Those regulations have now been made and came into force on 1st December 1986.[153]

19.57. Under section 30 of the 1946 Act the outgoing tenant is obliged to produce to the arbiter a statement of the sales of sheep from the stock whose value has been submitted for determination, together with such sales notes or other evidence as the arbiter may require to vouch the accuracy of the statement.

19.58. Under section 2 of the 1937 Act a case may be stated by the arbiter at his or her option, or on the direction of the sheriff if either of the parties so requests, for the opinion of the sheriff on any question of law arising in the course of the arbitration.

19.59. The arbiter is required by section 1(1) of the 1937 Act to —

'show the basis of valuation of each class of stock and state separately any amounts included in respect of acclimatisation or hefting or of any other consideration or factor for which he has made special allowance.'

If this is not done, the award may be set aside by the sheriff under subsection (2) of that section,[154] though the exercise of the power is

---

[153] Hill Farming Act 1946 (Variation of Second Schedule) (Scotland) Order 1986 (S.I. 1986 No. 1823).
[154] As in *Paynter* v. *Rutherford* 1940 S.L.T. (Sh. Ct.) 18.

discretionary.[155] It is not competent for an arbiter to lodge a minute offering to make good any failure to indicate the basis of the valuation,[156] or to give evidence explaining the meaning of the text of the award,[157] but questions may be asked to ascertain whether or not he or she acted within his or her jurisdiction in making the valuation.[158]

[155] *Dunlop* v. *Mundell and Others* 1943 S.L.T. 286 at 287.

[156] *Duke of Argyll* v. *MacArthur and Campbell* (*supra* note 148).

[157] *Dunlop* v. *Mundell and Others* (*supra* note 155); *McIntyre* v. *Forbes* 1939 S.L.T. 62.

[158] *Dunlop* (*supra* note 155).

CHAPTER TWENTY

INDUSTRIAL ARBITRATION

Introduction

20.1. Under this heading are gathered the various procedures under which disputes between employees or their trade unions on the one hand and employers or their associations on the other are determined by a decision reached by third parties. Most of these procedures have a rather loose connection with the legal system, which is rarely called upon either to enforce awards or to regulate proceedings or to interpret arbitration agreements, in spite of the fact that the state has since the end of the eighteenth century[1] given some encouragement to the settlement of industrial conflict by arbitration. Since 1919 it has maintained a permanent arbitral tribunal to which trade unions and employers may have resort,[2] and under pressure of war it has from time to time included the designation 'arbitration' in the title of a statutory tribunal with compulsory jurisdiction in certain kinds of industrial dispute.[3]

20.2. In Scotland, industrial arbitration has hitherto been ignored by the principal writers on the law of arbitration, and until the juridification of industrial relations began in earnest in the late 1960s it attracted little attention from the academic legal profession in general.[4] As a result, the extent to which the ordinary

---

[1] Combination Act 1800 (39 & 40 Geo. III) c. 106, ss. 18–22. Arbitration was established even earlier in particular trades: Bagwell P. S., *Industrial Relations in 19th Century Britain*, Irish University Press, 1974, 28.

[2] Industrial Courts Act 1919 s. 1. It was succeeded briefly by the Industrial Arbitration Board established under the Industrial Relations Act 1971, the present body being the Central Arbitration Committee, established under s. 10 of the Employment Protection Act 1975.

[3] National Arbitration Tribunal established under the Conditions of Employment and National Arbitration Order 1940 (S.R.& O. 1940 No. 1305) made under reg. 58AA of the Defence (General) Regulations 1939 (S.R. & O. 1939 No. 927) as amended by Order in Council (S.R.& O. 1940 No. 1217), made under the Emergency Powers (Defence) Act 1940. N.B. also Munitions of War Acts 1915–7.

[4] The great pioneer among lawyers was Professor K. W. Wedderburn (now

Scots law of arbitration applies in the industrial context has not been examined. The Employment Protection Act 1975[5] provides that Part I of the Arbitration Act 1950 does not apply to proceedings under it which are regulated by English law, but its only reference in this context to Scots law[6] states merely that in the application of section 3 to Scotland, 'references to an arbitrator shall be construed as references to an arbiter.' Given the nature of certain forms of industrial arbitration and the lingering questionmark over the office of 'arbitrator' in Scots law,[7] the precise implications of this provision for the arbitration of interest disputes are difficult to determine.

The classification of industrial disputes

20.3. Industrial disputes may be classified in two main ways for the purposes of analysing the procedures established for settling them. They may be distinguished first with regard to the relevance of norms, that is, whether they are about rights or interests; and second, with regard to the involvement of organisations, that is, whether they are between trade unions on the one hand and employers or employers' associations on the other — 'collective disputes' — or between one or more employees as individuals on the one hand and their employer on the other — 'individual disputes'.[8] The first classification was not much used in Great Britain until fairly recently, because the distinction tended to be blurred in industrial relations practice,[9] but it is now accepted at least as a tool of academic analysis.[10]

20.4. Disputes about rights are disputes concerning the meaning or application of or compliance with rules, whether those rules are derived from the general law, or from the individual contract, or from a collective agreement. For this purpose it does not matter whether a collective agreement is legally enforceable or not.

Lord Wedderburn). N.B. in particular Wedderburn and Davies, *Empl. Griev. Proc.*, Chapter 9.
[5] S. 3(5) and Schedule 1 paragraph 26.
[6] Subsection 3(6).
[7] For a discussion, see paragraphs 1.3–1.4, 2.12–2.14, 2.34 and 2.52 above.
[8] Zack, *Griev. Arb.*, 3.
[9] Kahn-Freund O., *Labour and the Law*, London, 2nd edn. 1977, 54.
[10] Wood Sir J., 'Last Offer Arb.' 415.

Disputes about interests are disputes which have no reference to positive rules, though the parties may base their arguments on equitable principles. For example, a dispute over a claim by workers to higher wages is a dispute about interests, assuming of course that the claim is not based on some law or agreement which, say, guarantees an increase when the cost of living rises by a specified amount.

20.5. Individual disputes — or at least those which come to be the subject of grievance procedures — are usually though not necessarily about rights. The Examination of Grievances Recommendation of the 1967 General Conference of the International Labour Organisation of the United Nations goes so far as to define the grounds for a 'grievance' as —

> 'any measure or situation which concerns the relations between employer and worker or which affects or may affect the conditions of employment of one or several workers in the undertaking when that measure or situation appears contrary to provisions of an applicable collective agreement or of an individual contract of employment, to works rules, to laws or regulations or to the custom or usage of the occupation, branch of economic activity or country, regard being had to principles of good faith.'[11]

The fact that a dispute between an individual employee and his or her employer arises out of a clause in a collective agreement which has been incorporated in the contract of employment does not destroy its individual character.[12]

20.6. Collective disputes, by contrast, are very often about interests. This means that arbitration — which as a form of adjudication applies rules or principles in determining issues — is at first sight less suitable for dealing with collective than individual disputes. In Great Britain, however, individual disputes are usually either presented to an industrial tribunal or are transformed by the solidarity of workplace feeling into collective disputes, and the numbers submitted to arbitration are quite small.[13] It is collective disputes about interests which are generally referred to arbitration in this country, though in recent years there

---

[11] Art. 3: printed in Appendix 1 to Zack, *Griev. Arb.* p. 64.
[12] *O'Neill* v. *Scottish J.N.C.* 1987 S.C.L.R. 275.
[13] The Advisory, Conciliation and Arbitration Service (ACAS) in 1983

has been some growth in the proportion of 'rights' cases,[14] reflecting a tendency towards juridification in British industrial relations. Given that in 'interest' disputes there are by definition no positive rules to which reference can be made, the integration of the arbitration proceedings concerned into a juristic framework poses serious difficulties. Indeed, except to the extent that reference is made at least to equitable principles (when the dispute cannot be one of pure interest) the use of the title 'arbitration' would seem inappropriate.[15]

Arbitration in different types of industrial dispute

20.7. **Individual disputes**. Individual contracts of employment sometimes provide that disputes arising out of or in connection with the contract shall be referred to arbitration. Where this is done, whether by incorporation of a term in a collective agreement or otherwise, the proceedings are in almost all respects identical to ordinary arbitration, and are governed by the law relating to that institution. A distinction must of course be carefully drawn between any stages in proceedings which are of a conciliatory character and those which are arbitral. It has been held in England that statements made during a conciliation stage of proceedings following the plaintiff's dismissal were not privileged, though they would have been if they had been made in the later arbitration stage,[16] and there seems no reason to doubt that this decision would be followed in Scotland. It remains true, however, that the only legal speciality in individual industrial disputes is that the agreement to refer to arbitration cannot, except in certain special circumstances, prevent any person from presenting to an industrial tribunal a complaint arising out of an alleged infringement of rights under the Employment Protection (Consolidation) Act 1978.[17] Thus, where an employee who has been dismissed summarily or with notice demands arbitration of a grievance over the dismissal, and the employer's action is upheld

arranged for arbitration in only 51 individual disputes: ACAS, *Annual Report, 1983*, London, 1984, 74. See also Concannon, 'Dismissal Arb.', 13.

[14] Concannon, 'ACAS Arb.', at 16.

[15] Schmidt F., 'Conciliation, Adjudication and Administration: Three Methods of Decision-making in Labor Disputes', in Aaron, *Disp. Proc.*, 47.

[16] *Tadd* v. *Eastwood and Daily Telegraph Ltd.* [1983] I.R.L.R. 320.

[17] EPCA s. 140.

by the arbiter's award, the employee cannot normally be prevented from having the case reheard by an industrial tribunal. Only where an order has been made by the Secretary of State under either section 18 or section 65 of the 1978 Act designating a collective agreement as satisfying conditions specified in the Act can the jurisdiction of the tribunal be ousted.

20.8.   Though there are hardly any legal specialities, there are some non-legal ones. The arbitration of individual disputes often has what has been called a 'collectivist character'.[18] It is usually based on a collective agreement, even if the terms of the agreement have been to some extent individualised by their incorporation into a contract of employment; the worker is usually represented by a trade union official, who has probably been involved already in conciliation proceedings under the auspices of the Advisory, Conciliation and Arbitration Service (ACAS); and the arbiter selected either by the parties or by ACAS is likely to be sensitive to the industrial relations background, and to seek to arrive at a decision which will be broadly acceptable not only to the individual employee and the employer but also to the trade union involved. Where the dispute is over dismissal, reinstatement is more likely to be asked for and granted than in industrial tribunal proceedings.[19] Though reinstatement is no more enforceable in law when ordered by an arbiter at common law than by an industrial tribunal under statutory powers,[20] the arbiter's order is likely to be issued more quickly and to carry more weight in industrial relations terms.

20.9.   The collectivist character of individual grievance arbitration may affect proceedings in a number of other ways. First of all, the constitution of the arbitral tribunal is usually agreed between the employer and trade union concerned, with or without the help of ACAS. Technically, the agreement of the worker is formally obtained through his or her agreement to the terms of a contract of employment which incorporates provisions of a collective agreement, and indeed it is this which alone gives the arbitration award any legal force since collective agreements are

---

[18] Concannon H., 'ACAS Arb.' at 15.
[19] Rideout, R. W., 'Unfair Dismissal — Tribunal or Arbitration' (1986) 15(2) *Industrial Law Journal* 84 at 92.
[20] EPCA ss. 69–70.

not normally binding in law,[21] but in practice some categories of workers — those whose interests are in a minority within the union — may not have much more influence on the terms of the arbitration agreement than the tenants of a mediaeval lord had over arbitrations dealing with disputes between members of different kin.[22]

20.10.   Sometimes a single arbiter is appointed to deal with whatever grievances happen to occur within a specified period among the workers covered by the collective agreement; in other cases an arbiter or arbiters are appointed *ad hoc*. The former is regarded by some writers as preferable because it is more likely to prevent disputes about nomination holding up proceedings,[23] but it seems that in Britain the assistance of ACAS has usually enabled *ad hoc* appointments to be made without difficulty.

20.11.   Second, the collective agreement on which the arbitration is based may provide for representation only by officials of the union which is a party to it, without committing the union to represent all employees including non-members. In practice such agreements often allow the aggrieved worker to choose a representative from among fellow-employees, but the absence in this country of any legal duty of fair representation such as exists, for example, in the United States of America,[24] does enable the union to exercise greater influence over the outcome of disputes than would otherwise be possible.

20.12.   Third, the arbitrability of grievances is determined by the collective agreement. Though the union obviously has an interest in ensuring that most types of grievance and all workers whom it has or hopes to have in membership are covered, there is no legal obligation on it to extend the scope of the agreement further than its organisational interests dictate.

20.13.   These features of industrial grievance arbitration are mitigated in the case of some procedures by the statutory conditions imposed where the jurisdiction of the industrial

[21] Trade Union and Labour Relations Act 1974 s. 18.
[22] On the latter see paragraph 2.18 above.
[23] Zack, *Griev. Arb.*, at 26.
[24] *Steele* v. *Louisville and N.R.R.*, 323 U.S. 192 (1944); *Wallace Corp.* v. *National Labor Relations Board* 323 U.S. 248 (1944).

tribunals is excluded. Under section 65(2)(*c*) of the Employment Protection (Consolidation) Act 1978, a designated dismissal procedures agreement must be 'available without discrimination to all employees falling within any description to which the agreement applies'. Since no agreements seem yet to have been designated,[25] no opportunities have arisen for the meaning of this provision to be tested, but it is possible that it means no more than that all the workers covered by the agreement must have access to the procedure whether they are union members or not, and does not impose on the union any duty of fair representation. The provisions of section 18, which permit the jurisdiction of industrial tribunals to be excluded for the purposes of disputes concerning guarantee pay, are even less protective.

20.14. In spite of what appear from some points of view to be defects, individual grievance arbitration can have some advantages over industrial tribunal procedure for all parties including individual employees, at least in some larger undertakings and undertakings where the employer is a member of an employers' association which can provide expert assistance in establishing and maintaining an arbitration service. All significant kinds of dispute, not only those based on legislation, can be made arbitrable, and a wider range of outcomes is possible. Hearings can more readily be organised at or close to the workplace for the convenience of the parties. The procedures can be adapted to the circumstances. From the point of view of the individual worker, however, a great deal depends on the following essential conditions being satisfied —

(a) a fairly even balance must exist between the employer or employer's association and the union;

(b) the trade union must not only be independent[26] but also able to provide highly capable local officials backed by an expert central advice service; and

(c) the union must recognise and observe a duty of fair representation of all workers covered by arbitration agreements.

It is arguable that the duty of fair representation should be made a legal condition of the exclusion of the jurisdiction of courts and tribunals.

[25] No orders appear in Scottish Current Law up to the March 1987 issue.
[26] Defined in s. 30(1) of the Trade Union and Labour Relations Act 1974 (henceforth 'TULRA').

20.15. The Advisory, Conciliation and Arbitration Service (ACAS) can assist in providing arbitration services for the determination of individual as well as collective disputes, though it tends to be associated in the public mind mainly with the latter. The role of ACAS will be considered in the paragraphs which follow. There is, of course, no requirement that parties resort to ACAS for this purpose.

20.16. **Collective disputes**. There are a number of aspects of the arbitration of these disputes which require some discussion here as they have not hitherto been considered in the context of the Scots law of arbitration. These are, the place of this form of arbitration in the Scottish legal system including the enforceability of awards, some aspects of the terms of submissions, and the conduct of proceedings.

20.17. The question of the *enforceability* of awards handed down by industrial arbitrators is complicated by the fact that the arbitration of disputes between trade unions and employers has a very tenuous connection with the legal system. The jurisdiction of the arbitrator is normally based on a collective agreement,[27] and such agreements are not enforceable in law unless they comply with the very stringent conditions laid down in section 18 of the Trade Union and Labour Relations Act 1974, which few do. Application for a stated case for the opinion of the court on a question of law is incompetent in a dispute which is a 'trade dispute' in terms of the Industrial Courts Act 1919 or the Trade Union and Labour Relations Act 1974, or which arises out of a collective agreement.[28] Furthermore, though disputes between employers and trade unions often raise questions of right, questions of interest are equally if not more likely to be at stake. It is questionable whether, except in cases governed by special statutory provisions,[29] the awards given in such disputes would be enforceable in law even indirectly through the contract of employment whether the collective agreement on which the arbitration was based was enforceable or not.

---

[27] Also defined in s. 30(1) TULRA 1974.

[28] Administration of Justice (Scotland) Act 1972 s. 3(3); *O'Neill* v. *Scottish J.N.C. for Teaching Staff* 1987 S.C.L.R. 275.

[29] E.g. awards arising out of a complaint by a trade union of the employer's failure to disclose information: Employment Protection Act 1975 s. 21(6)–(8).

20.18. Because of its tenuous connection with the legal system in Britain, the *juristic character* of industrial arbitration is difficult to determine. Except where the dispute arises out of the interpretation or application of an agreement which is or could be enforceable at law, the proceedings amount at best to equitable arbitration, for the arbiters — or arbitrators as perhaps they should be called in this context — do not apply positive rules but 'strive to make just and equitable awards'.[30] The Industrial Court — a predecessor of the present Central Arbitration Committee — based its decisions variously upon criteria of 'subsistence', 'fairness' and 'the ability of the employer to pay'.[31] Other criteria sometimes used include changes in the cost of living, the right of workers to benefit from increased profits arising from improved productivity, comparability, and public interest.[32] Part of the difficulty in resolving industrial disputes is that, in contrast to those arising among merchants, the parties approach the issues from different moral standpoints. Even where they each accept the relevance of the criteria mentioned above, they rarely attach the same relative weight to them.

20.19. If reference to equitable principles rather than positive rules were always made, industrial arbitration in collective disputes might nevertheless not be very difficult to integrate into the legal system. Even ordinary arbitration may be used as a means of completing a contract if the decision is based on rules or criteria capable of objective expression.[33] The trouble is that this form of arbitration is often regarded in Britain as 'a process by which the parties seek a settlement which will make it possible for them to continue their relationship',[34] and therefore even equity is not always the ultimate point of reference. It has been remarked that the classic picture of the rational arbitrator deciding disputes by the application of rules and principles —

> 'has to be set alongside the practical game which an arbitrator may need to play. It is not merit but power which may often be the determinant. The arbitrator must gauge bargaining strengths, what the balance of power is, and produce an answer which fits the realities of power in the situation. He must also

[30] Gladstone, *Vol. Arb.*, 29.
[31] Sharp, *Ind. Arb.*, 358.
[32] Gladstone, *Vol. Arb.* 29–40.
[33] See paragraph 1.11 above.
[34] Concannon, 'ACAS Arb.' at 13.

gauge the consequences of his decision, what effect it will probably have on the efficiency of the enterprise, what effect on the attitudes of the parties. Above all is the question of what decision is practicable in the day-to-day conduct of industrial relations in the enterprise'.[35]

It was the prevalence of this conception of industrial arbitration that led the Swedish labour lawyer Folke Schmidt to suggest that it could not be regarded as a form of adjudication so much as what he called 'administration'.[36] Public policy may make the outcome of such 'administration' legally enforceable, on the basis that it is in the interests of industrial peace that the 'administrator' is in certain circumstances entitled to impose terms as if they had been agreed by the parties themselves, but it cannot properly be regarded as equivalent to a decree arbitral.

20.20. Given that parties involved in a collective industrial dispute generally do not trouble themselves about the precise function of the person to whom the dispute is referred for a decision, a reference in an industrial dispute is similar in character to the mediaeval submission to an 'arbiter, arbitrator and amicable compositor',[37] and the nature of the outcome is equally problematic. In cases where the collective agreement constituting the submission is legally enforceable — and as long as section 18 of the Trade Union and Labour Relations Act 1974 is on the statute book these will be very rare — the decision of a modern industrial referee (to use a neutral term) might be made legally enforceable as an award on much the same ground (and perhaps with as little practical effect) as that of a person acting as 'arbiter, arbitrator and amicable compositor' in former times. In the absence of written reasons and of power to compel the third party to explain the basis of the decision, it might be difficult to overcome a presumption, based on the acceptance of analogous decrees in former times, that it was the outcome of a procedure which could properly be regarded as arbitration and should be enforced as such. Yet as such antiquarian reasoning would be unlikely to carry much weight with a modern court, it is very doubtful indeed whether apart from special legislation the outcome of 'arbitration' proceedings in a

---

[35] *Ibid.* at 14.
[36] Schmidt F., 'Conciliation, Adjudication and Administration': Three methods of decision-making in labor disputes', in Aaron, *Disp. Proc.*, 47.
[37] See paragraph 2.17 above.

collective industrial dispute would be enforced by a Scottish court, even if the proceedings were regarded as having a sufficiently judicial character to ensure the protection of privilege for statements made by witnesses.[38]

20.21. **Terms of submissions.** An agreement to refer a collective dispute to arbitration must as a matter of practical necessity deal with many of the same issues with which ordinary submissions have to be concerned, namely the number of arbiters, the nature of the matters submitted, and the powers of the arbiter. In the majority of arbitrations arranged with the assistance of ACAS there is a submission to a single arbiter, though in major disputes a board of three persons is occasionally appointed.[39] ACAS maintains lists of persons available to act, and often at the request of both parties makes the appointment, much as in ordinary arbitration the sheriff or the president of a professional association does. In complex cases ACAS sometimes assigns one of its own officials to act as clerk (or, as he or she is more often called in this context, 'secretary',) to the arbiter. The submission — or 'request for arbitration' as it is sometimes called in this context, does not require to be in any special form, but where ACAS is involved it suggests the use of a form which it has designed. Occasionally, the parties simply write separate letters to ACAS, and if it appears that these indicate agreement between them on the issues and the appointment of arbiters these are regarded as acceptable.

20.22. The specification of the powers of the arbiter is a matter of considerable importance, and requires especial care in cases where the parties have agreed to adopt what is called 'pendulum' or 'last offer' or 'flip-flop' arbitration. This differs from what has hitherto been (and may remain) the more usual type, in that the arbiter is here required to choose between the final proposal of each party for terminating the dispute, instead of coming to his or her own view of what is the most equitable solution or at least the one most likely to prove acceptable to both sides. The object of 'last offer' arbitration is to encourage the parties to adopt reasonable positions

---

[38] For a brief discussion of the application of those rules in ordinary arbitration, see paragraph 13.49 above.
[39] This paragraph is based generally upon information contained in the pamphlet *The ACAS Role in Conciliation, Arbitration and Mediation* issued by ACAS.

in negotiation.[40] There is a natural tendency, where the normal system is used, for the trade union to seek more, and for the employer to offer less, than the amount which an arbiter might award, and this is thought to have a 'chilling effect' on prior negotiations. Also, where the parties resort frequently to the normal system of arbitration they may be inclined not to exert themselves to arrive at a negotiated solution — in other (American) words, there is a 'narcotic effect' upon negotiations. There are, however, some disadvantages in 'last offer' arbitration also. Probably the most difficult is that of determining what the last offer on each side actually is.[41] Another problem is that in disputes of any complexity the proposals of each side contain a number of items. The arbiter may regard almost all of the proposals of one side as preferable to the corresponding proposals of the other, but consider that one of the former's is quite impossible. If one of these positions must be chosen, there is a dilemma, but if the first party is allowed to amend the impossible article, the procedure ceases to be 'last offer' arbitration and loses the advantages associated with it. It is therefore highly desirable that in a submission to 'last offer' arbitration the parties agree to define the meaning of 'last offer' in very precise terms.

20.23.   In some agreements[42] the third party is expected to act as mediator or conciliator as well as arbiter. This may pose special problems, because some types of conduct such as separate private discussions between the conciliator and each of the parties in turn are acceptable and even desirable in conciliation but are improper in arbitration. Hence, if the same person acts in both roles there is a risk that either the conciliation process will be hampered or the arbitration process will be flawed, even if care is taken to keep them separate. Also, the parties may have different conceptions of what mediation or conciliation means in this context. One may take the view that it means that the third party should assist merely in clarifying the claims and defences being put forward on either side, the other that the third party has a much wider role. Nevertheless, it is often felt to be convenient to combine the functions of

[40] This paragraph is based generally upon Wood, 'Last Offer Arb.'.

[41] This faced Professor Kessler in the arbitration between Sanyo Industries (UK) Ltd. and EETPU in 1985: Gourlay D., 'Peace and Pendulum' in (1985/6) 3(1) *The Economic Bulletin*, Robert Gordon's Institute of Technology Business School, Aberdeen, 71 at 75.

[42] E.g. that between Sanyo Industries and EETPU: see Gourlay D., (*supra* note 41).

conciliator and arbiter in one person, and where the third party personally enjoys the great respect and trust of both parties the practice may have successful results.

20.24. **Proceedings**. The time and place of hearings, and the conduct of the proceedings, may be regulated by the collective agreement setting up the arbitration, but often this is at the discretion of the arbiter. Where the arbitration has been arranged with the assistance of ACAS[43] the time that elapses between the submission or request for arbitration and the hearing generally varies from two or three weeks in the case of proceedings before a single arbiter to three or four weeks in the case of those which involve a board. The hearing often takes place on the employer's premises, but the neutral ground of an ACAS office may be chosen. Normally the parties send written statements of their cases to the arbiter and to each other in advance of their appearance. The hearing itself is generally private and informal, the parties being allowed to bring such advisers and witnesses as they consider necessary. Representation by professional lawyers is rare and not encouraged.

20.25. **Awards**. The awards of British industrial arbiters have traditionally been fairly brief and have contained no reasons.[44] A trend towards reasoned awards has recently been observed, however,[45] and this may bring British practice more into line with what is normal elsewhere.[46] They are normally confidential to the parties — the main exception is that the awards of the Central Arbitration Committee (CAC) are published[47] — and in proceedings where ACAS is involved are usually issued to them within about a fortnight of the hearing. It is not unknown for a party to ask for clarification of some clause in an award. This is regarded by ACAS as permissible where the opponent agrees and where the request for clarification is not in reality an attempt to raise a new question.[48] The CAC has statutory power to entertain requests for interpretation.[49]

---

[43] This paragraph is broadly based on the ACAS pamphlet *The ACAS Role in Conciliation, Arbitration and Mediation*.
[44] Wedderburn and Davies, *Empl. Griev. Proc.*, 197; Sharp, *Ind. Arb.*, 358.
[45] Concannon, 'Dismissal Arb.', 17.
[46] As described in Gladstone, *Vol. Arb.*, 58.
[47] Employment Protection Act 1975 Schedule 1 paragraph 24.
[48] ACAS pamphlet (*supra*) at paragraph 21 note 35.
[49] Paragraph 23.

State arbitration institutions

20.26.   It has already been observed that in both individual and collective disputes arbitration may be arranged with the assistance of ACAS, which maintains its own lists of persons whom it regards as qualified for the purpose. ACAS has power under section 3 of the Employment Protection Act 1975 to refer to arbitration any 'trade dispute'[50] which exists or is apprehended, so long as the parties agree and provided any available procedures for settlement by conciliation or negotiation have been tried and have failed. The reference may be to a person appointed by ACAS itself (other than one of its own officials) or to the Central Arbitration Committee (CAC). That body is established under section 10 and Schedule 1 to the 1975 Act and consists of a chairman and members, the latter being divided into two panels, containing respectively persons whose experience is as representatives of employers and of workers. All are appointed by the Secretary of State after consultation, in the case of the members, with appropriate organisations.

20.27.   Except where the law provides otherwise the CAC is empowered to determine its own procedure.[51] In its notes for the guidance of parties it makes a number of points. These include the following:-

(a) Seven copies of written statements, which should be 'as brief as the full presentation of the case allows' should be sent to the Committee along with copies of any relevant agreements or other documents not later than 21 days before the date of the hearing, of which the parties are usually given 6 weeks' notice;
(b) The parties should exchange their statements before the hearing in sufficient time for each to prepare responses;
(c) Evidence is not given on oath and the cross-examination of witnesses is not permitted. The Committee asks questions of witnesses itself to clarify statements;
(d) Parties may be represented at a hearing by counsel or a solicitor, but should inform the Committee and the opponent of their intention;

If the Committee is unable to reach a unanimous decision on any matter properly referred to it, the chairman has the power of an

[50] Defined in TULRA 1974 s. 29.
[51] 1975 Act Schedule 1 paragraph 20.

oversman to make a decision.[52] Clerical slips in awards may be corrected,[53] and a party may apply to the Committee for an interpretation of a decision.[54] Decisions are published.[55]

20.28. The statutory functions of the CAC have recently been somewhat curtailed with the repeal by the Employment Act 1980 of section 98 and Schedule 11 of the Employment Protection Act 1975. They now comprise complaints under section 19 of the 1975 Act concerning an employer's failure to disclose information required by a trade union for collective bargaining purposes, and references under sections 3, 4 and 5 of the Equal Pay Act 1970. The role of the CAC in deciding complaints of infringement of the 1946 Fair Wages Resolution of the House of Commons has ceased with the rescission of that Resolution with effect from September 1983. The CAC may still entertain issues submitted to it voluntarily by the parties.

20.29. Complaints under the 1975 Act may be presented to the Committee only by an independent trade union,[56] but any person whom the Committee regards as having a proper interest in the complaint is entitled to be heard before it.[57] Only matters in respect of which it is 'recognised' by the employer[58] can be the subject of a complaint, 'recognition' being defined[59] as being for the purpose of negotiations concerning one or more of the categories of matters specified in section 29(1) of the Trade Union and Labour Relations Act 1974. Where a union is recognised for collective bargaining about some matters, and accepted as having the right to make representations over others, it has the right to disclosure of information only about the former.[60]

20.30. The Committee is required to consider whether the complaint is reasonably likely to be settled by conciliation, and if it thinks this is so it must refer it to ACAS.[61] If the Committee finds

[52] Schedule 1 paragraph 18.
[53] Paragraph 22.
[54] Paragraph 23.
[55] Paragraph 24.
[56] S. 19(1).
[57] S. 19(5).
[58] S. 17(2)(*a*).
[59] Ss. 11(2) and 126(1).
[60] *R* v. *CAC ex parte BTP Tioxide Ltd.* [1982] I.R.L.R. 60.
[61] S. 19(2).

the complaint well founded, and if, after such period as the Committee may have specified, the employer has still not provided the information, the union may present a further complaint to this effect.[62] Simultaneously with the second complaint or thereafter the union may present to the Committee a claim that the contracts of employment of specified groups of workers should include certain terms and conditions.[63] If the second complaint is upheld, the Committee may make an award requiring the employer to observe either the terms and conditions specified in the claim or such other terms as the Committee considers appropriate, provided that they relate to matters in respect of which the trade union is recognised by the employer.[64] The award then has effect as part of the contracts of employment of the workers concerned,[65] and can be enforced as such in the ordinary courts.

20.31. References to the Committee under section 3 of the Equal Pay Act 1970 may be made either by a party to the collective agreement concerned or by the Secretary of State, with the object of obtaining a declaration of what amendments have to be made to the agreement to remove discriminatory terms, but only where the agreement contains provisions applying specifically to men only or women only. Where the Committee declares that amendments are necessary, any terms of contracts of employment which are dependent on the collective agreement concerned have to be ascertained by reference to it as amended in accordance with the declaration. In appropriate cases, the Committee is willing to postpone the date for implementation of an award because of economic difficulties in the industry concerned.[66] References under sections 4 and 5 of the Act, relating to wages regulation orders and agricultural wages orders may only be made by the Secretary of State.

20.32. Decisions of the CAC are subject to the general power of judicial review possessed by the ordinary courts. As it normally sits in London it is not surprising that the Court of Session has not yet been called upon to exercise this power in relation to it, but the

[62] S. 20.
[63] S. 21(1).
[64] S. 21(3)(5).
[65] S. 21(6).
[66] *Scottish Knitwear Association and NUDBTW, NUGMW, NUH & KW and TGWU*, CAC Award No. 46/76.

Queen's Bench Divisional Court has done so in England in a number of cases, including one arising out of the CAC's jurisdiction under the Equal Pay Act 1970.[67] A trade union had complained that a certain employer's pay structure based on an agreed job evaluation exercise discriminated against women because there were no women in the two highest grades and no men in the two lowest. The CAC had upheld the complaint, and decided on certain amendments to the system. The Court held that the CAC had exceeded its jurisdiction under the 1975 Act because the collective agreement out of which the dispute arose did not contain any provision 'applying specifically to men only or to women only', and had exceeded its powers of amendment under section 3(4) of the Act. Browne, L. J. accepted[68] that

> 'there may be cases in which the agreement is a sham, in fact containing provisions which applied specifically only to women although on its face it does not',

and appeared to accept that in such cases the CAC might entertain a complaint, but he did not consider that the case then before the court came within that exception. It is probable that the Court of Session would come to a similar conclusion.

[67] *R* v. *CAC ex parte Hy-Mac Ltd.* [1979] I.R.L.R. 461.
[68] At 464.

APPENDIX I

STATUTORY PROVISIONS

I. *Articles of Regulation 1695*

Article 25. That for the cutting off of groundless and expensive pleas and processes in time coming, the Lords of Session sustain no reduction of any decreet arbitral that shall be pronounced hereafter on a subscribed submission at the instance of the parties submitters, upon any cause whatever, unless that of corruption, bribery, or falsehood to be alleged against the judges arbitrators, who pronounced the same.

II. *Arbitration (Scotland) Act 1894 (57 & 58 Vict. Ch. 13)*

(3rd July 1894) (as amended by the Statute Law Revision Act 1908 (c. 49) s. 1 and Schedule, and the Law Reform (Miscellaneous Provisions) (Scotland) Act 1980 (c. 55) s. 17(4))

1. An agreement to refer to arbitration shall not be invalid or ineffectual by reason of the reference being to a person not named, or to a person to be named by another person, or to a person merely described as the holder for the time being of any office or appointment.

2. Should one of the parties to an agreement to refer to a single arbiter refuse to concur in the nomination of such arbiter, and should no provision have been made for carrying out the reference in that event, or should such provision have failed, an arbiter may be appointed by the court, on the application of any party to the agreement, and the arbiter so appointed shall have the same powers as if he had been duly nominated by all the parties.

3. Should one of the parties to an agreement to refer to two arbiters refuse to name an arbiter, in terms of the agreement, and should no provision have been made for carrying out the reference in that event, or should such provision have failed, an arbiter may be appointed by the court, on the application of the other party, and the arbiter so appointed shall have the same powers as if he had been duly nominated by the party so refusing.

4. Unless the agreement to refer shall otherwise provide, arbiters shall have power to name an oversman on whom the reference shall be devolved in the event of their differing in opinion. Should the arbiters fail to agree in the nomination of an oversman, the court may on the application of any party to the agreement, appoint an oversman. The decision of such oversman, whether he has been named by the arbiters or appointed by the court, shall be final.

5. ... [Transitional provisions.]

6. For the purposes of this Act the expression 'the court' shall mean any sheriff having jurisdiction or any Lord Ordinary of the Court of Session, except that where —

(*a*) any arbiter appointed is; or
(*b*) in terms of the agreement to refer to arbitration an arbiter or oversman to be appointed must be,

a Senator of the College of Justice, 'the court' shall mean the Inner House of the Court of Session.

III. *Administration of Justice (Scotland) Act 1972 (Ch. 59)*

(9th August 1972) (as amended by the Trade Union and Labour Relations Act 1974 Schedule 3 paragraph 17 and Schedule 5, and the Employment Act 1982 (c. 46) Schedule 3 paragraph 11)

3. (1) Subject to express provision to the contrary in an agreement to refer to arbitration, the arbiter or oversman may, on the application of a party to the arbitration, and shall, if the Court of Session on such an application so directs, at any stage in the arbitration state a case for the opinion of that Court on any question of law arising in the arbitration.

(2) This section shall not apply to an arbitration under any enactment which confers a power to appeal to or state a case for the opinion of a court or tribunal in relation to that arbitration.

(3) This section shall not apply to any form of arbitration

relating to a trade dispute within the meaning of the Industrial Courts Act 1919 or relating to a trade dispute within the meaning of the Employment Protection Act 1975; or to any other arbitration arising from a collective agreement within the meaning of the Trade Union and Labour Relations Act 1974; or to proceedings before the Industrial Arbitration Board.[1]

(4) This section shall not apply in relation to an agreement to refer to arbitration made before the commencement of this Act.

[1] The reference to the Industrial Arbitration Board has to be construed as a reference to the Central Arbitration Committee, by virtue of the Employment Protection Act 1975 s. 10(2).

APPENDIX II

FORM OF OATHS[1]

Oath of witness

The witness should raise his or her right hand and repeat after the arbiter the following words:

'I swear by Almighty God that I will tell the truth, the whole truth, and nothing but the truth.'

Affirmation of witness

The witness should repeat after the arbiter the following words:

'I solemnly, sincerely and truly declare and affirm that I will tell the truth, the whole truth, and nothing but the truth.'

Oath or affirmation of interpreter or shorthand writer

For the words carrying the obligation to tell the truth, the following are substituted:

'I will faithfully discharge the duty of [interpreter or shorthand writer] in these arbitration proceedings.'

[1] Act of Adjournal (Form of Oaths) 1976, S.I. 1976 No. 172 (S. 11).

INDEX

427

Index

Index